The Music Lover's Guide to Europe

A Compendium of Festivals, Concerts, and Opera

ROBERTA GOTTESMAN, *Editor*

CATHERINE SENTMAN, *Associate Editor*

John Wiley & Sons, Inc.

New York · Chichester · Brisbane · Toronto · Singapore

To Michael, my lifelong traveling companion

In recognition of the importance of preserving what has been written, it is a policy of John Wiley & Sons, Inc. to have books of enduring value published in the United States printed on acid-free paper, and we exert our best efforts to that end.

Library of Congress Cataloging-in-Publication Data

The music lover's guide to Europe : a compendium of festivals, concerts, and opera / Roberta Gottesman, editor.
    p.   cm.
  Includes index.
  ISBN 0-471-53310-6
  1. Musical landmarks—Europe—Guidebooks. 2. Music festivals—Europe—Guidebooks. 3. Concerts—Europe—Guidebooks. 4. Opera—Europe—Guidebooks. 5. Europe—Description and travel—1971—Guidebooks. I. Gottesman, Roberta. II. Sentman, Catherine.
ML12.M87 1992
780.78'4—dc20   91-14409
                                              MN

Printed in the United States of America

10 9 8 7 6 5 4 3 2 1

Printed and bound by Courier Companies, Inc.

CONTRIBUTING EDITORS

Rebecca Broberg
  France
  Luxembourg
  Monaco
  Netherlands
  Scandinavia
  Switzerland
Therese Grundl
  Austria
  Germany
  Maps
Nancy Melville
  City Descriptions

Catherine Sentman
  Eastern Europe
  France
  Great Britain
  Greece
  Italy
  Monaco
  Spain and Portugal
Nancy Stagnitta
  Belgium
  Great Britain
  Ireland
  Switzerland

ACKNOWLEDGMENTS

We would like to thank the following friends and colleagues who have given us their advice and encouragement: Eugene Rotberg, David Fetter, Felice Homan, Linda Hurley, Dan Elswit, April Guice, Mary Mitchell, James Katchko, Bernice Smith, and Vivian Hogan.

The following members of the Washington diplomatic corps have graciously given their time and attention to this project: Mr. François Barras, Head, Cultural Affairs Office, the Embassy of Switzerland; Mr. Piergiuseppe Bozzetti of the Embassy of Italy; Ms. Andrea Murphy of the Embassy of Belgium; Mr. Bjarne R. Flolo of the Embassy of Norway; Ms. Pirkko-Liisa O'Rourke of the Embassy of Finland; Mr. Ulf Pacher of the Embassy of Austria; Dr. José Ramón Remacha of the Embassy of Spain; Dr. Josef Rusnak of the Embassy of the Federal Republic of Germany; Mr. Gordon Tindale, O.B.E., Cultural Counsellor, and Ms. Barbara Rosen, Cultural Affairs Officer, of the British Embassy; the Swedish Institute, Stockholm; the Swedish Embassy, Washington, D.C.

This book has greatly benefitted from the information provided by the Tourist Boards of all the countries represented.

FOREWORD

༺✿༻

I am happy to salute the appearance of *The Music Lover's Guide to Europe,* which will, I believe, be of extraordinary benefit to all those who have struggled in the past to learn about musical events in Europe when planning a trip abroad. This book will help avoid the frustration of expending time and financial resources during a European vacation to arrive at a venerated music center only to discover that a recital by world-renowned artists has been advertised there for some time and that all the tickets were sold a month ago.

I am happy to note that much of the research for this book was conducted by Peabody Institute graduate students who have themselves participated at some of the festivals listed. They have patiently read hundreds of brochures in many different languages in order to help bring together the wealth of information found here.

Thus I wish music lovers *bon voyage* with confidence that there can be more satisfying artistic journeys ahead, thanks to this unique new resource.

Robert O. Pierce, Director
The Peabody Institute of
The Johns Hopkins University
Baltimore, Maryland

PREFACE

On a summer evening in 1989 my husband and I found ourselves in the stately drawing room of an ancient Swiss castle on Lake Thun, with moonlight pouring through the windows as we listened to the plaintive chords of a Beethoven sonata. We had come upon this exquisite chamber music concert quite by accident, having noticed an advertisement for it posted on a tree near our hotel.

After the concert, which was one of the highlights of our trip, we remarked that we might have missed this musical jewel if we hadn't noticed the sign on the tree. We knew of no guide books that detailed musical events in Europe. There seemed no way to plan a trip around such events, nor, while traveling, to know what other musical events we were missing in the towns nearby.

Having gained so much pleasure from the Swiss concert, and remembering equally wonderful musical experiences that we had found by chance over the years in the grand cathedrals, Roman amphitheaters, castles, stately homes, and little medieval churches, I decided to research and write the first comprehensive music lover's guide to Europe—including not only the well-known festivals such as Glyndebourne and Salzburg, but the smaller ones like my Lake Thun concert.

When I returned home, I did a thorough investigation and confirmed that indeed there is no comprehensive guide to musical events in Europe. I contacted the Peabody Conservatory of Music in Baltimore, one of the leading conservatories of the world, and hired a great staff of multilingual graduate students who are dedicated musicians majoring in voice and instruments. Working together, we designed detailed questionnaires that we sent to festivals, opera houses, and concert halls across Europe. From over 1500 festival and concert season brochures in 10 different languages, we have produced *The Music Lover's Guide to Europe*.

The book can be used to plan a trip around specific musical events, or, for the traveler already abroad, to find a wonderful evening's entertainment nearby.

Fortunately for concert lovers like us, music is a universal language, so unlike most other forms of entertainment, there is no language barrier to our enjoyment. All we need is to know where and when, and we shall have music wherever we go.

Roberta Gottesman

CONTENTS

❦

How to Use This Book   1

AUSTRIA   **5**

Calendar   7

Bad Ischl	9	Millstatt	24
Baden	10	Mondsee	25
Bregenz	11	Mörbisch	25
Eisenstadt	12	Ossiach	26
Graz	15	Salzburg	27
Innsbruck	17	Spittal an der Drau	33
Linz	18	Upper Austria	34
Lower Austria	20	Vienna	35
Melk	23		

BELGIUM   **43**

Calendar   45

Antwerp	47	Ghent	57
Bruges	48	Kortrijk	58
Brussels	50	Liège	59
Dinant	55	Mechelen	60
Flanders	56	Wallonia	61

FRANCE   **63**

Calendar   65

Aix-en-Provence	68	Dijon	80
Albi	70	Divonne-les-Bains	81
Avignon	71	Evian-les-Bains	82
Beaune	73	Fontevraud l'Abbaye	82
Bordeaux	74	Fréjus	83
Brittany	75	Lille	84
Caen	75	Lyon	84
Cannes	77	Marseille	88
Chamonix	78	Menton	88
Chartres	79	Metz	89
Cordes-sur-Ciel	80	Mont Saint Michel	90

Montpellier	91	St.-Céré	105
Mulhouse	93	St.-Paul-de-Vence	106
Nancy	94	St.-Rémy-de-Provence	107
Nantes	95	Strasbourg	108
Nice	95	Sully-sur-Loire	110
Orange	97	Toulon	111
Paris	98	Les Vans	112
St.-Bertrand-de-		Vars (Dauphiné)	112
Comminges	105		

GERMANY   115

Calendar 117

Augsburg	121	Heilbronn	151
Bad Hersfeld	122	Hohenlohe	152
Bad Kissingen	123	Karlsruhe	153
Baden-Baden	124	Leipzig	154
Bamberg	125	Lower Saxony	155
Bayreuth	126	Ludwigsburg	156
Berlin	129	Mainz	157
Bonn	133	Mannheim	158
Cologne	134	Munich	158
Darmstadt	136	Nuremberg	164
Dresden	137	Osnabrück	166
Düsseldorf	139	Regensburg	167
Essen	140	Saarbrücken	169
Frankfurt	142	Schleswig-Holstein	170
Freiburg	144	Schwäbish Gmünd	172
Garmisch-		Stuttgart	172
Partenkirchen	145	Ulm	175
Göttingen	146	Wiesbaden	176
Hamburg	147	Würzburg	179
Hannover	148	Xanten	181
Heidelberg	150		

GREECE   183

Calendar 185

Athens	186	Patras	187

IRELAND   189

Calendar 191

Cork	191	Waterford	193
Dublin	192	Wexford	194

ITALY 195

Calendar 197

Aosta	199	Piacenza	223
Asolo	200	Ravello	223
Bergamo	201	Ravenna	224
Bologna	203	Reggio Emilia	225
Brescia	203	Rimini	226
Cagliari	204	Riva del Garda	227
Como	205	Rome	228
Cremona	206	Salerno	231
Fermo	207	Siena	232
Florence	208	Spoleto	234
Genoa	211	Stresa	235
Martina Franca	212	Taormina	236
Milan	213	Torre del Lago Puccini	237
Modena	216	Trieste	238
Naples	216	Turin	239
Orta San Giulio	218	Venice	241
Palermo	219	Verona	243
Parma	220	Vicenza	244
Pesaro	222		

LUXEMBOURG 245

Calendar 247

Echternach	247	Wiltz	249
Luxembourg City	248		

MONACO 251

Calendar 253

Monaco	253

THE NETHERLANDS 257

Calendar 259

Amsterdam	259	Rotterdam	264
Haarlem	262	Utrecht	265
The Hague	264		

SCANDINAVIA 267

Calendar 269

Denmark 270

Århus	270	Copenhagen	271

Finland 272

Helsinki	272	Naantali	275
Jyväskylä	273	Savonlinna	276
Lahti	274	Turku	276

Norway 277

Bergen	278	Oslo	278

Sweden 280

Stockholm	280	Visby	282

SPAIN AND PORTUGAL	**283**

Calendar 285

Spain 286

Barcelona	286	Montserrat	297
Canary Islands	289	San Sebastian	298
Cuenca	290	Santander	299
Figueras	291	Seville	300
Granada	292	Valencia	301
Madrid	294	Zaragoza	302
Mallorca	295		

Portugal 304

Estoril	304	Sintra	306
Lisbon	305		

SWITZERLAND	**309**

Calendar 311

Ascona	312	Lausanne	320
Basel	312	Lucerne	321
Berne	314	Martigny	323
Crans-sur-Sierre,		Montreux	324
Montana	315	Neuchâtel	325
Ernen	316	St. Gallen	326
Geneva	317	Sion	326
Gstaad	319	Zürich	328

UNITED KINGDOM	**331**

Calendar 334

England 337

Aldeburgh	337	Birmingham	342
Ambleside	339	Bournemouth	344
Arundel	340	Brighton	345
Bath	341	Bristol	347
Beverley	342	Buxton	348

Cambridge	348	Newbury	375
Canterbury	349	Nottingham	376
Cheltenham	351	Oxford	376
Chichester	351	Poole	378
Coventry	352	St. Albans	379
Cricklade	353	St. Endellion	380
Glyndebourne	354	Salisbury	381
Haslemere	355	Sevenoaks	382
Hereford	355	Stratford-upon-Avon	383
King's Lynn	357	Thaxted	384
Leeds	357	Tilford	384
Lichfield	359	Truro	386
Lincoln	360	Warwick	386
Liverpool	361	Winchester	387
London	363	Windsor	388
Ludlow	374	York	389

Northern Ireland 390

Belfast	390		

Scotland 392

Aberdeen	392	Glasgow	397
Dumfries	393	Orkney Islands	399
Edinburgh	394	Perth	400

Wales 401

Cardiff	401	Llangollen	404
Fishguard	403	Swansea	405
Gregynog	403		

EASTERN EUROPE   **409**

Calendar 411

Czechoslovakia 412

Bratislava	412	Prague	412

Hungary 413

Budapest	413	

Poland 413

Warsaw	413	

Yugoslavia 414

Dubrovnik	414	

Appendix A	European Government Tourist Boards—New York Offices	415
Appendix B	Opera in Europe	419
Index		429

HOW TO USE THIS BOOK

ᘓᕙᕗᘒ

The Music Lover's Guide to Europe presents a wide variety of music festivals and events, many held in spectacular locales: picturesque villages, castles, palaces, outdoor Roman theaters, coliseums, and famous cathedrals. Some of the festivals listed are world famous, others little known outside their own region. Did you know, for example, that there is a festival with world-famous artists in the Canary Islands during the entire month of January? Or that if you want to combine a trip to England's Lake District with a music festival in the area, you need to go in August? The listings and calendars in this guide will give you this information and much more.

Tickets for the well-known festivals and major opera houses are often difficult to obtain, and advance planning may be essential. The local festivals are well worth considering as an alternative, especially if you've been unable to plan ahead. Often they are conducted in venues that are themselves a treat: castles, palaces, stately homes, and even caves and a champagne cellar. Although they may not boast world-famous performers, the quality of performances is almost always highly professional. For example, during the summer months the top chairs in many European orchestras "moonlight" by performing as soloists or in chamber groups at these local festivals.

You will find two kinds of musical events in this book. The first are the special festivals, large and small, that take place across Europe. Second are the ongoing performances at opera houses, concert halls, and other sites, which contribute to the cultural life of the major cities.

Each country in this guide, with the exception of those in Scandinavia, those in Eastern Europe, and Portugal (combined with Spain), is covered in its own chapter. Every chapter begins with a map and a calendar of events that will aid you in planning your trip. Nothing is more frustrating than arriving in a lovely European village only to discover that you missed a festival held there two weeks before or, worse still, learning too late that the day you were wishing for music, there was an event just a few miles away. Armchair reading during the cold winter nights preceding your trip will enable you to identify the precise time for your visit and to map out

1

a specific itinerary based on where the festivals are located. The tourist offices listed in Appendix A can be of great help in providing timely information about the musical events you hope to attend.

You'll be most successful if you can plan your vacation many months in advance. This book lists box office addresses, telephone numbers, and, where applicable, fax numbers. Request that the box office send you the festival or season program, which is usually available four to six months in advance. These will provide you with the exact dates, performers, and programs and will usually include a ticket-order form. It is often wise to indicate your second and even third choice for tickets. We would have liked to include the upcoming performers and programs in this book, but such information simply isn't available far enough in advance for book publication. We have, however, listed recent performers so you can gauge the caliber of each event.

If you can't plan far ahead, it's still worthwhile to contact the box office as soon as you know when you'll be arriving. Tickets at world-famous events sell out weeks, even months, in advance, but those at many local festivals can be obtained even a day or two in advance. A call made a few days ahead of your arrival may spell the difference between getting tickets and arriving at a sold-out performance.

If you can't plan ahead at all, don't despair. Some events don't sell out until the day of the performance. And at some festivals the premiere events sell out, but there are fringe concerts, rehearsals, lectures, and similar performances that are accessible without advance reservations. What's more, the concierges at major hotels are often quite enterprising at producing tickets to sold-out events, albeit often at a premium (which can be substantial).

Plan ahead if you can, but if that's not possible, take the book along on your trip and search out the festivals, opera houses, and concert halls along your itinerary. The events described in *The Music Lover's Guide to Europe* are established, regularly scheduled programs. However, there are literally hundreds of wonderful found-at-the-last-minute musical offerings that can be discovered only by reading the current events listings, billboards, and even notices posted on trees and sides of buildings. If you need further guidance when planning your trip, you might wish to consult a travel agent who specializes in musical tours. Or contact us so that we can put you in touch with one.

ABBREVIATIONS

You will find a series of abbreviations beside each entry. These refer to the following categories: **Band** = band concerts; **Cham** = chamber music; **Child** = children's programs; **Chor** = choral music; **Dance** = ballet or modern dance; **Ex** = exhibitions; **Film** = film; **Folk** = folk music; **Fringe** = fringe events (the unofficial offerings that surround many of these festivals); **Jazz** = jazz; **Lec** = lectures; **Op** = opera and/or operetta; **Orch** = orchestral music; **Org** = organ music; **Rec** = recitals; **Read** = readings; **Sem** = seminars; **Th** = theater.

ADDRESSES AND TELEPHONE NUMBERS

The addresses and telephone numbers are almost always those for information and/or tickets. Be careful: they do not always correspond to the actual site of the performances.

Beware! Dialing from abroad can be quite different from dialing within a country—be sure that you are dialing the correct combination of numbers. *The numbers printed in this book assume that you are calling from within that country.* When dialing from the United States, the prefix is 011, followed by the country code. Country codes are indicated at the beginning of each chapter. When calling from another country (e.g., calling Germany from France), it is necessary to check with the local operator. City codes are often preceded by a prefix, but if you are dialing from abroad, this prefix is dropped (see notes at the beginning of each chapter). Remember, most European lunch hours are longer than those in the United States, and it is not wise to call box offices between 1 P.M. and 4 P.M. Many offices are open 10 A.M. to 1 P.M. and 4 P.M. to 7 P.M.; some are open mornings only, others only in the afternoons. The time difference between the United States and Europe varies, so check with your local operator before calling.

MILEAGES

The mileage indications to be found throughout the book are approximate and are to help in locating venues; they should not be used for navigational purposes.

GOVERNMENT TOURIST OFFICES

The government tourist offices located in many major U.S. cities can be of great help in planning your trip. They can often provide schedules of upcoming events in addition to information on accommodations and transportation. The main U.S. offices for many of the countries discussed here are based in New York, so we have listed contact information for those in Appendix A. If you live in a major metropolitan area, check your telephone book to see if there are European tourist boards in your city.

OPERA LISTINGS

Since opera lovers are often in a class by themselves, we have listed, by country, each festival that includes opera among its offerings, as well as the opera houses described in each city. This list is found in Appendix B.

We hope that *The Music Lover's Guide to Europe* will enable you to plan a magical musical tour, and that you will share your experiences with us. We would very much like to hear about your musical adventures and to include any annual events in upcoming editions of this book. You may write to us c/o Notes from Abroad, 3524 Pinetree Terrace, Falls Church, VA 22041. Keep your eyes and ears open and have fun!

Important. Every precaution has been taken to verify the information in this book. However, dates and telephone numbers change, programs are canceled, and the unexpected happens. Always write or call for specific information before traveling.

AUSTRIA

View of Salzburg from the Mirabell Gardens (courtesy of the Austrian National Tourist Office).

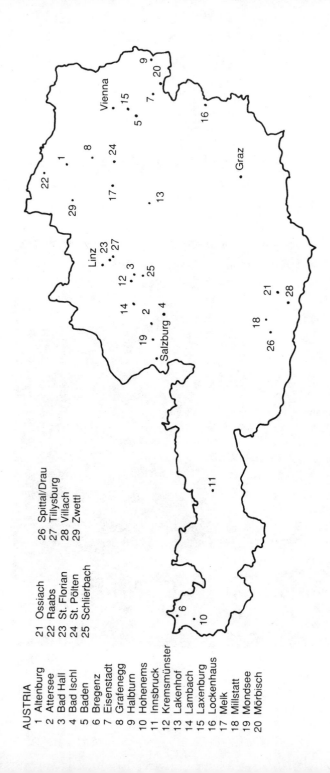

AUSTRIA

1 Altenburg
2 Attersee
3 Bad Hall
4 Bad Ischl
5 Baden
6 Bregenz
7 Eisenstadt
8 Grafenegg
9 Halbturn
10 Hohenems
11 Innsbruck
12 Kremsmünster
13 Lakenhof
14 Lambach
15 Laxenburg
16 Lockenhaus
17 Melk
18 Millstatt
19 Mondsee
20 Mörbisch

21 Ossiach
22 Raabs
23 St. Florian
24 St. Pölten
25 Schlierbach
26 Spittal/Drau
27 Tillysburg
28 Villach
29 Zwettl

CALENDAR

JANUARY

Mozart Week, **Salzburg** (Salzburg)

FEBRUARY

Haydn Festival, **Vienna** (Vienna)
Mozart Week, **Salzburg** (Salzburg)

MARCH

Salzburg Easter Festival, **Salzburg** (Salzburg)

APRIL

Salzburg Easter Festival, **Salzburg** (Salzburg)

MAY

Melk Abbey Whitsun Concerts, **Melk** (Lower Austria)
Millstatt International Music Weeks, **Millstatt** (Carinthia)
Raabs Cultural Summer, see **Lower Austria**
Vienna Festival, **Vienna** (Vienna)

JUNE

Bad Hall Operetta Festival, see **Linz** (Upper Austria)
Raabs Cultural Summer, see **Lower Austria**
Melk Abbey Whitsun Concerts, **Melk** (Lower Austria)
Millstatt International Music Weeks, **Millstatt** (Carinthia)
Schubertiade Hohenems, see **Bregenz** (Vorarlberg)
Styriarte Graz, **Graz** (Styria)
Upper Austrian Abbey Concerts, see **Upper Austria**
Vienna Festival, **Vienna** (Vienna)
Vienna's Musical Summer, **Vienna** (Vienna)
Zwettl Abbey Organ Festival, see **Lower Austria**

JULY

Altenburg Summer Music Academy, see **Lower Austria**
Attergau Summer of Culture, see **Upper Austria**
Bad Hall Operetta Festival, see **Linz** (Upper Austria)
Bad Ischl Music Days, **Bad Ischl** (Upper Austria)
Bad Ischl Operetta Weeks, **Bad Ischl** (Upper Austria)
Baden Operetta Summer, **Baden** (Lower Austria)
Bregenz Festival, **Bregenz** (Vorarlberg)
Carinthian Summer Festival, see **Ossiach** (Carinthia)
Chamber Music Festival at Tillysburg Palace, see **Linz** (Upper
     Austria)

Halbturn Palace Concerts, **Eisenstadt** (Burgenland)
Innsbruck Festival of Early Music, **Innsbruck** (Tyrol)
Lockenhaus Chamber Music Festival, see **Eisenstadt** (Burgenland)
Millstatt International Music Weeks, **Millstatt** (Carinthia)
Mörbisch Operetta Festival, **Mörbisch** (Burgenland)
Raabs Cultural Summer, see **Lower Austria**
Schubertiade Hohenems, see **Bregenz** (Vorarlberg)
Spectaculum, **Vienna** (Vienna)
Styriarte Graz, **Graz** (Styria)
Upper Austrian Abbey Concerts, see **Upper Austria**
Salzburg Festival, **Salzburg** (Salzburg)
Spittal an der Drau International Choir Competition, **Spittal an der Drau** (Carinthia)
Vienna's Musical Summer, **Vienna** (Vienna)
Zwettl Abbey Organ Festival, see **Lower Austria**

AUGUST

Altenburg Summer Music Academy, see **Lower Austria**
Attergau Summer of Culture, see **Upper Austria**
Austrian Chamber Music Festival, see **Baden** (Lower Austria)
Bad Hall Operetta Festival, see **Linz** (Upper Austria)
Bad Ischl Operetta Weeks, **Bad Ischl** (Upper Austria)
Baden Operetta Summer, **Baden** (Lower Austria)
Bregenz Festival, **Bregenz** (Vorarlberg)
Carinthian Summer Festival, see **Ossiach** (Carinthia)
Halbturn Palace Concerts, see **Eisenstadt** (Burgenland)
Hellbrunn Festival, **Salzburg** (Salzburg)
Innsbruck Festival of Early Music, **Innsbruck** (Tyrol)
Karthaus Gaming Chopin Festival, see **Lower Austria**
Millstatt International Music Weeks, **Millstatt** (Carinthia)
Mörbisch Operetta Festival, **Mörbisch** (Burgenland)
Raabs Cultural Summer, see **Lower Austria**
Salzburg Festival, **Salzburg** (Salzburg)
Vienna's Musical Summer, **Vienna** (Vienna)

SEPTEMBER

Austrian Chamber Music Festival, see **Baden** (Lower Austria)
Bad Ischl Operetta Weeks, **Bad Ischl** (Upper Austria)
Baden Operetta Summer, **Baden** (Lower Austria)
Haydn Festival, **Eisenstadt** (Burgenland)
International Bruckner Festival, **Linz** (Upper Austria)
Millstatt International Music Weeks, **Millstatt** (Carinthia)
Mondsee Music Days, **Mondsee** (Upper Austria)
Vienna's Musical Summer, **Vienna** (Vienna)

OCTOBER

International Bruckner Festival, **Linz** (Upper Austria)
Salzburg Culture Days, **Salzburg** (Salzburg)
Styrian Autumn, **Graz** (Styria)
Wien modern, **Vienna** (Vienna)

NOVEMBER

Schubert Festival, **Vienna** (Vienna)
Wien modern, **Vienna** (Vienna)

DECEMBER

Mozart Festival, **Vienna** (Vienna)
Schubert Festival, **Vienna** (Vienna)

The international telephone country code for Austria is (011) 43. City codes have the prefix 0, which is deleted when calling from abroad. The exception to this is Vienna, where the city code is 0222 when calling within Austria and 1 when calling from abroad.

BAD ISCHL (Upper Austria)
155 miles W of Vienna

Emperor Franz Joseph I selected Bad Ischl as his summer residence, making it a mecca for Europe's elite. The area's rich mineral deposits still entice people to vacation at the brine spas and health resorts that originally drew the Emperor.

FESTIVALS

Bad Ischl Music Days

5 Days	Musiktage Bad Ischl
Mid-July	Hütteldorferstrasse 252-4-1
	A-1140 Vienna

Orch, Cham

Philippe Entremont and the Vienna Chamber Orchestra are the featured artists here in performances that have included a Mendelssohn symphony, a Haydn violin concerto, and a Mozart string trio in the eighteenth-century parish church of Bad Ischl. **Venues:** St. Nicholas Parish Church and Parish Hall. **Performances:** nightly.

Operetta Weeks

8 Weeks	Operettengemeinde Bad Ischl
Early July–Early September	Herrengasse 32
	A-4820 Bad Ischl
Op	Tel: 06132/3839

Only operetta is celebrated during Bad Ischl's Operetta Weeks, specifically the enchanting masterpieces of Franz Lehár. Most of Lehár's operettas were composed here during a remarkable lifespan (1870–1948) that began in Franz Joseph's Austria and ended during the Cold War. Twelve years after his death, during the very month that the Berlin Wall was erected, this celebration of music from merrier times began. One of the two productions staged each summer is by Lehár. **Venue:** Kurhaus. **Performances:** 25; evenings.

BADEN (Lower Austria)
15 miles SW of Vienna

Discovered by the Romans in A.D. 100, the nurturing baths of Baden have long soothed illustrious visitors from near and far. The town's popularity reached its peak in the eighteenth and nineteenth centuries, initiated by Czar Peter the Great of Russia, who "discovered" Baden in the early eighteenth century. When the town became the summer residence of the Hapsburgs from 1803 to 1834, most of the Viennese aristocracy followed. Schubert was a frequent visitor, and Mozart is said to have composed his "Ave Verum" here. Beethoven stayed in Baden for three summers working on the Ninth Symphony. The house where he lived at 10 Rathausgasse is now the Memorial Museum to Beethoven. The tourist office has information on concerts given in the Kurpark.

FESTIVALS

Austrian Chamber Music Festival

3 Weeks	Kammermusik Festival
Mid-August–Early September	Austria
	Germergasse 16
Orch, Chor, Cham, Rec, Sem	A-2500 Baden
	Tel: 02252/89 3 20

This wide-ranging festival has featured the music of Janáček, Mozart, Britten, and Boccherini in abbeys and castles throughout Austria since 1979. **Recent Performers:** Musician's Chamber Orchestra, Prague String Quartet. **Venues:**

towns of Eggenburg, Gmünd, Horn, Weitra, and Zwettl; Breiteneich and Ottenstein castles; Altenburg, Geras, and Zwettl abbeys. **Performances:** 25; evenings and afternoons.

Baden Operetta Summer

2 Months	Badener Operetten Sommer
July–Mid-September	Theaterplatz
	A-2500 Baden
Op	Tel: 02252/48 5 47

Summer evenings can now be spent listening to Austrian operettas in the park of this famous spa town. Surrounded by peaceful old trees, audiences can enjoy works such as Johann Strauss's *Night in Venice* and Lehár's *Count von Luxembourg.* **Venue:** Kurpark. **Performances:** 57; evenings.

BREGENZ (Vorarlberg)
330 miles SW of Vienna

Situated amid the Alps on the shores of Lake Constance, Bregenz offers a magical setting for a festival. The provincial capital of Vorarlberg, this lavish, lakeside resort village can become quite busy around festival time, because it is internationally known as a vacation paradise. The Bregenz Festival facilities are used throughout the year for cultural activities. Contact the Bregenz Tourist Office for information.

FESTIVALS

Bregenz Festival

4 Weeks	Bregenzer Festspiel
Mid-July–Mid-August	Postfach 311
	A-6901 Bregenz
Op, Orch, Chor, Cham, Rec,	Tel: 05574/22 8110
Org, Th, Dance	

Off the shores of Lake Constance floats an enormous stage upon which dazzling opera is performed each summer. Not content with duplicating an ordinary theater stage, the Bregenz artists use their singular setting to produce extraordinary operas that redefine the term spectacle. The Vienna Symphony is the major orchestra, performing alone and with the opera, and chamber music is played throughout the town and in nearby Hohenems (see p. 12). Initiated in 1946 simply to offer the war-weary people pleasure, the Bregenz Festival enjoys enduring popularity with the local residents, some of whom are chorus members. Recent productions include

Der fliegende Hollander, Samson and Delilah, and *The Gypsy Baron.* **Recent Performers:** Conductors Erich Leinsdorf and Rafael Frübeck de Burgos, tenor Placido Domingo. **Venues:** Lake Constance Shoreline Stage, Grand Festival Hall, Theater am Kornmarkt, Martinsplatz, Mehrerau Abbey, Hohenems Palace. **Performances:** 80; evenings and some matinees.

IN THE AREA

Schubertiade Hohenems

2 Weeks	Schubertiade Hohenems
Mid-June–Early July	Postfach 100
	Schweizer Strasse 1
Orch, Chor, Cham, Rec	A-6845 Hohenems
	Tel: 05576/2091

Many an evening would find Franz Schubert playing for small gatherings of friends and admirers in their homes, and these occasions became known as Schubertiads. To recreate those events, the Renaissance palace at Hohenems, 6 miles S of Bregenz, was selected in 1976 for this refreshing festival. The elegant palace courtyard and the 300-seat Knight's Hall, with its carved mahogany ceiling, hunting tapestries, and stag heads, offer a delightful intimacy that suits the chamber music of Schubert. Larger works are presented in the nearby town of Feldkirch. World-renowned artists perform here, and the festival has been ranked as one of ten best music festivals worldwide by *Courvoisiers.* **Recent Performers:** Concertgebouw Orchestra Amsterdam, Tokyo String Quartet, baritone Dietrich Fischer-Dieskau. **Venues:** Hohenems Palace; towns of Feldkirch and Wolfegg. **Performances:** about 35; afternoons and evenings. Tickets should be ordered one year in advance.

EISENSTADT (Burgenland)
25 miles S of Vienna

The small town of Eisenstadt, the capital of Burgenland province, is a popular day-excursion from Vienna. Situated at the foot of the Leitha mountains and only a few miles from Lake Neusiedl, Eisenstadt is surrounded by vineyards and orchards. Music lovers will want to visit the Esterházy Palace, where Franz Josef Haydn served the Esterházy family for more than 30 years. Originally built as a medieval stronghold, the palace was refurbished in the seventeenth century in the lavish baroque style. Haydn's modest home is filled with interesting mementos of his life, and his white marble tomb can be seen at the nearby Bergkirche. Because the tourist office in Eisenstadt is the clearinghouse for events throughout the province, information can be obtained there for many regional events. Ask about occasional candlelight chamber or organ concerts at Halbturn Castle, Kittsee Castle, the Gothic church in Rust, Eisenstadt Bergkirche, and Donnerskirchen. Bus service from Vienna is available.

FESTIVALS

Haydn Festival

2 Weeks	Haydn Festspiele
Early September	Schloss Esterházy
	A-7000 Eisenstadt
Orch, Chor, Cham, Rec, Org	Tel: 02682/618 66
	Fax: 02682/618 05

Haydn spent most of his adult life here and maintained a fondness for Eisenstadt even after he left, declaring that it was where he wished to live and to die. Eisenstadt now returns that high regard with this festival, which, like "Papa" Haydn himself, is characterized by modestly presented brilliance. Local musicians collaborate with major recording artists to pay gracious tribute to the master during this event, which is also known as the Haydn Tage (Haydn Days). One day of the Festival is reserved to honor Franz Liszt, who lived in nearby Raiding (now in Austria, Raiding was part of Hungary when Liszt was born there in 1811). Beginning in 1991, the Festival also incorporates the International Joseph Joachim Violin Competition, held every four years in honor of the great virtuoso born in the Burgenland town of Kittsee in 1831.   **Recent Performers:** Michael Tilson Thomas conducting the London Symphony Orchestra, Moscow Philharmonic, Austrian-Hungarian Haydn Philharmonic.   **Venues:** Esterházy Palace, Bergkirche, Raiding Liszt House.   **Performances:** evenings and matinees, plus Sunday morning Mass.   Tickets for the Haydn Festival should be requested 9 months in advance.

ONGOING EVENTS

Austrian-Hungarian Haydn Philharmonic

Orch, Cham, Org	Österreichish-Ungarische
	Haydnphilharmonie
	Schloss Esterházy
	Postfach 95
	A-7000 Eisenstadt
	Tel: 0222/43 13 14 (Vienna)

Founded and conducted by Adam Fischer, the Haydn Philharmonic seeks to reproduce the sound of the eighteenth-century orchestra for which Haydn composed his symphonies. Programs of Haydn and Mozart are performed in both of the palaces used by the Esterházys during the years Haydn was employed by Hungary's benevolent princes. Organized in 1987, the orchestra is chiefly known for its esteemed recordings of Haydn symphonies. **Venues:** Esterházy Palace (Eisenstadt), Esterházy Palace (Fertöd, Hungary). **Performances:** 10; April, June, September. Bus service between Vienna, Eisenstadt, and Fertöd is available.

Esterházy Palace Chamber Concerts

Orch, Cham   Burgenland Tourist Office
                             Schloss Esterházy
                             A-7000 Eisenstadt
                             Tel: 02682/61866

Haydn's music is performed within the same cream and gold walls and beneath the same lustrous baroque ceiling where it first sounded. Three different chamber series are given in this hall, whose remarkable acoustics captivated Haydn. **Performances:** Tuesdays and Fridays, May–October: Haydn quartet performing in eighteenth-century costume; weekly, July–August: chamber orchestras and choirs.

IN THE AREA

Halbturn Palace Concerts

8 Concerts   Halbturner Schlosskonzerte
July–August   Halbturn Tourist Office
                             Budapester Strasse 35
Orch, Cham, Rec   A-7131 Halbturn
                             Tel: 02172/8645
                             or /8580
                             Fax: 0222/586 1900

Surrounded by a magnificent park, this hunting lodge 25 miles E of Eisenstadt became a favorite summer retreat of Empress Maria Theresa after it was redesigned in the flamboyant baroque style. Concerts featuring Debussy, Mozart, and Brahms now enable audiences to experience the ambience of an imperial house party. The artists and/or the artistic director give an informal introduction to the works on the program. The festival was founded in 1974 to combine yearly art exhibitions with performances by Austrian artists. **Venue:** Freskensaal of the Halbturn Palace. **Recent Performers:** Ensemble Classico, violinist Christian Altenburger, pianist Jörg Demus, soprano Gundula Janowitz. **Performances:** Saturday evenings.

Lockenhaus Chamber Music Festival

2 Weeks	Kammermusikfest
Early July	Lockenhaus
	A-7442 Lockenhaus
Cham	Tel: 02616/22 24

This festival is devoted to chamber music, and for more than a decade renowned artists have joined local musicians to bring small-scale masterpieces to life in this tiny village 30 miles S of Eisenstadt. Ensembles extend beyond the traditional string quartet, and programs are among the most comprehensive in Austria. Recent programs have featured music by Debussy, Beethoven, Ravel, Boulez, Smetana, Messiaen, Schubert, Janáček, and Vivaldi. **Recent Performers:** pianists Andras Schiff and Alfred Brendel, Moscow-Borodin Quartet, Darmstadt Concert Choir. **Venues:** Lockenhaus Castle, Lockenhaus Village Church. **Performances:** 25; daily, afternoons and evenings.

GRAZ (Styria)
90 miles SW of Vienna

A city of parks on the banks of the River Mur, Graz owes its name to the Slavic word for its fortress, built in the twelfth century. Only the bell tower of this medieval stronghold remains today, but the garden-covered hill on which it stood offers clear views of the city, the river valley, and the foothills of the Alps. Although it has become an industrial center, Graz preserves much of the elegance and grace that have characterized it since the Renaissance. Throughout the summer the Graz Congress and Graz Cathedral host concerts as part of the American Institute of Musical Studies.

FESTIVALS

Styrian Autumn

1 Month	Steirischer Herbst
October	Sackstrasse 17/1
	A-8010 Graz
Orch, Cham, Th, Lect, Ex	Tel: 0316/82 30 07
	Fax: 0316/83 57 88

The grandfather of avant-garde festivals, Styrian Autumn was founded in 1968 and has evolved into an internationally acclaimed celebration of contemporary music, literature, art, and theater. Each year performances and exhibitions revolve around a selected topic (in 1990 it was "Mobility: The Third Way"), and each program has a more specific theme such as "Space and Light" or "Goodbye Big Mac! The Slow Food Avant-garde." Over 200 events are held throughout the city, and admission to some is free. **Recent Performers:** Kronos Quartet, Ensemble Modern, Frankfurt Radio Symphony Orchestra. **Venues:** City Park, Mobile Hall. **Performances:** daily. Tickets are on sale during the festival and can be difficult to obtain.

Styriarte Graz

3 Weeks	Styriarte Graz
Late June–Mid-July	Palais Attems
	Sackstrasse 17
Op, Orch, Chor, Cham,	A-8010 Graz
Rec, Sem	Tel: 0316/81 29 41
	Fax: 0316/87 73 835

The locations are variable, but the high level of music making is constant at this summer festival. Each year programs focus on the music of one composer (Mendelssohn was a recent honoree) and include a four-day seminar that examines that musician's work. The venues themselves are an attraction, for they include the terraced Schlossberg; the Minoritensaal, formerly a ceremonial refectory; and the splendid baroque Eggenberg Palace. **Recent Performers:** Nicholas Harnoncourt conducting the Chamber Orchestra of Europe, pianist Martha Argerich, Arnold Schönberg Choir. **Venues:** Schlossberg, Congress, Minoritensaal, Orpheum, Eggenberg Palace, Stainz Parish Church. **Performances:** 26; evenings. Tickets for the festival are available one year in advance, and requests are accepted until mid-May. Space is always saved for visitors from abroad, and organizers claim that no one has yet been sent away. Bus service to Stainz is provided.

ONGOING EVENTS

Graz Opera

Op, Dance, Th, Child

Grazer Oper
Kaiser-Josef Platz
A-8010 Graz
Tel: 0316/82 74 22
Fax: 0316/82 64 51

Within a stately nineteenth-century opera house that is nearly as large as Vienna's State Opera, the Graz Opera performs a full season of opera, operetta, and ballet. This theater and the Play House constitute the Vereinigte Bühnen (United Stages) of Graz. Recent productions have included Berlioz' *Beatrice et Benedict*, Mozart's *Idomeneo*, and Puccini's *Tosca*. **Performances:** nearly 200; October–June.

INNSBRUCK (Tyrol)
240 miles SW of Vienna

Innsbruck is one of Austria's largest Alpine cities, spread out on both sides of the Inn River in the shadow of huge walls of jagged mountains. Innsbruck contains many reminders of imperial glory in its Hofkirche, Hofburg Palace, and the most famous of Innsbruck landmarks, the Golden Roof (a balcony in the center of the old town covered with gilded tiles). As one of Europe's great ski resorts and host to two recent Winter Olympics, Innsbruck's essence is a near-perfect combination of vitality and old-world charm. The Tourist Office publishes a list of classical and jazz concerts and theater, folk, and sporting events.

FESTIVALS

Festival of Early Music

8 Weeks
July–August

Op, Cham, Rec, Org

Festwochen der Alten Musik
Tourist Office
Burggraben 3
A-6021 Innsbruck
Tel: 0512/5356
Fax: 0512/535643

Because Innsbruck was a seat of the Hapsburgs during the sixteenth and seventeenth centuries, it became a center for European music, and since 1967 the city has revived that role with this celebration of music composed before 1750. International artists perform on period instruments, notably the restored 1558 organ in the Hofkirche, one of the most historically important organs in Europe. Productions of three early operas form the core of this festival, which balances vocal and instrumental works. Recent presentations have included Monteverdi's *Coronation of Poppea* and Purcell's *Dido and Aeneas*. Most concerts are given in the Imperial Riesensaal, providing suitable splendor for music originally heard in courtly settings. Incorporated into the festival are the concerts at Ambras Castle (2 miles SE of Innsbruck), which are held in a sixteenth-century Renaissance Spanish Hall known not only for its vivid frescoes but also for its fine acoustics. **Recent Performers:** London Baroque, Ensemble Mosaiques, Gesualdo Consort Amsterdam, Rameau Trio Leipzig. **Venues:** Hofburg (eighteenth-century Hapsburg Palace built by Maria Theresa), Hofkirche, Tirol Landestheater, Ambras Castle. **Performances:** 18, evenings.

LINZ (Upper Austria)
90 Miles W of Vienna

The Danube city of Linz was a Roman town in the first century and is now the capital of Upper Austria. Its great symbol, the Trinity column, stands in the city's Hauptplatz, a baroque combination of cherubs, swirls, and sun. The city houses several impressive museums, including the Neue Galerie der Stadt Linz, which contains some of Austria's best modern art. Although Linz was home to Beethoven while he wrote the Eighth Symphony, it is Anton Bruckner, born in nearby Ansfelden in 1824, who is the city's most famous musical son.

FESTIVALS

International Bruckner Festival

3 Weeks
Mid-September–Early
    October

Op, Orch, Chor, Cham, Rec,
    Org, Dance, Th, Ex, Film

Internationale Brucknerfest
Brucknerhaus
Untere Donaulände 7
A-4020 Linz
Tel: 0732/75225
Fax: 0732/283745

Anton Bruckner's roots are deep at Linz, for his ancestors settled in the area centuries before his birth, and he was always more comfortable here than in cosmopolitan Vienna. Since 1974 Linz has paid him homage with this festival, which offers such diverse programming as Stravinsky, Telemann, and Shostakovich in addition to Bruckner's own monumental works. Incorporated into the Brucknerfest are two "Cloud of Sound" (*Klangwolke*) performances, during which symphony concerts are transmitted live from the Brucknerhaus to the surrounding Danube Park. **Recent Performers:** London Symphony Orchestra, soprano Kiri Te Kanawa, pianist Rudolf Buchbinder. **Venues:** Brucknerhaus, St. Florian Abbey, Wilhering Abbey. **Performances:** 15; evenings.

ONGOING EVENTS

Brucknerhaus

Op, Orch, Chor, Cham, Rec, Brucknerhaus
Org, Dance, Th, Film Untere Donaulände 7
A-4020 Linz
Tel: 0732/275225
Fax: 0732/283745

With a curving glass facade that mirrors the broad Danube flowing below, this multipurpose facility plays many roles in Linz, housing social events, conventions, and year-round classical music concerts. Built in 1974, the Brucknerhaus was voted one of the top five concert halls in the world by the London Philharmonic Orchestra. Chamber music and organ recitals are also offered here. **Recent Performers:** Bruckner Orchestra Linz, oboist Heinz Holliger, violinist Shlomo Mintz, cellist Heinrich Schiff. **Performances:** September–June.

IN THE AREA

Bad Hall Operetta Festival

6 Weekends Operettenfestspiele Bad Hall
Late June–Early August Hauptplatz 5
A-4540 Bad Hall
Op Tel: 07258/22 55

Operetta brightens the summer for patients and visitors at this spa town, 15 miles S of Linz, which is famous for its iodine-rich brine. One production is staged each summer;

Kalman's *Czar Prince* and Zeller's *Bird Dealer* were recently performed. **Venue:** Kurtheater. **Performances:** 12; Friday and Saturday evenings.

St. Florian Organ Recitals

Org

St. Florian Organ Recitals
Tourist Office
Thannstrasse 2
A-4490 St. Florian
Tel: 0732/27 61 27

Although known today for his orchestral and choral works, Anton Bruckner was famed in his lifetime for his undisputed genius at the organ, and he performed throughout Europe as a celebrated soloist. He always retained a fondness for this Augustinian abbey 11 miles SE of Linz, where he served as a choirboy and for which he later composed his *St. Florian Requiem*. At his request, Bruckner is buried in the crypt beneath this 7000-pipe, 103-rank organ, which was always his favorite instrument.

Chamber Music Festival at Tillysburg Palace

4 Days
Mid-July

Cham, Read

Kammermusikfest auf
Schloss Tillysburg
Postfach 57
Untere Donaulände 7
A-4010 Linz
Tel: 0732/275 230

Since 1985 candlelight chamber concerts featuring works such as the Bolling *Jazz Suite* along with Schumann and Beethoven string quartets have been offered in the inner courtyard of this baroque palace 8 miles SE of Linz.

LOWER AUSTRIA (Also see Melk and Vienna)

This land of castles, abbeys, and vineyards is Austria's northernmost province. Its name comes from its geography, which includes the lower portion of the Danube River valley. The foothills of the Alps rise to the south, the forested slopes of the Waldviertel roll toward Czechoslovakia to the north, and the Vienna Woods surround Vienna to the east.

FESTIVALS

Altenburg Abbey Music Academy

2 Weeks
Late July–Early August

Orch, Chor, Cham, Rec,
Org, Sem

Stift Altenburger Musik
Akademie
A-3591 Altenburg
Tel: 02982/3451

Music for the keyboard is explored here in a twelfth-century Benedictine abbey 4 miles SW of Horn (50 miles NW of Vienna) that was extensively rebuilt in the rococo style during the seventeenth and eighteenth centuries. Organized by the Viennese organization Friends of Piano Music, the festival presents piano, harpsichord, and organ recitals at this still-functioning abbey. Other programs are given throughout the year, and the Altenburg Boys Choir regularly sings masses here in addition to their concert performances throughout Austria and abroad. **Recent Performers:** Swiss Ensemble Classico, composer Gottfried von Einem, pianist Robert Lehrbaumer. **Venue:** Altenburg Abbey. **Performances:** 8. Address written ticket requests to Freunde der Claviermusik/Kostlergasse 3-10; A-1060 Vienna.

Kartause Gaming Chopin Festival

3 Days
Late August

Orch, Cham, Rec, Lect

Bookshop
Kartause Gaming
Tel: 07485/354

International Chopin Society
Biberstrasse 4
A-1010 Vienna
Tel: 0222/512 23 74

Ninety miles SW of Vienna, music now resounds through halls that for more than four centuries knew only silence. The cloister of Kartause Gaming was founded in 1332 by Hapsburg Duke Albrecht II and for 450 years belonged to the Carthusian (Kartause) order of silent monks. Since 1984 European artists, many from Chopin's native Poland, have performed works by Chopin and his contemporaries. Information is available from the International Chopin Society in Vienna and from Kartause Gaming, which is near the pretty town of Lackenhof.

Raabs Cultural Summer

11 Concerts	Raabser Kultursommer
May–August	Lower Austria Tourist Office
	Heidenschuss 2
Orch, Chor, Cham, Rec, Ex	A-1010 Vienna
	Tel: 02846/365

Spanish guitar music, Mozart's Requiem, and chamber music from the Middle Ages were recently heard in the medieval castle of Raabs, which lies along the river Thaya 55 miles NW of Vienna. **Recent Performers:** pianist Elisabeth Leonskaja, Krems Chamber Orchestra, guitarist Stefan Fuchs. **Performances:** 11; evenings.

ONGOING EVENTS

Grafenegg Castle Concerts

Orch, Cham, Rec	Grafenegger Schlosskonzerte
	A-3485 Haitzendorf

Piano recitals, Beethoven's Symphony no. 3, and Schrammel music are among the varied offerings in this castle 50 miles W of Vienna. Although there has been a structure on the site since 1294, the fine Victorian castle seen today was completed between 1840 and 1873. A special Advent program is always given here, the details for which are available by late November. Information may be obtained directly from the castle or by contacting the Lower Austria Tourist Office. **Recent Performers:** Budapest Symphony, Mozarteum Orchestra Salzburg. **Performances:** 18; weekend evenings, April–December.

St. Pölten Gala Concerts

Orch, Cham, Rec	Gala Konzerte
	Prandtauerstrasse 2
	A-3100 St. Pölten
	Tel: 02742/52531 411
	Fax: 02742/52531 492

These programs were organized in 1988 soon after this handsome town 40 miles W of Vienna was named the capital of Lower Austria. Designed to bring high-quality cultural events to the new provincial seat, the concerts are given in the sixteenth-century Town Hall. Special "Festival Weeks" take place in May and June. Concerts are also given in the synagogue and Grosse Stadtsaal. The cathedrals of

St. Pölten and nearby Herzogenburg and Lilienfeld host the International Church Music Days in September and October. **Recent Performers:** tenor Peter Schreier, cellist Heinrich Schiff, Vienna Schubert Trio. **Venue:** Rathaus. **Performances:** 9; November–June.

Zwettl Abbey Organ Festival

6 Weekends	Orgelfest Stift Zwettl
Mid-June–Late August	Zwettl Tourist Office
	A-3910 Zwettl
Orch, Chor, Cham, Org	Tel: 02822/24 14 29

The centerpiece for the concerts at this Cistercian monastery 70 miles NW of Vienna is the organ built in 1731, the largest of its kind in Austria. The monastery itself was founded in 1138, and although several of the original Romanesque buildings remain, the church nave is a fine example of the Gothic style. **Recent Performers:** Saxon Virtuosos, English Brass Ensemble, organist Roland Goetz. **Venues:** Zwettl Abbey, Ottenschlag Parish Church. **Performances:** 6; Saturday or Sunday.

MELK (Lower Austria)
50 miles W of Vienna

The tidy riverside village of Melk is a charming introduction to the wine-producing Wachau region. Dominating the town is one of Europe's great religious institutions, the Melk Abbey, an astounding baroque edifice that Umberto Eco used as the setting for his novel *The Name of the Rose*. Rising from atop a bluff overlooking the Danube, the Abbey was a center of knowledge and enlightenment during the Middle Ages and is justifiably one of Austria's most visited sites. Choral and organ concerts and art exhibitions are held regularly in the Abbey.

FESTIVALS

Melk Abbey Whitsun Concerts

1 Week	Pfingstkonzerte im Stift Melk
Late May–Early June	Rathaus
	A-3390 Melk
Orch, Chor, Cham, Rec,	Tel: 02752/2307
Org, Jazz, Ex	Fax: 02752/2307 27

The spectacular Benedictine Melk Abbey opens many of its wondrous rooms to celebrate Pentecost with these concerts, which began in 1978. Sacred music is performed on the weekend, but during the week the repertory encompasses selections such as Russian songs, chamber music by Schubert, and works for solo guitar by Villa-Lobos. **Recent Performers:** Philippe Entremont conducting the Vienna Chamber Orchestra, Vienna String Quartet, bass Robert Holl. **Venues:** Melk Abbey, Linzerstrasse Museum. **Performances:** 9. Because Pentecost (Whitsun) is a movable holiday, the days of this festival vary, but tickets are always available by April 1.

MILLSTATT (Carinthia)
150 miles SW of Vienna

Millstatt is the most prominent town on Millstätter See, a beautiful lake popular for its water sports. Aside from the lake, Millstatt's other great attraction is its eleventh-century abbey, which features remarkable elements of Romanesque, Gothic, and baroque architecture.

FESTIVALS

Millstatt International Music Weeks

May–June; July–August; September	Internationalen Musik-wochen
	Stiftsgebäude
Orch, Chor, Cham, Rec, Org	A-9872 Millstatt
	Tel: 04766/21 65

Millstatt hosts essentially three separate festivals: Musical Spring (May–June), International Music Weeks (July–August), and Musical Autumn (September), all offering similar programs. A Benedictine abbey filled with Renaissance frescoes and Gothic vaults provides the stage for these concerts. In 1977 a magnificent Danish organ was installed, and it is featured in most programs. Much sacred baroque and classical music is presented, with recent productions including Handel's *Judas Maccabeus,* Mozart's C Major Missa Brevis, and Haydn's *Theresa Mass.* The repertory has also included Brahms and Poulenc. **Recent Performers:** Salzburg Wind Quintet, Bavarian Brass Ensemble, Seoul Sinfonietta.

Venue: Stiftskirche. **Performances:** 40; evenings and Sunday Mass.

MONDSEE (Upper Austria)
140 miles SW of Vienna

Mondsee ("moon lake") is named for the placid, crescent-shaped lake upon whose shores it rests. The lake is the warmest and third largest of several lakes that dot the Salzkammergut countryside, making this a favorite summer holiday area. Mondsee is a peaceful village of colorful flowers and historic houses framed by jagged mountain slopes.

FESTIVALS

Mondsee Music Days

1 Week	Musiktage Mondsee
Early September	Postfach 31
	A-5310 Mondsee
Cham, Rec	Tel: 06232/22 03 37
	Fax: 06232/31 51 17

Under the artistic direction of pianist Andras Schiff, renowned artists collaborate for concerts that have recently garnered international praise. The programs are always focused on two composers—in 1990 music by Bartók and Bach was performed, and in 1991 the focus was on Schubert and Janáček. Because the artists are in residence throughout the festival, audiences are able to meet and mingle with the performers. **Recent Performers:** Takacs Quartet, oboist Heinz Holliger, violinist Christian Altenburger. **Venues:** Parish Church, Palace. **Performances:** 12.

MÖRBISCH (Burgenland)
30 miles SE of Vienna

Mörbisch is one of several small, picturesque villages of whitewashed houses along the shores of Lake Neusiedl near the Hungarian border. The attraction of the large, shallow lake (average depth is only 4 feet) brings visitors year-round to this town of narrow streets and fertile vineyards.

FESTIVALS

Mörbisch Operetta Festival

7 Weeks	Mörbisch Seefestspiele
Mid-July–Late August	Schloss Esterházy
	A-7000 Eisenstadt
Op	Tel: 02682/66 210
	02682/66 211

Let the strains of an Austrian operetta beguile you as you sit on the banks of Lake Neusiedl. Since 1957 operettas by composers such as Lehár and Kalman have been performed on a floating stage reminiscent of the one at Bregenz. Each performance closes with a fireworks display. **Venue:** Lake Neusiedl floating stage. **Performances:** 15; Saturday and Sunday evenings. Transportation from Vienna is available. During the festival, the box office may be contacted:

> Seestrasse 4
> A-7072 Mörbisch
> Tel: 02685/8232
> 02685/8855

OSSIACH (Carinthia)
150 miles SW of Vienna

Ossiach is one of the tiny villages that line the shores of the serene Ossiacher See, Carinthia's third largest lake. This scenic area is a popular vacation resort among Austrians, who visit as much for the sensational surroundings as for the warmth of the lake, which may reach 79 degrees Fahrenheit during the summer.

FESTIVALS

Carinthian Summer Festival

2 Months	Carinthischer Sommer
July-August	A-9570 Ossiach
	Tel: 04243/510
Op, Orch, Chor, Rec, Org,	04243/502
Sem, Child	

An inviting series of diverse concerts offered in two Alpine towns, Ossiach and Villach, draws enthusiastic audiences into the quiet region of Carinthia. Since its founding in 1969, the combination of renowned artists and varied programs has won this festival international respect. Recent performances have included music by Palestrina, Messiaen, Kodály, and Schubert. **Recent Performers:** Vienna Boys' Choir, Bruckner Orchestra Linz, pianist Rudolf Buchbinder. **Venues:** eleventh-century Ossiach Abbey, Villach conference center. **Performances:** almost daily; afternoons and evenings.

SALZBURG (Salzburg)
160 miles SW of Vienna

When viewed from its Old Town, this entrancing small city on the banks of the Salzach river seems to exist for sheer aesthetic delight. The birthplace of Mozart, Salzburg was governed for centuries by Prince Archbishops who enriched its many churches and gave a baroque elegance to its spacious squares and historic buildings. The town is dominated by the imposing, medieval fortress of Hohensalzburg, which towers 400 feet above the old city from the top of the Mönchsberg. Mozart's spirit is kept alive everywhere, from the house where he was born in 1756 to the home where he lived until he left to seek his musical fortune in Vienna at the age of 24. Music seems to waft from any space in which a group can gather, and visitors who arrive ticketless can often enjoy concerts in the Mirabell Gardens or at the Mozarteum.

FESTIVALS

Easter Festival

9 Days	Oster Festspiele Salzburg
Palm Sunday–Easter Monday	Festspielhaus
	A-5010 Salzburg
Op, Orch, Chor, Cham	Tel: 0662/84 25 41 361

Herbert von Karajan conceived this celebration of Easter in 1967 and forged it into one of Europe's premier music festivals. With the Berlin Philharmonic and Vienna State Opera Chorus as the two resident ensembles, it is small wonder that the performances are superb and prices steep. Recent repertoire has included Bach's B Minor Mass, Beethoven's *Fidelio*, Stravinsky's *Firebird*, and Wagner's *Ring of the*

Nibelungen. **Recent Performers:** Berlin Philharmonic, Vienna State Opera Chorus. **Venue:** Large Festival Theater. **Performances:** about 8 evenings, Easter matinee. Tickets are sold only in series; bookings are accepted a year in advance.

Hellbrunn Festival

2 Weekends	Fest in Hellbrunn
Early August	Postfach 47
	A-5027 Salzburg
Op, Orch, Cham, Rec, Dance,	Tel: 0662/787 84
Child, Read	Fax: 0662/883 220

Best known for the elaborate, whimsical fountains in its extensive gardens, the Italianate Hellbrunn Palace 3 miles SE of Salzburg is the site for this musical celebration. Viennese songs, fireworks, and Offenbach operettas are among the offerings to be enjoyed in the seventeenth-century palace and at the open-air Stone Theater, the stage where the first opera was performed in Austria in 1617 (Monteverdi's *Orfeo*). **Recent Performers:** English Brass Ensemble, Collegium Musicum Juvarense. **Venue:** Hellbrunn Palace and Park. **Performances:** 25.

Mozart Week

10 Days	Mozartwoche
Late January–Early February	International Stiftung
	Mozarteum
Op, Orch, Chor, Cham, Rec	Postfach 34
	Schwarzstrasse 26
	A-5024 Salzburg
	Tel: 0662/73154
	Fax: 0662/88 2419

Since 1956 Mozart's birthday (January 27, 1756) has been celebrated by the Mozarteum Foundation with this festival, which is nearly as luminous as the Salzburg Festival itself. Programs feature his lesser-known compositions as well as such perennial favorites as *Don Giovanni*. Mass with orchestra and soloists is celebrated on both Sundays, and evening dress is formal. **Recent Performers:** Zubin Mehta conducting the Vienna Philharmonic Orchestra, pianists Richard Goode and Andras Schiff, Salzburg Marionettes. **Venues:** Mozarteum, Large Festival Theater, Landestheater, Franciscan Church, Cathedral, University, Mozart's residence. **Performances:** 35; afternoons and evenings.

Salzburg Culture Days

2 Weeks	Salzburger Kulturtage
Late October	Salzburg Kulturvereinigung
	Waagplatz 1a Trakl Haus
Op, Orch, Chor, Cham	Postfach 42
	A-5010 Salzburg
	Tel: 0662/845 346

This autumnal event is cosponsored by six Salzburg music societies. Performances are evenly divided among opera, symphony, and chamber music. Recent productions have included Verdi's *Otello,* Dvořák's *New World* Symphony, and the Berlioz Requiem. **Recent Performers:** Mozarteum Orchestra, National Orchestra of Bordeaux, European Chamber Ensemble, Antidogma Musica. **Venues:** Large Festival Theater, Residenz Palace, Mozarteum, University. **Performances:** 18; evenings.

Salzburg Festival

5 Weeks	Salzburger Festspiele
Late July–August	P.O. Box 140
	A-5010 Salzburg
Op, Orch, Chor, Cham, Rec,	Tel: 0662/84 25 41
Dance, Th, Ex	Fax: 0662/89 11 14

Salzburg is transformed into a glittering mecca for the music world during this festival, which has grown into one of Europe's favorite and most respected celebrations. The spirit of the festival suffuses the whole town, and visitors who have not been able to secure tickets can still enjoy excellent performances that are not formally part of the program. Hugo von Hofmannsthal's modern morality play, *Everyman* (which, ironically, is a nonmusical event), was the centerpiece of the first festival in 1920, and its stark presentation on the steps of the Cathedral has become a hallowed tradition. Although not the intent of the founders, the festival has become Salzburg's grand homage to Mozart and is sometimes mistakenly referred to as the "Mozart Festival." Although there is more music by Mozart than any other single composer, the repertory is broad. Sadly, with the passing of Herbert von Karajan in 1989 an era closed, for the force of his presence was stamped on every festival for over two decades. **Recent Performers:** Riccardo Muti with the Berlin Philharmonic, sopranos Jessye Norman and Kathleen Battle, flutist James Galway, pianist Alfred Brendel, Kronos Quartet, English Baroque Soloists. **Venues:** Large and Small Festival Theaters, Felsenreitschule (see below under "Festival Theaters"), Cathedral, University Church, Landestheater, Mozarteum, St. Peter's Church. **Performances:** many daily. Tickets can be expensive and usually sell out by February. Ticket requests must be in writing and must be received by mid-January. If received later, they will be processed by April, at which time a list of remaining tickets is available and can be sent upon request. Formal dress for the major events is requested.

ONGOING EVENTS

Festival Theaters

Op, Orch, Cham, Rec
Hofstallgasse 1
A-5020 Salzburg
Tel: 0662/84 25 41

In addition to housing the Salzburg Festival, these three theaters maintain year-round concert schedules. All three are located at the base of the Mönchsberg in the same space that in the seventeenth century served as horse stables for the Prince Archbishops. Their growth has matched that of the Festival. *Felsenreitschule* (Rock Riding School): In the quarry where the rock for the Salzburg Cathedral was cut, a riding school was created in the seventeenth century by carving 96 boxes in three tiers out of the cliff wall. In 1924 this dramatic arena provided the first permanent home for the fledgling Festival. *Small Festival Theater* (Kleines Festspielhaus): In 1928, as the Salzburg Festival continued to grow, this hall was created by adapting part of the horse stables into a theater that remains essential to the Festival. *Large Festival Theater* (Grosses Festspielhaus): The baroque facade of the old stables graciously masks the generous proportions of this theater, which was built right into the cliff face between 1956 and 1960. With its vast stage, excellent acoustics, and state-of-the-art technology, this theater easily accommodates grand operas and symphonies. The stage equipment is comparable to that of the Vienna State Opera, and many productions are shared between the two houses.

Mozart Serenades

Cham
Mozart Serenaden
Residenzplatz 4
A-5071 Salzburg
Tel: 0662/89 1087
0662/89 1168

Varied chamber ensembles participate in this series, with at least one work by Mozart on each program. The Gothic arches of St. Blaise Church, the elegance of the famed Mozarteum, and the exuberant excesses of Hellbrunn Palace Gardens make delightful settings for these concerts. Special programs include candlelight performances at Christmastime and recitals with performers in period dress. **Recent Performers:** Vienna Quintet, Munich Leopold Quartet. **Performances:** 90; May–December (daily in August).

Mozarteum

Orch, Chor, Cham, Rec, Org	Mozarteum Hochschule für Musik Mirabellplatz 1 A-5020 Salzburg Tel: 0662/75 53 40
Orch, Chor, Cham, Rec, Org	International Stiftung Mozarteum Postfach 34 Schwarzstrasse 26 A-5024 Salzburg Tel: 0662/73154 Fax: 0662/88 2419

"Mozarteum" in Salzburg can mean several things. The term is most accurately applied to a complex of three buildings bordering the Mirabell Palace Gardens. It also refers to both the renowned Academy of Music (Hochschule für Musik) and the International Mozarteum Foundation (Stiftung), which use these buildings.

The building at Schwarzstrasse 24 is a lovely baroque concert hall seating 800 that is one of Salzburg's main concert venues and home of the Mozarteum Orchestra. This professional ensemble specializes in the interpretation of Mozart while maintaining a well-rounded concert repertoire.

The Academy offers countless faculty and/or student recitals called *Vortragsabends* that provide visitors the best chance to happen upon a pleasing performance. These concerts are given in the newer building at Mirabellplatz 1 and in the classical building at Schwarzstrasse 26. Programs also take place at Frohnburg Palace, which appeared in *The Sound of Music* as the Von Trapp family home and is now a student dormitory. Announcements for these concerts are posted throughout the complex, and admission is free or nominal.

The International Mozart Foundation is dedicated to maintaining Mozart's art, deepening knowledge of his personality, and upholding his memory. The Foundation is at the forefront of the seemingly endless tribute Salzburg pays to Mozart in what appears to be compensation for the indifference shown here during his lifetime. From September to May, the Foundation sponsors seven series of fine chamber and symphony concerts, not only at the Mozarteum but at Mozart's residence and St. Peter's Church. **Recent Performers:** Julliard String Quartet, cellist Yo-Yo Ma, Vienna Chamber Orchestra. **Performances:** afternoons and evenings. The Academy and the Foundation are interdependent organizations that both utilize all of the Mozarteum venues. It is therefore recommended that both offices be contacted.

Salzburg Fortress Concerts

Cham

Salzburger Festungskonzerte
A.-Adlasser-Weg 22
A-5020 Salzburg
Tel: 0662/82 58 58

Mozart is included in each of these concerts given in the Prince's Chamber or the Hall of Arms of Europe's largest completely preserved fortress. Area musicians are featured on the programs, which include special performances at Christmas and New Year's. Recent repertory has included Mozart's "Eine kleine Nachtmusik" and piano concertos by Mozart and Beethoven. **Recent Performers:** Salzburg Mozart Ensemble, Hohensalzburg Piano Trio. **Performances:** Most evenings; June–August.

Salzburg Marionettes

Salzburger Marionetten-
theater
Schwarzstrasse 24
A-5024 Salzburg
Tel: 0662/72 4 06

Begun in 1913 as a personal entertainment by Anton Aicher, the Salzburg Marionettes have become one of Salzburg's most endearing companies. Music is broadcast through a multichannel recording system as the meticulously carved marionettes impersonate the characters of operas and fairy tales. The elegant theater is small (335 seats) and the troupe often on tour, so tickets may be difficult to obtain. Recent repertoire has included *The Magic Flute, Don Giovanni, The Marriage*

of Figaro, The Barber of Seville, Snow White, The Nutcracker.
Performances: 20 per month; year-round, afternoons and evenings.

Salzburg Palace Concerts

Cham

Makartplatz 9
A-5024 Salzburg
Tel: 0662/72 7 88

Crystal chandeliers gracefully illuminate sculpted cream walls and a vast overhead fresco in the seventeenth-century Residenz Palace, where accomplished instrumentalists perform in these chamber music concerts. Programs are also given in the Marble Hall of the Mirabell Palace, which was built in 1606 as a private residence and now houses the mayor's offices. When the weather obliges, concerts are sometimes held outdoors by the brightly lit Residenz Fountain. Programs here, more varied than those found on the Mozart Serenade series, have recently included not only Mozart, but Brahms, Webern, Vivaldi, Grieg, Dvořák, and Bartók. **Recent Performers:** Vienna String Quartet, Alban Berg Quartet, soloists from the Berlin and Vienna Philharmonic Orchestras. **Venues:** Mirabell Palace, Residenz Palace. **Performances:** year-round; almost nightly.

SPITTAL AN DER DRAU (Carinthia)
180 miles SW of Vienna

Considered the gateway to Carinthia, Spittal is one of the region's loveliest towns, attracting visitors from near and far to its main attraction: the magnificent Porcia Palace, a sixteenth-century Italianate palace that is considered one of Austria's finest Renaissance structures. The enchanting courtyard and lavish gardens are particularly delightful. Classical and folk concerts are given in Porcia Palace throughout the year.

FESTIVALS

International Choir Competition

4 Days
Early July

Chor

Internationaler Chorbewerb
Schloss Porcia
Burgplatz 1
A-9800 Spittal an der Drau
Tel: 04762/3420

Choirs from the Philippines, Scandinavia, Europe, and the United States compete here in two categories: classical/

modern and folksong. For more than 25 years, the setting for these open-air concerts has been the three-story arcaded courtyard of the Porcia Palace, built in 1597.

UPPER AUSTRIA (Also see Bad Ischl, Linz, Mondsee)

The Danube flows through Upper Austria toward Vienna, passing on its way through the provincial capital of Linz. South of the Danube is the fertile land where the abbeys hosting the Upper Austrian Abbey Concerts are found, and further south still is Attersee, in the heart of the scenic Salzkammergut. This area of Alpine lakes is a vacation wonderland year-round, and its rich salt deposits made it a prized and closely guarded possession of the Hapsburgs.

FESTIVALS

Attergau Summer of Culture

6 Weeks	Attergauer Kultursommer
Mid-July–Late August	St. Georgen Tourist Office
	A-4880 St. Georgen im
Rec, Cham, Read	Attergau
	Tel: 07667/386

Since 1981 world-famous artists have appeared in such simple rural settings as a thirteenth-century farmhouse converted into a concert hall (Narzbergergut) and two parish churches. These lovely provincial sites are located in Attergau, the area around Attersee, Austria's largest Alpine lake. The modest surroundings belie the sophistication of the programs, which feature stellar international performers. Recent concerts have included music by Liszt, Mozart, Vivaldi, and Couperin, as well as readings by well-known European actors. **Recent Performers:** Academy of St. Martin in the Fields, pianists Vladimir Ashkenazy and André Previn, cellist Heinrich Schiff. **Venues:** St. George Parish Church, Narzbergergut am Kronberg, Vöcklamarkt Parish Church. **Performances:** 10–15; evenings.

Upper Austrian Abbey Concerts

7 Weekends	Oberösterreichische
Mid-June–Late July	Stiftskonzerte
	Domgasse 12
Orch, Chor, Cham, Rec	Postfach 116
	A-4010 Linz
	Tel: 0732/27 61 27

Within the halls, not the churches, of four remarkable abbeys are heard the varied sounds of chamber music that has included Brahms piano sonatas, medieval madrigals, Respighi dances, and Mozart wind serenades. The richly ornamented Marble Hall at St. Florian has been used as a concert hall since it was built over 200 years ago, and the Emperor's Hall at Kremsmünster (named for the portraits that line the walls) reveals the baroque glory that now characterizes this Benedictine abbey founded in the eighth century. The other abbeys are those of Schlierbach and Lambach, founded in the eleventh century. **Recent Performers:** Bruckner Orchestra Linz, Budapest Wind Ensemble, pianist Elisabeth Leonskaja. **Venues:** Kremsmünster Imperial Hall, Lambach Summer Refectory, St. Florian Marble Hall, Schlierbach Bernhard Hall. **Performances:** 16; evenings and afternoons. Written ticket requests are preferred, but any remaining tickets are available 1 hour before the performances.

VIENNA (Vienna)

Once the jewel of the Hapsburg Empire, Vienna remains one of the great music capitals of the world. The list of classical composers and musicians who have passed through this city is astounding. Brahms, Strauss, Schubert, Beethoven, and Mozart are names of streets, halls, cafes, and pastries. Less renowned but equally Viennese are the Schrammel ensembles that are heard throughout the city. This distinctive local form of chamber music evolved in the late nineteenth century when the Schrammel brothers, both violinists, joined forces with a guitarist and clarinetist. Strolling ensembles made up of these instruments perform waltzes and other light tunes.

Tickets for the State Opera, Volksoper, and Burgtheater (drama) are handled by the State Theater Booking Office. Written ticket requests must be received 14 days before a performance, and box office sales begin 7 days before a performance. Telephone sales begin 6 days prior to a performance (0222/513 1513).

State Theater Booking Office
Hanuschgasse 3
A-1010 Vienna
Tel: 0222/514 44 0
Fax: 0222/514 44 2969

At the American Express Tourist Office on Kärtnerstrasse, individuals post notices of tickets that they are unable to use. This is often the best chance of hearing the Philharmonic or getting a seat at the Opera. Inexpensive Standing Room Only tickets are sold at the State Opera and Volksoper one hour before each performance, but a line will form about two hours before curtain. If you try this alternative, be sure to bring a scarf or large handkerchief, for once inside the hall your place can be secured only by fastening something around your part of the railing. Desperate and unprepared opera fans have been seen using their belts.

The Tourist Office publishes a complete list of events in all major venues.

The telephone city code for Vienna is 0222 when dialing from within Austria and 1 when calling from abroad.

FESTIVALS

Schubert Festival

1 Week	Schubert Festival
Late November–Early	Wiener Musikverein
December	Bösendorferstrasse 12
	A-1010 Vienna
Orch, Cham, Rec	Tel: 0222/65 8190

Since 1983 Vienna's festival for Schubert has offered a chronological presentation of Schubert's works—the original goal of the Schubertiade Hohenems (see p. 12). Herman Prey, who founded and managed the Hohenems festival until 1980, organized Vienna's tribute to Schubert. **Recent Performers:** Baritone Herman Prey, violinist Christian Altenburger. **Venue:** Musikverein.

Spectaculum

4 Days	Gesellschaft für Musik-
July	theater
	Turkenstrasse 19
Op, Dance	A-1090 Vienna
	Tel: 0222/340 699

The spectacle that was baroque opera is recreated in the baroque Jesuit church in the Old University Quarter. Only historical instruments are used, and each performance lasts from early afternoon until late at night.

Vienna Festival

6 Weeks
Mid-May–Mid-June

Op, Orch, Chor, Cham, Rec,
Jazz, Dance, Th

Wiener Festwochen
Lehárgasse 11
A-1060 Vienna
Tel: 0222/586 09 23
Fax: 0222/586 16 76 49

Vienna bursts with good music during this comprehensive celebration of all the arts in a city already charged with vitality. Also called Vienna Weeks (Wiener Festwochen), this festival is less centralized than most because each of Vienna's major concert halls contributes to the event with independent festivities that together constitute a 6-week gala to close the regular concert and opera seasons. Information may also be obtained from each individual venue. **Recent Performers:** James Levine and Daniel Barenboim conducting the Vienna Philharmonic Orchestra, Cleveland Symphony Orchestra, pianists Alfred Brendel and Murray Perahia. **Venues:** State Opera, Volksoper, Burgtheater, Theater an der Wien, Konzerthaus, Messepalast, Vienna University, Rathaus, Academietheater, Franciscan Cultural Institute.

Vienna's Musical Summer

10 Weeks
Late June–Mid-September

Op, Orch, Chor, Cham, Rec,
Org, Band, Jazz, Th

Wiener Musik Sommer
Friedrich-Schmidt Platz 5
A-1082 Vienna
Tel: 0222/42 800 2741
Fax: 0222/4000 7217

One of Austria's longest festivals, Vienna's Musical Summer fills the void left by the closing of Vienna's regular musical season. Myriad popular and classical performances are evenly spread among the premier concert sites in the city, including the magnificent eighteenth-century Schönbrunn Palace. In keeping with the theme of celebrating Vienna are the outdoor Schrammel concerts that somehow reflect the affability of this unique city and nicely bridge classical and popular trends. **Recent Performers:** Vienna Symphony, London Symphony, flutist Jean-Pierre Rampal, Manhattan Transfer. **Venues:** Konzerthaus, Rathaus, Schönbrunn Palace (where the 6-year-old Mozart played for Empress Maria Theresa), Augustinian Church, Musikverein,

State Opera, Schubert and Haydn residences, various Viennese mansions. **Performances:** many daily.

Wien modern

4 Weeks
Late October–Late November

Wien modern
Kulturabteilung der Stadt
Wien

Op, Orch, Cham, Dance,
Lect, Ex

Friedrich Schmidt Platz
A-1082 Vienna
Tel: 0222/42 800 2741

Although this event was initiated by Claudio Abbado in 1987, the idea of a festival for music composed in the twentieth century was originally conceived by Arnold Schönberg. Unfortunately, Schönberg's contemporaries were not receptive, and his festival lasted only three songs into its first concert, after which the audience protested so strongly that the rest was canceled. In contrast, Abbado's 1987 festival was acclaimed in Vienna and throughout Europe. Geared to performances of "classic" modern music rather than to premieres of new works, Wien modern spotlights three or four composers each year. Stockhausen, Boulez, Ligeti, Stravinsky, and Cerha are among those recently featured. **Venues:** Konzerthaus, Musikverein, Secession. **Performances:** 30; afternoons and evenings.

ONGOING EVENTS

Jugendstil Theater

Op, Orch, Cham, Rec,
Dance, Th

Jugendstil Theater
Baumgartner Hohe 1
A-1145 Vienna
Tel: 0222/922 24 92
Fax: 0222/911 24 93

In 1989 a new Viennese opera house was built in the Steinhof, a psychiatric hospital in Vienna's 14th district. Situated near Otto Wagner Church (also part of the Steinhof), the theater was created to entertain patients during their stay at the hospital and to employ young talent in the productions. Performances are open to the general public. Recent offerings include Mozart's *Idomeneo,* Britten's *Let's Make an Opera,* and Stravinsky's *A Soldier's Tale.* **Venues:** Jugendstil Theater, Otto Wagner Church. **Performances:** 120; year-round. Tickets should be purchased 2 weeks in advance.

Konzerthaus

Orch, Chor, Cham, Rec, Org   Konzerthausgesellschaft
Lothringerstrasse 20
A-1030 Vienna
Tel: 0222/712 46 86-0
Fax: 0222/713 17 09

Built in 1913 to satisfy the demand for more publicly accessible concerts, the Konzerthaus has always championed innovative music. Mahler, Berg, and Webern found acceptance here, and this was the site of Vienna debuts for Leonard Bernstein, Claudio Abbado, and Pierre Boulez. The plain Empire style building houses the Great Hall (seating 1800), Mozart Hall (seating 760), and Schubert Hall (seating 360). The Konzerthaus is home for the Vienna Symphony, the ensemble that premiered, among many other works, Bruckner's Ninth Symphony and Ravel's Piano Concerto for the Left Hand. **Recent Performers:** Claudio Abbado conducting the Chamber Orchestra of Europe, tenor Peter Schreier, violinist Gidon Kremer. **Performances:** 130 (orchestral); September–June.

Musikverein

Orch, Chor, Cham, Rec, Org   Musikverein
Bösendorferstrasse 12
A-1010 Vienna
Tel: 0222/505 86 9220

During 1869 the Viennese witnessed not only the opening of their beloved Opera, but, on December 31, the inaugural concert of the Musikverein, which was erected to house concerts, a conservatory, and archives. It quickly established itself as a preeminent venue for Viennese concert life, with Johannes Brahms as the first director and Johann Strauss, Jr. composing a waltz for the opening ceremonies. The ornate Golden Hall is the home of the Vienna Philharmonic, founded in 1842. Tickets may be difficult to obtain because most seating is by subscription, but it is possible to hear the many guest ensembles that fill out the season. The Vienna Serenade Orchestra, which plays lighter repertoire from Viennese operettas, and the Lower Austrian Musicians Orchestra (Tonkünstlerorchester) also perform regularly in the Golden Hall, which contains an enormous organ. Chamber concerts are heard in the more intimate Brahms Room, seating 598. **Recent Performers:** Claudio Abbado conducting the Chamber Orchestra of Europe, pianists Andras Schiff and Martha Argerich, soprano Kiri Te Kanawa. **Performances:** daily; September–June.

State Opera

Op

Staatsoper
1 Opernring, 2
A-1010 Vienna

The State Opera is simply the heart of Vienna. It is said that when Allied bombs destroyed it in 1948 even Viennese who had never been inside wept in the streets. It was one of the first rebuilding projects to be completed, and now major artists accompanied by the Vienna Philharmonic combine to give incomparable performances in one of the world's great opera houses. The illustrious history of the Staatsoper is reflected by the list of its past directors: Christoph Willibald Gluck (1754–64), Antonio Salieri (1774–90), Gustav Mahler (1897–1907), Richard Strauss (1919–24), and Herbert von Karajan (1956–64). The schedule for one recent month alone included *La Bohème, Die Zauberflöte, L'Italiana in Algeri, Così fan tutte, La Traviata, Turandot, Carmen, Don Carlos,* and *La Forza del Destino*. **Performances:** almost daily; September–June. Opera films (August) and performances by the Volksoper take place during the summer. See p. 35 for information on advance ticket sales through the State Booking Office.

Theater an der Wien

Op, Dance, Th

Theater an der Wien
Linke Wienzeile 6
A-1060 Vienna
Tel: 0222/58830
Fax: 0222/587 9844

Opened in 1801, this is the oldest of Vienna's temples to music. Beethoven's Fifth and Sixth Symphonies, Johann Strauss's *Fledermaus,* and Lehár's *Merry Widow* were premiered here. During the 1950s the theater was neglected, but it has recently been restored. Musicals are the usual fare, but classical performances are sometimes heard, especially during the Vienna Festival. **Performances:** almost daily; September–June.

Vienna Choir Boys

Chor

Wiener Sängerknaben
Hofmusikkapelle
Hofburg
A-1010 Vienna

Reisebüro Mondial
Faulmanngasse 4
A-1040 Vienna
Tel: 0222/58804
Fax: 0222/587 1268

Perhaps Vienna's most widely known ensemble, the Vienna Choir Boys can be heard regularly in two different settings. Each Sunday morning from September through June High Mass is celebrated at the Hofburg Royal Chapel (Hofmusikkapelle) with the Choir and members of the Vienna Philharmonic. The Choir has sung Mass here for over 500 years. Tickets are scarce, and written ticket reservations must be received at least 8 weeks in advance. The Choir can also be heard at the Konzerthaus on Friday afternoons in May, June, September, and October singing motets, madrigals, folk songs, and works by Mozart, Schubert, and Brahms. Contact the Mondial Travel Agency (Reisebüro) for tickets for the Konzerthaus concerts, which should be obtained one month in advance. The Choir is often on tour, so it is necessary to plan ahead.

Volksoper

Op

Volksoper
Währinger Strasse 78
A-1090 Vienna
Tel: 0222/343627

In Vienna an important distinction is made between operetta and opera. Only the happy stories, light voices, and lively music of operetta will be heard at the ornate, round Volksoper Hall. Broadway musicals can trace their heritage to Austrian operettas, and they sometimes appear on the schedule. **Recent Productions:** *Der Fledermaus, Tales of Hoffmann, My Fair Lady.* **Performances:** almost daily; September–June. See p. 35 for ticket information.

IN THE AREA

Laxenburg Castle Concerts

Orch, Chor, Cham, Rec, Jazz   Lower Austria Tourist Office
Heidenschuss 2
A-1010 Vienna
Tel: 0222/533 29 53

For 10 years performances ranging from solo guitar to Haydn's *Creation* to Renaissance brass music have been given in Laxenburg, an unforgettable town 9 miles S of Vienna. The castle complex is comprised of an Old (fourteenth-century) and New (baroque) Palace and an enchanting neo-Gothic castle on an island in the Great Pond (Grosser Teich). **Recent Performers:** Vienna Schubert Trio, English Brass Ensemble, Dixieland All-Stars. **Venues:** Imperial Castle Theater. **Performances:** 10; July, August, October, November, March–May. Transportation from Vienna is available.

BELGIUM

Concert in an Antwerp church (courtesy of Antwerp Information Service).

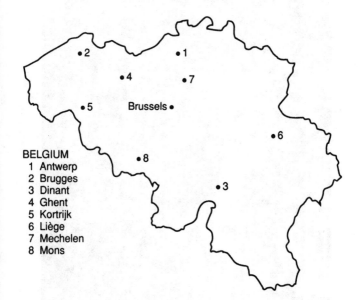

BELGIUM
1 Antwerp
2 Brugges
3 Dinant
4 Ghent
5 Kortrijk
6 Liège
7 Mechelen
8 Mons

CALENDAR

APRIL

Flanders Festival, see **Flanders** (northern provinces)
Flanders Festival, **Kortrijk** (West Flanders)
Queen Elisabeth Competition, **Brussels** (Brabant)

MAY

Flanders Festival, see **Flanders** (northern provinces)
Flanders Festivial, **Kortrijk** (West Flanders)
Queen Elisabeth Competition, **Brussels** (Brabant)

JUNE

Festival of Wallonia, see **Wallonia** (southern provinces)
Flanders Festival, see **Flanders** (northern provinces)
Flanders Festival, **Kortrijk** (West Flanders)
Queen Elisabeth Competition, **Brussels** (Brabant)

JULY

Arriaga Festival, **Bruges** (West Flanders)
Bruges Early Music Festival, **Bruges** (West Flanders)
Été Mosan Festival, **Dinant** (Namur)
Festival of Wallonia, see **Wallonia** (southern provinces)
Flanders Festival, **Flanders** (northern provinces)
Musical July in Aulne, **au Mons** (Hainaut)

AUGUST

Bruges Early Music Festival, **Bruges** (West Flanders)
Èté Mosan Festival, **Dinant** (Namur)
Festival of Wallonia, see **Wallonia** (southern provinces)
Flanders Festival, see **Flanders** (northern provinces)

SEPTEMBER

Èté Mosan Festival, **Dinant** (Namur)
Europalia, **Brussels** (Brabant)
Festival of Wallonia, see **Wallonia** (southern provinces)
Flanders Festival, see **Flanders** (northern provinces)
Flanders Festival, **Antwerp** (Antwerp)
Flanders Festival, **Brussels** (Brabant)
Flanders Festival, **Ghent** (East Flanders)

OCTOBER

Europalia, **Brussels** (Brabant)
Festival of Wallonia, see **Wallonia** (southern provinces)

Flanders Festival, see **Flanders** (northern provinces)
Flanders Festival, **Antwerp** (Antwerp)
Flanders Festival, **Brussels** (Brabant)
Flanders Festival, **Ghent** (East Flanders)
International Organ Week, **Brussels** (Brabant)

NOVEMBER

Europalia, **Brussels** (Brabant)

DECEMBER

Europalia, **Brussels** (Brabant)

The international telephone country code for Belgium is (011) 32. City codes have the prefix 0, which is omitted when calling from abroad.

ANTWERP (Antwerp)
25 miles N of Brussels

As the third-largest seaport in all of Europe, the Flemish city of Antwerp prospers as an industrial and trade center. Antwerp was the birthplace of Peter Paul Rubens, and the artist's well-preserved house, where many other well-known Flemish painters came to study, is now a museum. Many of these artists' paintings (including some of Rubens' finest) are displayed in the Cathedral of Our Lady, a Gothic masterpiece in itself and the largest cathedral in Belgium. Antwerp was home to several of the most famous sixteenth-century Flemish composers, including Ockeghem and Obrecht, and in the seventeenth and eighteenth centuries it was an important center for the building of harpsichords. In addition to classical music, Antwerp hosts the Middleheim Jazz Festival, which takes place every other August (odd years) in the scenic Middleheim Open Air Sculpture Museum.

FESTIVALS

Flanders Festival—Antwerp

1 Month
Early September—Early
   October

Op, Orch, Chor, Cham, Rec,
   Org, Dance, Th

Flanders Festival—Antwerp
Theaterwinkel
Sint-Jacobsmarkt 74
B-2000 Antwerp
Tel: 03/233 71 60
Fax: 03/232 28 85

Initially, Antwerp's role in the Flanders Festival consisted entirely of the International Theatre Festival. Gradually classical music concerts of all genres were added, and the festival continued to exist in this twofold capacity until 1976, when theater was abandoned and music became its exclusive focus. Several composers are featured each year, and one week of the month-long festival is dedicated to the presentation of early music by specialists at several of the city's historic sites. **Recent Performers:** London Symphony Orchestra, Flanders Royal Philharmonic Orchestra, tenor Luciano Pavarotti, London Baroque. **Venues:** Queen Elisabeth Hall, Concert Hall DeSingel, seventeenth-century St.-Charles Borromeo's Church, Our Lady's Cathedral, Rubens' seventeenth-century home, Butchers' Hall Museum (a splendid Gothic structure constructed by the Butchers' Guild). **Performances:** about 3 each week.

ONGOING EVENTS

De Vlaamse Opera (Also see Ghent)

Op, Orch, Chor

De Vlaamse Opera
Frankrijklei 3
B-2000 Antwerp
Tel: 03/233 66 85
Fax: 03/232 26 61

This company's impressive schedule incorporates operas from the standard repertoire, as well as several works from both baroque and contemporary eras. Productions recently offered include Monteverdi's *L'Orfeo,* Verdi's *Don Carlo,* and Richard Strauss's *Ariadne auf Naxos.* **Recent Performers:** sopranos Eva Marton, Janet Hardy, Sue Patchell. **Venue:** Antwerp Opera, Ghent Opera. **Performances:** 8 productions, October–June, 5–7 presentations of each production.

Royal Philharmonic Orchestra of Flanders

Orch, Chor, Cham, Rec

Royal Philharmonic Orch-
estra of Flanders
Britselei 80
B-2000 Antwerp
Tel: 03/231 37 37
Fax: 03/231 91 26

Formed in 1957 as the Antwerp Philharmonic, the name was changed and the orchestra augmented in 1983. With a season that now also includes several chamber music concerts, the orchestra offers two series in Antwerp and also tours extensively. **Recent Performers:** flutist Jean-Pierre Rampal, pianist Vladimir Ashkenazy, soprano Lucia Popp. **Venues:** Queen Elisabeth Hall, DeSingel Hall. **Performances:** 24, September–June.

BRUGES (West Flanders)
55 miles NW of Brussels

It is hard to imagine a more perfectly preserved medieval village than Bruges. Tranquil canals weave past ornate squares graced with palaces, churches, and guildhalls that seem untouched by time. Because Bruges had access to both the Baltic and North Seas, it was considered Western Europe's most important trading port during the Middle Ages, and it enjoyed at the election of a new pope. This competition is a favorite event among concert-goers, and the audience/performer relationship here is a unique one; the level of emotion is riveting as the jury comes closer to its decision. First prize winners have included pianist Leon Fleisher, the first American winner, and violinist Berl Senofsky. **Venue:** Palais des Beaux-Arts. **Performances:** many throughout the competition.

ONGOING EVENTS

Balconop Ballets, Concerts, and Opera (Also see Liège)

Op, Orch, Rec, Dance

Balconop
Artistic Services
Office of Promotion of
Tourism
Rue Marché-aux-Herbes, 61
B-1000 Brussels
Tel: 02/518 14 94
Fax: 02/513 69 50
02/514 53 35

Balconop, an organization of the Artistic Section of the Office of Promotion of Tourism of the French community of Belgium, sponsors package programs to first-rate performances in Brussels and Liège. These packages include features such as a seat at a ballet, concert, or opera performance; an overnight stay; and breakfast. Performances are produced by the Philharmonic Society of Brussels, the Théâtre Royal de Monnaie, and the Opéra Royal of Wallonie in Liège. Standard operatic, orchestral, and dance repertoire is presented, as are contemporary works, musical theater, and vocal recitals. **Recent Performers:** Brussels Festival Orchestra, Production de l'Opéra de Marseille, Béjart Ballet Lausanne. **Venues:** Théâtre Royal de la Monnaie, Cirque Royal, Brussels; Théâtre Royal de Liège, Palais des Sports de Liège. **Performances:** number depends on package chosen.

European Galas

Orch

European Galas
Flanders Festival
E. Flageypl., 18
B-1050 Brussels
Tel: 02/649 20 80 (1425)

The European Galas represent a series of four prestigious concerts sponsored jointly by the Philharmonic Society of Brussels and the Flanders Festival. Each year, four of the

wealth and prosperity commensurate with its prestige. But when accumulating silt denied passage to the North Sea, the city seemed to become frozen in time. Today Bruges remains one of the most romantic cities of Europe.

FESTIVALS

Arriaga Festival

1 Week	Arriaga Festival
Late July	International Mozart Society of Belgium
Cham, Rec	Elzenlaan 29
	B-8500 Kortrijk
	Tel: 056/22 38 75

This festival, sponsored by the International Mozart Society of Belgium, takes place in the romantic and spectacular Swaene Hotel. Both Belgian and international performers are featured, and repertoire stays mostly within the classical and romantic eras. Patrons may attend individual concerts or may choose a package that includes all concerts and a room at the Swaene. **Recent Performers:** Arriaga String Quartet, pianist Anna Yaschy. **Venue:** Swaene Hotel. **Performances:** every evening, 8:30 P.M.

Bruges Early Music Festival—"Musica Antiqua" (Flanders Festival)

2 Weeks	Bruges Early Music Festival
Late July–Mid August	Collaert Mansionstraat 30
	B-3000 Brugge
Chor, Cham, Rec, Org,	Tel: 050/33 22 83
Lect, Ex	Fax: 050/34 52 04

This portion of the Flanders Festival revolves solely around early music. The foremost interpreters and scholars gather here to concertize and to offer classes and lectures on authentic interpretation. The public can attend competitions featuring voice, organ, harpsichord and old instruments, melody instruments, lute, ensembles, and Flemish polyphonic music held in magnificent historic buildings throughout the city. Two series of concerts are offered, one at lunchtime and the other in the evenings, each centering around a particular theme. Recent topics have included the age of the troubadours and the music of Latin nations. Repertoire spans the sixteenth century through Mozart's time. **Recent Performers:** The King's Consort; The Tallis Scholars; New College Choir Oxford. **Venues:** Provincial Palace,

Ryelandt Hall, many historic cathedrals and other buildings throughout the city. **Performances:** 2 daily, 11:30 A.M. and 8:30 P.M., plus competition events, lectures, and courses.

BRUSSELS (Brabant)

In the center of this sophisticated, international city, home of the Common Market and the headquarters of NATO, exists one of the most stunningly beautiful squares in all of Europe, the Grand Place. The sight of the astounding varieties of Gothic and baroque architecture, the exotic and tantalizing smells of Brussels' famous cuisine, and the sound of countless languages heard above the faint, perpetual percussion of fluttering pigeon wings converge here in perfect harmony.

FESTIVALS

Europalia

10 Weeks
Late September–
    Mid-December

Op, Orch, Chor, Cham, Rec,
    Dance, Th, Film, Ex

Europalia Festival
Palais des Beaux-Arts
Rue Ravenstein 23
B-1000 Brussels
Tel: 02/512 50 45

Mounted every two years, this comprehensive festival is dedicated to the culture of a particular country at each biennial celebration (odd-number years). Based in Brussels, events also take place in many other cities. Although the arts are featured, other aspects such as education, religion, and literature are also explored. A recent festival was devoted to the culture of Japan; it featured liturgical Buddhist chants, ritual drums, traditional instruments and dances, and contemporary Japanese music and jazz, as well as Japanese soloists appearing with Belgian orchestras. **Recent Performers:** Orchestre National de Belgique, Tokyo Philharmonic, Tokyo String Quartet, Pro Musica Nipponia. **Venues:** many locations throughout Belgium, including the Palais des Beaux-Arts. **Performances:** many daily.

Flanders Festival—Brussels

1 Month
September–October

Op, Orch, Chor, Cham Rec,
    Dance

Flanders Festival—Brussels
Place E. Flagey, 18
B-1050 Brussels
Tel: 02/512 85 54

The city that saw the birth of the Flanders Festival continues its great tradition with superb performances and diverse programming. The spectacular Palais des Beaux-Arts hosts most concerts, and many performances take place in surrounding historic towns and villages. **Recent Performers:** London Classical Players conducted by Roger Norrington, tenor Luciano Pavarotti, cellist Heinrich Schiff. **Venues:** Palais des Beaux-Arts, Cirque Royal, Museum of Ancient Art, many other locations. **Performances:** approximately 5–6 concerts weekly.

International Organ Week in Brussels

1 Week
Late October

Orch, Chor, Org, Rec

International Organ Week in
    Brussels
Domstraat 8
B-1712 Vlezenbeek
Tel: 02/532 50 80

This series of organ recitals features a performer from a different country each day. Programs have also focused upon the instruments themselves and their histories. **Recent Performers:** organists Gustav Leonhardt (Amsterdam), Joseph Sluys (Brussels), Boris Romanov (Moscow), Istvan Bella (Budapest). **Venues:** many churches and cathedrals in Brussels, including St. Michael's and St. Catherine's. **Performances:** one concert each evening, more throughout the weekend.

The Queen Elisabeth International Music Competition of Belgium

4 Weeks
Late April–Early June
    (variable)

Orch, Rec

The Queen Elisabeth International Competition of
    Belgium
Rue aux Laines 20
B-1000 Brussels
Tel: 02/513 00 99
Fax: 02/514 32 97

One of the premier competitions in the world, the Queen Elisabeth Competition is renowned for the success of its winners, as well as for the strict rules by which it is run. Instituted in 1937 by Queen Elisabeth, who was herself a talented musician and a pupil of the famed violinist Eugène Ysaÿe, the four-year cycle of competitions rotates yearly between violin, piano, composition, and voice, with a year of rest separating each cycle. The twelve finalists spend 8 days in seclusion while preparing for the final round, and the jurors ob serve a silence that has been compared to that which e

world's finest orchestras, along with international soloists, offer performances at the splendid Palais des Beaux-Arts. Music lovers may attend single concerts, or they may choose to purchase a "Gala Card," which entitles them to the same seat at all concerts, free parking, cloak room, program, champagne cocktail, and a souvenir compact disc. Programs have included orchestral works by Haydn, Beethoven, Brahms, Mahler, Strauss, and Ives. **Recent Performers:** Vienna Philharmonic conducted by André Previn, Cleveland Orchestra conducted by Christoph von Dohnanyi, London Symphony Orchestra conducted by Michael Tilson Thomas, cellist Yo-Yo Ma, flutist James Galway. **Venue:** Palais des Beaux-Arts. **Performances:** 4 concerts, usually February, April, May, and November.

Palais des Beaux-Arts

Orch, Chor, Cham,   Palais des Beaux-Arts
    Rec, Dance, Th, Film   Booking Office
    Rue Ravenstein, 23
    B-1000 Brussels
    Tel: 02/512 50 45
    Fax: 02/514 30 44

This magnificent theater houses a large concert theater and a smaller recital hall, as well as two additional theaters, several exhibition rooms, and a film museum. The glorious main hall, the Grand Salle Henry Le Boeuf, holds an audience of 2000 and was designed by the famous Belgian architect Victor Horta. The recital hall holds 480 seats and was renovated in 1988. The Grand Salle provides the setting for many of Belgium's most significant artistic events, including concerts that are part of the Flanders Festival, the final round of the Queen Elisabeth Competition, and concerts by the Philharmonic Society of Belgium. It is also the home of the Belgian National Orchestra, which presents 25 performances of the standard orchestral repertoire with soloists of international standing. **Performances:** September–June (no performances in July and August).

Philharmonic Society of Brussels

(closed in July)   Philharmonic Society of
    Brussels
Orch, Chor, Cham, Rec   Bureau de Location
    Palais des Beaux-Arts
    Rue Ravenstein 23
    B-1000 Brussels
    Tel: 02/512 50 45

This society sponsors a wide variety of concerts, from solo piano to full orchestra. **Recent Performers:** Orchestre National de Belgique, London Symphony Orchestra conducted by Michael Tilson Thomas, Tokyo String Quartet, violinist Pinchas Zuckerman. **Venue:** Palais des Beaux-Arts: Grand Salle Henry Le Boeuf and Salle de Musique de Chambre. **Performances:** 70; September–May.

Pullman Astoria Hotel

Orch, Chor, Cham, Rec   Pullman Astoria Hotel
                               Rue Royal 103
                               B-1000 Brussels
                               Tel: 02/217 62 90
                               Fax: 02/217 11 50

This is one of Brussels' last elegant "grand hotels." It was opened in 1909 and was completely renovated in 1987, preserving its turn-of-the-century character. Concerts are held in the Grand Salle Waldorf, where majestic mirrors and 8 Venetian chandeliers provide a stunning backdrop for quality classical concerts. **Performances:** September–June, including concerts every Sunday morning, 11 A.M.–12:30 P.M., sponsored by the "Astoria Concerts" (closed July and August).

Théâtre Royal de la Monnaie

Op, Orch, Chor, Cham, Rec,   Théâtre Royal de la Monnaie
Dance   Ticket Office
                               Rue de la Reine
                               B-1000 Brussels
                               Tel: 02/218 12 66

La Monnaie is regarded as one of Europe's most sublime concert halls, and has enjoyed a rich history since it first opened in 1700. It is the home of the National Opera de la Monnaie, which is committed to presenting traditional operatic repertoire in innovative productions and to staging the operas of contemporary composers. Recent programs have included operas of Mozart, Verdi, Janáček, and John Adams; symphonic music of Beethoven, Mahler, and Bruckner; and chamber music of Schumann. The Monnaie's resident dance company is well known for its highly original work. The theater is also used for orchestral and chamber music concerts. **Recent Performers:** opera companies of Théâtre des Amandiers (Nanterre, France) and Brooklyn Academy of Music, Orchestre Symphonique de la Monnaie, soprano Felicity Lott, mezzo-soprano Christa

Ludwig, baritone José Van Dam.   **Performances:** 12 opera and dance productions, 30 concerts, September–July.

DINANT (Namur)
40 miles SE of Brussels

Dinant and Namur are the two principal cities of the province of Namur, often referred to as Belgium's "chateau country." Both cities sit on the River Meuse, which runs through the province, and both preserve eleventh-century fortresses that cap rocky peaks. Not only do the streets of these towns reflect their medieval heritage, but the surrounding countryside is also filled with history and beauty. Turreted castles perch on hilltops and on riverbanks, evoking the pageantry of the past.

FESTIVALS

Été Mosan Festival

8 Weeks	Festival de L'Été Mosan
Mid-July–Mid-September	Rue des Fossés, 30
	B-5500 Dinant
Orch, Chor, Cham, Rec	Tel: 082/22 45 53

Founded in 1978, this festival features baroque, classical, and Romantic music presented in intimate, memorable settings throughout the province of Namur, including abbeys, chateaus, churches, private homes, and various pastoral surroundings. The programs feature a wide range of ensembles and repertoire, from Mozart chamber music to the Brahms Requiem. Among the highlights are a sound and light show to the music of Handel and a recital offered by the winner of the Queen Elizabeth Competition (see p. 51).   **Recent Performers:** Flanders Symphony Orchestra, Trio Moussorgski, pianist Jörg Demus.   **Venues:** Chateau de Fontaine, Donjon of Crupet, Abbaye de Floreffe, many other locations.   **Performances:** 14; afternoons and evenings.

IN THE AREA

Musical July in Aulne

11 Concerts	Juillet Musical d'Aulne,
June–September	A.S.B.L.
	62, Route de Thuin
Orch, Cham, Rec, Org	B-6558 Lobbes
	Tel: 071/59 10 01

These concerts offer first-rate performers and diverse programming presented in the Abbey d'Aulne, a seventh-century Cistercian monastery (restored in 1896) 25 miles NW of Dinant. Recent performances have included piano music of Beethoven, Ravel, and Scriabin, string quartets of Mozart and Tchaikovsky, and orchestral music of Brahms and Johann Strauss. **Recent Performers:** Brussels Philharmonic Orchestra, Quator de Moscou, Trio Amati, Queen Elisabeth Competition winners. **Venue:** Abbaye d'Aulne. **Performances:** most in July, several in June and September.

FLANDERS (Also see Antwerp, Bruges, Ghent, Kortrijk, Mechelen)

The canals and rivers that connect Flanders with the North Sea once made this northern, Dutch-speaking part of Belgium Europe's wealthiest region. Though somewhat more industrial than the southern region of Wallonia, the provinces that compose Flanders contain some of the world's best-preserved medieval and Renaissance towns and villages. Belgium's bustling coastline is entirely within Flanders, and the resorts, casinos, and hotels that line the broad beaches make this one of northern Europe's most popular vacation spots.

FESTIVALS

Flanders Festival

7 Months
April–October

Orch, Chor, Cham, Rec,
    Org, Dance, Film, Ex

Flanders Festival
Algemeen Secretariat
Eugene Flageyplein 18
. B-1050 Brussels
Tel: 02/649 20 80
        02/648 14 84
Fax: 02/649 75 49

The Flanders Festival is one of Belgium's leading cultural events, taking place throughout the northern Flemish provinces. Its international stature has grown enormously because of its consummate blend of diversity, quality, and historical character. The festival began in 1958, when a Flanders music program was presented at the World's Fair in Brussels. Festival organizers from neighboring cities then decided to band together under the appellation "Festival of Flanders" in order to bring international classical music to Flemish audiences. The host cities are closely united under this auspice but still maintain their own highly individual seasons. A salient feature throughout is the presentation of music from all periods in historic settings that include churches, castles, museums, abbeys, concert halls, and stadiums. The festival is particularly noted for its presentation of early music and for special anniversary celebrations of composers and their music. Artists are of the highest caliber, and programs differ from year to year. **Recent Performers:** Vienna Philharmonic, Tokyo String Quartet, violinist Pinchas Zuckerman, Stockholm Bach Collegium, Béjart Ballet Lausanne. **Towns:** *Antwerp, *Bruges, *Brussels, *Ghent, *Kortrijk, *Mechelen, Hasselt, Kraainem, La Hulpe, Leuven, Lier, Limburg, Oostende, Tongeren, Turnhout, and other locations (*further information can be found under the city listing). **Performances:** events occur steadily April–October, although each city has its own major season.

GHENT (East Flanders)
30 miles NW of Brussels

Ghent was an industrial town centuries before the industrial revolution shook much of Europe. During the Middle Ages thousands of weavers and dyers produced the Flemish cloth prized throughout the continent, and Ghent at that time rivaled Paris in size and importance. The city possesses a rich artistic heritage, and a significant number of Belgium's greatest art treasures are to be found here. Painter Van Eyck's stunning masterpiece, The Adoration of the Mystic Lamb, is housed in the breath-taking Cathedral of St. Bavo. Central to Ghent's heritage is its medieval port, which contains many of the city's most ancient buildings.

FESTIVALS

Flanders Festival—Ghent

1 Month	Flanders Festival
September–October	Graaf van Vlaanderen
	plein 37
Orch, Chor, Cham, Rec,	B-9000 Ghent
Org, Dance	Tel: 091/25 77 80

This active section of the Flanders Festival opens with what is referred to as a "Great Happening," which serves to announce the arrival of the year's festival. Held in the exquisite St. Peter's Church, this all-day event includes various musical performances held in different parts of the church, costumed musicians playing ancient instruments, mimes, brass bands, and a jazz concert in the church's open courtyard. The remainder of the festival brings an equally diverse array of musical offerings. **Recent Performers:** Boston Symphony Orchestra, orchestra and chorus of La Scala, soprano Jessye Norman. **Venues:** Opera House of Ghent, St. Bavo's Cathedral, Sports Palace, other locations. **Performances:** many weekly.

ONGOING EVENTS

De Vlaamse Opera

Op

De Vlaamse Opera
Schouwburgstraat 3
B-9000 Ghent
Tel: 091/25 24 25

See Antwerp for information on this company, which performs in both cities.

KORTRIJK (West Flanders)
45 miles W of Brussels

A center of the cloth industry since the fifteenth century, Kortrijk is a prosperous town on the Lys River with numerous pedestrian promenades lined with an array of luxury shops. The towers of the thirteenth-century Church of Notre Dame provide a focal point and seem to invite the visitor to explore the riches within, which include a celebrated painting by Van Eyck, the Raising of the Cross. Nearby is a thirteenth-century convent (Béguinage), a small oasis of peace and calm in the midst of the surrounding urban bustle.

FESTIVALS

Flanders Festival—Kortrijk

3 Months
April–June

Flanders Festival—Kortrijk
Jan Breydellaan 12
B-8500 Kortrijk

Orch, Chor, Cham, Rec, Org

Tel: 056/22 28 29
Fax: 056/22 05 02

The Flanders Festival opens in this town, and, although a great variety of repertoire is represented, the focus here is on choral music. **Recent Performers:** Academy of St. Martin in the Fields, Cleveland Quartet, violinist Joshua Bell. **Venues:** Kortrijk Municipal Theater, Church of Notre Dame, others. **Performances:** many weekly.

LIÈGE (Liège)
55 miles E of Brussels

Known as "the ardent city" for its high spirits and love of freedom, Liège lies in the French-speaking region of Wallonia. A city that both works hard and plays hard, Liège is an industrial center and the home of a large university that contributes much to its cultural (and café) life. The River Meuse meanders through the town, giving its name to Outre Meuse, a small island in the center of the city filled with narrow alleys and cobblestone streets. This city, with its love of art and music, was the birthplace of two important composers, André Grétry and César Franck.

ONGOING EVENTS

Opéra Royal de Wallonie

Op

> Opéra Royal de Wallonie
> Théâtre Royal de Liège
> Place de la République-
>   Française
> B-4000 Liège
> Tel: 041/ 23 59 10

The early nineteenth-century theater where this company performs seats just over 1000 and is an appropriate setting for productions that feature young singers. The repertoire is broad and stagings imaginative, with emphasis on traditional favorites. The company tours throughout the French-speaking provinces of Belgium and also appears abroad. **Venue:** Théâtre Royal de Liège. **Performances:** 5–7 of each of about 12 operas and operettas; September–June.

Orchestre Philharmonique de Liège

Orch

> Orchestre Philharmonique
>   de Liège
> 11, Rue Forgeur
> B-4000 Liège
> Tel: 041/23 67 74

At the end of the nineteenth century, in an attempt to enrich the musical life of Liège, a series known as "Nouveaux

Concerts" was formed by Sylvain DuPuis at the Conservatory. Gustav Mahler and Richard Strauss conducted their first works here, and yet Liège still hungered for a professional orchestra. It was not until 1960 that the needed funds were procured, and the Orchestre Philharmonique de Liège was born. The ensemble has earned a worldwide reputation and now performs its broad repertoire throughout Belgium and abroad. Recent programs have included works by Mozart, Beethoven, Schumann, Ravel, and Martinu. **Recent Performers:** composer Luciano Berio, cellist Janos Starker, Trio Amati. **Venues:** Liège Conservatory. **Performances:** 70, 30 of which take place in Liège; September–June.

MECHELEN (Antwerp)
15 miles N of Brussels

The sixteenth century was Mechelen's Golden Age, when Margaret of Austria, aunt of Charles V, held court here surrounded by artists, philosophers, and musicians that included Josquin des Prez, Erasmus, and Thomas More. When the court moved to Brussels in 1531, Mechelen maintained its importance as an ecclesiastical center (it is still the seat of the archbishop). A tranquil town on the River Dyle, Mechelen is famed for its magnificent fifteenth-century Tower of St. Rombaut, perhaps the most beautiful in all of Belgium. The city is a center for tapestry making, and products of its tapestry studios have been Belgium's gift to numerous international organizations. Mechelen, like Lier and Oostende, is famed for its Carillon concerts.

ONGOING EVENTS

Carillon Recitals

Tourist Office
Stadhuis
Grote Markt
B-2800 Mechelen
Tel: 015/20 85 11
      015/21 18 73

International College for
      Carillon Art
Frederick de Merodestraat 63
B-2800 Mechelen
Tel: 015/20 47 92

Mechelen's carillon is one of the most famous, largely because of the added activity of the Royal Carillon School "Jef Denyn," an International College for Carillon Art, and to the Triennial International Carillon Competition it sponsors in mid-July. The instrument itself is housed in St. Rombaut's tower, constructed during the late Middle Ages and once referred to as the "eighth wonder of the world." The tower holds two carillons, one historic (with a bell dating back to 1480) and one modern, constructed in 1981. The latter is often celebrated as the purest and most brilliant carillon in Europe. Its beauty can be enjoyed during Mechelen's famous summer evening recitals. Both carillons are composed of 49 bells and are the heaviest in Europe, weighing 40 tons. **Performances:** Monday evenings, 8:30–9:30 P.M.; June–mid-September.

WALLONIA (Also see Dinant, Liège)

So different from Flanders is the southern region of Wallonia that the need for regional designations seems entirely logical. The most obvious distinction is that Wallonia is French, culturally and linguistically. Yet the geographical differences between north and south are equally profound. In contrast to the flat terrain of the north are the lush forests and mysterious hills found in one of Wallonia's most beautiful areas, the Ardennes. The inspiration for the Forest of Arden in Shakespeare's *As You Like It,* this area is brimming with castles, chateaus, and medieval abbeys. The nearby valley of the Meuse is famed for its abundant architectural treasures.

FESTIVALS

Festival of Wallonia

5 Months
June–October

Op, Orch, Chor, Cham, Rec,
    Org, Dance, Th, Lect,
    Child, Ex

Festival of Wallonia
Rue Sur-les-Foulons 11
B-4000 Liège
Tel: 041/22 32 48
    041/22 33 67

This vibrant festival takes place throughout Wallonia, and since 1971 has united all the festivals within the region from spring through fall. A unique feature here is that music lovers may meet and talk with world-class performers. This, coupled with the spectacular historical settings in which concerts are presented, makes for a profoundly gratifying musical experience. From baroque to contemporary, each city or province has individual charms and surprises. In Brussels, most concerts are presented at the magnificent Palais des Beaux-Arts, and in Chimay, one can enjoy "music and café" in the Château Chimay, an eighteenth-century castle whose intimate 250-seat theater lends itself perfectly to chamber music and recitals. The versatile festival "Les Nuits de Septembre" in Liège involves performances by international orchestras and theater companies, and at Luxembourg's "Juillet Musical de Saint-Hubert" workshops in music and dance are offered. Choral music, presented in the impressive Abbaye de Floreffe, is the focus in Namur, and in Stavelot the ancient abbey provides the setting. Programs have included orchestral music of Bach, Berlioz, and Tchaikovsky, string quartets of Beethoven and Berg, and songs of Franck and Bernstein. **Recent Performers:** Orchestre National de Belgique, Munich's Orchestre Pro Arte, flutist Jean-Pierre Rampal, Scottish Baroque Ensemble, Medici String Quartet. **Towns:** Brussels (Palais des Beaux-Arts), Chimay, Hainaut, Huy-Durbury (Collegiate Church), Liège, Modare (Château), Mons, Namur (Abbey of Floreffe), Stavelot (Abbey), Tournai (Cathedral), Villers-la-Ville (Roman Church), Brabant Wallon region, Saint-Hubert (Luxembourg). **Performances:** daily concerts, both morning and evening.

ONGOING EVENTS

Chamber Orchestra of Wallonie

Orch

Chamber Orchestra of
    Wallonie
Rue Neuve 5
B-7000 Mons
Tel: 065/35 31 20
Fax: 065/35 63 36

Conducted by George Octors, this orchestra performs in its home base of Mons but also tours extensively. International soloists are engaged, and repertoire has recently included works by such composers as Vivaldi, Beethoven, Shostakovich, and Bartók. **Recent Performers:** trumpeter Maurice André, pianist Paola Volpe. **Venues:** Auditorium Abel Dubois, Collège Saint-Stanislas. **Performances:** 6–10 concerts each month in various cities; one monthly concert in Mons at 12:15 P.M. (day varies); no concerts in August.

FRANCE

St.-Guilhem-le-Désert (courtesy of Association des Amis de St.-Guilhem-le-Désert).

63

FRANCE
1 Aix-en-Provence
2 Albi
3 Ambronay
4 Avignon
5 Beaune
6 Bordeaux
7 Caen
8 Cannes

18 Lille
19 Lourmarin
20 Menton
21 Metz

29 St.-Céré
30 St.-Germer-de-
   Fly
31 St.-Guilhem-le-
   Désert

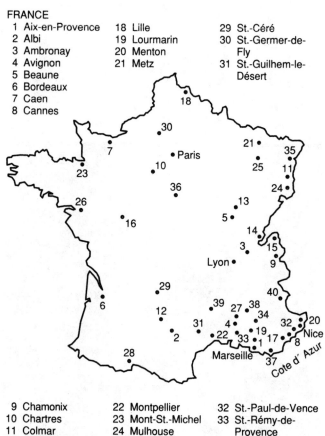

9 Chamonix
10 Chartres
11 Colmar
12 Cordes
13 Dijon
14 Divonne-
   les-Baines
15 Evian-les-
   Baines
16 Fontevraud
   l´ Abbaye
17 Fréjus

22 Montpellier
23 Mont-St.-Michel
24 Mulhouse
25 Nancy
26 Nantes
27 Orange
28 St. Bertrand-de-
   Comminges

32 St.-Paul-de-Vence
33 St.-Rémy-de-
   Provence
34 Simiane
35 Strasbourg
36 Sully-sur-Loire
37 Toulon
38 Vaison-la-Romain
39 Les Vans
40 Vars

CALENDAR

MARCH

Aspects of Contemporary Music, **Caen** (Normandy)
Manca Festival, **Nice** (Provence)

APRIL

Manca Festival, Nice (Provence)

MAY

Mulhouse Bach Festival, **Mulhouse** (Alsace)
Musical Encounters, **Evian** (Savoy)
Strasbourg Bach Festival, **Strasbourg** (Alsace)
Toulon Festival, **Toulon** (Provence)

JUNE

Ambronay Abbey Festival, see **Lyon** (Lyonnaise)
Avray Music Festival, see **Paris** (Ile-de-France)
Beaune International Meeting of Baroque and Classical
    Music, **Paris** (Ile-de-France)
Châteaux en Fête, see **Brittany**
Divonne Festival, **Divonne** (Bresse)
Festival Atlantique, **Nantes** (Brittany)
International String Quartet Festival, see **Avignon** (Provence)
Lyon Symphony Nights, **Lyon** (Lyonnaise)
Mulhouse Bach Festival, **Mulhouse** (Alsace)
Music at St.-Guilhem-le-Désert, see **Montpellier** (Languedoc)
Sacred Music Festival, **Nice** (Provence)
Sceaux Orangerie Festival, **Paris** (Ile-de-France)
Strasbourg Music Festival, **Strasbourg** (Alsace)
Sully International Music Festival, **Sully-sur-Loire** (Loire
    Valley)
Toulon Festival, **Toulon** (Provence)

JULY

Aix-en-Provence Festival, **Aix-en-Provence** (Provence)
Albi Festival of Music, **Albi** (Albigeois)
Ambronay Abbey Festival, see **Lyon** (Lyonnaise)
Avignon Festival, **Avignon** (Provence)
Beaune International Meeting of Baroque and
    Classical Music, see **Paris** (Ile-de-France)
Cannes American Festival, **Cannes** (Côte d'Azur)
Cévennes Festival, **Les Vans** (Ardèche)
Chartres Organ Festival, **Chartres** (Ile-de-France)

Châteaux en Fête, see **Brittany**
Chorégies d'Orange, **Orange** (Provence)
Comminges Festival, **St.-Bertrand-de-Comminges** (Midi-
    Toulousain-Pyrénées)
Cordes-sur-Ciel Festival, **Cordes-sur-Ciel** (Albigeois)
Festival Atlantique, **Nantes** (Brittany)
Festival of Radio France and Montpellier, **Montpellier**
    (Languedoc)
Festival Weeks of Mont Blanc, **Chamonix** (Savoy)
Fréjus Forum for the Arts and Music, **Frejus** (Provence)
International String Quartet Festival, see **Avignon** (Provence)
Lyon Symphony Nights, **Lyon** (Lyonnaise)
Maeght Foundation Concerts, see **Nice** (Provence)
Music at St.-Guilhem-le-Désert, see **Montpellier** (Languedoc)
Musical Evenings in Mazauges, see **Aix** (Provence)
Musical Hours of Mont-St.-Michel, **Mont-St.-Michel**
    (Normandy)
Organa, **St.-Rémy-de-Provence** (Provence)
St.-Céré Festival, **St. Cere** (Périgord)
St.-Germer-de-Fly Festival, see **Paris** (Ile-de-France)
Sceaux Orangerie Festival, **Paris** (Ile-de-France)
Simiane Festival, see **Aix** (Provence)
Strasbourg Music Festival, **Strasbourg** (Alsace)
Sully International Music Festival, **Sully-sur-Loire** (Loire
    Valley)
Summer Music at the Château of Lourmarin, see **Aix**
    (Provence)
Sylvanès Abbey Summer Music, see **Albi** (Albigeois)
Toulon Festival, **Toulon** (Provence)
Tourettes-sur-Loup Festival, see **Nice** (Provence)
Vaison-la-Romaine Festival, see **Orange** (Provence)

AUGUST

Albi Festival of Music, **Albi** (Albigeois)
Avignon Festival, **Avignon** (Provence)
Cévennes Festival, **Les Vans** (Ardèche)
Chartres Organ Festival, **Chartres** (Ile-de-France)
Chorégies d'Orange, **Orange** (Provence)
Comminges Festival, **St.-Bertrand-de-Comminges** (Midi-
    Toulousain-Pyrénées)
Cordes-sur-Ciel Festival, **Cordes-sur-Ciel** (Albigeois)
Festival Atlantique, **Nantes** (Brittany)
Festival of Radio France and Montpellier, **Montpellier**
    (Languedoc)
Festival Weeks of Mont Blanc, **Chamonix** (Savoy)
International String Quartet Festival, see **Avignon** (Provence)

Menton Festival of Music, **Menton** (Provence)
Music at St.-Guilhem-le-Désert, see **Montpellier** (Languedoc)
Musical Evenings in Mazauges, see **Aix** (Provence)
Musical Hours of Mont-St.-Michel, **Mont-St.-Michel**
    (Normandy)
Organa, **St.-Rémy-de-Provence** (Provence)
St.-Céré Festival, **St.-Céré** (Périgord)
St.-Germer-de-Fly Festival, see **Paris** (Ile-de-France)
Sceaux Orangerie Festival, **Paris** (Ile-de-France)
Simiane Festival, see **Aix** (Provence)
Summer Music at the Château of Lourmarin, see **Aix**
    (Provence)
Sylvanès Abbey Summer Music, see **Albi** (Albigeois)
Tourettes-sur-Loup Festival, see **Nice** (Provence)
Vaison-la-Romaine Festival, see **Orange** (Provence)
Vars International Piano Festival, **Vars** (Dauphiné)

SEPTEMBER

Ambronay Abbey Festival, see **Lyon** (Lyonnaise)
Berlioz Festival, **Lyon** (Lyonnaise)
Comminges Festival, **St.-Bertrand-de-Comminges** (Midi-
    Toulousain-Pyrénées)
Ile-de-France Festival, see **Paris** (Ile-de-France)
International String Quartet Festival, see **Avignon** (Provence)
Music at St.-Guilhem-le-Désert, see **Montpellier**
    (Languedoc)
Organa, **St.-Remy-de-Provence** (Provence)
Paris Autumn Festival, **Paris** (Ile-de-France)
Sceaux Orangerie Festival, **Paris** (Ile-de-France)

OCTOBER

Festival of Sacred Music, **Paris** (Ile-de-France)
Festival of String Quartets, see **Cannes** (Provence)
Ile-de-France Festival, see **Paris** (Ile-de-France)
Lille Festival, **Lille** (Picardy)
Paris Autumn Festival, **Paris** (Ile-de-France)

NOVEMBER

Festival of Sacred Music, **Paris** (Ile-de-France)
International Meeting of Contemporary Music, **Metz**
    (Lorraine)
Ile-de-France Festival, see **Paris** (Ile-de-France)
Lille Festival, **Lille** (Picardy)
Music of Old Lyon, **Lyon** (Lyonnaise)
Paris Autumn Festival, **Paris** (Ile-de-France)

DECEMBER

Festival of Sacred Music, **Paris** (Ile-de-France)
Forum for Musical Composition, **Paris** (Ile-de-France)
Music of Old Lyon, **Lyon** (Lyonnaise)
Paris Autumn Festival, **Paris** (Ile-de-France)

The international telephone country code for France is (011) 33. Telephone numbers in France all have 8 digits, which include the city codes. The exception to this is Paris. When calling Paris from abroad, 1 is added before the 8-digit number. When calling Paris from another province in France, 16 1 is added before the 8-digit number. When calling from Paris to another province, 16 is added to the 8-digit number. When calling within Paris, use only the 8-digit number.

AIX-EN-PROVENCE (Provence-Côte d'Azur)
465 miles SE of Paris

To say that Provence is "the Italy of France," as composer Charles Gounod did, is to pay equal homage to both places. The fifteenth-century university lends a cultural and intellectual note to an otherwise carefree atmosphere of fountains, cafes, and light Mediterranean breezes. It was here that Aix native Paul Cézanne developed his appreciation for the sublime. Cézanne's studio is open to the public, kept as it was found at his death in 1906. Aix was also the birthplace of composer Darius Milhaud, born here in 1892.

FESTIVALS

Aix-en-Provence Festival

3 Weeks	Festival d'Aix
Mid-July	Palais de l'Ancien
	Archêveché
Op, Orch, Chor, Cham	13100 Aix-en-Provence
	Tel: 42 23 11 20

A major event with a distinguished history, the Aix-en-Provence Festival has presented operatic and concert works since 1941 with a strong emphasis on vocal music. International singers appear in three opera productions each year, as well as in masterpieces of the oratorio literature. Operas by Mozart and Rossini have been complemented by Bach's *Magnificat*, Haydn's *Creation*, and Mozart's *C Minor*

Mass, along with orchestral works by Brahms, Bizet, and Mahler. **Recent Performers:** Jeffrey Tate conducting the English Chamber Orchestra, sopranos Dawn Upshaw and June Anderson, baritone José van Dam. **Venues:** Théâtre de l'Archêveché, Cathédrale Saint-Sauveur. **Performances:** 15 opera performances; 8 concerts; in addition, informal concerts and recitals are given by guest artists almost daily at noon or 6 P.M.

IN THE AREA

Musical Evenings in Mazauges

4 Concerts
Mid-July–Late August

Orch, Cham, Rec

Les Nuits Musicales
de Mazaugues
Town Hall of Mazaugues
83136 Mazaugues
Tel: 94 86 95 03
(Monday–Friday, 3–6 P.M.)

A single performance by a young French pianist in 1983 drew such enthusiastic support from the public and press that an annual series has evolved at this chateau 30 miles SE of Aix. Programs now range from Handel to Liszt, and are given by renowned artists from many countries. **Recent Performers:** Gewandhaus Chamber Orchestra, pianists Jean-Philippe Collard and Mikhail Rudy. **Venue:** Théâtre de Verdure, in the Chateau.

Simiane Festival

7 Concerts
Late July–Mid-August

Cham

Festival de Simiane
Secretariat du Festival
04150 Simiane-la-Rotonde
Tel: 92 75 90 14
(after January 6: 11–Noon;
4–6 P.M.)

Vocal and instrumental chamber music of the medieval, Renaissance, baroque, and classical periods is presented by candlelight in Simiane-la-Rotonde, a twelfth-century castle 50 miles N of Aix. Although the village itself has only 450 inhabitants, the Festival has enjoyed widespread regional support since its founding in 1983 because of the fine artists it presents and the rare pleasure of hearing them in such a memorable setting. **Recent Performers:** Boston Camarata, Ars Antiqua of Paris. **Venue:** Salle Romane, in the Castle Rotonde. **Performances:** all begin at 9 P.M.

Summer Music at the Château of Lourmarin

7 Weeks
Early July–Late August

Cham, Rec, Org, Dance

Musique d' Été au Chateau
de Lourmarin
Chateau de Lourmarin
84160 Lourmarin
Tel: 90 68 15 23

Twenty miles N of Aix-en-Provence lies the lovely Château of Lourmarin, the historic site of this series of chamber music concerts. French artists predominate, and although most programs feature an instrumental soloist with piano, more diverse combinations, such as flute and harp, piano four hands, and vocal soloists, add to the series' appeal. The music is varied, but the emphasis is on Bach, Beethoven, and Brahms. The château itself is open daily for visitors. **Recent Performers:** pianists Beatrice Hsi Chen Long and Gisèle Magnan. **Venues:** Lourmarin Castle, Catholic and Protestant churches. **Performances:** 12; all at 9:15 P.M.

ALBI (Albigeois)
440 miles S of Paris

The picturesque red-brick town of Albi is perched above the Tarn River, providing a beautiful setting for its many Renaissance architectural gems. The success of the town's textile, glass, and chemical industries have not encroached on the historic buildings, and a fine Gothic cathedral towers over streets still lined with medieval houses. Albi possesses among its art treasures an impressive collection of the works of post-impressionist painter Henri de Toulouse-Lautrec (born here in 1864) in the museum that bears his name.

FESTIVALS

Albi Festival of Music

3 Weeks
Mid-July–Early August

Op, Orch, Chor, Cham,
Rec, Org

Albi Festival de Musique
Office de Tourisme
Palais de la Berbie
81000 Albi
Tel: 63 54 28 88

Since its founding in 1974, this festival has gained international acclaim for its artistic originality and the splendor of its historic settings. Its operatic productions have been televised, recorded, and restaged following the festival in such sites as Versailles and the Côte d'Azur. **Recent Productions/Performers:** *Così fan tutte, The Rape of Lucrezia;* cellist Mstislav Rostropovich, trumpeter Maurice André. **Venues:** thirteenth-century Palais de la Berbie (former Bishop's Palace), twelfth-century Cathedral St.-Cecile, Eglise de la Madeleine. **Performances:** 10–15; all at 9 P.M.

IN THE AREA

Sylvanès Abbey Summer Music

1 Month
Mid-July–Mid-August

Orch, Chor, Cham, Rec,
Org, Lec

Rencontres Culturelles de
l'Abbaye de Sylvanès
Abbaye de Sylvanès
12360 Camares
Tel: 65 49 52 52
65 99 51 83
Fax: 65 49 54 52

This remarkable twelfth-century Cistercian abbey 50 miles E of Albi was largely in ruins in the late 1970s when the joint efforts of Father André Gouzes (a composer), Michel Wolkowitsky, and several other artists resulted in the creation of this festival and the restoration of the abbey. The festival reflects the abbey's mission to renew the ties between liturgical life and artistic expression. Nine months of various cultural activities culminate in the month-long festival, which combines sacred music, the visual arts, lectures, and exhibitions. Each year the festival commissions a new sacred work. Recent programs have included Berlioz' *L'Enfance du Christ*, Honegger's *Le Roi David*, and Verdi's Requiem. **Recent Performers:** Orchestre Baroque de Montréal, Ensemble Clément Janequin, soprano Gladys de Bellida. **Performances:** 12.

AVIGNON (Provence)
430 miles SE of Paris

Avignon holds an important place in European history, having been the home of the fourteenth-century French popes. The medieval papal palace is an immense, walled fortress built by Beniot XII, and tours of the ornate palace are given frequently. Avignon was a favored city for the medieval troubadours, and much later was home to Rameau for the year that he spent directing the local choir school (1702–1703).

FESTIVALS

Avignon Festival

1 Month	Festival d'Avignon
Early July–Early August	B.P. 92
	84006 Avignon Cedex
Op, Orch, Chor, Cham,	Tel: 90 82 67 08
Th, Dance, Film, Lect	

Theater and music are both at the forefront of this festival, which in the course of its 40-year history has incorporated the past while focusing on the present. Theater productions range from Euripides to Shakespeare to Chekhov to George Perec, while musical programs include the songs of Wolf and Brahms as well as pop music from Pakistan. The principal emphasis, however, is on contemporary music. **Recent Performers:** Pierre Boulez conducting the Ensemble Intercontemporain, Arditi Quartet, soprano Phyllis Bryn-Julson. **Venues:** Chapels, chambers, and cloisters in and around the fourteenth-century Papal Palace. **Performances:** Many daily.

ONGOING EVENTS

Opéra d'Avignon et des Pays de Vaucluse

Op, Orch, Chor, Rec, Dance	Opéra d'Avignon et des Pays de Vaucluse
	B.P. 111
	84007 Avignon Cedex
	Tel: 90 82 23 44
	Fax: 90 85 04 23

There is far more than opera on stage here. Symphony concerts, vocal ensembles, recitals by well-known singers and instrumentalists, ballet, and theater productions fill the program. Operas include *Rigoletto*, *Faust*, and *Madama Butterfly*, while orchestral concerts offer Beethoven, Dvořák, Mozart, and Shostakovich. **Recent Performers:** Orchestre Lyrique de Région Avignon-Provence, Ysaÿe Quartet, pianist Yefim Bronfman. **Performances:** Nearly 100, October–June.

IN THE AREA

International String Quartet Festival

Cham

Festival International de
Quatuors à Cordes
Les Amis de la Musique de
Luberon
Roussillon
84220 Gordes
Tel: 90 75 89 60

Of the many tiny villages tucked away in the Provençal hills, those hosting the International String Quartet Festival are particular gems. Roussillon is memorable for its colors—red, pink, and gold—provided by the surrounding quarries. Neighboring Fontaine de Vaucluse is one of the great sites of this region, with its magnificent waterfall cascading in vivid colors from a cliff 750 feet high. Though a festival in name, this program is organized as a series, with each of eight string quartets presenting three concerts throughout the summer. The standard repertoire is played by artists from around the world, including the recipients of the first prize at the prestigious Evian Competition. **Recent Performers:** Talich Quartet, Parisii Quartet, Sine Nomine Quartet. **Venues:** Churches in Roussillon, Goult, and Fontaine de Vaucluse, and the cloister in Silvacane's Abbey. **Performances:** 24, mid-June–mid-September.

BEAUNE (Burgundy)
200 miles SE of Paris

The small town that the Dukes of Burgundy left in the fourteenth century in favor of nearby Dijon has since become one of the most beautiful towns in Burgundy. Surrounded by the famed vineyards, Beaune is an important center in the wine trade, and is filled with artistic treasures, including Flemish painter Rogier van der Weyden's celebrated "Last Judgement." Most compelling is the Hôtel-Dieu, the princely complex constructed in the fifteenth century as a hospital for the poor. Perfectly preserved, the turrets, traceries, and brilliantly colored tiled roofs of the Hospices de Beaune (as it is also called) still evoke the medieval world.

FESTIVALS

Beaune International Meeting
of Baroque and Classical Music

Weekends
Late June–Mid-July

Op, Chor, Cham, Rec

Rencontres Internationales
de Musique Baroque et
Classique de Beaune
2, square St.-Irénée
75011 Paris
Tel: 16 1/43 57 46 97

Since 1983 this festival has offered performances noted for authenticity in original, historic performance practices. Programming is varied, from Rameau to Tchaikovsky, and standards are uniformly high. **Recent Performers:** USSR Symphony Orchestra conducted by Evgeny Svetlanov, La Petite Bande led by Sigiswald Kuijken, countertenor Jeffrey Gall. **Venues:** Hospice de Beaune, Notre Dame Basilica. **Performances:** 2–3 each weekend.

BORDEAUX (Bordelais)
360 miles SW of Paris

A stroll through the city of Bordeaux reveals an elegance and refinement that perfectly reflect this region's agricultural prize—the grape vines. A sampling of vintage varieties can be had anywhere in town, including a mandatory visit to the Maison du Vin, but one need not be a *vin* connoisseur to enjoy the pleasures of Bordeaux. The old section of town, Vieux Bordeaux, is filled with cobblestone streets and graceful eighteenth-century homes embellished with ornamental ironwork. The imposing eighteenth-century Grand Theater and two impressive museums at the Palais de Rohanis contribute to Bordeaux's image as one of France's most sophisticated cities.

ONGOING EVENTS

Grand-Théâtre de Bordeaux

Op, Dance

Grand-Théâtre de Bordeaux
Place de la Comedie
33074 Bordeaux-Cedex
Tel: 56 48 58 54

Opera, operetta, and ballet are all in the spotlight here. Recent productions include *Aida*, *Elektra*, and *Manon*, and operettas by Offenbach and Messager. **Recent Performers:** Bolshoi Ballet and Orchestra, Orchestre National de Bordeaux Aquitaine, soprano Leonie Rysanek. **Performances:** 14 productions, each with numerous performances.

BRITTANY
200–300 miles W of Paris

Brittany's scenic coastal towns and prehistoric megaliths are steeped in a rich tradition of Celtic folklore, providing the unique flavor that permeates its cultural offerings. As the country's westernmost province, Brittany is secluded but not remote, its regions poetically distinguished as Armor— "land of the sea" and Argoat— "land of the forest." Historic castles and chateaus dot the countryside, offering romantic refuge from the sweeping Atlantic winds.

FESTIVALS

Châteaux en Fête

2 Months	Châteaux en Fête
Mid-June–July	ARCODAR
	1, rue du Prieure
Orch, Chor, Cham, Rec,	35410 Chateaugiron
Dance	Tel: 99 37 34 58

This special festival has dual aims—to celebrate the architectural richness of the chateaus, chapels, and churches of Brittany and to present concerts featuring French artists. Each concert takes place in a different, outstanding locale, with programs ranging from the baroque to the most modern, including jazz and rock. **Recent Performers:** Western Baroque Ensemble, in a production of Marais' opera *Alcione;* String Quartet of the National Orchestra of France; Celtic harpist Myrdhin. **Venues:** castles, churches, historic houses and buildings. **Performances:** 10; evenings.

CAEN (Normandy)
150 miles W of Paris

Though Caen sustained substantial damage during World War II and is now a largely contemporary town, the war spared some of the most historic buildings. William the Conqueror was born nearby and was buried in Caen in 1087, and one may still marvel at the abbeys and castle that he founded.

The Romanesque naves of the Abbaye aux Hommes and Abbaye aux Dames are particularly beautiful, and are fine examples of Norman architecture. The castle, founded by William in 1060 and now an awesome ruin, contains within its enclosure several later buildings, including the baroque Governor's Palace, now restored, which houses the Normandy Museum.

FESTIVALS

Aspects of Contemporary Music

1 Week	Aspects de la Musique
Mid-March	Contemporaine
	Théâtre Municipal de Caen
Cham, Lect, Th, Ex	BP 217
	14007 Caen Cedex
	Tel: 31 86 42 00

This festival seeks to promote contemporary music by presenting works by living composers and by inviting the composers themselves to take part. Audiences are encouraged to explore the realm of new music through educational programs that examine new trends in the arts and their influence on both performers and the public. A recent festival focused on electroacoustical music, inviting the Groupe de Recherches Musicales (GRM) of Paris, the Centre International de Recherche Musicale (CIRM) of Nice, and the Groupe de Réalisation et de Recherche Appliquée en Musiques Electroacoustiques (GRAME) of Lyon. **Recent Performers:** Saxophonist Daniel Kientzy, violinist Rodrigue Milosi, soprano Liliane Mazeron. **Venue:** Grand Auditorium. **Performances:** 5.

ONGOING EVENTS

Théâtre Municipal de Caen

Orch, Chor, Cham, Rec	Théâtre Municipal de Caen
	BP 217
	14007 Caen Cedex
	Tel: 31 86 12 79

The box office of this theater handles tickets for the Orchestre de Caen and a range of musical events that includes oratorios, chamber music, and recitals. The Orchestre de Caen is joined by internationally acclaimed performers for concerts that present the standard orchestral repertory in the Grand Auditorium of the Conservatoire de Region. **Recent Perform-**

ers: pianist Charles Rosen, soprano Katia Ricciarelli, pianist Mikhail Rudy.   **Performances:** 18; October–July.

CANNES (Provence-Côte d'Azur)
560 miles SE of Paris

Though Cannes' annual film festival has earned this town the somewhat dubious reputation of being the "très chic" playground of the rich, its sweeping coral views of the Mediterranean, pleasant climate, and tiny surrounding cliffside villages provide a special type of wealth, clearly illustrating that Cannes need not depend on the movie industry for its splendor.

FESTIVALS

Cannes American Festival

10 Programs
July

Rec, Dance, Jazz

Festival Americain de
Cannes
Cannes Tourist Board
Esplanade Président Georges
Pompidou
La Croisette
06400 Cannes
Tel: 93 39 01 01

Since 1985 Cannes has celebrated its connection with American artists and expatriates by inviting some of the best-known to perform in these programs. Well-known classical performers join popular music, jazz, and modern dance artists to provide the sparkling entertainment.   **Recent Performers:** Soprano Julia Migenes, Alvin Ailey Dance Theater, Merce Cunningham Dance Company.

ONGOING EVENTS

Orchestre Régional de Cannes Provence Alpes Côte d'Azur

Orch

Orchestre Régional de Cannes
Provence
Alpes Côte d'Azur
Palais des Festivals et des
Congrès
Esplanade Président Georges
Pompidou
06400 Cannes
Tel: 92 98 62 77

Under the direction of resident conductor Philippe Bender and guest conductors, this orchestra presents repertoire from Bach to Milhaud. In addition to its performances in its home town, the ensemble is in great demand at festivals throughout the region. **Recent Performers:** conductor Tibor Varga, soprano Gundula Janowitz, flutist Ransom Wilson. **Venue:** Théâtre Claude Debussy. **Performances:** 15; October-June.

IN THE AREA

Festival of String Quartets

1 Week	Festival of String Quartets
Late October	Office du Tourisme
	83440 Fayence
Cham	Tel: 94 76 20 08

This festival provides an ideal opportunity to explore the villages of Provence during the autumn grape harvest. The Romanesque and Gothic churches of the region provide the settings for six evenings of concerts by young artists from France and other countries, performing music for string quartet that ranges from Mozart to Webern. **Recent Performers:** Fine Arts Quartet, Ysaÿe Quartet, Orlando Quartet. **Venues:** Churches in Fayence, Montauroux, Tourrettes, others. **Performances:** nightly; 9 P.M.

CHAMONIX (Savoy)
390 miles SE of Paris

Chamonix is the jewel of the French Alps, known as much for unparalleled skiing as for the astounding beauty of the jagged, sloped glaciers that surround the resort village. Skiers and nonskiers alike can enjoy a breathtaking ride in the telepherique to the Auguille du Midi for an unforgettable view of Europe's highest mountain, Mont Blanc, which towers above the village.

FESTIVALS

Music Weeks of Mont Blanc

9 Concerts	Office of Tourism
Mid-July–Mid-August	Place de l'eglise
	BP 25
Orch, Cham	74400 Chamonix Mont Blanc
	Tel: 50 53 00 24
	50 54 02 14

Since 1969 these concerts have been among the high points of the summer season in Chamonix. Each year the programs draw a range of international performers, including at least one of "star" status. The standard chamber music repertoire is enlivened by an occasional foray into jazz. **Recent Performers:** Warsaw Chamber Orchestra, violinist Yehudi Menuhin, pianist Jörg Demus, Claude Bolling Trio. **Venue:** Grande Salle of the Chamonix Majestic. **Performances:** All begin at 9 P.M.

CHARTRES (Ile-de-France)
50 miles SW of Paris

Dominated by one of the world's most magnificent cathedrals, Chartres is a graceful village filled with the same medieval spirit that permeates the cathedral. This village of pretty, gabled rooftops and steep, narrow streets possesses a timeless dignity that is further enhanced by several other churches of historic interest. And then of course, there is the Cathedral, an architectural masterpiece and art historian's shrine, known the world over for its soaring towers and supremely crafted stained-glass windows.

FESTIVALS

Chartres Organ Festival

2 Months	Festival d'Orgue
July-August	Association des Grandes
	Orgues de Chartres
Org	75 rue de Grenelle
	75007 Paris
	Tel: 45 48 31 74

The grand organ of Chartres Cathedral is the instrument featured during this festival, and the glorious twelfth-century cathedral itself is the venue. Organists from around the world can be heard here, including prizewinners of the "Grand Prix du Chartres" competition. The finals of this annual event take place during the first week of the festival, and are open to the public. Both the festival and the competition have been regular events since the early 1970s. **Recent Performers:** Organists who hold some of Europe's most prestigious organ posts, including Notre Dame and Saint Sulpice in Paris, as well as Chartres itself. **Performances:** 11; all are free and take place between 4:45 and 5:45 P.M.

CORDES-SUR-CIEL (Albigeois)
425 miles S of Paris

When enshrouded by the mists from the River Cerou, this fairy-tale village 12 miles NW of Albi resembles a floating ethereal image, thus earning its nickname "Cordes-sur-Ciel" (Cordes in the Sky). Founded in 1222 as a fortified medieval "bastide," Cordes' heritage is manifested in the lovely Gothic houses and half-timbered craft shops along the Grand-Rue as well as in the town's unique old covered market.

FESTIVALS

Cordes-sur-Ciel Festival

5 Concerts	Festival de Musique de
Early July–Mid-August	Cordes-sur-Ciel
	ACADOC
Orch, Chor, Cham, Org	Maison Gaugiran
	81170 Cordes
	Tel: 63 56 00 75

Taking place under the auspices of the Regional Cultural Center for Ancient and Contemporary Music, these concerts emphasize the music of the baroque. This still allows for diversity, however, and performers range from choirs to baroque orchestra to sackbut ensemble, featuring that most notorious of the medieval wind instruments. More contemporary music is offered in performances that include Honegger, Debussy, and de Falla. The festival takes place in the medieval parish church. **Recent Performers:** Baroque Orchestra of Toulouse, violinist Pierre Amoyal, the Soloists of Salzburg. **Venue:** thirteenth-century Church of Saint Michel. **Performances:** all begin at 9 P.M.

DIJON (Burgundy)
225 miles SE of Paris

A culinary paradise, Dijon is most commonly associated with its most popular export, mustard. There are other crops growing here as well, and the fertile soil of the countryside produces excellent grapes for Burgundy wines. But gastronomic gallivanters will find plenty to do in this ancient city between meals. Once the stronghold of the Dukes of Burgundy, Dijon is brimming with royal residences, the most exquisite of which is the former ducal palace, now an impressive museum of fine arts.

ONGOING EVENTS

Grand Théâtre de Dijon

Op, Dance, Rec

Grand Théâtre de Dijon
2, rue Longepierre
21000 Dijon
Tel: 80 67 23 23

Offering opera, operetta, and ballet, this theater has recently produced *La Traviata* and *Norma*. Operas are occasionally presented in French rather than their original language, as was the case with *The Magic Flute* and Menotti's *The Saint of Bleeker Street*. **Performances:** Approx. 40; October–April.

DIVONNE-les-BAINS (Bresse)
315 miles SE of Paris

Divonne-les-Bains is an exclusive mineral spring spa that sits just a few kilometers from the Swiss border, at the foot of one of the Jura mountain range's highest peaks. The resort's impressive golf course, casino, and sailing facilities, as well as the famous nurturing springs, attract travelers from all over the world.

FESTIVALS

Divonne Festival

2 Weeks
Late June

Orch, Cham, Rec

Divonne Festival
T.T.H.
01220 Divonne-les-Bains
Tel: 50 40 34 52
Fax: 50 40 34 23

The magnificent scenery and the resort setting are matched by the music making at this festival, which brings a cultural note to the glittering casino. Chamber music concerts present an interesting variety of ensembles—duo pianists, chamber orchestra, and solo voice with piano, as well as string trios and quartets. The music is as varied as the ensembles, ranging from Vivaldi to Messaien. **Recent Performers:** soprano Lucia Popp, violinist Josef Suk, pianist Martha Argerich, duo pianists Kalia and Marielle Labeque. **Venue:** nineteenth-century Casino Theater. **Performances:** 15, all at 8:30 P.M.

EVIAN-LES-BAINS (Savoy)
365 miles SE of Paris

Known internationally for the bottled mineral water that carries the town's name, Evian is one of the great spa villages of Europe. Situated on the south shore of Lac Leman, Evian provides a variety of water sports and boat excursions, and is just a few scenic hours' drive from the French and Italian Alps.

FESTIVALS

Musical Encounters

2 Weeks	Rencontres Musicales
Mid-May	d'Evian
	47, rue de Ponthieu
Op, Orch, Cham, Rec	75008 Paris
	Fax: 42 25 60 66

Under the direction of Mstislav Rostropovich, this festival brings together many of the world's finest young musicians at the threshold of their performing careers. Prizewinners of many international competitions are joined in performance by established artists, and a prestigious string quartet competition takes place during the festival's first week. Orchestral and chamber concerts feature the masterpieces of the standard repertoire. **Recent Performers:** flutist Jean-Pierre Rampal, pianist Alicia de Larrocha, violinist Isaac Stern. **Venues:** Auditorium Rostropovich, Théâtre Antoine Riboud. **Performances:** 20; 5 or 8 P.M. (No ticket sales by phone).

FONTEVRAUD L'ABBAYE (Maine)
190 miles SW of Paris

Used today to showcase the performing arts, the Fontevraud Abbey is a fascinating example of medieval architecture. Its striking design is most evident in an octagonal Romanesque tower. Contained in this once powerful abbey are the tombs of two English kings, Henry II and his son, Richard the Lion-Hearted.

ONGOING EVENTS

Cultural Center for Western France

Op, Orch, Chor, Cham, Rec,	Centre Culturel de l'Ouest
Dance, Lect, Th, Film	Abbaye Royale de Fontevraud
	49590 Fontevraud l'Abbaye
	Tel: 41 53 73 52

Established in 1975 to protect and promote the spectacular Fontevraud Abbey, the Cultural Center sponsors a broad range of cultural activities. Choral music from Gregorian chant to the baroque is the primary focus, with outstanding ensembles presenting such neglected masterpieces as Purcell's *King Arthur*. In addition to concerts, the Center presents films, lectures, evening tours of the illuminated Abbey, and special "Days of National Heritage." **Recent Performers:** Academy of St. Martin in the Fields, the Tallis Scholars, Taverner Consort. **Performances:** 16; year round.

FRÉJUS (Provence-Côte d'Azur)
540 miles SE of Paris

Fréjus is one of the small inland villages along the Côte d'Azur, between St.-Tropez and Cannes. Its Roman ruins date back to 49 A.D., when the town was settled by Julius Caesar. A more recent and therefore better preserved monument to Fréjus' heritage is its tenth-century cathedral, where superb cloisters and a lovely garden provide a peaceful refuge for tired travelers.

FESTIVALS

Fréjus Forum for the Arts and Music

1 Month	Comité d'Animation et
July	d'Action Culturelles
	Hôtel de Ville
Orch, Chor, Cham, Rec,	83600 Fréjus
Dance, Ex, Jazz, Folk	Tel: 94 53 56 45
	94 51 20 36

Founded in 1977, Forum of the Arts integrates various styles of art, classical music, and dance in its activities, presenting works from the Middle Ages to the present. It is possible to enjoy contemporary choreography while listening to the music of Marais and Purcell and to visit many ancillary art exhibits. Also taking place in July is the Session of Choral Singing, where masterclasses result in performances of works such as Fauré's Requiem. The venues include an early Gothic cathedral and an ancient amphitheater that once held 10,000 spectators. **Recent Performers:** I Solisti Veneti, Ysaÿe Quartet, baritone Michel Piquemal. **Venues:** Cathedral, Roman Theater, Town Hall. **Performances:** 15.

LILLE (Picardy)
135 miles N of Paris

Though it is now a bustling, commercial city, Lille has successfully preserved much of its history, most notably the seventeenth-century Stock Exchange and Vauban citadel. The city's Fine Arts Gallery has an impressive collection of primitives. Lille is a cultural city, offering great theater and music. Not to be missed is the classical Theatre de la Salamandre and an opportunity to hear the young, vibrant Orchestre National de Lille.

FESTIVALS

Lille Festival

6 Weeks	Festival de Lille
Mid-October–Late November	2, rue des Bons Enfants
	59800 Lille
Op, Orch, Chor, Cham,	Tel: 20 06 88 04
Rec, Jazz, Th, Film	

From *Madama Butterfly* to the Japanese *No* play, from Byzantine choirs to songs of Debussy, this far-ranging festival gathers together stellar performers in programs that explore the cultural riches of many lands. In addition to music, the festival sponsors dance, theater, and film, all relating to a central chosen theme such as the interchange between East and West. **Recent Performers:** Lille Opera, Tokyo Philharmonic Orchestra, violinists Anne-Sophie Mutter and Pinchas Zukerman, tenor Alfredo Kraus, composer Iannis Xenakis. **Venues:** about 20 in and around Lille. **Performances:** 40; evenings and some afternoons.

LYON (Lyonnaise)
465 miles SE of Paris

Once the ancient capital of the Gauls, Lyon is now a bustling French city in the southeastern part of the country, where the Saône and Rhône rivers meet. The city is the second largest in France, and possesses outstanding architectural treasures, which include the Roman remains on Fourvière Hill, a major Gallo-Roman museum and basilica, flamboyant Gothic churches, a seventeenth-century town hall, and a Benedictine abbey housing one of France's finest art museums.

FESTIVALS

Berlioz Festival

2 Weeks
Late September (odd-
    numbered years)

Op, Orch, Chor, Cham

Festival Berlioz
Maison de Lyon
69002 Lyon
Tel: 72 40 26 26

This biennial event focuses mainly on the work of its honoree, from the operas and large-scale choral works to songs for solo voice. Musical programs are augmented by conferences and lectures. **Recent Performers:** Orchestre National de Lyon directed by John Nelson, Georges Pretre conducting the Bamberg Orchestra. **Venues:** Maurice Ravel Auditorium, others. **Performances:** 24; afternoons and evenings.

Lyon Symphony Nights

2 Weeks
Late June–Mid-July

Orch, Chor, Cham, Rec,
    Film, Child

Les Nuits Symphoniques de
    Lyon
Auditorium Maurice Ravel
149 rue Garibaldi
69431 Lyon Cedex 03
Tel: 78 60 37 13
Fax: 78 60 13 08

This festival celebrated its inaugural season in 1990 with the theme "America, America," following the next year with "Mozart, Mozart." The energetic young event is given in the historic heart of Lyon. **Recent Performers:** Orchestre National de Jazz, soprano Julia Miguenes, pianist Ray Charles. **Venues:** seventeenth-century Hôtel de Ville. **Performances:** 10–15.

Music of Old Lyon

2 Weeks
Late November–Early
    December

Chor, Cham

Festival de Musique du
    Vieux-Lyon
Société de Musique du
    Lyonnais
BP 5064
69245 Lyon Cedex 05
Tel: 78 42 26 49
    78 28 34 12
    (after October 4)

Both baroque and classical music enjoy the spotlight at these concerts, which place a special emphasis on sacred choral music. Mozart masses, Handel oratorios, and choral and instrumental works by Vivaldi, Scarlatti, and their contemporaries have been featured here since 1983. **Recent Performers:** Les Arts Florissants, The King's Consort, International Vocal Ensemble of Lausanne. **Venues:** Churches throughout Lyon. **Performances:** 10; mostly evenings.

ONGOING EVENTS

L'Auditorium Maurice Ravel

Op, Orch, Cham, Rec, Org

149 Rue Garibaldi
69431 Lyon Cedex 3
Tel: 78 60 37 13
(Monday–Saturday, 12–7 P.M.)

Home of the Lyon Orchestra and the site of many of the Lyon Opera's productions, this facility also hosts a broad range of guest artists and ensembles, and is the centerpiece of musical life in Lyon. Programs include guest orchestras and world-renowned soloists. **Recent Performers:** violinist Iona Brown leading the Academy of St. Martin in the Fields, Scottish Chamber Orchestra, flutist Jean-Pierre Rampal. **Performances:** nearly 100, September–June.

Les Grands Interprètes

Orch, Chor, Cham, Rec

Les Grands Interprètes
B.P. 1083
69202 Lyon Cedex 01
Tel: 78 27 11 36

These concerts present world-renowned artists performing repertory from Vivaldi concerti to Mozart masses to Chopin mazurkas. **Recent Performers:** Auverne Orchestra, trumpeter Maurice André, violinist Isaac Stern, pianist Samuel Sanders. **Venue:** Auditorium Maurice Ravel. **Performances:** 8; October–June.

Orchestre National de Lyon

Orch, Chor

Orchestre National de Lyon
Auditorium Maurice Ravel
149 Rue Garibaldi
69003 Lyon
Tel: 78 60 37 13
(12–7 P.M.)

Music Director Emmanuel Krivine, guest conductors, and stellar performers collaborate on programs that present both traditional orchestral literature and twentieth-century compositions. In addition, special series explore contemporary music, choral music, chamber music, and pops. **Recent Performers:** conductors Rafael Frühbeck de Burgos and Gennady Rozhdestvensky, pianist Martha Argerich, cellist Yo-Yo Ma. **Venue:** Auditorium Maurice Ravel. **Performances:** 60, September–July (including "Les Nuits Symphoniques de Lyon," in June and July).

L'Opéra de Lyon

Op, Orch, Cham, Rec, Dance   L'Opéra de Lyon
                                 9, Quai Jean Moulin
                                 69001 Lyon
                                 Tel: 78 28 09 60

In addition to 10 opera productions (from Donizetti's *Don Pasquale* to Schoenberg's *Moses and Aaron*), L'Opéra hosts the Lyon Ballet, concerts by the opera orchestra, chamber music performed by members of the orchestra, and recitals by major singers. **Recent Performers:** conductors John Eliot Gardiner and Sergio Commissiona, sopranos Maria Ewing and Margaret Price. **Venues:** Numerous historic sites in Lyon. **Performances:** nearly 100, September–May.

IN THE AREA

Ambronay Abbey Festival

4 Weekends   Festival de L'Abbaye
June, July, September   d'Ambronay
                                 Place de l'Abbaye
Orch, Chor, Cham, Rec   01500 Ambronay
                                 Tel: 74 35 08 70

The special focus of this festival, 30 miles NE of Lyon, is on early music played on original instruments, but this does not preclude the programming of more modern music as well. Recent festivals have juxtaposed the music of Bach and Scarlatti with opera choruses of Verdi, Gounod, and Wagner. **Recent Performers:** the chorus and orchestra of the Paris Opera, Les Arts Florissants, soprano Ann Monoyios. **Venue:** thirteenth-century Benedictine Abbey of

Ambronay.   **Performances:** 14; afternoons, evenings, and midnight (!).

MARSEILLE (Provence-Côte d'Azur)
480 miles SE of Paris

Bordered by the Mediterranean, this largely commercial city derives its identity not from an entrenchment in French culture, like Paris, but from the exotic influences afforded by its accessible location. Marseille's Old Port (Vieux Port) is its thriving central focus, and the bustling shopping street, La Canebière, is an unrivalled spot for people watching. The Office of Tourism publishes a monthly booklet, *Nouvelles de Marseille*, listing cultural and tourist activities.

ONGOING EVENTS

Opéra de Marseille

Op, Orch, Chor, Rec

Opéra de Marseille
1, rue Molière
13001 Marseilles
Tel: 91 55 00 70
Fax: 91 54 94 15

In addition to 8–10 major productions, L'Opéra offers a series of concerts by the Marseille Philharmonic Orchestra in April, and occasional recitals by such well-known artists as mezzo-soprano Marilyn Horne and pianist Martin Katz. **Recent Productions:** *Le Nozze di Figaro, La Cenerentola, Fidelio, Pélléas et Mélisande, Tosca.*   **Venue:** Opera House. **Performances:** 55–60; October–June.

MENTON (Provence)
600 miles SE of Paris

Menton is a small, flower-filled town on the French Riviera close to the Italian border. Famous for its lemon and orange trees and its exceptional climate, it has for centuries been the haven of Europe's royal families, whose palaces still remain among more modern buildings. The music festival takes place in the heart of the red-roofed Old Town.

FESTIVALS

Menton Festival of Music

1 Month	Festival de Musique de
August	Menton
	Palais de L'Europe
Op, Orch, Chor, Cham, Rec	Avenue Boyer, BP 111
	06503 Menton Cedex
	Tel: 93 35 82 22
	93 57 57 00
	Fax: 93 57 51 00

An enchanting plaza flanked by two baroque churches and old fishermen's houses has been the site of this star-studded festival since 1950, when artistic director André Borocz was captivated by its charm. Overlooking the Mediterranean, the courtyard forms an ideal spot for candlelit programs of chamber music by Beethoven, Mozart, and Schubert performed by some of the world's great artists. **Recent Performers:** mezzo-soprano Marilyn Horne, violinist Schlomo Mintz, cellist Mstislav Rostropovich. **Venue:** Parvis St.-Michel. **Performances:** 3 each week.

METZ (Lorraine)
230 miles E of Paris

Although it is one of the Lorraine's most important commercial centers, Metz is filled with buildings and sites of historic interest. Most dramatic is the monumental, twelfth-century Metz cathedral, one of France's grandest. The cathedral's spectacular stained-glass windows are of a more recent vintage, some having been designed by Marc Chagall in this century. Still standing are the remains of the 10 gates (some turreted) that once surrounded the town, beyond which lies the gentle countryside of the Moselle Valley.

FESTIVALS

International Meeting of Contemporary Music

1 Weekend	Rencontres Internationales de
Late November	Musique Contemporaine
	2, rue de Paradis
Op, Orch, Chor, Cham, Rec,	57000 Metz
Org, Dance, Th, Film	Tel: 87 55 54 70
	Fax: 87 36 02 11

Founded in 1972, this festival annually presents an international panorama reflecting the multifarious trends in contemporary music. More than 200 works have been performed since the festival's founding, most of them world premieres. **Recent Performers:** Orchestre de l'Opéra de Lyon, Chorus of University Ljubljana, Ensemble Köln, Musique Oblique, organist Zsigmond Szathmary. **Venues:** Arsenal Concert Hall, the Theatre, various churches. **Performances:** 10.

ONGOING EVENTS

Théâtre Municipal de Metz

Op, Orch, Dance, Th, Lect   Théâtre Municipal
                                             de Metz
                                   4-5, place de la Comédie
                                   57000 Metz
                                   Tel: 87 75 40 50

The Metz Theatre, built in 1752, is the oldest and smallest theatre in France. Remarkable for the period, its architectural design has served as a model for many small theaters throughout the country. The theater is contemporary in spirit, however, and is the first in France to be guided by a female artistic director, Christiane Issartel. The theatre hopes to excite audiences with its operatic offerings, producing approximately 12 different productions each year. Recent offerings include *Manon, Albert Herring, Die Walküre,* and *La Cenerentola*. Lectures on particular operas are sometimes offered. The theater is also home to a ballet company and an active dramatic season. **Performances:** Almost 70; September–May.

MONT SAINT MICHEL (Normandy)
230 miles NW of Paris

The magnificent island that is Mont St.-Michel rises from the edge of the Normandy Coast in majestic Gothic grandeur. The imposing architecture of the island's abbey, cloisters, and medieval buildings admittedly draw the inevitable tourists and souvenir vendors in droves, but their presence shouldn't detract from the enjoyment of exploring the myriad historic treasures.

FESTIVALS

Musical Hours of Mont Saint Michel

8 Concerts	Les Heures Musicales du
Late July–Late August	Mont Saint Michel
	Syndicat d'Initiative
Chor, Cham, Rec	d'Avranches
	50300 Avranches
	Tel: 33 58 00 22

Only two of these concerts actually take place on the spectacular granite isle, while the others are given in equally historic settings on the mainland of Normandy. Despite the ancient sites, the repertory is not limited to early music, and one is as likely to hear the New American Chamber Orchestra playing Shostakovich as Les Arts Florissants presenting M. A. Charpentier. The festival has been in existence since 1968. **Recent Performers:** Oxford Cathedral Choir, Enesco String Quartet. **Venues:** various. **Performances:** all begin at 9 P.M.

MONTPELLIER (Languedoc)
470 miles S of Paris

Montpellier is a lively university town whose medical school is one of the best in France. The city's old town possesses an impressive collection of seventeenth- and eighteenth-century mansions, and the pedestrian promenades and courtyards in the town give this regional capital of Bas Languedoc an air of spacious elegance.

FESTIVALS

Festival of Radio France and Montpellier

3 Weeks	Festival International de
Mid-July–Early August	Radio France et de
	Montpellier
Op, Orch	Service Location
	7, Boulevard Henri IV
	34000 Montpellier
	Tel: 67 52 07 07

Since 1985, this festival has celebrated the importance of Radio France. There is a special interest in promoting forgotten or ignored works of major composers in addition to the standard repertoire. Recent operatic revivals have included Bellini's *La Straniera* and Saint-Saëns' *Henry VIII* along with *The Marriage of Figaro* and *Salome*. **Recent Performers:** Orchestre National de France conducted by Lorin Maazel, London Baroque, Russian Vocal Quartet of Nice. **Venues:** two dozen abbeys, cathedrals, churches, and theaters in Montpellier and the surrounding area of Languedoc Roussillon. **Performances:** 85; afternoons and evenings.

ONGOING EVENTS

Montpellier Opera

Op, Orch, Cham, Rec, Dance, Lect, Film	Opéra de Montpellier Boulevard Victor Hugo 34000 Montpellier Tel: 67 66 00 92

In addition to standard repertory such as *I Vespri Siciliani, Tannhäuser*, and *Les Huguenots*, L'Opéra offers its audiences the chance to explore the riches of baroque opera, with productions of *Atys, Platée, Anacréon/Actéon, David et Jonathas*, and Monteverdi's *Orfeo*, and *L'Incoronazione di Poppea*. L'Opéra also offers concerts and recitals of baroque music, as well as lectures, debates, and films on related subjects. The new Opera House, L'Opéra Berlioz, opened its doors in 1990. **Recent Performers:** Ensemble Clément Janequin, Les Arts Florissants, mezzo-soprano Marilyn Horne with pianist Martin Katz, pianist Sviatoslav Richter. **Venues:** Opéra-Comédie, Opéra Berlioz, Notre Dame des Tables. **Performances:** 10–12 productions; October–June.

Montpellier Philharmonic Orchestra

Orch, Chor	Orchestre Philharmonique de Montpellier CORUM Allée de l'Esplanade 34000 Montpellier Tel: 67 66 38 19

In addition to its important role in the Montpellier opera company productions, the ensemble presents an ambitious season of orchestral and choral concerts. Recent repertoire has included Bach's Mass in B Minor, the world premiere of Xenakis' *Kyania*, and major works by Mozart, Beethoven, Brahms, and Ravel. **Recent Performers:** conductors Franz Brüggen and Thomas Fulton, cellist Matt Haimowitz, pianist

Nikita Magaloff. **Venues:** L'Opéra-Berlioz Corum, Eglise Sainte Thérèse. **Performances:** 33 concerts plus five opera productions; weeknights at 8:30, Saturday at 5, Sunday at 10:45; September–July.

IN THE AREA

Music at Saint-Guilhem-le-Désert

2 Months
Late June–Late August

Chor, Cham, Rec, Org, Ex

Association des Amis de
Saint-Guilhem le Desert
165, rue Michel-Ange
34000 Montpellier
Tel: 67 63 14 99

Twenty-five miles NW of Montpellier lies the ancient Abbey of Saint-Guilhem-le-Désert, built in the eleventh century on the site of an earlier monastery founded by one of Charlemagne's knights in 804. It houses a magnificent eighteenth-century organ, which figures prominently in the concerts held in this memorable space. Baroque music is what you will most commonly find here, played by chamber ensembles as well as by organ soloists. **Recent Performers:** Tokyo Baroque Ensemble, Manfred Quartet, harpsichordist Gustav Leonhardt. **Performances:** 11; all at 9:15 P.M.

MULHOUSE (Alsace)
330 miles SE of Paris

Lying just 50 miles downstream from Strasbourg on the River Ill, Mulhouse shares the same bilingual heritage as its more cosmopolitan neighbor to the north. The combination of French and German cultures unique to the Alsace-Lorraine region infuses most aspects of the lifestyle here, including food, architecture, and tradition. Of particular interest are Mulhouse's museums, which feature renowned collections of antique cars, railroad artifacts, and Dutch and Flemish paintings.

FESTIVALS

Mulhouse Bach Festival

5 Concerts
Late May–Late June

Op, Orch, Chor, Cham

Festival Bach Mulhouse
B.P. 5
68390 Sausheim
Tel: 89 61 76 61
        89 61 78 10

Although music by Bach may be only a small portion of the program here, the fine programming and stellar performers are sure to please even those who expected more music by the Leipzig master. The offerings are often unusual—the Basler Bach Choir recently performed Bellini's Te Deum and Donizetti's Requiem, while another program featured concertos for one, two, three, four, and six trumpets. Mozart's *Marriage of Figaro* and Purcell's *Dido and Aeneas* have been presented in concert versions. **Recent Performers:** Concerto Köln, La Follia Instrumental Ensemble, flutist Jean-Pierre Rampal. **Venue:** Temple Saint-Etienne. **Performances:** 5; once a week at 9 P.M.

NANCY (Lorraine)
180 miles E of Paris

An intriguing city of architectural diversity, Nancy contains a significant mix of some of France's most important art movements, and its magnificent Museum of the School of Nancy celebrates the Art Nouveau. The center of sightseeing is the Place Stanislas, named for the last Duke of Lorraine, a former king of Poland. This magnificent eighteenth-century square features imposing buildings of classical and rococo design, many decorated with the attractive Art Nouveau grid ironworks that are abundant throughout the entire city.

ONGOING EVENTS

Opéra de Nancy et de Lorraine

Op, Orch

Opéra de Nancy et de
    Lorraine
1, rue Sainte-Catherine
54000 Nancy
Tel: 83 32 04 43
Fax: 83 35 38 26

The season in this theater, constructed in 1919, includes a comprehensive operatic repertoire ranging from Wagner and Verdi to the light-hearted works of Offenbach. The company offers six operas each season, and is particularly proud to offer at least one modern work each year. Striking productions of Prokofiev's *La Cantata d'Octobre* and Tippett's *King Priam* have been highlights of recent seasons that also offered *Otello* and *Thais*. **Performances:** approx. 40; October–June.

NANTES (Brittany)
230 miles SW of Paris

Once considered the capital of Brittany, this small city on the Loire River is filled with wide boulevards and beautiful old mansions. Most notable among the numerous historical and cultural attractions of Nantes are the fifteenth-century Ducal Castle of Anne of Brittany, the nineteenth-century shopping arcade, the Passage Pommeragye, and the highly recommended Fine Arts Museum.

FESTIVALS

Festival Atlantique

2 Months	Festival Atlantique
Mid-June–Mid-August	7 quai de Versailles
	44000 Nantes
Op, Rec	Tel: 40 35 46 46
	Fax: 40 12 09 10

Begun in 1983 by a passionate lover of the vocal arts, Pierre Gire, and led by the great French singer Mady Mesplé who serves as its president, this event has been graced by renowned singers from around the world. Far from the stiff proprieties of the concert hall, established artists and young singers collaborate to learn and to perform. The festival is associated with an international vocal competition that takes place here in August. **Recent Performers:** soprano June Anderson with the Warsaw Orchestra, tenor José Carreras, soprano Shirley Verrett. **Venues:** a medieval castle, an Italian renaissance villa, an eighteenth-century chapel. **Performances:** 8.

NICE (Provence-Côte d'Azur)
520 miles SE of Paris

Overlooking the gentle Baie des Anges (Bay of Angels), Nice captures the romance of the Mediterranean without spoiling it with the frequent madness of the Côte d'Azur. Even though this city's prime location does attract its share of sun and celebrity worshippers, Nice maintains an air of dignified sanity. The shops and bistros along the lively Promenade de Anglais play host to Nice's cafe society, and ruins of a fortress high on a hill preside over the enchanting Old City (La Vieille

Ville), where narrow cobblestone streets and alleys reveal a Nice of yesteryear.

FESTIVALS

Manca Festival

10 Days	Festival Manca
Late March–Early April	33, Avenue Jean Medecin
	06000 Nice
Orch, Cham, Jazz	Tel: 93 88 75 04
	93 88 74 68

Manca—Musiques Actuelles Nice Côte d'Azur—brings together an interdisciplinary mix of music, dance, visual arts, theater, and film, all with an emphasis on the contemporary. Many of Europe's foremost musical innovators participate in the programs, joined by American colleagues. The festival has been in existence since 1979, and is augmented by a three-day film festival that runs concurrently. **Recent Performers:** composer/conductors Luciano Berio, Alex Grillo, Paul Bowles. **Venues:** Palais des Arts, Opera House, others. **Performances:** 13; one each evening, with some afternoon programs.

Sacred Music Festival

3 Weeks	Opéra de Nice
Mid-June	Festival de Musique Sacrée
	4, rue Saint-François de
Orch, Chor, Cham, Org	Paule
	06300 Nice
	Tel: 93 85 67 31

Since 1975 this festival has provided an invigorating overview of sacred music. From Byrd to Negro spirituals and Monteverdi to Delalande, the programs cover the repertoire while also providing a musical tour of the churches of Nice. **Recent Performers:** Nice Philharmonic, Golden Gate Vocal Quartet, organist Michel Chapuis. **Venues:** churches throughout Nice. **Performances:** 14; usually at 8 P.M.

ONGOING EVENTS

Théâtre de l'Opéra de Nice

Op, Orch, Chor, Cham,	Théâtre de l'Opéra de Nice
Rec, Dance	4, rue St.-François de Paule
	06300 Nice
	Tel: 93 80 59 83
	Fax: 93 80 34 83

This theater is home to the Nice Opera, with productions ranging from Cimarosa's *Il Matrimonio Segreto* to Berg's *Wozzeck*, as well as orchestral and chamber music concerts, recitals, and dance. The Broadway Musical Company of New York recently presented *West Side Story,* and the resident orchestra has been joined by renowned soloists in a repertoire ranging from Purcell to Parmegiani. **Recent Performers:** tenor Gérard Souzay with pianist Dalton Baldwin, violinist Pinchas Zukerman, soprano Lucia Popp. **Performances:** Approx 100; September–June.

IN THE AREA

Tourettes-sur-Loup Festival

6–10 Concerts
Late July–Mid-August

Chor, Cham, Rec

Société des Arts de
    Tourettes sur Loup
2247, route de Grasse
06140 Tourrettes sur
    Loup
Tel: 93 24 11 32
    93 24 18 93

This colorful village 16 miles W of Nice has survived centuries of war and famine to become a peaceful town where the main occupation is the cultivation of violets. It is also a gathering place for artists, with over two dozen studios and galleries dotting its ancient streets. Its festival draws musicians often heard on the nearby Côte d'Azur. What makes the performances here unique is the intimate charm of this hilltop town. **Recent Performers:** Shostakovich Trio, Wind Quartet of Paris, Russian Vocal Quartet of Nice. **Venues:** Church, Chateau Mairie. **Performances:** all begin at 9 P.M.

ORANGE (Provence-Côte d'Azur)
410 miles SE of Paris

The small town of Orange is known for its remarkable Roman theater, Théâtre Antique, which is the best preserved in the world. This amphitheater was built before the birth of Christ and features an enormous "screen," or wall, which stands 120 feet tall and forms a dramatic backdrop for the operas and other productions. Also noteworthy in Orange are the medieval cathedral and the Municipal Museum, which features Roman stonework.

FESTIVALS

Chorégies d'Orange

4–5 Performances
July–Early August

Op, Orch, Chor

Chorégies d'Orange
B.P. 180
84105 Orange Cedex
Tel: 90 34 24 24

These programs are limited only in number—in every other respect they are truly grand. The productions, the artistic rosters, and the site–the ancient Roman amphitheater—are indeed impressive. Major artists appear in productions such as Wagner's Ring Cycle, Verdi's Requiem, and symphonies by Mahler and Bruckner. **Recent Performers:** soprano Eva Marton (singing all three Brünnhildes), bass Simon Estes, conductor Claudio Abbado, mezzo-soprano Christa Ludwig. **Venue:** Théâtre Antique, noted for its outstanding acoustics. **Performances:** evenings. Tickets are often sold out by May.

IN THE AREA

Vaison-la-Romaine Festival

1 Month
Early July–Early August

Op, Orch, Cham, Rec,
    Dance, Jazz

Vaison-la-Romaine Festival
Bureau du Festival
84110 Vaison-la-Romaine
Tel: 90 36 24 79
(after mid-April)

A little bit of everything can be found at this festival 15 miles NE of Orange–opera *(Cendrillon)*, drama (Molière), a modern setting of the twelfth- and thirteenth-century sources for the Tristan and Isolde legend, as well as orchestral performances of Strauss, Beethoven, and Mozart. Founded in 1953, the Festival is notable for the diversity of its performances. **Recent Performers:** Nantes Opera, National Ballet of Marseille, pianists Gustavo Romero and Jean-Philippe Collard. **Venues:** Théâtre Antique and Théâtre du Nymphée. **Performances:** 15; evenings.

PARIS (Ile de France)

Elegant, eccentric, eclectic, enticing. One could spend a lifetime in this romantic city and still not see it all. This is due not only to an abundance of riches, but to the city's uncanny penchant for re-creating itself. A chameleon spirit flits amid the lofty monuments of Paris like a jovial muse bantering among the gods. This is the spirit that metamorphosed the city's magnificent new Musée D'Orsay from an old railroad station, and is continuously rebuilding Louis XIV's palace (also known as The Louvre) to accommodate its always expanding art collection. And in this sense, Paris ultimately imitates life— balancing the beauty and dignity of age with the brilliance and romance of youth.

Current information on cultural events in Paris can be found in several weekly publications, including *L'Officiel des Spectacles*, *Pariscope*, and *7 à Paris*. As in all major centers, there are innumerable concerts held in small but spectacular venues. Among the most memorable are the candlelight concerts at the Sainte-Chappelle.

A note of Parisian telephone numbers: when calling Paris from abroad, 1 is added before the 8-digit number. When calling Paris from another province in France, 16 1 is added before the 8-digit number. When calling from Paris to another province, 16 is added to the 8-digit number. When calling within Paris, use only the 8-digit number.

FESTIVALS

Festival of Sacred Music

3 Months
October–December

Chor, Cham, Rec

Festival d'Art Sacré
4, rue Jules-Cousin
74004 Paris
Tel: 16 1/42 33 43 00

These concerts present sacred music from the Renaissance to the present day, including organ recitals, chamber concerts, and liturgies. The choral works range from the very grand to the most intimate, and may include Bach cantatas, Byrd masses, or Bruckner motets. **Recent Performers:** European Community Baroque Orchestra, Choir of Winchester Cathedral, Chamber Orchestra of Cologne. **Venues:** historic churches throughout Paris. **Performances:** 24; October–December.

L'Ile-de-France Festival

2 Months
Mid-September–Late
November

Orch, Chor, Cham, Rec, Jazz

Festival de L'Ille de France
4, rue de la Michodière
75002 Paris
Tel: 16 1/42 65 07 22

All styles of music, from baroque to jazz, are represented in this festival, which takes advantage of many unique settings throughout this historic region of Paris and its environs. French artists predominate in programs ranging from harpsichord recitals to Beethoven piano concertos. **Recent Performers:** Orchestra of the Auvergne, Ysaÿe Quartet, pianist Catherine Collard. **Venues:** Chateaus, chapels, churches, and concert halls throughout the region, including Versailles. **Performances:** 50; schedule is variable.

Paris Autumn Festival

3 Months
Late September–Late
    December

Op, Orch, Chor, Cham,
    Rec, Th, Dance, Film

Festival d'Automne à Paris
156, rue de Rivoli
75001 Paris
Tel: 16 1/42 96 12 27
Fax: 16 1/40 15 92 88

The best of the contemporary arts are represented in this important festival, which is as international in its sponsorship as in its artistic roster. The musical program is especially notable for presenting an extraordinary number of world premieres. The festival was begun in 1972. **Recent Performers:** composers Luciano Berio, Pierre Boulez, Gyorgy Ligeti, Luigi Nono, Steve Reich. **Venues:** various sites, including the Opéra Comique and the Pompidou Centre. **Performances:** more than two dozen musical events, scores of theater and dance performances.

Sceaux Orangerie Festival

Weekends
Early June–September

Orch, Cham, Rec

Saison Musicale d'Eté de
    Sceaux
B.P. Postale 52
92333 Sceaux Cedex
Tel: 16 1/47 02 95 91

The site of these concerts is the newly restored Orangerie in the Chateau de Sceaux, built by J. H. Mansart in 1685 and situated on 200 acres of parkland just outside Paris. Since 1969 over 200,000 visitors have attended these chamber music programs, which feature primarily French artists in repertoire from Mozart to contemporary music. **Recent Performers:** Chamber Orchestra of Cologne, Versailles, and Caen, prize winners of the Jean-Pierre Rampal Competition. **Performances:** 30; Saturday and Sunday, usually at 5:30 P.M.

ONGOING EVENTS

Ensemble InterContemporain

Orch, Chor, Cham, Lec

Ensemble Inter-
Contemporain
9, rue de l'Echelle
75001 Paris
Tel: 16 1/42 61 56 75 or
42 60 94 27

Founded in 1976 by the Ministry of Culture, the Ensemble InterContemporain was formed to afford composers the resources to create new works in accordance with their artistic intents. The aim of the ensemble is to foster audience understanding of the evolution of twentieth-century music, featuring contemporary composers such as Iannis Xenakis, Heinz Holliger, and Gyorgy Ligeti, and predecessors such as Debussy, Stravinsky, and Messiaen. **Recent Guest Performers:** BBC Orchestra, Chorus, and Singers; London Voices; pianist Maurizio Pollini; soprano Phyllis Bryn-Julson. **Venues:** George Pompidou Center, Théâtre Renaud-Barrault, Théâtre des Champs-Elysées, Salle Pleyel, Théâtre du Châtelet, Opéra Comique, Radio-France Auditorium. **Performances:** approx. 25 in Paris; October–June.

Musique en Sorbonne

Op, Orch, Cham, Rec

Musique en Sorbonne
2, rue Francis de Croisset
75018 Paris
Tel: 16 1/42 62 71 71

The active musical life of this celebrated institution is often augmented by special events such as the 1990 Schumann Festival, which presented his rarely heard scenes from *Faust* as well as the beloved chamber music and songs. Regular events include such large-scale performances as the Berlioz Requiem and the Beethoven Triple Concerto, as well as chamber music by Debussy and Strauss. **Recent Performers:** Choir and Orchestra of the University of Paris-Sorbonne, Arpeggione Quartet (quartet in residence at the Sorbonne), pianist Nöel Lee. **Venues:** Amphitheatre Richelieu, Grand Amphitheatre. **Performances:** several each month during the academic year.

Opéra Comique

Op, Orch, Rec, Dance

Opéra Comique
5, rue Favart
75002 Paris
Tel: 16 1/42 86 88 83
Fax: 16 1/42 86 85 78

This exquisite theater, also known as the Salle Favart, has been one of main opera houses in Paris for over a century. Originally intended for operas with spoken dialogue (as opposed to the completely sung productions staged at the Salle Garnier), the works were not necessarily humorous. Bizet's *Carmen* stretched the sensibilities of audiences accustomed to "family entertainment" and caused a scandal when it was premiered here in 1875. Now the theater offers concerts and dance productions in addition to opera. **Performances:** September–July.

Opéra Bastille de Paris

Op, Orch, Cham, Rec

Opera Bastille de Paris
Service Location
120 rue de Lyon
75012 Paris
Tel: 16 1/40 01 17 89
Fax: 16 1/40 01 19 46

The Bastille Opera was surrounded by controversy over its building, programming, and management before the doors opened in 1990 with Berlioz' *Les Troyens*, but the spectacular season of opera, orchestral concerts, and recitals now offered is likely to mollify even the fiercest critics. The operatic repertoire encompasses favorites such as *Otello* and *The Marriage of Figaro*, lesser-known works like Leoš Janáček's *Katia Kabanova*, and new operas, including Luciano Berio's *Un Re in Ascolto*. Recitals feature singers of international standing, including mezzo-soprano Christa Ludwig and soprano Katia Ricciarelli. Ten concerts are given by the Orchestre National de L'Opéra de Paris, conducted by the musical director of the Paris Opera, Myung-Whun Chung. The Orchestre Philharmonique de Radio France offers a series of six concerts, and there are also concerts by visiting ensembles and artists. In addition to the 2700-seat main hall, the glassy, circular building houses a 500-seat amphitheater and a 237-seat studio theater where chamber music, contemporary works, recitals, and lectures are given in appropriately intimate surroundings. **Recent Performers:** Kurt Masur conducting the Gewandhaus Orchestra of

Leipzig, tenor Placido Domingo, soprano Ruth-Ann Swenson. **Performances:** 150; September–July, no performances on Sunday.

Salle Pleyel

Orch, Chor, Cham, Rec,
Dance, Film

Salle Pleyel
252, rue du Faubourg-Saint-
Honoré
75008 Paris
Tel: 16 1/45 61 06 30
Fax: 16 1/45 61 46 87

The present Salle Pleyel, built in 1927, is the third to bear this name. The present building has become much more than a concert hall—its three theaters, Salle Pleyel, Salle Chopin, and Salle Debussy, are home to nine ensembles and concert series, and the complex contains an exhibition gallery, two musical instrument and record shops, and more than 30 studios offering instruction in an impressive range of music and dance. This activity supports the Salle Pleyel's other name: Centre Artistique de Paris. Among the resident ensembles is the highly respected Orchestre de Paris, founded in 1967 as an offshoot of the Société des Concerts du Conservatoire. Resident conductor Semyon Bychkov continues the work of his predecessors, who include Charles Munch, Herbert von Karajan, George Solti, and Daniel Barenboim in 60 concerts each season. Another resident ensemble is the Ensemble Orchestral de Paris, which presents 40 programs ranging from a concert version of Mozart's *Idomeneo* to the Schumann Piano Quintet to Schönberg's "Transfigured Night." Thursday afternoon chamber music concerts and Sunday afternoon orchestra programs are sponsored by the Concerts Lamoureux. Other resident ensembles include the Orchestre National de'Ile de France, and the Orchestre Symphonique Français. **Recent Performers:** National Symphony Orchestra conducted by Mstislav Rostropovich, cellist Yo-Yo Ma, pianist Emanuel Ax, violinist Isaac Stern, soprano Phyllis Bryn-Julson. **Performances:** almost 200; September–June.

IN THE AREA

Avray Music Festival

1 Week
Mid-June

Orch, Chor, Cham, Rec,
Dance

Festival de Ville d'Avray
10 rue de Marnes
92410 Ville d'Avray
Tel: 16 1/47 50 44 28

Since it was established in 1979, the festival in this town 8 miles W of Paris has dedicated its programs of each season to an early twentieth-century French composer—Poulenc, Roussel, Hahn, Ibert, and Massenet have been among those so honored. This musical heritage has enriched not only the concert programs, but reached a wider audience, for the festival has provided the impetus for a number of new recordings. **Recent Performers:** Jean-Louis Petit Chamber Orchestra, Erwartung Ensemble, Albert Roussel Quartet. **Venues:** castles and churches. **Performances:** 7–15.

Forum for Musical Composition
"The Composer in the City"

1 Month	"Le Compositeur dans la
December	Ville"
	34 rue Corot
Chor, Cham, Rec, Org, Dance	92410 Ville-d'Avray
	Tel: 16 1/47 50 44 28

"Le Compositeur dans la Ville," conceived by its artistic director Jean-Louis Petit in 1980, is an organization that commissions, presents, and researches new works, expanding the frontiers of modern music. Most concerts are given in the Château de Ville d'Avray, though many are given in the more than 30 towns and villages of the Haut de Seine. **Recent Performers:** Ensemble InterContemporain directed by Pierre Boulez, Atelier Musique de Ville D'Avray, soprano Phyllis Bryn-Julson. **Performances:** 10–15.

St.-Germer-de-Fly Festival

2 Weeks	Festival de St.-Germer-de-Fly
Late July–Mid-August	44, rue du Commandant
	Kieffer
Chor, Cham, Rec	95240 Cormeilles-en-Parisis
	Tel: 39 78 43 45

Olivier Messiaen is among the artistic directors of this chamber music festival, which since 1983 has presented concerts in spectacular settings 50 miles NW of Paris. The range of repertoire is broad, including Bach, Beethoven, Chopin, and jazz. **Recent Performers:** Gregg Smith Singers, pianist Claude Bolling, soprano Mady Mesplé. **Venues:** twelfth-century Benedictine abbey, thirteenth-century Sainte-Chappelle (a replica of the famous one in Paris). **Performances:** 8; afternoons and evenings.

ST.-BERTRAND-DE-COMMINGES
(Midi-Toulousain-Pyrénées)
505 miles SW of Paris

On a rocky bluff above the Garonne River one finds this tiny village, where prehistoric paintings, Roman ruins, and a treasure-filled cathedral combine to make this the art and history center of the central Pyrénées. The famed cave paintings of Gargas are less than 5 miles from the village, and in the lower part of the town are the remains of Roman and Christian basilicas, baths, a forum, and a theater, all sacked by the Vandals in the fifth century. The Cathedral of St. Marie is in the upper town, and contains the tomb of the Saint who gave his name to the town.

FESTIVALS

Comminges Festival

6 Weeks	Festivals du Comminges
Mid-July–Early September	31260 Mazère sur Salat
	Tel: 61 88 32 00
Orch, Cham, Rec, Org	61 95 81 25

The magnificent organ in the Cathedral of St. Marie is in part responsible for the tremendous success of this early music festival, which since 1979 has also included more recent music in its programs. In addition to music played on the 400-year-old organ, famed for its opulent sound and splendidly ornate case, programs include chamber and orchestral music of all eras as well as works commissioned by the festival from both established and rising young composers. Another remarkable instrument used in these programs is a 1774 Kroll harpsichord. **Recent Performers:** Hesperion XX, Parisii Quartet, soprano Lucia Popp. **Venues:** Cathedral of St. Bertrand of Comminges, Collegiale of St. Gaudens, Basilica of St. Just of Valcabrère. **Performances:** 21; 9 P.M.

ST.-CÉRÉ (Périgord)
340 miles S of Paris

A charming town just west of the Segala Mountain region of Auvergne, St.-Céré is notable for its fifteenth-, sixteenth-, and seventeenth-century houses. Nearby are some of the limestone caves for which the area is famous, and above ground is the even more famous locale cuisine—truffles, foie gras, and fattened poultry are served at village inns throughout the region.

FESTIVALS

St.-Céré Festival

1 Month
Mid-July–Mid-August

Op, Orch, Chor, Cham

Festival de Musique de
St.-Céré
Centre International
d'Exchanges Musicaux
64, rue Saint-Honoré
75001 Paris
Tel: (1) 40 26 77 94

Although this festival presents a range of choral and orchestral concerts, the heart of its programming is opera. Productions are created for the courtyard of a magnificent twelfth-century fortress, and, after the festival, travel to locations throughout France. Since its founding in 1961, the Saint-Céré Festival has encouraged young artists, placing its greatest emphasis on French performers. **Recent Productions:** *Lucia di Lammermoor, Don Quichotte* (Massenet), *Les Contes d'Hoffman*. **Venues:** Château de Castelnau, historic sites in the surrounding area. **Performances:** 40.

ST.-PAUL-DE-VENCE (Provence–Côte d'Azur)
575 miles SE of Paris

This is a small Côte d'Azur town whose charms attracted artists in search of a colony. Here they created one out of a fortified, medieval village. Chagall, Signac, and Bonnard all resided here at one point or another, and the town is still a favorite haunt of writers, artists, and poets.

FESTIVALS

Maeght Foundation Concerts

5 Concerts
Mid-July

Cham, Ex, Film, Dance

Nuits de la Fondation
Maeght
Fondation Maeght
06570 Saint-Paul-de-Vence
Tel: 93 32 81 63

In keeping with the Maeght Foundation's mandate to promote contemporary art, these concerts present twentieth-century music, with homage to composers as diverse as Charles Ives and Luciano Berio, and to the national music of Spain and Cuba. The Foundation is perhaps the most important cultural center in southern France, and the exhibitions in its museum have brought international praise. The building itself is a strikingly modern structure built in the 1960s. **Recent Performers:** Musicus Concentus of Florence, Nash Ensemble of London, Grupo Circulo of Madrid. **Venue:** Fondation Maeght. **Performances:** all begin at 9 P.M.

ST.-RÉMY-de-Provence (Provence)
440 miles SE of Paris

The artistic associations of this tiny town are remarkable. Gounod wrote his opera *Mireille* here, and less than a mile south is the monastery where Vincent van Gogh spent the last year of his life in a nursing home. St.-Rémy-de-Provence was the birthplace of both Nostrodamus, the Renaissance physician-astronomer, and Frédéric Mistral, the most celebrated of the Provençal poets.

FESTIVALS

Organa

2 Months	Organa
Mid-July–Mid-September	Office de Tourisme
	13210 St.-Rémy-de-Provence
Cham, Rec, Org	Tel: 90 92 05 22

The great organ of the Collégial Saint-Martin is the centerpiece of this festival, which also features chamber music and masterclasses at the nearby Charles Gounod School of Music. The organists are both renowned artists and gifted young players, and the repertoire spans the centuries from Buxtehude to the present, including prize winning works from the biennial competition for organ compositions held in conjunction with the festival. **Recent Performers:** organists Thomas Schäfer, Yves Castagnet, pianist Catherine Collard, cellist Génévieve Teulièves. **Venues:** Collégiale Saint-H. Martin, Auditorium Rolland. **Performances:** 24; including weekly Saturday concerts at 5:30 P.M.; most concerts are free.

STRASBOURG (Alsace)
300 miles E of Paris

Strasbourg is a marketplace of sensory delights, showcasing the historic, architectural, and gastronomic riches of the surrounding Lorraine-Alsace region, over which the city so elegantly presides. The city's main attraction is its imposing Gothic cathedral, which houses a sixteenth-century astronomer's clock.

FESTIVALS

Bach Festival

1 Week	Festival Bach
Mid-May	Wolf Musique
	24, rue de la Mésange
Orch, Chor, Cham, Rec	67081 Strasbourg Cedex
	Tel: 88 32 43 10

This venerable program was begun in 1926, and includes the music of Bach's contemporaries as well as that of the master himself. **Recent Performers:** Stuttgart Chamber Orchestra, flutist Jean-Pierre Rampal, organist Marie-Claire Alain. **Venues:** Palais De la Musique et des Congres, Cathedral, churches. **Performances:** 12; afternoons and evenings.

Strasbourg Music Festival

1 Month	Strasbourg Music
Early June–Early July	Festival
	Wolf Musique
Op, Orch, Chor, Cham, Rec	24, rue de la Mésange
	67081 Strasbourg Cedex
	Tel: 88 32 43 10

One of the oldest of the French festivals (founded in 1932), Strasbourg has recently expanded its offerings to include operas of Mozart and Rossini along with its primarily nineteenth-century orchestral and chamber music programs. A week-long jazz festival follows the classical program. **Recent Performers:** Concertgebouw of Amsterdam under Nikolaus Harnoncourt, the Melos Quartet, pianist Claudio Arrau. **Venues:** Cathedral, concert halls, churches. **Performances:** 24; evenings.

ONGOING EVENTS

Concerts Ajam

Cham

AJAM
6, Rue du Maroquin
67000 Strasbourg
Tel: 88 22 19 22

The purpose of these concerts is to advance the careers of young performers, many of whom are winners of international competitions. **Venues:** chateaus and historic buildings in and around Strasbourg. **Performances:** More than 30; November–April.

Orchestre Philharmonique de Strasbourg

Orch

Orchestre Philharmonique
de Strasbourg
Palais de la Musique et des
Congres
Avenue Schutzenberger
67082 Strasbourg Cedex
Tel: 88 37 67 87
Fax: 88 37 09 43

This orchestra seeks diversity, and finds it in both repertoire and guest artists. In addition to the standard orchestral works, a number of "modern classics" such as Stravinsky's *Pulcinella* Suite and Prokofiev's Symphony-Concerto are featured. **Recent Performers:** conductors Evgeny Svetlanov and Lukas Foss, oboist Heinz Holliger, pianist Lazar Berman. **Venue:** Palais de la Musique et des Congres. **Performances:** 27; October–May.

Wolf Musique

Orch, Chor, Charm

Wolf Musique
24, rue de la Mésange
67081 Strasbourg Cedex
Tel: 88 32 43 10

The concerts sponsored by this organization present international artists performing music from Bach to Bruch. **Recent Performers:** Mozarteum Orchestra, cellist Yo-Yo Ma, the King's Singers, Emerson String Quartet. **Venue:** Palais de la Musique et des Congres. **Performances:** 15; October–May.

Théâtre Municipal

Op, Dance

Théâtre Municipal
19, place Broglie
67008 Strasbourg Cedex
Tel: 88 75 48 23

With productions given in Strasbourg, Mulhouse, and Colmar, the resident opera company of this theater, Opéra du Rhin, prides itself on discovering and supporting new talents. Since 1865, great artists such as Célestine Galli-Marié (the first Carmen and Mignon), Régine Crespin, Rachel Yakar, and Karita Mattila have begun their careers in this theater. Recent productions include *Parsifal,* Martinu's *Passion Grecque, Don Giovanni*, and Saint-Saëns' *Samson et Delila.* The ballet company offers three productions each season. **Resident Companies:** Opéra du Rhin, Ballet du Rhin. **Performances:** 80–90 of 8 operas; October–June.

SULLY-SUR-LOIRE (Loire Valley)
90 miles S of Paris

The village of Sully has blossomed along with its agriculture, industry, commerce, and tourism in the heart of a fertile valley. However, its prime situation on the river and its position at the juncture of many significant routes are responsible not only for its development, but also for many battles over possession of the town and its fourteenth-century château, rebuilt in the seventeenth century by Henry IV's minister, Sully.

FESTIVALS

Sully International Music Festival

1 Month
Mid-June–Mid-July

Op, Orch, Chor, Cham,
Rec, Jazz, Dance

Festival de Sully, Orléans,
and Lorient B.P. 58
45600 Sully-sur-Loire
Tel: 38 36 23 46
Fax: 38 36 53 32

Since 1973 this festival has presented renowned performers in spectacular venues from Sully to Orleans. Chamber music and recitals are among the offerings at the superb château of Sully, where concerts and operas are presented in the fourteenth-century castle's keep and in the specially designed outdoor Espace Auditorium. In St.-Benoit-sur-Loire the featured venue is the remarkable Benedictine abbey, a Romanesque structure that houses the relics of St. Benedict himself. The nearby church of Germigny-des-Prés is one of the oldest in France, dating back to the ninth century. This intimate space (seating 350) is especially suited to early music, which one can enjoy while admiring the Byzantine mosaic ornamenting the apse. In Orleans the venues include the medieval cathedral of Sainte-Croix, the adjoining Campo Santo (a recently restored Gothic cloister), and the Church of St.-Pierre-le-Puellier, one of Orleans' most ancient and beautiful churches. **Recent Performers:** The London Classical Players directed by Roger Norrington; Hanover Band; Alban Berg Quartet; jazz player, Dizzy Gillespie. **Performances:** 15–20; mostly on weekends.

TOULON (Provence)
520 miles SE of Paris

This is the home of France's major naval base, and the sparkling harbor is almost permanently dotted with naval ships and pleasure craft alike. Lively open markets and colorful cafes abound in the historic waterfront section, and a variety of historic buildings and churches are scattered throughout the entire town. Surrounding the city are ridges of Provençal limestone mountains.

FESTIVALS

Toulon Festival

8 Weeks	Festival de Musique de
Late May–Mid-July	Toulon
	Palais de la Bourse
Orch, Chor, Cham, Rec	Avenue Jean Moulin
	83000 Toulon
	Tel: 94 93 52 84

This well-established festival has brought a variety of musical activities to Toulon since 1951, and now sponsors an international competition for wind instruments. Guest artists come from throughout Europe to present music of all eras, from the baroque to contemporary. **Recent Performers:** conductor Karl Munchinger, Talich Quartet, pianist Eugene Istomin. **Venue:** Opera House, churches. **Performances:** 10–12; evenings only.

ONGOING EVENTS

Toulon Opera

Op, Operetta	Toulon Opéra
	Boulevard de Strasbourg
	8300 Toulon
	Tel: 94 92 70 78

This company mounts an impressive season of both opera and operetta, sung primarily by international artists. Eight opera productions and nine operettas span the repertoire from Verdi's *Otello* to Offenbach's *La Vie Parisienne*. **Recent Performers:** sopranos Yoko Watanabe and Miao Qing. **Performances:** 45; October–April.

LES VANS (Ardèche)
475 miles S of Paris

Hiking trails wind through the enchanted forests and startling rock formations of the Vans region, a naturalist's dream. The stone houses and elegant fountains of Les Vans embody the charm of the entire region.

FESTIVALS

Cévennes Festival

10 Days	Festival en Cévennes
Late July–Early August	Château de Banne
	07460 Banne
Orch, Chor, Cham, Rec	Tel: 75 39 81 20
	75 39 81 35

Founded in 1987 by Claude Carasso and Thérèse Dussaut, this event draws both artists and audiences to an area known for its extraordinary beauty. The programs here are quite varied, and have included a Liszt recital, an evening of songs by Schumann, Schubert, Brahms, and Wolf, and works by Shostakovich and Ysaÿe.   **Recent Performers:** Budapest Trio, Orpheus Quartet, violinist Vartan Manoogian.   **Venue:** Castle of Banne near Les Vans.   **Performances:** 6.

VARS (Dauphiné)
450 miles SE of Paris

Vars is one of the delightful tiny towns that dot France's Queyras Valley, a region steeped in a heritage of woodworking and known for its refreshing natural beauty. The high elevation of nearby Vars Pass makes Vars a wonderful winter sports resort.

FESTIVALS

Vars International Piano Festival

2 Weeks	Académie de Musique et de
Early–Mid-August	Théatre de Vars
	Office du Tourisme–Festival
Cham, Rec, Lec, Th, Sem	de Piano
	05560 Vars
	Tel: 92 46 51 31

The objective of this festival is to unite renowned artists in a unique natural setting near the Alps. Since 1980 the sunny surroundings of Vars have been host not only to sports enthusiasts, but to a loyal and rapidly growing audience for music and theater. Varied programming has ranged from Bach to Hindemith. A summer music academy runs concurrently with the festival, featuring language courses and masterclasses with professors from the Paris Conservatory. **Recent Performers:** pianists Catherine Collard, Anne Marie Ghirardelli, Aldo Ciccolini.   **Venue:** Théâtre Mont-Dauphin. **Performances:** 20; all at 9 P.M.

GERMANY

Festspielhaus, Bayreuth (courtesy of the German Information Center).

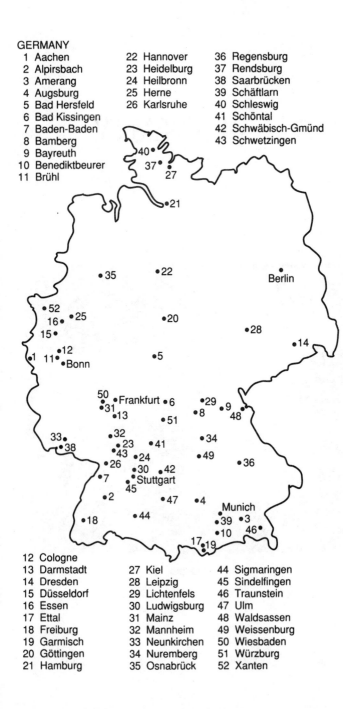

GERMANY

1 Aachen
2 Alpirsbach
3 Amerang
4 Augsburg
5 Bad Hersfeld
6 Bad Kissingen
7 Baden-Baden
8 Bamberg
9 Bayreuth
10 Benediktbeurer
11 Brühl

22 Hannover
23 Heidelburg
24 Heilbronn
25 Herne
26 Karlsruhe

36 Regensburg
37 Rendsburg
38 Saarbrücken
39 Schäftlarn
40 Schleswig
41 Schöntal
42 Schwäbisch-Gmünd
43 Schwetzingen

12 Cologne
13 Darmstadt
14 Dresden
15 Düsseldorf
16 Essen
17 Ettal
18 Freiburg
19 Garmisch
20 Göttingen
21 Hamburg

27 Kiel
28 Leipzig
29 Lichtenfels
30 Ludwigsburg
31 Mainz
32 Mannheim
33 Neunkirchen
34 Nuremberg
35 Osnabrück

44 Sigmaringen
45 Sindelfingen
46 Traunstein
47 Ulm
48 Waldsassen
49 Weissenburg
50 Wiesbaden
51 Würzburg
52 Xanten

CALENDAR

Karlsruhe Handel Festival, **Karlsruhe** (Baden-Württemberg)

MARCH

Karlsruhe Handel Festival, **Karlsruhe** (Baden-Württemberg)

APRIL

Schwetzingen Festival, see **Heidelberg** (Baden-Württemberg)

MAY

Benediktbeuer Concerts, **Munich** (Bavaria)
Dresden Music Festival, **Dresden** (Eastern Germany)
International May Festival, **Wiesbaden** (Hesse)
Ludwigsburg Castle Festival, **Ludwigsburg** (Baden-Württemberg)
Music in the 20th Century, **Saarbrücken** (Saarland)
Musica Bayreuth, **Bayreuth** (Bavaria)
Schwetzingen Festival, see **Heidelberg** (Baden-Württemberg)
Summer Music between the Inn and Salzach, see **Munich** (Bavaria)

JUNE

Amerang Castle Concerts, see **Munich** (Bavaria)
Augsburg Open-Air Stage, **Augsburg** (Bavaria)
Bad Hersfeld Festival Concerts, **Bad Hersfeld** (Hesse)
Benediktbeuer Concerts, **Munich** (Bavaria)
Days of Old Music, **Bamberg** (Bavaria)
Days of Old Music, **Regensburg** (Bavaria)
Dresden Music Festival, **Dresden** (Eastern Germany)
Festival Weeks of the Jacques Offenbach Society, **Bad Ems** (Rhineland-Palatinate)
Göttingen Handel Festival, **Göttingen** (Lower Saxony)
Hohenlohe Cultural Summer, **Hohenlohe** (Baden-Württemberg)
International Organ Weeks, **Nuremberg** (Bavaria)
Kissingen Summer, **Bad Kissingen** (Bavaria)
Ludwigsburg Castle Festival, **Ludwigsburg** (Baden-Württemberg)
Mendelssohn-Bartholdy Festival, see **Saarbrücken** (Saarland)
Music and Theater in Herrenhausen, **Hannover** (Lower Saxony)

Nordelbischen International Organ Concerts, see **Schleswig-Holstein**

Nymphenburg Summer Festival, **Munich** (Bavaria)

Regensburg Days of Old Music, **Regensburg** (Bavaria)

Rhine Music Festival, see **Wiesbaden** (Hesse)

Rhinegau Music Festival, see **Wiesbaden** (Hesse)

Rhineland Music Festival, **Düsseldorf** (North Rhineland-Westphalia)

Schleswig-Holstein Music Festival, see **Schleswig-Holstein**

Schwetzingen Festival, see **Heidelberg** (Baden-Württemberg)

Richard Strauss Days, **Garmisch-Partenkirchen** (Bavaria)

Summer Music between the Inn and Salzach, see **Munich** (Bavaria)

Upper Main Musical Summer, see **Bamberg** (Bavaria)

Weekend for New Music, **Bayreuth** (Bavaria)

Würzburg Mozart Festival, **Würzburg** (Bavaria)

JULY

Amerang Castle Concerts, see **Munich** (Bavaria)

Augsburg Open-Air Stage, **Augsburg** (Bavaria)

Bad Gandersheim Cathedral Festival, **Bad Gandersheim** (Lower Saxony)

Bad Hersfeld Festival Concerts, **Bad Hersfeld** (Hesse)

Baden-Baden Musical Summer, **Baden-Baden** (Baden-Württemberg)

Bayreuth Festival, **Bayreuth** (Bavaria)

Bell'Arte Musical Summer, **Munich** (Bavaria)

Benediktbeuer Concerts, **Munich** (Bavaria)

Berlin Bach Days, **Berlin** (Berlin)

Ettal Abbey Summer Concerts, see **Garmisch-Partenkirchen** (Bavaria)

European Church Music, **Schwäbisch Gmünd** (Baden-Württemberg)

Heidelberg Castle Festival, **Heidelberg** (Baden-Württemberg)

Hohenlohe Cultural Summer, **Hohenlohe** (Baden-Württemberg)

International Organ Weeks, **Nuremberg** (Bavaria)

Kissingen Summer, **Bad Kissingen** (Bavaria)

Ludwigsburg Castle Festival, **Ludwigsburg** (Baden-Württemberg)

Munich Opera Festival, **Munich** (Bavaria)

Music and Theater in Herrenhausen, **Hannover** (Lower Saxony)

Nordelbischen International Organ Concerts, see **Schleswig-Holstein**

Nymphenburg Summer Festival, **Munich** (Bavaria)

Rhine Music Festival, see **Wiesbaden** (Hesse)
Rhinegau Music Festival, see **Wiesbaden** (Hesse)
Schleswig-Holstein Music Festival, see **Schleswig-Holstein**
Summer Music between the Inn and Salzach, see **Munich** (Bavaria)
Upper Main Musical Summer, see **Bamberg** (Bavaria)
Weissenburg Summer Festival, see **Nuremberg** (Bavaria)

AUGUST

Amerang Castle Concerts, see **Munich** (Bavaria)
Augsburg Mozart Summer, **Augsburg** (Bavaria)
Augsburg Open-Air Stage, **Augsburg** (Bavaria)
J. S. Bach Summer Academy, **Stuttgart** (Baden-Württemberg)
Bad Hersfeld Festival Concerts, **Bad Hersfeld** (Hesse)
Bayreuth Festival, **Bayreuth** (Bavaria)
Benediktbeuer Concerts, **Munich** (Bavaria)
Ettal Abbey Summer Concerts, see **Garmisch-Partenkirchen** (Bavaria)
European Church Music, **Schwäbisch Gmünd** (Baden-Württemberg)
Festival Summer Concerts in the Court Church, **Würzburg** (Bavaria)
Heidelberg Castle Festival, **Heidelberg** (Baden-Württemberg)
Hohenlohe Cultural Summer, **Hohenlohe** (Baden-Württemberg)
Lower Saxony Music Days, see **Lower Saxony**
Ludwigsburg Castle Festival, **Ludwigsburg** (Baden-Württemberg)
Nordelbischen International Organ Concerts, see **Schleswig-Holstein**
Opera in the Abbey Ruins, **Bad Hersfeld** (Hesse)
Music and Theater in Herrenhausen, **Hannover** (Lower Saxony)
Rhine Music Festival, see **Wiesbaden** (Hesse)
Rhinegau Music Festival, see **Wiesbaden** (Hesse)
Schleswig-Holstein Music Festival, see **Schleswig-Holstein**
Summer Music between the Inn and Salzach, see **Munich** (Bavaria)
Upper Main Musical Summer, see **Bamberg** (Bavaria)
Xanten Summer Festival, **Xanten** (North Rhineland-Westphalia)

SEPTEMBER

Amerang Castle Concerts, see **Munich** (Bavaria)
Augsburg Mozart Summer, **Augsburg** (Bavaria)

Augsburg Open-Air Stage, **Augsburg** (Bavaria)
J. S. Bach Summer Academy, **Stuttgart** (Baden-
Württemberg)
Benediktbeuer Concerts, **Munich** (Bavaria)
Days of Old Music, see **Osnabrück** (Lower Saxony)
European Church Music, **Schwäbisch Gmünd** (Baden-
Württemberg)
International Beethoven Festival, **Bonn** (North Rhineland-
Westphalia)
Lower Saxony Music Days, see **Lower Saxony**
Ludwigsburg Castle Festival, **Ludwigsburg** (Baden-
Württemberg)
Music and Theater in Herrenhausen, **Hannover** (Lower
Saxony)
Nordelbischen International Organ Concerts, see **Schleswig-
Holstein**
Summer Music between the Inn and Salzach, see **Munich**
(Bavaria)
Upper Main Musical Summer, see **Bamberg** (Bavaria)

OCTOBER

International Beethoven Festival, **Bonn** (North Rhineland-
Westphalia)
Lower Saxony Music Days, see **Lower Saxony**
Nordelbischen International Organ Concerts, see **Schleswig-
Holstein**

NOVEMBER

Wiesbaden Bach Weeks, **Wiesbaden** (Hesse)
Würzburg Bach Days, **Würzburg** (Bavaria)

DECEMBER

Days of Old Music, see **Essen** (North Rhineland-Westphalia)
Wiesbaden Bach Weeks, **Wiesbaden** (Hesse)
Würzburg Bach Days, **Würzburg** (Bavaria)

The international telephone country code for western Germany is (011) 49. For eastern Germany, the code is (011) 37.
The 49 and 37 codes must also be used within Germany when
calling between the western and eastern portions of the country. Western city codes have the prefix 0, which is deleted
when calling from abroad (or from eastern Germany). Eastern
city codes have no prefixes.

Opera in the Abbey Ruins

2 Weeks
Mid-August

Op, Rec

Oper in der Stiftsruin
Pavillon am Marktplatz
Postfach 91
D-6430 Bad Hersfeld
Tel: 06621/720 66

Essentially a continuation of the Bad Hersfeld Festival Concerts, these performances concentrate on the voice, whereas the Festival Concerts are instrumental. At night the ruins are lit to startling effect and create an especially dramatic backdrop for productions such as Mozart's *The Magic Flute*, Smetana's *The Bartered Bride*, and Monteverdi's *Il combattimento di Trancredi e di Clorinda*. Lieder recitals and performances of early music are given in the more intimate settings of the Stadtkirche and Parish House. **Venues:** Stiftsruin (outdoors), Stadtkirche, Parish House. **Performances:** nightly with some matinees.

BAD KISSINGEN (Bavaria)
50 miles E of Frankfurt

Nestled in the basin of the Saale River Valley, this cozy little village is one of Bavaria's most beloved spas. Although the hot springs here are said to cure a multitude of ailments, the serenity of this environment is perhaps equally nurturing. Surrounding a central marketplace of small curiosity shops and enchanting medieval buildings are lavish gardens and parks, beyond which lie the mysterious Franconian Woods.

FESTIVALS

Kissingen Summer

3 Weeks
Late June–Mid-July

Orch, Cham, Th, Lect

Kissinger Sommer
Postfach 2260
D-8730 Bad Kissengen
Tel: 0971/80 70

If the mud baths and mineral waters fail to heal you, these concerts will. You can take your musical cure in magnificent buildings and lovely outdoor settings, where the programs and the surroundings are equally colorful. In addition to the expected eighteenth and nineteenth-century German composers, works by Glazunov, Liszt, Dutilleux,

Shostakovich, Donizetti, and many others have been recently heard. **Recent Performers:** Czech Philharominic, pianist Vladimir Ashkenazy, cellist Heinrich Schiff. **Venues:** Kurtheater, St. Jakobus Church, Regent's Hall, Palace Park, Redeemer Church, Bildhauser Cloister. **Performances:** daily; evenings and matinees.

BADEN-BADEN (Baden-Württemberg)
90 miles S of Frankfurt

Although settled first by the Romans, this lavish spa town reached the height of its prosperity in the nineteenth century when the aristocracy rediscovered it and built many fine royal residences. Where there was royalty, there were musicians, and Baden-Baden drew the finest. Liszt and Paganini played here, and Brahms spent his summers at the spa between 1864 and 1872. Berlioz presided over the summer festival in 1853 and again from 1856 to 1863. He wrote his last work, *Béatrice et Bénédict*, for the opening of the theater in 1862. Between 1892 and 1927 the festival again drew stellar names, including Fritz Kreisler, Pablo Casals, and Ferruccio Busoni.

FESTIVALS

Musical Summer

3 Weeks	Musikalischer Sommer
July	Postfach 540
	Augustaplatz 8
Orch, Cham, Rec, Org	D-7570 Baden-Baden
	Tel: 07221/27 52 28
	Fax: 07221/27 52 02

French and English madrigals, Offenbach selections, and Handel's *Water Music* were among the recent offerings at this festival designed to relax and divert vacationers during their sojourn at this elegant health resort, a magnet for Europe's elite since imperial days. **Recent Performers:** George Enescu Philharmonic Bucharest, Baden-Baden Orchestra, Deller Consort London. **Venues:** Kurhaus, Kurgarten, St. Jacob's, New Castle Courtyard, Brenner's Park Hotel, Evangelical Stadtkirche. **Performances:** 23; evenings, some matinees.

BAMBERG (Bavaria)
200 miles E of Frankfurt

This grand Imperial city is a historian's delight. Settled in the
second century A.D., Bamberg's rise was marked by its status
in the eleventh century as the seat of the Holy Roman Emperor Heinrich II. His majestic cathedral is one of the town's
main attractions. The Regnitz River divides the city into
the Bishop's town and the Burgher's town, both filled with
cobblestone streets that meander between gabled houses. A
mecca for beer enthusiasts, Bamberg has more breweries than
Munich and is famous for its smokey Rauchbier. An operatic
note: The inspiration for Offenbach's opera *Tales of Hoffman*
was writer, poet, and critic E. T. A. Hoffman, who hailed
from Bamberg and whose tiny house still stands, open to
visitors.

FESTIVALS

Days of Old Music

4 Days   Tage Alter Musik in
Mid-June   Bamberg
                                    Musica Canterey Bamberg
Chor, Cham, Rec, Org   Amalienstrasse 20
                                    D-8600 Bamberg
                                    Tel: 0951/275 45

Bamberg's famed baroque architecture complements the
seventeenth-century music that is performed during this celebration, which presents baroque cantatas, chamber music,
and madrigals. The venues include an enormous baroque
palace (New Residenz) and the city's glorious cathedral.
Recent Performers: Mensa Sonora Freiburg, Cantus Cölln.
Venues: New Residenz, Cathedral, St. Martin's, Dominican
Cloister, Geyersworth Castle. **Performances:** evenings; 1 afternoon.

IN THE AREA

Upper Main Musical Summer

3 Months   Musiksommer Obermain
Mid-June–Late September   Kronacher Strasse 30
                                    D-8620 Lichtenfels
Orch, Chor, Rec, Folk   Tel: 09571/1 82 33

These festival concerts were founded in 1971 to celebrate the beauty of the baroque architecture found in this area of the upper Main river and to encourage travelers to enjoy the region. Recent programs have included Russian balalaika music, Ravel and Kodály choral pieces, and Mozart serenades. Each year, locations vary among the towns listed, although the five cities underlined below are always included. **Recent Performers:** Nuremberg Baroque Orchestra, Prague Chamber Choir. **Towns:** Bamberg, Banz, Coburg, Egloffstein, Forchheim, Gössweinstein, Kronach, Lahm, Lauenstein, Lichtenfels, Ludwigsstadt, Mitwitz, Neustadt, Rodach, Rödental, Sesslach, Sonnefeld, Staffelstein, Tettau, Untersiemau, Vierzehnheiligen, Wallenfels. **Performances:** 15 evenings.

BAYREUTH (Bavaria)
130 miles E of Frankfurt

Bayreuth was a center for the arts for a century before Richard Wagner turned this Franconian town into a mecca for opera lovers. Schutz and Telemann composed for the city, and the baroque Margrave Opera House was the ideal setting for operas by Rameau, Handel, and Mozart. Eventually, the opera house proved inadequate for Wagner's vast music dramas, and the importunate musician prevailed upon Ludwig II of Bavaria to finance the building of the Festspielhaus, where the now legendary Wagner Festival takes place. Wagner, his wife Cosima, and Cosima's father Franz Liszt are all buried in Bayreuth. The Wagner home, Villa Wahnfried, is now open as a museum.

FESTIVALS

Musica Bayreuth

10 Days	Musica Bayreuth
Early May	Ludwigsstrasse 26
	D-8580 Bayreuth
Orch, Chor, Cham, Rec, Org	Tel: 0921/67 3 67

Music composed by Richard Wagner will *not* be heard at this festival, which has long been overshadowed by its venerable counterpart, the Bayreuth Festival. For three decades European artists have presented programs of instrumental and choral music from the baroque to the twentieth century. **Recent Performers:** Cologne Academy of Music Orchestra, trumpeter Maurice André. **Venues:** Margrave Opera House, Stadtkirche, City Hall, Parish House, Hospital Church. **Performances:** nightly.

Richard Wagner Festival

5 Weeks	Richard Wagner Festspiele
Late July–Late August	Postbox 100262
	D-8580 Bayreuth 1
Op	Tel: 0921/2 02 21

Better known as the Bayreuth Festival, this celebration continues a tradition envisioned by Richard Wagner and launched by him in 1876. Only Wagner's operas are performed here in the austere hall where the *Ring* Cycle was first heard in its entirety. The acoustics are uniquely suited to Wagner's music, and the functional design and deliberate lack of decoration focus attention on the unfolding music drama. Today the festival is one of Europe's largest and most elite, drawing the world's leading dramatic singers for performances that are broadcast worldwide. **Recent Performers:** conductors James Levine, Giuseppi Sinopoli, Daniel Barenboim. **Venue:** Bayreuth Festival Hall. **Performances:** 30 evenings (formal attire suggested). Only written ticket requests are accepted, and the waiting period can be several years. The written request must be renewed each year in October.

Weekend for New Music

3 Days	Wochenende für Neue Musik
Late June	Pianohaus Steingraeber
	Friedrichstrasse 2
Chor, Cham, Rec, Org	D-8580 Bayreuth

Since 1987 this event has filled a summer weekend with concerts devoted to chamber music of the twentieth century. **Recent Performers:** Stuttgart Philharmonic Trio, Ensemble Musica Viva. **Venues:** Steingraeber House, Schlosskirche, Redeemer's Church. **Performances:** 8.

ONGOING EVENTS

Margrave Opera House

Cham	Margräfliches Opernhaus
	Opernstrasse
	D-8580 Bayreuth
	Tel: 0921/2 54 16

Bedecked with flowers, the unassuming facade of this famous opera house gives little indication of the sumptuous rococo interior, where figures bound from the walls and gold leaf reflects every surface. The intimate size suits the chamber music for which the theater is now primarily used. **Recent Performers:** baritone Hermann Prey, Lions Charity Musica. Ticket information may also be obtained from the Stadthalle.

Stadthalle

Op, Orch, Cham, Rec, Jazz,   Stadthalle
    Dance, Th   Luitpoldplatz 9
                             D-8580 Bayreuth
                             Tel: 0921/6 90 01

Most of the year-round musical events in Bayreuth are held in this modern concert hall, which has two theaters—one large and one small. In addition to performances by international artists of standard orchestral and operatic repertoire, the calendar has included Arthur Miller's *Death of a Salesman*, *The Rocky Horror Picture Show*, and a concert by the Bayreuth Zither Club. Performances are also given in the Sportpark. **Recent Performers:** Beaux Arts Trio, soprano Margaret Price, Bamberg Symphony. **Performances:** 90; September–May.

IN THE AREA

Waldsassen Basilica Concerts

Org, Orch, Chor, Rec   Basilika Konzerte
                             Postfach 1228
                             D-8595 Waldsassen
                             Tel: 09632/21 28

An immense organ surrounded by blue marble and countless chubby cherubs resounds with the measured brilliance of sacred music during these concerts in a monastery 45 miles E of Bayreuth. One may hear a Bruckner symphony, Mozart's Requiem, or solo organ recitals by European artists. Special Advent and Christmas performances are offered each year. **Recent performers:** Nürnberg Symphony, Augsburg Boys' Choir. **Performances:** 8 evenings; March, May-August, November, December.

BERLIN (Berlin)
260 miles NE of Frankfurt

The city of Berlin has long nurtured artistic genius. Over the centuries famous musicians, composers, painters, architects, and writers have left behind a rich heritage and the seeds for an ever-flowering cultural life. From the very traditional to the avant-garde, everything can be found, and the cultural scene has been greatly enriched by the reunification. Because each side had much to offer before, the downfall of the wall has now doubled the pleasures. There are exquisite theaters with longstanding traditions, a number of superb orchestras, and three opera houses with some of the world's best singers performing every night. Not to be forgotten are the famous cabarets, night clubs, the circus, and the ballets.

FESTIVALS

Berlin Bach Days

9 Days
Early July

Orch, Chor, Cham, Rec, Org,
    Lect, Carillon

Bach Tage Berlin
VDMK Berlin
Bismarckstrasse 73
D-1000 Berlin 12
Tel: 030/312 36 77
Fax: 030/312 60 28

This is an intellectual celebration of Johann Sebastian Bach, with time devoted to lectures and lecture/recitals nearly equaling that given to performances. Programs are wide ranging and encompass music not only by Bach but by composers from many eras, with a surprising number of twentieth-century pieces included. **Recent Performers:** Bach Ensemble of New York, London Oboe Band, soprano Emma Kirkby. **Venues:** Philharmonic Hall, Charlottenburg Castle (a scaled-down version of Versailles that was the residence of the Prussian rulers in the 18th century), St. Matthew's Church, Musical Instrument Museum. **Performances:** daily, evenings and afternoons.

Berlin Festival Weeks

1 Month
September

Op, Orch, Chor, Cham, Rec,
    Dance, Th

Berliner Festwochen
Budapester Strasse 50
D-1000 Berlin 30
Tel: 030/2 54 840
Fax: 030/2 54 8911

Organized in 1950 to soothe the severed city, the Berlin Festival features renowned international artists in nearly every venue in the city. The Berlin Philharmonic presents a number of concerts with some of the world's most famous conductors, and guest ensembles have included the Leipzig Gewandhaus Orchestra and Amsterdam Concertgebouw Orchestra. The busy chamber music schedule offers an equally glittering roster, with soloists and ensembles from around the world. Much contemporary music is performed, and programs include drama and dance productions. **Recent Performers:** Sergiu Celibidache conducting the Munich Philharmonic Orchestra, Takacs Quartet, soprano Lucy Shelton, pianist Vladimir Ashkenazy. **Venues:** Philharmonic Hall, Hebbel Theater, Berlin Gallery, GrundkreditBank, Academy of Arts, National Gallery, Renaissance Theater, St. Matthaus Church, German Opera of Berlin. **Performances:** many daily.

ONGOING EVENTS

Berlin Comic Opera

Op, Orch, Cham, Dance

Komische Oper Berlin
Behrenstrasse 55/57
Postfach 1311
O-1086 Berlin
2/2 292 555

Built in 1947 on the ruins of Berlin's old Music Revue Theater, the Comic Opera was founded to offer accessible productions of light opera. The gently curving, neo-baroque interior is unexpected, given the theater's modern, block-style exterior. In 1966 the ballet company was added, and chamber music concerts are offered in the foyer. **Recent Performers:** Berlin Horn Quartet, mezzo-soprano Brigitte Fassbänder. **Performances:** September–July.

Berlin Radio Symphony Orchestra

Orch, Chor, Cham

Radio Symphonie Orchester
Berlin
Kaiserdamm 26
D-1000 Berlin 19
Tel: 030/302 72 42
Fax: 030/301 95 41

Under the direction of Vladimir Ashkenazy since 1989, the Radio Symphony Orchestra includes a fair sampling of twentieth-century works within its comprehensive programs.

A veteran of international tours and several recordings, the orchestra divides its concerts in Berlin evenly between two venues. Soloists from the ensemble play in a corresponding chamber music series. **Recent Performers:** cellist Lynn Harrell, baritone Dietrich Fischer-Dieskau, pianist Rudolf Buchbinder. **Venues:** Philharmonic Hall, Broadcast House. **Performances:** 45; September–June. Tickets are available 14 days before each concert.

German Opera of Berlin

Op, Dance, Cham, Rec, Child
    Deutsche Oper Berlin
    Bismarkstrasse 35
    D-1000 Berlin 10
    Tel: 030/34 38 1
    Fax: 030/34 38 232

The white, pebbly walls of this building house an opera company whose life has always been entwined with the political fortunes of Berlin. After its opening in 1912, Puccini, Bruno Walter, Otto Klemperer, and others helped establish a flourishing opera tradition that was broken when the Nazis drove out most artists in the 1930s. The building was destroyed in World War II, and 18 years later in 1961, the German Opera was proudly reborn in its current 1885-seat home. That premiere came 5 weeks after the Berlin Wall was erected, a development that isolated the opera from most of its audience and stimulated Western nations to support the company. Today it is known for masterful realizations of Wagner's operas and innovative productions of standard and contemporary repertoire. One consistently sold-out production is that of Wilhelm Dieter's *Sinking of the Titanic*, which is staged in the foyer, bar, stairwells, and courtyard. **Recent Productions:** Wagner's *Ring*, Stravinsky's *Rake's Progress*, Puccini's *La Boheme*, R. Strauss' *Elektra*. **Recent Performers:** soprano Julia Varady, mezzo-soprano Teresa Berganza, baritone Dietrich Fischer-Dieskau. **Performances:** nearly daily, August–June. Written ticket requests should be sent to Richard Wagner Strasse 10, D-1000 Berlin 10. Tickets are available 10 days in advance, and many performances sell out early.

German State Opera

Op, Orch, Cham, Dance
    Deutsche Staatsoper
    Unter den Linden 7
    O-1086 Berlin
    Tel: 2/200 47 62

Long known as the "Linden Opera," this majestic building with its tall colonnades and classic statuary stands in what was once East Berlin. The house opened in 1742 with Graun's *Cleopatra and Caesar*, and Meyerbeer, Mendelssohn, and Richard Strauss are among those who have conducted here. The theater was destroyed in 1945 and reopened in 1955. Extensive reconstruction was completed in 1986. The impressive roster of productions here is one of the most extensive in Europe, covering all periods and styles of opera. **Performances:** September–July.

Philharmonic Hall

Orch, Chor, Cham, Rec, Org   Philharmonie
Matthaikirchstrasse 1
D-1000 Berlin 30
Tel: 030/2 54 88 0
Fax: 030/2 61 48 87

A distinctive scalloped roof identifies this building, which was built between 1960 and 1963 specifically to house the Berlin Philharmonic Orchestra. The Philharmonic performs in the larger of the theater's two halls, which seats 2400, and the Chamber Orchestra of Europe, which is mainly heard during the Berlin Festival, performs in the Chamber Music Hall. Both halls are pentagonally shaped and are designed with spare clean lines and little ornamentation. If the Philharmonic is on tour, still check for other performances, for the halls are seldom quiet. **Recent Performers:** Vienna Boys Choir, soprano Jessye Norman, guitarists Pepe and Angel Romero, violinist Itzak Perlman. **Performances:** almost daily; (Philharmonic: September–June).

Sender Freies Berlin

Orch, Chor, Cham   Sender Freies Berlin
Masurenallee 8-14
D-1000 Berlin 19
Tel: 030/303 10
Fax: 030/301 50 62

Also called the Haus des Rundfunks (Broadcast House), this radio and television broadcasting headquarters presents orchestral concerts, choral works, and chamber music in its Large Studio Hall and Small Studio Hall. The complex was built in 1931 with an interior that is a study in squares—square tiers and balconies, square chandeliers, honeycomb railings, square windows, and square skylights.

Recent Performers: Radio Symphony Orchestra of Berlin, Netherlands Chamber Choir, organist Joachim Dalitz. **Performances:** year-round.

Theater des Westens

Op

Theater des Westens
Kantstrasse 12
D-1000 Berlin 12
Tel: 030/31903 193

Operettas and musicals are given in this theatre, one of the few buildings in Berlin to survive World War II intact. Built in 1896, the theater housed the Deutsche Oper Berlin from 1945 to 1967. **Performances:** January–December.

BONN (North Rhineland-Westphalia)
80 miles NW of Frankfurt

Selected as capital of West Germany after World War II, Bonn was to serve as a provisional substitute for Berlin, and the bureaucratic atmosphere of the city does not overshadow its other, more permanent aspects. The thriving university, attended by Karl Marx and Heinrich Heine, provides a refreshing vitality and nightlife, and among the attractive baroque buildings of the Old Town is the Beethoven House, where the composer was born in 1770.

FESTIVALS

International Beethoven Festival

3 Weeks
Mid-September–Early October
(Triennial, 1992, 1995, etc.)

Internationales Beethovenfest
Mulheimer Platz 1
D-5300 Bonn
Tel: 0228/774533

Orch, Cham, Chor, Rec

International stars gather in Bonn for a festival that in its third decade has grown into a significant tribute to Beethoven, Bonn's native son. A wide sampling of Beethoven's music is complemented by carefully selected music by other composers. **Recent Performers:** pianist Alicia de Larrocha, Kronos Quartet, Riccardo Chailly conducting the Royal Concertgebouw Orchestra. **Venues:** Beethoven Hall, Beethoven House, Kreuzkirche, Bruckenforum Beuel. **Performances:** 30; evenings or matinees.

ONGOING EVENTS

Beethoven Hall

Orch, Cham, Org, Chor, Rec   Beethovenhalle
Mulheimer Platz 1
D-5300 Bonn 1
Tel: 0228/77 36 66

Bonn constructed its first Beethoven Hall at the urging of Franz Liszt in 1845, barely 20 years after Beethoven's death. That hall was subsequently demolished as a fire hazard, but in 1959 Bonn opened this new hall that sits along the banks of the Rhine. The stadium-like building was built primarily for the International Beethoven Festival and is home for the Orchestra of the Beethoven Hall, conducted by Dennis Russell Davies. The repertoire is broad and fine guest artists plentiful. Chamber concerts are sponsored here and throughout Bonn. **Recent Performers:** cellist Janos Starker, pianist Rudolf Buchbinder, flutist Jean-Pierre Rampal. **Performances:** 200; September–June.

Bonn Opera

Op, Dance, Rec   Oper Bonn
Am Boeselagerhof 1
D-5300 Bonn 1
Tel: 0228/77 36 66 7

Overlooking the Rhine just south of the Beethoven Hall, the Bonn Opera offers a repertoire of well-known works from the opera and ballet literature as well as pieces by Bohuslav Martinu and Philip Glass. Although guest conductors are often featured, Dennis Russell Davies is music director, and his Beethoven Hall Orchestra plays for the opera. Seven outstanding song recitals should not be overlooked. **Recent Productions:** *Aida, Madama Butterfly*, Wagner's *Ring* Cycle. **Recent Performers:** mezzo-sopranos Marilyn Horne, Teresa Berganza, Grace Bumbry. **Performances:** 64; September–June.

COLOGNE (North Rhineland-Westphalia)
90 miles NW of Frankfurt

Although Cologne (Köln) was an unfortunate casualty of World War II, its greatest monument, the Gothic cathedral, miraculously escaped without damage. Begun in 1248 and completed in 1880, the cathedral graces the town square as a symbol of perseverance. And what is relatively new in

Cologne seems to embrace this message of endurance and persistance: museums contain old and new treasures, cable cars efficiently trundle people around town, and nightlife in the city's shopping district vibrates with entertainment and activity.

ONGOING EVENTS

Cologne Opera

Op, Rec, Dance, Child

Oper der Stadt Köln
Offenbachplatz
Postfach 18 02 41
D-5100 Cologne
Tel: 0221/221 8210

Cologne's opera house was obliterated during World War II, but the new building, which opened in 1957, is home to one of Germany's finest opera companies. With conductor James Conlon and director Michael Hampe, the Cologne Opera is establishing an international reputation and touring schedule. In addition to performances in this 1400-seat theater, the company has been heard in London, Paris, Washington, and Edinburgh. **Performances:** almost daily, September–June. Tickets are available 14 days before a performance.

Philharmonic Hall

Orch, Chor, Cham, Rec, Org, Dance, Jazz

Kölner Philharmonie
Bishofsgartenstrasse 1
D-5000 Cologne
Tel: 0221/221 8400

Quality and variety characterize the programs offered in this modern hall, which opened in 1986. Symphonic and chamber music by Schubert, pieces by Philip Glass, and recitals on an extraordinary organ can be heard during the regular season, which runs September–June. **Recent Performers:** violinist Nadja Salerno-Sonnenberg, Alban Berg Quartet, soprano Lucia Popp. **Performances:** nearly daily; year-round.

IN THE AREA

Brühl Palace Concerts

Orch, Cham, Rec, Org

Brülher Schlosskonzerte
Schlossstrasse 2
D-5040 Brühl
Tel: 02232/43 1 83

Music by Bach is featured along with classical and romantic works at the Augustusburg Palace in Brühl, 8 miles S of Cologne. Built in the early eighteenth century as residence for the Cologne archbishops, the imposing palace reflects the transition from baroque to rococo. These concerts, which are performed in conjunction with Cologne's Philharmonic Hall, have been held since 1958. **Recent Performers:** Cologne Chamber Orchestra, guitarist Pepe Romero, Vienna String Sextet. **Venues:** Augustusburg Castle, Cologne Philharmonic Hall. **Performances:** 50; May–October.

DARMSTADT (Hesse)
20 miles S of Frankfurt

This city has a proud cultural history and at the begining of this century was a center of Art Nouveau. Darmstadt now hosts various writing organizations, including the Academy of Language and Poetry and the German PEN Center. Both the town's Luisenplatz and Schloss section feature attractive historic buildings dating back to the sixteenth century. The Tourist Office publishes a comprehensive list of classical concerts entitled "Konzerte in Darmstadt—Algemeiner Terminkalendar" and a monthly brochure entitled "Lebendiges Darmstadt," which includes not only concerts but exhibitions, lectures, and plays.

ONGOING EVENTS

Blickpunkt Orangerie

Orch, Cham, Rec, Dance, Th,　　Blickpunkt Orangerie
　　Film, Read, Child　　　　　　Lucasweg 23
　　　　　　　　　　　　　　　　D-6100 Darmstadt
　　　　　　　　　　　　　　　　Tel: 06151/42 28 21

Music from the Middle Ages through the nineteenth century is performed on historical instruments in the Darmstadt Orangerie. Light streams through the large, graceful windows of this eighteenth-century baroque greenhouse originally constructed to cultivate orange trees. The centrally placed stage is still brightened by a few orange trees for presentations that vary from Renaissance dance music to puppets performing "Babar the Elephant" to music of minnesinger Neidhart von Reuental. **Recent Performers:** Munich Philharmonic, Musica Antiqua of Cologne, Il Giardino Armonico. **Performances:** 16–20; October–April.

Chamber Concerts in the Castle

Cham, Rec

Kammerkonzerte im Schloss
Rehkopfweg 9
D-6100 Darmstadt
Tel: 06151/4 77 56

Music for small ensembles is performed in this sixteenth century castle. Spanish solo piano music, a Bach cello suite, and a Brahms' violin sonata were recently featured. **Recent Performers:** Southwest German Piano Quartet, Krommelbein Quartet. **Performances:** 5; August, December–March.

Darmstadt State Theater

Op, Orch, Th

Staatstheater Darmstadt
Postfach 111 432
D-6100 Darmstadt
Tel: 06151/2811 213

The State Theater offers a full season utilizing its three halls, with productions that have included Strauss's *Arabella*, Lerner and Loewe's *My Fair Lady*, and Puccini's *Madama Butterfly*. **Performances:** nearly daily September–June, closed Monday.

DRESDEN
230 miles NE of Frankfurt

Once the majestic capital of Saxony, Dresden was filled with vast art treasures and an architectural splendor that earned it the nickname of "Florence on the Elbe." But in one dreadful night in 1945 the city was virtually leveled by a devastating air raid that has since been compared to Hiroshima. Although the losses of the attack were tremendous, painstaking restoration efforts have earned Dresden a new nickname—"the city that rose from the ashes." Much of the elegant rococo architecture that once graced the entire city has been miraculously restored, and the baroque buildings of the Zwingen Palace now house a wealth of treasures that survived the war. Of international renown is the Palace's Gallery of Old Masters, which features masterpieces by Raphael, Rubens, and Rembrandt. And reflecting the city's tradition of commitment to the arts, the Semper Opera House, where many of Richard Strauss's operatic works were introduced, has been brought back to life and is one of Dresden's most celebrated revivals.

FESTIVALS

Dresden Music Festival

2 Weeks
Late May–Early June

Op, Orch, Chor, Cham,
    Rec, Dance

Besucherdienst der Dres-
    dener Musikfestspiele
Postfach 110
O-8012 Dresden
Tel: 51/495 50 25
Fax: 51/459 37 38

Since 1978 Dresden has hosted one of Germany's largest festivals, with performances by international companies that focus each year on a specific theme. The 1991 celebration of "The Heritage of Mozart in Dresden" included productions of five of the master's operas by the Dresden State Opera as well as *Idomeneo* by the Hamburg State Opera and *Magic Flute* in an imaginative version by the Düsseldorf Marionette Theatre. Although the emphasis is on opera, outstanding orchestral and chamber concerts fill the busy schedule. Past themes have included "Verdi and Wagner in Dresden," and "Dresden Opera Traditions." **Recent Performers:** Berlin Philharmonic Orchestra, New York Philharmonic Orchestra, Bolshoi Ballet. **Venues:** Semper Opera House, Cultural Palace of Dresden, Albrechtsburg Meissen and Jagdschloss Moritzburg castles, theaters, baroque parks. **Performances:** 70.

ONGOING EVENTS

Dresden State Theater

Orch, Cham

Staatstheater Dresden
Julian Grimau Allee 27
O-801 Dresden
Tel: 51/486 60

Founded in 1548, the Dresden State Orchestra is one of Europe's oldest orchestras, and it performs primarily in the modern House of Culture, which opened in 1969. In addition to playing for the Dresden State Opera, the ensemble gives several orchestral and chamber music concerts each season. The past conductors of this ensemble include Heinrich Schütz, Carl Maria von Weber, Richard Wagner, Karl Böhm, and Herbert Blomstedt.

Semper Opera House

Op

Semper Opera House
2 Theaterplatz
O-801 Dresden
Tel: 51/484 20

Gottfried Semper built Dresden's grand opera house in 1878, and it soon established itself as a major European opera center. Richard Strauss's *Salome*, *Elektra*, and *Der Rosenkavalier* were premiered here. The building was destroyed in the 1945 bombing, but the plucky Dresden people rebuilt their opera house in 1985 after a painstaking, detailed restoration. **Performances:** September–July.

DÜSSELDORF (North Rhineland-Westphalia)
110 miles NW of Frankfurt

This is a city of epicurean delights, which can be found along the fashionable Konigsalle promenade, lined with fine shops and cafes, as well as in the rollicking nightlife of the city's Altstadt district, where ethnic food, pubs, and live music abound. Düsseldorf has always been an important cultural center, and has produced such eminent artists as Heinrich Heine, Robert Schumann, and Felix Mendelssohn. The Tourist Office publishes a list of classical concerts given in the city.

FESTIVALS

Rhineland Music Festival

10 Days	Rheinisches Musikfest
Early June	Postfach 1210
	D-5100 Aachen
Orch, Chor, Cham, Org,	Tel: 0241/432 4101
Jazz, Film, Lect, Dance	

Founded in 1984, this festival rotates each year among the three Rhineland cities of Aachen, Cologne, and Düsseldorf. A striking array of programs has included organ recitals, selections by Count Basie, Renaissance mandolin music, and Orff's *Carmina Burana*. **Recent Performers:** Aachen Chamber Orchestra and Choir, organist Donald Sutherland, Ballroom Stompers. **Venues:** major halls and churches in each city. **Performances:** many daily.

ONGOING EVENTS

Tonhalle

Orch, Rec, Cham, Chor, Org	Tonhalle
	Ehrenhof 1
	D-4000 Düsseldorf 30

Built in the mid-1920s, this immense modern hall sheathed in wood paneling is home to the Düsseldorf Symphony. Founded in 1864, the Symphony presents the standard repertoire and features contemporary composers conducting their own works. A full complement of symphony, chamber music, and children's concert series is offered. Soloists are often world renowned. **Recent Performers:** David Zinman conducting the Düsseldorf Symphony, violinist Shlomo Mintz, pianist Mitsuko Uchida. **Performances:** 45; August–June.

German Opera on the Rhine

Op, Dance   Deutsche Oper am Rhein

Opera House
Heinrich-Heine Alee 16 A
D-4000 Düsseldorf
Tel: 0211/8908211
Fax: 0211/329051

Theater
Neckarstrasse
D-4100 Duisburg 1
Tel: 0203/3009100
Fax: 0203/3009200

The twin cities of Düsseldorf and Duisburg share the internationally acclaimed Opera on the Rhine, founded in 1956. Little known works as well as standard repertoire are included in a broad range of opera and ballet productions. The theaters in both cities were destroyed during World War II, and both were rebuilt in the 1950s. **Recent Productions:** Britten's *The Rape of Lucretia*, Verdi's *La Traviata*, Schubert's *Genoveva*. **Recent Performers:** baritone Sherrill Milnes, bass Kurt Moll, soprano Myung-Whun Chung. **Performances:** over 400; January–December. Tickets are available 30 days before each performance.

ESSEN (North Rhineland-Westphalia)
115 miles NW of Frankfurt

Essen is the prosperous capital of the Ruhr region. At the forefront of the city's cultural community are the highly regarded Ruhr State College of Music and Folkwang Academy of Music. Historic buildings and churches in town serve as venues to musical productions, and the Essen Minster, built between the ninth and fourteenth centuries, is one of the country's oldest cathedrals.

ONGOING EVENTS

Aalto Theater

Op, Orch, Chor, Cham, Rec, Th

Theater and Philharmonie Essen
Rolandstrasse 10
D-4300 Essen 1
Tel: 0201/81 22 200
Fax: 0201/81 22 172

The asymmetrical, curving Aalto Theater is stage for the busy opera season in Essen. Although the opera lover's expectations are met with performances of the standard fare of Wagner, Mozart, and Strauss, Essen specializes in nineteenth-century French opera. The ten productions in one recent season included *Pélléas et Mélisande*, *The Magic Flute*, *Der Rosenkavalier*, *Aida*, and *La Cage aux Folles*. The performers include many international stars, and recitals have recently been given by tenor Nicolai Gedda, bass Kurt Moll, and soprano Lucia Popp. **Recent Productions:** *Orpheus in the Underworld, Aida, La Cage aux Folles*. **Recent Performers:** baritone Hermann Prey, pianist Alfred Brendel, cellist Heinrich Schiff. **Performances:** over 200; September–June. Tickets are available three months before each performance.

IN THE AREA

Days of Old Music in Herne

4 Days
Early December

Tage Alter Musik in Herne
Postfach 18 20
D-4690 Herne 1

Cham, Rec, Org, Ex

Founded in 1975, this enthusiastic and well-researched festival of pre-baroque music held 10 miles NE of Essen focuses each year on a specific theme such as "Italy—Music and Musicians" or "Cembalo and Virginal." Concerts are combined with an exhibition of early musical instruments, and both are sponsored by the West German Broadcasting Company. **Recent Performers:** Fitzwilliam String Quartet, Amsterdam Schönbrunn Ensemble. **Venues:** Cultural Center, Strunkede Palace. **Performances:** 10.

FRANKFURT (Hesse)

Like other German cities that sustained heavy damage during World War II, Frankfurt has spent the last half-century rebuilding, physically and spiritually. The city has risen to become one of Germany's prominent commercial and industrial centers, and although prosperity has brought urban expansion, Frankfurt has preserved its human dimension. Parks, gardens, and pedestrian arcades abound, and the innumerable outdoor cafes are always filled with an international mix of residents and tourists. Sites of interest include Goethe's House and Museum, and Alt-Sachsenhausen, a charming village of half-timbered houses, cobblestone streets, pubs, and cafes.

ONGOING EVENTS

Hesse Broadcasting Company

Orch, Chor, Cham, Rec, Org, Child

Hessicher Rundfunk
Bertramstrasse 8
D-6000 Frankfurt 1
Tel: 069/15 51

Bach cantatas, Shostakovich chamber music, and Schubert symphonies can be heard in the concerts sponsored not only in Frankfurt but in cities throughout the province of Hesse. The Radio Symphony Orchestra of Frankfurt is the Broadcasting Company's largest ensemble, and it has recently appeared with guest conductors Erich Leinsdorf, Placido Domingo, and Andrew Davis. **Recent Performers:** Gächinger Kantorei, Auryn Quartet, cellist Heinrich Schiff. **Venues:** Old Opera, New Broadcast Hall, Finkenhof, Academy of Music. **Performances:** 105; year-round.

Hoechst Century Hall

Orch, Chor, Cham, Jazz, Dance

Jahrhunderthalle Hoechst
Pfaffenwiese
D-6230 Frankfurt 80
Tel: 069/3601 240
Fax: 069/3601 222

Located on the western outskirts of Frankfurt, this 2000-seat multipurpose hall hosts a roster of internationally acclaimed artists. **Recent Performers:** Canadian Brass, cellist

Heinrich Schiff, Alvin Ailey Dance Theater. **Performances:** 100; October–May.

Municipal Stages

Op, Orch, Cham, Dance   Städtische Bühnen
Theaterplatz
D-6000 Frankfurt 1
Tel: 069/25 62 434

Two theaters and an opera house are found in this impressive new performing arts complex, the home of the Frankfurt Opera. The opera company offers creative productions of a vast repertoire and has established an international reputation. Chamber concerts are held in the smaller of the two theaters. **Recent Performers:** Leonard Slatkin conducting the Frankfurt Opera House Orchestra. **Performances:** 150; year-round.

Music in St. Katherine's Church

Chor, Rec, Org   Musik in St. Katherinen
Leerbachstrasse 18
D-6000 Frankfurt 18
Tel: 069/728094

These concerts feature the organ in St. Katherine's Church and focus on the works of Bach and Reger. **Recent Performers:** St. Katherinen Cantorei. **Performances:** first and third Friday evenings; year-round.

Old Opera

Orch, Chor, Cham, Rec   Alte Oper
Opernplatz 8
D-6000 Frankfurt 1
Tel: 069/13 40 4000

With its inscription "to all that is true, beautiful, and good" intact, the Old Opera of Frankfurt was reopened in 1981 as a concert hall and convention center (opera is given in the new opera house at the Municipal Stages). Reconstruction after World War II followed the original designs that made this theater one of Europe's most beautiful when it was first opened by Kaiser Wilhelm I in 1880. Concerts by well-known recording artists are given in the building's three halls. **Recent Performers:** Phillipe Entremont conducting the Orchestre National de France, Juilliard String Quartet, pianist Emmanuel Ax. **Performances:** almost daily.

FREIBURG (Baden-Württemberg)
150 miles S of Frankfurt

Freiburg is a congenial modern town set in the heart of the
Black Forest. As in many German cities, the cathedral in
Freiburg survived attacks that otherwise did heavy damage to
the town during World War II. Thus this Gothic structure with
its 386-foot tower is a cherished and well-preserved monument to Freiburg's medieval heritage. The cathedral's Silber-
mann organ, dating from 1714, is the oldest of 31 crafted
by the master organ builder. A sixteenth-century merchants'
hall, the Kaufhaus, sits across from the cathedral and is now
a renowned festival hall. Medieval and baroque art can be
found in great abundance at the renowned Augustiner Museum, and dozens of architectural gems line the city streets.
Freiburg has a tradition of choral music, so ask the tourist
office for the current programs, especially at Mundenhof,
Schlossberg, and the Rathaus.

ONGOING EVENTS

Albert Concerts

Orch, Cham

Albert Konzerte
Bertoldstrasse 10
D-7800 Freiburg
Tel: 0761/490 94 12

Both orchestral and chamber music are presented at these
irregularly scheduled concerts. World-class artists offer refreshingly diverse programs, which have included chamber
music by Debussy and orchestral works by Prokofiev and Al-
beniz. **Recent Performers:** Moscow Philharmonic Orchestra, Cleveland Quartet, pianist Alicia de Larrocha. **Venue:**
Stadthall, Paulussaal. **Performances:** about 2 evenings each
month, September-June.

Freiburg Theater

Op, Orch, Cham, Dance, Th

Freiburger Theater
Bertoldstrasse 46
D-7800 Freiburg
Tel: 0761/31 96 260
Fax: 0761/31 96 459

Comprised of four venues located in one complex,
the Theater is Freiburg's musical hub. The Freiburg Opera
presents standard repertoire but is known for unconventional
productions of the classics and its championing of contempo-

rary musical theater. Now 100 years old, the Freiburg Philharmonic Orchestra boasts a repertoire that spans the centuries from Gabrielli to the present, with an enthusiastic endorsement of twentieth-century avant-garde composers. **Recent Productions:** *Peter Grimes, Hansel and Gretel, The Mikado.* **Performances:** almost daily; September–July.

IN THE AREA

Alpirsbach Cloister Concerts

Rec, Cham, Org, Chor,   Alpirsbacher Klosterkonzerte
   Guitar   Am Marktplatz
                            D-7297 Alpirsbach
                            Tel: 07444/23 52

Organ concerts, recitals of small wind ensembles, and such ambitious pieces as Penderecki's *Lukas Passion* and Verdi's Requiem were recently featured in this late Romanesque cloister nestled in the Black Forest 60 miles NE of Freiburg. **Recent Performers:** Maulbronn Chamber Choir, Bonn Camerata. **Performances:** 30 evenings, mid-March–mid-October, December.

GARMISCH-PARTENKIRCHEN
(Bavaria) 220 miles SE of Frankfurt

The neighboring towns of Garmisch and Partenkirchen joined in 1936 to host the Winter Olympics, and the area has become the ski capital of the Bavarian Alps. Germany's highest mountain, the Zugspitze, towers above the numerous baroque churches of the predominantly modern town, while the frequent appearance of inhabitants dressed in native costume remind one that some Bavarian customs are timeless. Of particular beauty is the nearby church of St. Anton, an ornate vision of silver and pink set like a gem, sparkling in the brilliant Alpine sun. Central Garmisch is a fashionable and often vibrant resort village surrounded on all sides by towering, jagged mountains.

FESTIVALS

Richard Strauss Days

5 Days   Richard Strauss Tage
Early June   Partnachauenstrasse 5
                            D-8100 Garmisch-
Orch, Cham, Rec, Lect   Partenkirchen

World-class artists come to celebrate the music of Richard Strauss, who resided in Garmisch and died here in 1949. Because Garmisch-Partenkirchen lacks a suitable stage, opera cannot be performed, but Strauss's lush symphonic and chamber works can be accommodated in varying locations throughout these twin towns. Only music by Strauss is performed. **Recent Performers:** Vladimir Ashkenazy with the London Philharmonic Orchestra, pianist Martha Argerich, hornist Hermann Baumann. **Venues:** Werdenfels Festival Hall, Richard Strauss Hall, Olympic Ski Stadium. **Performances:** 7. Telephone bookings begin in April.

IN THE AREA

Ettal Abbey Summer Concerts

6 Concerts	Ettaler Sommerkonzerte
Mid-July–Late August	Pienzenauerstrasse 12
	D-8000 Munich 80
Orch, Chor, Cham, Rec, Org	Tel: 08821/744 30 (Ettal)
	or 089/9828676 (Munich)

Sacred music for varied ensembles is emphasized at this fourteenth-century Benedictine abbey tucked into the South Bavarian Alps 10 miles N of Garmisch. Originally of Gothic design, Ettal was rebuilt in the baroque style in the early eighteenth century. Bach organ music, Mozart's Missa Brevis in C Major, and Portuguese baroque trumpet pieces were recently programmed. **Recent Performers:** Tobias Reiser Ensemble, Regensburg Boys Choir. **Performances:** Saturday or Sunday evenings.

GÖTTINGEN (Lower Saxony)
110 miles NE of Frankfurt

Situated just off of the newly designated "Fairytale Road," Göttingen contains all of the charm and romance of which fairytales are made. The half-timbered houses and Gothic buildings here seem right out of a Brothers Grimm story and could possibly have inspired a few of their tales, since the prolific duo taught and worked for the library at the university.

FESTIVALS

Handel Festival

1 Week
Early June

Göttingen Handel Society
Hainholzweg 3-5
D-3400 Göttingen

Chor, Orch, Cham, Org, Lect

During this festival the visitor is transported in time to experience a typical seventeenth-century concert. There is much organ music, choral music, and concert presentations of operas, and many baroque composers are heard in addition to Handel and Bach. The historic venues include St. John's Church, with its distinctive octagonal towers, and the fourteenth-century City Hall. **Recent Performers:** John Elliot Gardiner conducting the English Baroque Soloists, Monteverdi Choir. **Venues:** St. John's Church, City Hall, St. Jacob's Church, University, Brewery. **Performances:** 15; evenings, some matinees.

HAMBURG (Hamburg)
250 miles N of Frankfurt

Germany's second largest city (after Berlin), Hamburg is one of Europe's most sophisticated seaports. Situated just inland of the North Sea on the River Elbe, Hamburg's busy harbor is filled with seafaring ships and pleasure craft, bringing a lively flow of visitors to town. The city is known for its nightlife as well as for its exotic seafood dishes, which are standard fare at most of the hundreds of restaurants. Hamburg was a center for German opera in the seventeenth and eighteenth centuries and it was here that Handel first developed his operatic gifts.

ONGOING EVENTS

Hamburg State Opera

Op, Dance

Hamburgische Staatsoper
Dammtorstrasse 28
D-2000 Hamburg 36
Tel: 040/35 17 21

Hamburg's ballet and opera companies are vital to the cultural life of the city and have earned international reputations. Tenor Placido Domingo began his career here. Recent productions have included Mozart's *Idomeneo*, Wagner's *Tannhäuser,* and Shostakovitch's *Lady Macbeth of the Mzensk District.* **Performances:** September–June. Performances often sell out, so advance reservations are strongly recommended.

Music Hall

Orch, Cham, Rec

Musikhalle
Karl-Muck Platz
D-2000 Hamburg
Tel: 040/34 69 20

The smaller of this building's two halls features chamber music, and the larger is home not only to the three orchestras based in Hamburg (Hamburg Symphony, NDR Symphony Orchestra, and Philharmonic State Orchestra) but to guest orchestras from around the world.   **Recent Performers:** Daniel Barenboim conducting the Berlin Philharmonic, violinist Nadja Salerno-Sonnenberg, pianist Martha Argerich **Performances:** September–June.

Office for Church Music

Chor, Org

Amt für Kirchenmusik
Uhlandstrasse 49
D-2000 Hamburg 76
Tel: 040/2 20 51 31

A detailed listing of sacred music throughout Hamburg is published by this organization. The main churches in Hamburg are St. Jacobi, St. Katharinen, St. Marien, St. Michaelis, St. Nikolai, St. Petri, and the Russian Orthodox Cathedral of St. Propopius.

HANNOVER (Lower Saxony)
165 miles NE of Frankfurt

Parks and elegant buildings abound in this verdant city, capital of Lower Saxony. Especially beautiful are the three main gardens—the Royal Gardens of Herrenhausen, the Grosse Garten, and the Berggarten. They are magnificent masterpieces of baroque design, with mazes, fountains (including the highest-shooting fountain in Europe), and a variety of exotic flowers. Monthly listings of opera and theater performances are available from the Tourist Office.

FESTIVALS

Music and Theater in Herrenhausen

6 Weeks
Late June–Early September

Op, Orch, Jazz, Cham, Dance,
Th

Musik und Theater in
Herrenhausen
Ernst-August Platz 8
D-3000 Hannover
Tel: 0511/168 3903

These festivities take full advantage of a vast baroque garden with flawless lawns, geometric flower beds, and symmetrically scattered statues. Participants can hear opera in the Orangerie and jazz in the gallery or picnic to a Chopin piano concerto. Incorporated into the celebration are the Hannover Light Festivals (Lichterfeste), which are illuminations of the garden culminating in an authentic baroque fireworks display accompanied by Handel's *Music for the Royal Fireworks*. **Recent Performers:** Munich Philharmonic Brass, clarinetist Sabine Meyer, Prague Chamber Orchestra. **Venue:** Herrenhausen Great Garden. **Performances:** daily, except Monday; evenings and matinees (5 Light Festivals each summer).

ONGOING EVENTS

Lower Saxon State Theater

Op, Dance, Th, Orch

Niedersächsische Staats-
theater
Opernplatz 1
D-3000 Hannover
Tel: 0511/368 17 11
Fax: 0511/368 17 68

Within this three-tiered sandstone opera house the Lower Saxon State Opera Company offers an impressive season of 40 highly imaginative productions. *Parsifal* and *Die Zauberflöte* are complemented by less conventional works such as Stravinsky's *Oedipus Rex* and Pfitzner's *Palestrina*, and ballet and theater works are an important part of the schedule. The Lower Saxon State Orchestra presents eight concerts from September to May. In addition to the Opera House, (seating 1207), there is a chamber music hall, the Ballhof (seating 406). Tickets are available 4 days before a performance. **Performances:** 300; September–July.

HEIDELBERG (Baden-Württemberg)
50 miles S of Frankfurt

Once the capital of the Palatinate, Heidelberg is now a university town presided over by one of Europe's most romantic ruins—the Heidelberg Castle. The original castle was considered "the most beautiful Renaissance structure north of the Alps" before its near destruction in the mid-1700s. In its heyday it was the site of spectacular pageants that included music, dance, and masquerades. This tradition continues with the festival and other events that take advantage of the castle's hillside view of the town and the river Neckar below.

FESTIVALS

Heidelberg Castle Festival

4 Weeks	Heidelberg Schloss Spiele
Late July-Late August	Konzertkasse
	Theaterstrasse 8
Op, Chor, Cham, Jazz, Folk	D-6900 Heidelberg
	Tel: 06221/583521

A beguiling program that promises fun is offered by an energetic company of local artists and the resident orchestra—that of Rochester, New York's Eastman School of Music. Recent repertoire has included Britten's *Albert Herring*, Donizetti's *Elixir of Love*, and orchestral music by Mendelssohn, Dvořák, Bach, and Villa-Lobos. **Recent Performers:** Cleveland Quartet, Eastman Philharmonia, Darmstadt Concert Choir. **Venues:** Heidelberg Castle Ruin (in case of rain, King's Hall). **Performances:** about 20; evenings (except Monday) and Sunday matinees.

International Festival of Women Composers

4 Days	Internationalen Festival
Variable	Komponistinnen
	Henriette-Feuerbach Haus
Cham, Rec, Org, Sem, Ex	Theaterstrasse 11
	D-6900 Heidelberg
	Tel: 06221/16 68 61

Contemporary works and those of Eastern European composers are featured in this festival emphasizing music written by women. Pieces by Sofia Gubaidulina, Fanny Mendelssohn, and Clara Schumann were recently programmed. The performance sites include Germany's oldest University, a museum housed in a former palace, and the fourteenth-century Church of the Holy Ghost, where not so holy activities once included the burning of witches and the torture of criminals. The festival was founded in 1985. **Venues:** University, Heiliggeistkirche, Kurpfälzisches Museum, Kunst Verein. **Performances:** 8.

IN THE AREA

Schwetzingen Festival

2 Months	Schwetzinger Festspiele
Late April–Mid-June	Postfach 1941
	D-6830 Schwetzingen
Op, Orch, Chor, Cham, Rec,	Tel: 06202/4933
Dance	

Many of the world's great performers have gathered since 1952 for this festival held in the palace 8 miles W of Heidelberg where Voltaire once took refuge and the 7-year-old Mozart played in 1763. Dresden court music, lieder recitals, and contemporary opera have recently held the stage here. Concerts also make use of the magnificent park, replete with formal French gardens, small winding streams, and temples to the Greek gods. **Recent Performers:** Neville Marriner conducting the Stuttgart Radio Symphony Orchestra, Cleveland Quartet, soprano Lucia Popp. **Venues:** Schwetzingen Palace. **Performances:** 35.

HEILBRONN (Baden-Württemberg)
70 miles S of Frankfurt

Built on the banks of the Neckar River, Heilbronn is the largest producer of the Neckar Valley's distinctive wine. This thriving city is perhaps most famous for the magnificent St. Killian's Church. The ornate 210-foot tower of this church was one of the earliest works of Renaissance architecture north of the Alps. The tourist office can provide information on the city's most important classical music venue, the Harmony Festival Hall.

ONGOING EVENTS

St. Killian's Church

Chor, Org	Tourist Office
	Rathaus, Marktplatz
	D-7100 Heilbronn
	Tel: 07131/56 22 70

Contact the Tourist Office for information on church music concerts at St. Killian's Church throughout the year.

Harmonie Festival Hall

Orch, Cham, Rec   Harmonie Festival Hall
                                    Allee
                                    D-7100 Heilbronn
                                    Tel: 07131/56 22 70

This large concrete and glass building houses two concert halls and is also host to conventions, balls, banquets, and exhibitions. The Heilbronn Symphony Orchestra performs six concerts here between September and April, and the Württemberg Chamber Orchestra is also in residence. The Heilbronn Cultural Association sponsors concerts by major orchestras from abroad, and other programs include chamber music and recitals by internationally acclaimed artists. **Recent Performers:** flutist James Galway, pianist Rudolf Buchbinder, Moscow Philharmonic, trumpeter Maurice André.

HOHENLOHE (Baden-Württemberg)
100 miles SE of Frankfurt

The cozy towns and villages of the Hohenlohe region speak of a time when Gothic churches and romantic castles presided over the serene German countryside. Essentially the eastern watershed of the Neckar river, Hohenlohe is bordered by the Swabian Forest and the Taube Valley, beyond which lies the nearby Romantic Road.

FESTIVALS

Hohenlohe Cultural Summer

3 Months   Hohenlohe Kultursommer
Mid-June–Early September   D-7109 Schöntal
                                    Tel: 07943/20 83

Orch, Cham, Rec, Schrammel,
    Ex, Lect

Nestled in the Hohenlohe plain is a wealth of beautiful abbeys, castles, and churches where Renaissance choral music, Johann Strauss songs, and the Schumann piano quintet were recently heard. The venues for this regional celebration change each year, taking advantage of towns throughout Hohenlohe. **Recent Performers:** Salzburg ProArte Quartet, Werneck Castle Chamber Orchestra. **Towns:** Ingelfingen, Künzelsau, Laibach, Neuenstein, Niedernhall, Öhringen, Pfedelbach, Schöntal, Waldenburg. **Performances:** 28.

KARLSRUHE (Baden-Württemberg)
80 miles S of Frankfurt

Located in the foothills of the Black Forest near the Rhine, Karlsruhe's atmosphere is a pleasant mix of old and new, reflecting the successful rebuilding that took place after World War II. The streets of the city are arranged in the shape of a fan, all leading to the eighteenth-century palace that now houses the Baden Provincial Museum. The large universities of art and music here contribute to the vibrant cultural community, and several impressive museums display the works of important German masters.

FESTIVALS

Handel Festival

12 Days	Handel Festspiele
Mid-February–Early March	Internationale Handel Akademie
Op, Chor, Cham, Th, Sem	Postfach 14 49
	Baumeisterstrasse 11
	D-7500 Karlsruhe
	Tel: 0721/152 1

This festival featuring the works of Handel and his contemporaries follows a series of seminars on the music of these masters. Vocal and choral pieces are emphasized, and original instuments are played whenever possible. Recent productions have included Handel's *Admeto* and *Imeneo*. Organized by Karlsruhe's International Handel Academy, this festival began in 1985. **Recent Performers:** London Baroque Ensemble, Roy Goodman conducting the German Handel Soloists. **Venues:** Baden State Theater, Gottesaue Mansion. **Performances:** 13; evenings.

ONGOING EVENTS

Baden State Theater

Op, Orch, Cham, Rec, Dance,   Badisches Staatstheater
Th   Karlsruhe
                               Baumeisterstrasse 11
                               D-7500 Karlsruhe 1
                               Tel: 0721/60 20 2
                               Fax: 0721/37 32 23

Opera is clearly the focus in this theater, with thoughtful productions of favorites from the repertoire as well as less well known operas such as Prokofiev's *War and Peace* and Chayne's *Erzebet*. Built between 1970 and 1975, this modern, angular structure contains a Large House (seating 1002), Small House (seating 330), and foyer that are all used for performances. Recent productions include *Lucia di Lammermoor, Lohengrin, Hello Dolly!*, and Offenbach's *Bluebeard*. Fifteen symphony concerts and 5 chamber concerts are given by the Baden State Band (Badisches Staatskapelle). **Recent Performers:** soprano Kathleen Cassello, mezzo-soprano Theodora Hanslow, violinist Christian Altenburger. **Performances:** daily; September–July. Tickets are available 1 week before a performance.

LEIPZIG
180 miles NE of Frankfurt

Since the sixteenth century Leipzig has played host to Europe's most renowned trade fairs, and each year in March and September hundreds of tradespeople gather here from east and west for the traditional event. In addition to its famous fairs, Leipzig is simply steeped in musical tradition. Bach spent his most productive years in Leipzig from 1723 to 1750 and is buried in St. Thomas Church, where he was choirmaster. Richard Wagner was born here, just 63 years after the death of Bach. Schiller composed his "Ode to Joy" in a house just outside of town, and the local university's most renowned graduate, Goethe, used a local restaurant (still open) as the setting for Faust's meeting with the Devil. Though Leipzig sustained tremendous damage during World War II, much of the town's historic treasures have been well preserved. An appropriate starting place for exploration of the city's heritage is the Musikinstrumenten-museum, which displays musical instruments from the sixteenth through nineteenth centuries.

ONGOING EVENTS

Gewandhaus

Orch, Cham

Gewandhaus
Postfach 35
O-7010 Leipzig

During the eighteenth century, when cloth makers and wool merchants gathered for trade fairs in Leipzig's Cloth Hall (Gewandhaus), its great central hall hosted the first "Gewandhaus Concerts" of the Leipzig orchestra. Under Felix Mendelssohn (1835–47), the Gewandhaus Orchestra was molded into one of Europe's finest ensembles. The young Johannes Brahms came to Leipzig in 1853, and the subsequent tumultuous relationship between Brahms, Leipzig, and the Gewandhaus Orchestra spanned 40 years. He performed 20 times as pianist and conductor between 1853 and 1885, and his Violin Concerto and *German Requiem* received only tepid receptions at their premieres. Today this ensemble claims to be the oldest concert orchestra in Germany, and it performs in the new Gewandhaus building, constructed in 1977. **Performances:** 150. Tickets are sold largely by subscription. The tourist office may be able to furnish ticket information.

Leipzig Opera

Op, Rec, Dance

Oper Leipzig
Postfach 35
O-7010 Leipzig
Tel: 7168/258
Fax: 7168/293 633

Although its basic structure survived World War II, the Leipzig opera house was effectively silenced by Allied bombs and was not reopened until 1960. Operas, ballets, and musicals are now produced by a versatile company, and the repertoire of twentieth-century works is especially strong. Performances are given in the Large Stage and Cellar Theater. Five song recitals are offered each season. **Performances:** 190.

LOWER SAXONY
(also see Göttingen, Hannover, Osnabrück)

Lower Saxony is Germany's second most northern province, bordered by Schleswig-Holstein to the north and North Rhineland-Westphalia and Hesse to the south. The lowland region between the Elbe and Ems Rivers is covered with heath and moor, and the forests and fertile river basins are dotted with towns whose agricultural economy is dependent on the fertile land.

FESTIVALS

Lower Saxony Music Days

2 Months	Niedersächsische Musiktage
Mid-August–Late October	Niedersächsische
	Sparkassenstiftung
Orch, Cham, Rec, Jazz, Chor,	Schiffgraben 6
Rock, Org	D-3000 Hannover 1
	Tel: 0441/2 69 92
	(in Oldenburg)

The most ambitious of Germany's many regional festivals, Lower Saxony Music days boasts 64 concerts in 54 places. Programs range widely from Mozart through Stravinsky, Kodály, and Poulenc, and much early music on original instruments is featured. "Lower Saxons play for Lower Saxons" is the festival slogan. Organizers prefer tickets to be purchased at each town—ask for the "Gesamtprogram" with detailed schedules and addresses. **Recent Performers:** Ma'alot Quintet, Gothic Voices, clarinetist Sabine Meyer. **Performances:** 65; evenings and afternoons.

LUDWIGSBURG (Baden-Württemberg)
90 miles S of Frankfurt

Situated just a few miles from Stuttgart, Ludwigsburg is a testimony to the prosperity of Duke Eberhard Ludwig of Württemburg, who chose this spot in the early eighteenth century to build his palace. The town that took his name still centers around this lavish baroque and rococo palace, the Residenzschloss, where sumptuous gardens and numerous wings invite hours of wandering. Parks and baroque buildings are in abundance in this town, which is also the home of several universities.

FESTIVALS

Ludwigsburg Castle Festival

5 Months	Ludwigsburger
May–September	Schlossfestspiele
	Postfach 1022
Op, Orch, Chor, Cham, Rec,	D-7140 Ludwigsburg
Org, Dance, Jazz, Th	Tel: 07141/28000

Ludwigsburg has organized an intriguing musical menu in an ambitious regional festival encompassing seven towns in southern Germany. Concerts include much music of the Renaissance and many twentieth-century works, in addition to more familiar repertoire. Imaginative venues include ornate theaters, Gothic churches, The Old Wine Press at Bietigheim, and the Fruit Bin at Haigerloch. The variable locations and times may be difficult to locate, but the programs and outstanding artists are worth the effort. **Recent Performers:** Cleveland Quartet, cellist Yo-Yo Ma, flutist James Galway, soprano Kathleen Battle. **Towns:** Ludwigsburg, Bad Teinach, Bietigheim, Haigerloch/Bad Imnau, Schwäbisch Hall, Schwaigern, Wolfegg/Allgäu. **Performances:** almost nightly, except for one quiet week in August.

MAINZ (Rhineland-Palatinate)
20 miles SW of Frankfurt

Located on the banks of the Rhine River at its intersection with the Main, the town of Mainz is a center for the Rhine wine trade and is the economic base for the Rhine-Main region. The city holds a unique place in history, for it was here that Johannes Gutenberg set up his press in 1450. The imposing eleventh-century cathedral dominates a historic old section of town that was restored as a thriving marketplace after severe bombing during World War II.

ONGOING EVENTS

Mainz State Theater

Op, Orch, Th

Staatstheater Mainz
Gutenbergplatz 7
D-6500 Mainz 1
Tel: 06131/12 33 65
Fax: 06131/12 27 06

The State Theater Philharmonic Orchestra offers 18 concerts from September to May with recent repertoire including Mahler's Symphony no. 5, Barber's *Essays,* and Beethoven's Piano Concerto no. 2. In addition, the orchestra plays for the 12 operas that are staged each season. Recent productions include *Parsifal, Don Giovanni, La Cage aux Folles.* **Recent Performers:** tenor Peter Schreier, pianist Lazar Berman. **Performances:** 40; evenings.

MANNHEIM (Baden-Württemberg)
45 miles S of Frankfurt

An important center for the arts since its founding in the seventeenth century (Schiller's plays were first performed here), Mannheim benefits from its location at the convergence of the Rhine and Neckar rivers and is one of the largest river ports in Europe. Hopelessly confused travelers may find refuge in its logically planned streets, with the *Quadrastadt* ("squared town") at its center. The city is famous in the history of music as the home of the Mannheim Orchestra, the "army of generals" that so impressed and influenced the young Mozart and that played such an important role in the transition from baroque to classical style in the mid-eighteenth century.

ONGOING EVENTS

National Theater

Op, Dance, Th   Nationaltheater
                                 Am Goetheplatz
                                 D-6800 Mannheim 1
                                 Tel: 0621/248 44
                                 Fax: 0621/1680 385

Built in 1957 and dedicated to the beloved poet and playwright Friedrich von Schiller, this gleaming white Bauhaus-style theater has its own drama and opera companies. In addition to standard repertoire, operettas and musicals are sometimes offered. **Performances:** September–June.

MUNICH (Bavaria)
200 miles SE of Frankfurt

Munich is Germany's vibrant Bavarian metropolis. Situated just a stone's throw from the Alps, Munich's museums, gardens, magnificent baroque architecture, and, of course, beer make this city the appropriate home for one of Europe's biggest bashes—Oktoberfest—which, contrary to its name, is celebrated in September. One of the great sights of the city is the magnificent Residenz, which after centuries of expansion (and reconstruction after World War II), now contains several of Munich's most important theaters and 7 interior courtyards. Munich was a capital city when the Kingdom of Bavaria was an independent state, and it was here that Wag-

ner's *Tristan und Isolde, Die Meistersinger, Das Rheingold,*
and *Die Walküre* all had their premieres, underwritten by the
treasuries of the beneficent King Ludwig II.

FESTIVALS

Bell'Arte Musical Summer

8 Days	Bell'Arte Musicalischer
July	Sommer
	Schongauer Strasse 22
Rec, Org, Jazz	D-8000 Munich
	Tel: 089/71 80 41

These entertaining concerts run the gamut from Bach
and Handel to the Beatles and Count Basie. They are held
in the spacious fountain courtyard of the Residenz, the extraordinary palace that the Dukes of Wittelsbach continually
enlarged and enriched from the fourteenth through the eighteenth centuries. Performances are held in the Hercules Hall
if it rains. **Recent Performers:** Sabine Meyer Wind Ensemble, Prague Swing Big Band. **Venue:** Residenz Brunnenhof
Performances: evenings.

Munich Opera Festival

1 Month	Münchner Opern-Festspiele
July	Maximillianstrasse 11
	D-8000 Munich 2
Op, Cham, Rec, Dance	Tel: 089/22136

Extraordinary casts are assembled by the Bavarian State
Opera to create an illustrious celebration of opera that has
become one of Europe's largest festivals. Founded in 1901
as a homage to the music of Mozart and Wagner, the repertoire is now broader, with Verdi, Rossini, and Tchaikovsky
recently included. Although song recitals and ballet are offered, opera is the mainstay, with special attention given to
works by Munich natives Richard Strauss and Carl Orff. **Recent Performers:** soprano Margaret Price, tenor Peter Schreier,
baritone Hermann Prey, bass Kurt Moll. **Venues:** National
Theater, Cuvilliés Theater, Residenz. **Performances:** 35.

Nymphenburg Summer Festival

3 Weeks	Nymphenburger Sommer-
Mid-June–Early July	spiele
	Zuccalistrasse 21
Orch, Chor, Cham	D-8000 Munich 19

Surrounded by a park filled with fountains and sweeping lawns, the seventeenth-century Nymphenburg Palace is actually a group of buildings notable for their grace and balance. Inside, billowing decorations of cream and gold swirl around the murals and long windows of the rooms where music from Buxtehude to Brahms is presented by outstanding artists. Founded in 1945, the festival features German music, although Italian madrigals and oratorios were recently heard. **Recent Performers:** Carmina Quartet, Segovia Guitar Quartet, soprano Emma Kirkby. **Venue:** Nymphenburg Palace. **Performances:** 12; evenings.

ONGOING EVENTS

Blutenburg Concerts

Orch, Chor, Cham, Jazz

Blutenburger Konzerte
Sipplinger Strasse 8
D-8000 Munich 60
Tel: 089/834 49 45

Blutenburg Castle is only one of many intriguing castles and churches to host these diverse concerts. Baroque brass, eighteenth-century French symphonies, gypsy swing music, and even Saint-Exupery's *A Little Prince* can be heard in the three "seasons" that comprise the offerings here: Blutenburg Herbst (Fall), Blutenburg Frühling (Spring), and a summer program begun in 1984 called IGA Park Festival Days. **Recent Performers:** Munich Chamber Orchestra, Salzburg Chamber Soloists, Veterinary Street Jazz Band. **Venues:** Blutenburg Castle, Pasing Island Castle and Maria Schutz Church, Dachau Castle, Schwaneck Castle. **Performances:** 50; January–December.

Gasteig

Orc, Cham, Rec, Org, Jazz,
  Dance, Th, Ex, Film

Gasteig
Rosenheimer Strasse 5
D-8000 Munich 80
Tel: 089/48098 600
Fax: 089/48098 632

The Gasteig is a massive brick and glass cultural center commanding a ridge overlooking Munich, and it houses the Munich Philharmonic, Munich Public Library, Munich Adult Education College, Richard Strauss Conservatory, year-round conventions, and a shopping mall. Chief among its seven performance halls is the Philharmonie, the 2400-seat home of the Munich Philharmonic. The orchestra is often on tour, but fine guest ensembles and soloists fill out the schedule. Renowned artists are heard throughout the Gasteig, and the repertoire encompasses nearly every style and ensemble. "Gasteig" is a contraction of "gacher Steig," which is the name of the steep path ("Steig") climbed by painters and sculptors throughout the centuries to reach the crest above the Isar river now occupied by this cultural conglomerate, which opened in 1985. **Recent Performers:** Christopher Hogwood conducting the Academy of Ancient Music, violinist Anne-Sophie Mutter, pianist Daniel Barenboim. **Performances:** daily; year-round (Philharmonic: September–July).

Munich Chamber Orchestra

Orch

Munich Chamber Orchestra
Elilandstrasse 6
D-8000 Munich 90
Tel: 089/697 13 11

Founded in 1950, this ensemble is committed to introducing the public to lesser-known works for chamber orchestra as well as the classics. Recent programs have included a C. P. E. Bach cello concerto, a concertino by Pergolesi, and Eder's "Pastorale for Strings." **Recent Performers:** trumpeter Maurice André, hornist Hermann Baumann. **Venue:** Academy of Music. **Performances:** 15; September–August.

National Theater

Op, Orch, Cham, Rec, Dance

National Theater
Maximillianstrasse 11
D-8000 Munich 22
Tel: 089/2185 368
Fax: 089/2185 304

Located in the magnificent Residenz complex, the National Theater is the home of the Bavarian State Opera, Orchestra, and Ballet. This 2100-seat theater has been an important musical center since it first opened in 1818, and it was here that four of Richard Wagner's operas were premiered. Almost completely destroyed in World War II, it was rebuilt in 1963 according to the original, neoclassical designs and is the largest theater in Germany. The Bavarian State Opera has long been one of Europe's most esteemed companies— Richard Strauss served as its conductor, and both Jenny Lind and Enrico Caruso graced its productions. Today major artists join the company in a repertoire encompassing 70 operas and

25 ballets. The National Theater should be distinguished from two other theaters within the Residenz complex: the Residenz Theater, which features drama productions, and the rococo Old Residenz Theater (or Cuvilliés Theater), which presents chamber operas and concerts. The Bavarian State Orchestra plays in the National and Cuvilliés Theaters. **Recent Performers:** sopranos Mirella Freni and Julia Varady, tenor Placido Domingo. **Performances:** almost daily; September–July. Written ticket requests should be sent 4 weeks in advance of a performance.

State Theater on the Gärtnerplatz

Op, Dance, Child

Staatstheater am Gärtner-
platz
Postfach 140 569
D-8000 Munich 5
Tel: 089/201 6767

Sometimes called "the little sister" of the National Theater, the Gärtnerplatz Theater is proud to be Munich's "second" opera house—a position that allows presentation of often unconventional scores in German translation. Although the repertoire of 37 operas, operettas, and musicals includes such familiar productions as *Don Giovanni, La Boheme,* and *Rigoletto,* there is an emphasis on works heard less often in Germany, including those of Cimarosa, Britten, Monteverdi, and Smetana, presented in highly imaginative productions. More than half of its opening nights are devoted to music by twentieth-century composers. **Performances:** Almost daily; September–July.

IN THE AREA

Amerang Castle Concerts

3 Months
Late June–Early September

Op, Orch, Cham, Dance, Th

Konzerte auf Schloss
Amerang
Konzertbüro
Schloss Amerang
D-8201 Amerang
Tel: 08075/1507
Fax: 08075/481

Fresh flowers cascade between marble columns as three stories of candlelit arcades rise above a small stage in the central courtyard of this castle 30 miles E of Munich. This romantic setting has been the stage since 1965 for a diverse group of ensembles performing music that ranges from opera to chamber music. The courtyard can be covered in case of rain, and evenings are likely to be cool, even during the summer. **Recent Performers:** Salzburg Chamber Orchestra, Berlin Philharmonic Winds, Vienna Horn Quartet. **Venue:** Amerang Castle Courtyard. **Performances:** 20; Friday–Saturday, some weekdays.

Benediktbeuer Concerts

11 Weekends	Benediktbeuer Konzerte
Mid-May–Mid-September	Widenmayerstrasse 42
	D-8000 Munich 22
Orch, Chor, Cham, Org	Tel: 089/29 26 27

Programs emphasizing classical and romantic music are presented within this simple Benedictine cloister 32 miles S of Munich. The *Carmina Burana* is a collection of thirteenth-century songs preserved in and named for this cloister, and it was this rich source that Carl Orff used for his 1937 oratorio of the same name. In addition to Orff's masterpiece, recent performances have included Brahms' *German Requiem*, chamber music by Mozart, and Chopin piano preludes. **Recent Performers:** Berlin Brass, Budapest Mandel Quartet. **Venues:** Basilica, Baroque Hall, Inner Courtyard. **Performances:** 18; evenings.

Schäftlarn Concerts

Orch, Chor, Cham, Rec, Org	Schäftlarner Konzerte
	D-8026 Schäftlarn
	Tel: 08178/3435

The baroque church of this monastery 10 miles SW of Munich is the site of these concerts, which feature music of the classical era performed by well-known soloists as well as instrumentalists from Munich orchestras. **Recent Performers:** trumpeter Maurice André. **Performances:** twice a month; May–July; September, October. Tickets available in April, and concerts can sell out.

Music Summer between the Inn and Salzach

4 Months	Musiksommer zwischen Inn
Mid-May–Early September	und Salzach
	Ludwig Thoma Strasse 2
Orch, Chor, Cham, Org	D-8220 Traunstein
	Tel: 0861/5 83 19

The little corner of Germany SE of Munich bounded by the Salzach and Inn rivers is the setting for this jewel of a festival that presents not only well-known works but revives forgotten pieces of classical music in the places where they were created. Remote Benedictine monasteries (which cultivated a strong musical tradition in the eighteenth century), old parish and collegiate churches, and romantic castles are the sites where these carefully chosen programs are presented. Because the festival was founded on the belief that high-quality music is "neither privilege nor luxury ...nor a monopoly of the large cities," entrance fees are moderate. **Recent Performers:** Bavarian Chamber Orchestra, Aachen Chamber Choir. **Towns:** Altotting, Bad Reichenhall, Berchesgaden, Inzell. **Performances:** 30; evenings.

NUREMBERG (Bavaria)
120 miles SE of Frankfurt

Nuremberg is one of Bavaria's largest cities, second only to Munich. Music and the arts have thrived here since the Middle Ages, when poet-musicians like Tannhauser and Hans Sachs helped to pioneer the German musical tradition continued by the Meistersingers of the fifteenth and sixteenth centuries. Nuremberg's most famous native son is artist Albrect Dürer, whose house is one of the city's major attractions. Although evidence of the city's dubious associations with Adolf Hitler and the Third Reich are for the most part gone, they are by no means forgotten, and one can still visit such sites as the Justice Palace, where the War Crimes Tribunal was held in 1946.

FESTIVALS

International Organ Weeks

2 Weeks	Internationale Orgelwoche
Late June–Mid-July	Nürnberg
	Bismarkstrasse 46
Chor, Org, Comp, Sem	D-8500 Nürnberg 20
	Tel: 0911/16 35 28

Founded in 1951, this is one of Europe's oldest festivals of sacred music. Organs in five churches and the Meistersinger Hall are played by international artists in concerts that offer music from the fifteenth to mid-twentieth centuries. A contest for organ improvisation is part of each festival, and excerpts of festival events are broadcast worldwide. **Re-**

cent **Performers:** Taverner Consort, organist Nicholas Danby. **Venues:** St. Egidien Church, thirteenth-century St. Sebald Church, Meistersinger Hall. **Performances:** 40.

ONGOING EVENTS

Meistersinger Hall

Orch
Nürnberg Symphony
Kongresshalle
Bayernstrasse 100
D-8500 Nürnberg
Tel: 0911/47 40 140
Fax: 0911/47 40 160

Performances are heard here from September to July, and although the Nürnberg Symphony is the principal ensemble, popular music concerts are also given. The symphony offers the standard repertoire: Borodin's *Prince Igor,* Saint-Saens' *Carnival of the Animals,* and Beethoven's Symphony no. 3 were recently heard. **Recent performers:** Choral Society of Southern California, trumpeter Carol Dawn Reinhard. **Performances:** 70.

Municipal Theaters

Op
Municipal Theaters
Richard Wagner Platz 2
D-8500 Nürnberg
Tel: 0911/163 808

Three performance spaces make up the municipal theaters—the 1082-seat Opera House, the 539-seat Theater, and the intimate 197-seat Workshop Theater. Recent productions in these halls have included Wagner's *Lohengrin,* Verdi's *Nabucco,* and Massenet's *Don Quixote.*

IN THE AREA

Weissenburg Summer Festival

1 Month
July

Op, Child
Weissenburg Festspiel-
sommer
Postfach 569
D-8832 Weissenburg
Tel: 09141/907 123

Open-air performances of light operas are given here, 25 miles S of Nuremberg, in a theater that was once a quarry. Recent productions have included Johann Strauss's *Gypsy Baron* and Verdi's *Il Trovatore*. **Venue:** Bergwald Theater. **Performances:** 9; evenings and matinees.

OSNABRÜCK (Lower Saxony)
150 miles N of Frankfurt

Set beside the lush Teutoburg Forest and lovely Wiehengebirge Hills, Osnabrück is a cosmopolitan city whose central historic old town contrasts with the surrounding urban development. Restored gabled houses and a fifteenth-century town hall are just a few of the historic attractions, while the newly established university (1971) provides a vital academic atmosphere.

ONGOING EVENTS

Forum Artium

Orch, Cham, Rec

Forum Artium
Musikhaus Bossmann
Neuer Graben
D-4500 Osnabrück
Tel: 0541/2 74 49

This organization sponsors a series of concerts in Osnabrück and neighboring Georgsmarienhütte that emphasizes early music. Recent programs featured Bach's *Brandenburg* Concertos, baroque cembalo music, and a Beethoven piano sonata. **Recent Performers:** Musica Antiqua Cologne, Young Bach Collegium. **Venues:** sixteenth-century Town Hall, Aula Castle, Georgsmarienhütte Lutheran Church, Forum Artium. **Performances:** 6; December–February; April–June.

Osnabrück Town Hall

Orch, Cham, Rec

Stadthalle Osnabrück
Neuer Graben 22
D-4500 Osnabrück
Tel: 0541/2 74 49

With such a high caliber of both artists and programs here, one can only lament that the concerts are so few. For over 20 years internationally renowned artists have presented works such as Tchaikovsky's Symphony no. 6, Strauss's *Four Last Songs*, and Verdi's String Quartet in E Minor. **Recent Performers:** Juilliard String Quartet, oboist Heinz Holliger, soprano Lucia Popp. **Performances:** 8; October–December, February.

IN THE AREA

Days of Old Music

3 Weeks	Tage Alter Musik
September	Forum Artium
	Am Kasinopark 1
Cham, Rec, Chor, Org, Sem	D-4504 Georgsmarienhütte
	Tel: 05401/34160

The region surrounding Osnabrück reverberates with the sounds of this festival established in 1988 to celebrate early music. Programs feature music of the Middle Ages, Renaissance, and baroque and are held in small, local churches. Complementing the concerts are courses on performance practice and interpretation. Some twentieth-century music also appears on the concert programs. **Recent performers:** Amsterdam Baroque Orchestra, Hilliard Ensemble London, Musica Antiqua Cologne. **Towns:** Bad Essen, Bad Iburg, Bersenbrück, Börstel, Georgsmarienhütte, Hagen, Melle, Osnabrück, Quakenbrück. **Performances:** 30 evenings; some matinees.

REGENSBURG (Bavaria)
170 miles SE of Frankfurt

Regensburg is one of the few ancient German cities to emerge from World War II virtually unscathed. Thus, this former Celtic settlement founded 500 years before the birth of Christ is brimming with historic buildings representing nearly every architectural style to appear in this part of Europe since the Roman age. The churches of Regensburg are the most compelling of the city's sites. Gothic spires, Romanesque cloisters, and dramatic medieval stained-glass windows are nearly everywhere, testifying to the city's status as the site from which Christianity was launched in Germany.

FESTIVALS

Days of Old Music

3 Days	Tage Alter Musik
Early June	Regensburg
	Luitpoldstrasse 3
Cham, Rec, Org	D-8400 Regensburg
	Tel: 0941/5 26 87
	Fax: 0941/5 30 94

Regensburg draws various ensembles, including several from the United States, to create an invigorating celebration of Renaissance and early baroque music in several of the city's fine churches and halls. **Recent Performers:** New York Cornet and Sackbut Ensemble, San Francisco Baroque Orchestra, Ensemble Alcatraz. **Venues:** Minorettenkirche, Rathaus, Dominican Church, Duke's Hall. **Performances:** 10; evenings and afternoons.

ONGOING EVENTS

City Theater

Op, Orch, Chor, Cham, Rec, Dance, Th, Child	Stadttheater Bismarkplatz 7 D-8400 Regensburg Tel: 0941/507 24 27

The Regensburg Ballet, Philharmonic Orchestra of the City of Regensburg, Regensburg Opera, and Regensburg Theater each give about 6 performances every year at this theater built in 1852. Recent productions include Debussy's *Pelléas et Mélisande,* Shakespeare's *King Lear,* and Rimsky-Korsakov's *Scheherazade.* **Performances:** September–July. Tickets are available 7 days before a performance.

Cultural Events

Tourist Office
Altes Rathaus
D-8400 Regensburg
Tel: 0941/507 2141
Fax: 0941/507 2929

Regensburg has an active musical life that is administered largely by the Tourist Office. Performances at the majestic thirteenth-century Cathedral of St. Peter and myriad other churchs are given year-round. The Rathaus and Music Society also offer recital series. Two large choirs (Regensburg Kantorei and Regensburger Chorkreis) and the Philharmonic Orchestra of Regensburg perform throughout the city; the Regensburger Kantorei offers concerts every evening during Holy Week. As might be expected in a city with so many churches, organ recitals are presented throughout the year. The Tourist Office publishes a monthly listing for all cultural events.

Master Concerts

Orch, Cham, Rec   Regensburger Meisterkonzerte
                                 Villsstrasse 7
                                 D-8400 Regensburg

Stellar concerts ranging from Strauss's *Ein Heldenleben* to Mozart songs are sponsored by this organization. **Recent Performers:** Bamberg Symphony, violinist Pinchas Zuckerman, tenor Peter Schreier. **Venue:** University of Regensburg. **Performances:** 6; evenings.

Regensburg Boys Choir

Chor   Regensburger Domspatzen
                                 Reichsstrasse 22
                                 D-8400 Regensburg
                                 Tel: 0941/79 82 94

With a tradition that reaches back over a thousand years to the cathedral school founded in 975, this ensemble continues today as one of the world's foremost boys' choirs. In addition to concerts, the Domspatzen ("Cathedral Sparrows") are regularly heard on television and radio broadcasts and have recorded widely, winning several coveted Grand Prix du Disque awards for recordings of Monteverdi and Bach. Like its famous Viennese counterpart, the choir is often on tour, so it is necessary to write ahead for concert schedules.

SAARBRÜCKEN (Saarland)
200 miles SW of Frankfurt

Nestled in a western corner of Germany on the border with France, Saarbrücken takes its name from the bridge that the Romans built over the River Saar. Prosperity in the eighteenth century resulted in the profusion of baroque buildings that still grace the town, which is now the cultural and economic center for the province of Saarland.

FESTIVALS

Music in the Twentieth Century

4 Days   Musik im 20. Jahrhundert
Late May   Saarländischer Rundfunk
                                 Funkhaus Halberg
Orch, Cham   D-6600 Saarbrücken
                                 Tel: 0681/60 20

Organized by the radio broadcasting system, this festival has celebrated contemporary music for 20 years. Messiaen, Kurtag, and van Bose are among the composers recently featured. Oboist Heinz Holliger conducts and is the featured soloist in some performances. **Venues:** Funkhaus Halberg, Convention Hall, Academy of Music. **Performances:** 8; evenings and matinees.

IN THE AREA

Felix Mendelssohn-Bartholdy Festival

1 Month	Felix Mendelssohn-Bartholdy
June	Festival
	Buchelstrasse 7
Orch, Org, Chor, Rec, Cham,	Postfach 1162
Lec	D-6680 Neunkirchen
	Tel: 0682/20 53 42

Held in 12 towns scattered throughout Saarland province, this festival celebrates music by Felix Mendelssohn and his sister Fanny. Other pieces recently included in the nicely balanced programs were Hindemith's *Symphonic Metamorphoses,* a Weber clarinet concerto, and Bernstein's *Age of Anxiety.* **Recent Performers:** Cleveland Orchestra Chorus, hornist Hermann Baurmann. **Towns:** Blieskastel, Dillengen, Dudweiler, Homburg, Mettlach, Neuenkirchen, Saarbrücken, Saarlouis, St. Ingbert, St. Wendel, Völklingen, Wadern. **Performances:** 20; evenings and matinees.

SCHLESWIG-HOLSTEIN

Schleswig-Holstein, Germany's northernmost province, could be described as the tale of two seas. The stormy shores of the North Sea to the west are wind-swept and dramatic, in contrast to the balmy and mild beaches of the Baltic Sea to the east. Nestled between the two are dozens of sleepy fishing villages set amid an attractive lake region.

FESTIVALS

Nordelbischen International Organ Concerts

5 Months	Nordelbische Internationale
June–October	Orgelkonzerte
	Süderdomstrasse 11
Org, Rec, Chor, Cham, Jazz	D-2380 Schleswig
	Tel: 04621/2 55 40

These concerts celebrating the great German tradition of organ playing are evenly spread among evangelical churches in 35 towns throughout Schleswig-Holstein. Aside from an occasional chamber music recital, all performances feature the organ. The range of music offered is staggering—Renaissance songs, a thorough representation of the baroque and classical periods, "Ol' Man River," and gospel tunes. Dating from 1466, the organ at St. Jakobei Church in Lübeck is the oldest instrument heard, but most were built after 1960. Artists have come from Budapest, Memphis, Dresden, Utrecht, Boston and Warsaw. **Recent performers:** organists Dagmar Holtz and Max Yount, Moscow Virtuosi. **Towns:** Bad Oldesloe, Bosau, Bredstedt, Büsum, Burg, Flensburg, Garding, Gleschendorf, Hamburg, Heide, Heiligenhafen, Helgoland, Itzehoe, Keitum, Kiel, Langenhorn, Lübeck, Lübeck-Travemünde, Meldorf, Morsum, Neuenkirchen, Neustadt-Pelzerhaken, Nieblum, Nortorf, Oldenburg, Petersdorf, Plön, Rendsburg, Schleswig, Schönkirchen, Schulau/Wedel, Silent, St. Peter-Ording, Wesselburen, Westerland. **Performances:** nearly daily, evenings and matinees.

Schleswig-Holstein Music Festival

7 Weeks	Schleswig-Holstein Musik
Late June–Mid-August	Festival
	Postfach 38 40
Orch, Cham, Rec, Sem, Chor	D-2300 Kiel 1
	Tel: 0431/56 70 80

Begun in 1986, this festival immediately earned the international acclaim usually reserved for festivals decades older. Bordering Denmark, Schleswig-Holstein is best known for its peerless scenery. The festival's founder, pianist Justus Frantz, declared "my first wish was to make people aware of the region's great physical beauty." Accordingly, he devised a festival held throughout the province in remote castles, large cities, mansions, and even a sixteenth-century barn. Frantz insists that concerts be open to everyone and ticket prices remain moderate, a feat accomplished with the help of substantial contributions from private industry. The music is as varied as the surroundings, and careful programming yields rich rewards: Verdi's Requiem in Lübeck Cathedral, Vaughn Williams' *The Wasp* on the open-air stage at Eutin, or a Brahms cello sonata on the resort island of Westerland. Most towns are no more than a one-hour drive apart and may be contacted directly, but it is best to use the central office in Kiel. Beware of the variable Northern climate—one July day can offer heat, rain, chill, gusty winds, and sunshine. **Recent Performers:** Giuseppe Sinopoli conducting the Philharmonia Orchestra of London, flutist Jean-Pierre Rampal, Tokyo String Quartet, Philippe Entremont with the Vienna Chamber Orchestra. **Towns:** Altenhof, Bad Segeberg, Bordesholm, Eutin, Flensburg, Föhr, Glücksburg, Hamburg, Hasselburg, Heide, Husum, Itzehoe, Kiel, Lübeck, Lüneburg, Meldorf, Neumünster, Norderstedt, Plön, Reinbek, Rellingen, Rendsburg, Salzau, Schleswig, Schönau, Westerland, Wotersen. **Performances:** 180.

SCHWÄBISH GMÜND (Baden–Württemberg)
150 miles SE of Frankfurt

The 3 summits of nearby Kaiserberge rise above Schwäbish Gmünd, renowned for its gold- and silversmiths. The metal industry is the mainstay of the economy, which is also fed by glass and jewelry making. The market square is of predominantly baroque design, though a number of medieval half-timbered buildings have been well-preserved.

FESTIVALS

European Church Music

2 Months	Europäische Kirchenmusik
Early July–Early September	Tourist Office
	Postfach 1960
Org, Chor, Cham, Rec, Orch,	D-7070 Schwäbisch Gmünd
Sem, Comp	Tel: 07171/60 34 15

The rich repertoire of sacred music composed before the seventeenth century is thoroughly explored here in many hallowed environs. The organ is featured, and along with choirs and small ensembles, engaging programs are offered in this city, which has been associated with church music since the High Middle Ages, when a school was founded here. The venues listed here are always used, but many smaller churches are sometimes included. **Recent Performers:** Deller Consort of London, Stuttgart Radio Symphony Orchestra. **Venues:** Holy Cross Minster, St. John's Church, Augustinian Church. **Performances:** 30 evenings.

STUTTGART (Baden-Württemberg)
90 miles S of Frankfurt

Situated in the lush Swabian Hills, Stuttgart is both a cultural and industrial center, equally famous for renowned ballet and opera companies and for industries such as Mercedes-

Benz, which makes its headquarters here. More than half of Stuttgart is devoted to parks and vineyards, and the Old Town is a pleasant plaza of shops and galleries dominated by the Old Palace, a magnificent mix of Gothic and Renaissance architecture.

FESTIVALS

J. S. Bach Summer Academy

3 Weeks	Sommer Akademie J. S. Bach
Mid-August–Early September	Internationale Bachakademie Stuttgart
Rec, Cham, Chor, Orch, Sem, Org	Johann Sebastian Bach Platz D-7000 Stuttgart 1 Tel: 0711/6 19 21 32 Fax: 0711/6 19 21 23

"The contemplation of music" is the mission of this specialized festival, which combines performances with extensive courses. Founded in 1979, the Academy is geared toward professional performers and historians as well as the general public. The repertoire extends beyond Bach to include works by Couperin, Berg, and Brahms. **Recent Performers:** tenor Peter Schreier, Cleveland Quartet, Stuttgart Chamber Orchestra. **Venues:** Liederhalle, Stiftskirche, Leonhardskirche, Neues Schloss, St. Eberhard Church. **Performances:** several daily.

ONGOING EVENTS

International Bach Academy

Orch, Chor, Cham, Rec, Sem	Internationale Bachakademie Stuttgart Johann Sebastian Bach Platz D-7000 Stuttgart 1 Tel: 0711/6 19 32 Fax: 0711/6 19 23

The Academy was founded in 1981 by Helmuth Rilling "to promote and network Bach research worldwide." It manages three resident ensembles: the Gächinger Kantorei, the Bach Collegium, and the Stuttgart Chamber Orchestra. Named for the small village in the Swabian Alps where it was founded in 1954, the Gächinger Kantorei is an *a cappella* choir that has been called the "Stradivarius of choirs." Its instrumental counterpart is the Bach Collegium, established in 1965. The third company is the Stuttgart Chamber Orchestra, founded by Karl Münchinger in 1945. This last ensemble has won international recognition through its many recordings and since 1986 has been associated with the Academy. The Italian Renaissance headquarters of the Academy once housed a publishing house and now contains a modern concert hall, library, administrative offices, and practice rooms.

Lieder Hall

Orch

Liederhalle
Schickhardtstrasse 5
D-7000 Stuttgart 1
Tel: 0711/640 7534
Fax: 0711/649 3535

Rebuilt in 1955-56, Stuttgart's chief concert hall is a modern composite of glazed brick, quartz, and mosaic. This is the home of the Stuttgart Philharmonic, whose programs have recently included Mozart symphonies, Rossini's *Stabat Mater*, and a Bartók piano concerto. **Recent Performers:** Beaux Arts Trio, pianist Rudolf Buchbinder. **Performances:** 70; September–July (Philharmonic only).

State Theater

Op, Orch, Dance, Th

Staatstheater
Postfach 10 43 45
D-7000 Stuttgart 10
Tel: 0711/22 17 95

Expect fresh, bold opera, drama, and ballet here in the city that has been called "the home of European avant-garde music." Opera repertoire includes works by Philip Glass, Niccolo Jommeli, and Hans Werner Henze in addition to many by Mozart and Wagner. The Stuttgart State Orchestra offers six concerts between October and July. Tickets may be bought 10 days before a performance. **Recent Productions:** *Elektra, Tosca*, Philip Glass's *Einstein on the Beach*. **Performances:** nearly daily; September-July.

IN THE AREA

Sindelfingen City Hall

Op, Orch, Cham, Dance, Th, Child

Stadthalle
Tourist Office
P.O. Box 180
D-7032 Sindelfingen
Tel: 07031/94 322
Fax: 07031/94 787

When confronted with the soaring plate glass facade of this modern convention center 8 miles SW of Stuttgart, one might not expect the classic programs or the international artists that appear within. Rebuilt in 1989, the City Hall hosts an ambitious and varied season of instrumental music, theater, and opera in its Grand Hall. **Recent productions:** Mozart's *Marriage of Figaro,* Tchaikovsky's "Nutcracker," Shakespeare's *All's Well That Ends Well.* **Recent performers:** Academy of St. Martin in the Fields, hornist Barry Tuckwell, trumpeter Hakan Hardenberger. **Performances:** 40; November–May.

ULM (Baden-Württemberg)
130 miles SE of Frankfurt

Perched along the Danube where it meets the River Blau, Ulm's strategic location has allowed the town to prosper since the Middle Ages. Dominating the picturesque city is the towering spire of Ulm Minster, which, at 530 feet, is one of the world's highest. Ulm was the birthplace of Albert Einstein.

ONGOING EVENTS

Ulm Theater

Op, Orch, Cham, Th, Dance, Child	Ulmer Theater Olgastrasse 73 D-7900 Ulm Tel: 0731/161 4400 Fax: 0731/137

On 17 Aug 1641 the Ulm Theater staged its first production, and despite the ravages of many wars, the show has gone on through four centuries. Ulm is the oldest established theater in Germany, and today at least eight opera productions, eight drama productions, and three ballets are offered each season along with chamber and symphony concerts by the Orchestra of the City of Ulm. **Recent productions:** *Aida, Hansel and Gretel, Evita.* **Performances:** nearly daily; September-June. Tickets may be bought 20 days before a performance, although most performances have free admission.

IN THE AREA

Society for Art and Culture

Rec, Orch, Th, Ex, Lec, Child	Gesellschaft für Kunst und Kultur Karlstrasse 26 D-7480 Sigmaringen Tel: 07571/13081

Thirty miles SW of Ulm, the imposing Sigmaringen Castle literally grows out of the cliff rock, commanding a stretch of the Danube flowing below. This is the dramatic setting for several of the concerts sponsored by the Society for Art and Culture, which has organized innovative cultural offerings since 1949 that combine art exhibitions, chamber music, children's theater, and symphony concerts. **Recent Performers:** Melos Quartet, Bodensee Symphony Orchestra. **Venues:** Sigmaringen Castle, City Hall, Old School. **Performances:** 21; September–November, January–June.

WIESBADEN (Hesse)
20 miles W of Frankfurt

Rivaled in Germany only by Baden-Baden, Wiesbaden is one of Europe's most elegant spa-resort towns, offering over 26 nurturing hot springs. Lying at the foot of the rolling Taunus hills, the town's lush surroundings attract an elite clientele, and an abundance of cultural activities is provided to entertain residents and visitors alike. Wiesbaden is the capital of the province of Hesse and as such is the center for many arts organizations, including the German Film Industry. The Tourist Office publishes a comprehensive semiannual listing of classical concerts in churches and mansions throughout Wiesbaden.

FESTIVALS

International May Festival

1 Month	Internationalen Maifestspiele
May	Hessisches Staatstheater
	Wiesbaden
Op, Orch, Rec, Dance, Th	Postfach 32 47
	D-6200 Wiesbaden l
	Tel: 06121/13 21
	(Tuesday–Friday, 11A.M.–
	1:30 P.M.; Saturday–Sun-
	day, 11 A.M.–12:30 P.M.,
	information only)
	Fax: 06121/132337

Founded in 1896, the International May Festival is the second oldest music festival in western Germany, for only the Bayreuth Festival has a longer history. The focus on international artists was underscored when in 1950 the first post-war program proclaimed "what is separated by the word is joined by music." This sentiment remains at the heart of the festival today, as artists from all parts of the world appear in works such as Verdi's *Rigoletto,* Mussorgsky's *Khovantschina,* and Mahler's Symphony no. 2. **Recent Performers:** Berlin Opera, Bolshoi Ballet, Budapest Katona Theater. **Venue:** Hesse State Theater. **Performances:** 40. Only written ticket requests are accepted.

Wiesbaden Bach Weeks

3 Weeks
Mid-November–Early
   December

Wiesbadener Bachwochen
Bernhard-Schwarz Strasse 25
D-6200 Wiesbaden

Op, Chor, Rec, Cham, Org

Music by Bach is the focus here, but the programs also offer works by his contemporaries. Organ music is especially emphasized in this program, which began in 1981. **Recent Performers:** Wiesbaden Bach Choir, Musica Alta Ripa Hanover. **Venues:** Kurhaus, Lutherkirche, Bergkirche, Marktkirche, Christopheruskirche. **Performances:** 23.

ONGOING EVENTS

Henkell Champagne Cellar

Cham

Sektkellerei Henkell
Biebricher Allee 142
D-6200 Wiesbaden
Tel: 0611/63218
Fax: 0611/63350

Performances are held in the entrance hall of this elegant mansion, which is the headquarters of Henkell Trocken, Germany's renowned sparkling wine. Since 1983 young winners of national and international awards have performed pieces such as a Pierné flute sonata, a Verdi string quartet, or Paganini violin caprices. Gracefully decorated with red Greek marble and green English floor tiles, the Marble Hall is actually the entrance to the stairway that leads down 7 floors to the cellars. Free Henkell champagne is served at intermission. **Recent Performers:** Cologne Sinfonietta, Domus Piano Quartet London. **Venue:** Marble Hall. **Performances:** 8; evenings; September–April.

Kurhaus

Orch, Cham, Rec

Kurhaus Wiesbaden
D-6200 Wiesbaden
Tel: 06121/31 81 65

Situated by the healing springs of Wiesbaden (which means "baths in the meadow"), the imposing Kurhaus was reopened in 1987 as a convention and concert center. The warm apricot and gold decor of the Friedrich von Thiersch Concert Hall provides an elegant setting for music of Mozart, Bach, Chopin, and Schubert. During the summer, concerts are also given in the Kurpark ("Spa Park"), where fireworks illuminate the evening. **Recent Performers:** Virtuosi Saxoniae, Linos Ensemble. **Performances:** September–April.

Hesse State Theater

Op, Cham, Dance, Th, Child

Hessiches Staatstheater
 Wiesbaden
Christian Zais Strasse 1-5
Postfach 32 47
D-6200 Wiesbaden
Tel: 06121/1 32 1

Together with the adjacent Kurhaus, this 1890s structure is the center of Wiesbaden's cultural life. Opera and ballet are presented in the lavish 1041-seat Large House, and theater and children's programs are given in the Small House (seating 328) and Studio (seating 89), built in the 1950s. Chamber concerts are given in the neo-baroque foyer, where the decor features intricate traceries and vibrant colors. **Performances:** 100; September–May. Tickets are available 4 weeks in advance.

IN THE AREA

Rhinegau Music Festival

2 Months
Late June–Late August

Orch, Cham, Rec

Rheingau Musik Festival
Kartenvorverkauf im
 Carsch-Haus
Kirchgasse 28
D-6200 Wiesbaden
Tel: 0611/376 444 or
 304 808
Fax: 0611/599 895

Renowned chamber ensembles and soloists are featured during this festival held in castles, abbeys, and towns throughout the Rhine valley. Baroque music is emphasized in such memorable sites as the pristine twelfth-century Eberbach Cloister Church, Wiesbaden's landmark Market Church, and Metternich's Johannisberg Mansion. **Recent Performers:** Moscow Virtuosos, Dresden Baroque Soloists, tenor Peter Schreier. **Performances:** 40; evenings.

WÜRZBURG (Bavaria)
60 miles SE of Frankfurt

This magnificent baroque city, the first of many along Germany's famous "Romantic Road," is known for its majestic Marienburg Fortess, perched above the Main River. The Franconian Museum of the Main is housed here, and its holdings include a collection of sixteenth-century sculpture by "the Master of Würzburg," Tilman Riemenschneider. Würzburg is surrounded by Germany's largest vineyards, and it is the center of wine production for the region of Franconia.

FESTIVALS

Festival Summer Concerts in the Court Church

6 Days	Festliche Sommerkonzerte
Mid-August	in der Hofkirche
	Kerzenleite 26
Orch, Cham, Rec	D-8707 Veitshöchheim
	Tel: 0931/917 06

Since 1977 concerts featuring baroque and classical music have been held in the church of the Residenz, the palatial eighteenth-century home of the area's prince-bishops. **Venue:** Residenz Church. **Performances:** evenings.

Würzburg Bach Days

10 Days	Würzburger Bachtage
Late November–Early	Hofstallstrasse 5
December	D-8700 Würzburg
	Tel: 0931/522 41
Chor, Cham, Org	

The master of the baroque—Johann Sebastian Bach—is celebrated in Würzburg with a festival featuring his work.

Local artists present an ample program of baroque music with a few later composers also included. Expect to hear everything from oratorio to string suites to organ fantasias. **Venues:** St. Johann Church, Academy of Music, Residenz. **Performances:** daily; evenings and matinees.

Würzburg Mozart Festival

1 Month	Mozartfest
June	Haus zum Falken
	D-8700 Würzburg
Op, Orch, Cham, Rec	Tel: 0931/3 73 36

International artists lend polish and well-planned programs lend substance to this pleasing homage to Mozart. Founded in 1922, this festival, like the Bach Days held later in the year (see preceding), makes use of the spectacular eighteenth-century residence of Prince-Bishop Johann Franz von Schönborn. *Courvoisiers* has listed this festival among the world's ten best music festivals. All music heard here is by Mozart. **Recent Performers:** Herbert Blomstedt conducting the Bamberg Symphony Orchestra, Prague Chamber Orchestra, pianists Alicia de Larrocha and Rudolf Buchbinder. **Venues:** Residenz, Imperial Hall and Garden, Opera House. **Performances:** 28; evenings and matinees.

ONGOING EVENTS

Academy of Music Master Concerts

Orch, Cham, Rec	Hochschule für Musik
	Meisterkonzerte
	Hofstallstrasse 6-8
	D-8700 Würzburg
	Tel: 0931/506 41

Sponsored by the conservatory of music in Würzburg, these concerts draw well-known artists to participate in both chamber music and orchestral programs. **Recent Performers:** Stockholm Sinfonietta, Cherubini Quartet, tenor Peter Schreier.

Main-Franconian Museum Concerts

Orch, Cham	Mainfrankisches Museums-
	konzerte
	Festung Mareinberg
	D-8700 Würzburg
	Tel: 0931/430 16

Chamber music is performed by candlelight in the Knight's Hall and Schönborn Hall of the Main-Franconian Museum, which is housed in the medieval Marienberg Fortress. **Recent Performers:** Leopold Quartet, South German Vocal Ensemble.

Würzburg City Theater

Op, Orch

Stadttheater Würzburg
Theaterstrasse 21
D-8700 Würzburg
Tel: 0931/58686

A wide selection of operas and plays is offered during this theater's extremely busy season. The City Philharmonic Orchestra plays for the operas and gives four concerts with programs emphasizing nineteenth-century German composers. **Recent Productions:** *Carmen, Don Giovanni,* Kern's *Show Boat.* **Venues:** City Theater, Academy of Music (symphony). **Performances:** 450; September–July.

XANTEN (North Rhineland-Westphalia)
150 miles NW of Frankfurt

This ancient town on the Rhine River is said to have been the birthplace of Siegfried, hero of the *Niebelungenlied* and Wagner's *Ring* Cycle. Efforts are being made to reconstruct the town's Roman heritage, and an amphitheater and inn are already in place in the Archeological Park. The city itself is dominated by the imposing thirteenth-century Gothic Cathedral of St. Victor. The Tourist Office publishes a list of events.

FESTIVALS

Summer Festival in the Archeological Park

4 Days
August

Op

Sommerfestspiele im
Archaologischen Park
Tourist Office
Karthaus 2
Postfach 11 64
D-4232 Xanten 1
Tel: 02801/37 2 38
Fax: 02801/37 2 09

The cries of Roman gladiators have long been silent, but since 1983 the soaring melodies of nineteenth-century opera have filled this amphitheater. By a twist of fate, modern Xanten developed adjacent to a Roman frontier outpost, so when excavations began in the twentieth century, an intact ancient Roman city was unearthed—the only one north of the Alps. The amphitheater seats 3000 and is uncovered.   **Venue:** Roman Amphitheater.   **Performances:** 4; evenings.

GREECE

Herod Atticus Theatre, Athens (courtesy of the Greek National Tourist Organization).

GREECE

CALENDAR

JUNE

Athens Festival, **Athens**
Patras International Festival, **Patras**

JULY

Athens Festival, **Athens**
Patras International Festival, **Patras**

AUGUST

Athens Festival, **Athens**
Patras International Festival, **Patras**

SEPTEMBER

Athens Festival, **Athens**

The international telephone country code for Greece is (011) 30. City codes have the prefix 0, which is deleted when calling from abroad.

ATHENS

Although incessant traffic jams and a permanent cloud of pollution indicate that Athens is, indeed, of this century, the profound presence of the ancient monuments diverts one's attention from the adverse elements of this age. The Corinthian columns of the Temple of Olympian Zeus, the compelling Hadrian's Arch, and the sixth century B.C. Theater of Dionysus are awesome testaments to the beginning of western literature, drama, philosophy, and spirituality. And rising above the urban sprawl is the glorious Acropolis, commanding the rapt attention of all visitors who behold it. It is from here, when the air is tinted mauve by the Mediterranean morning sun, that Athens seems to glow under the rose-colored fingertips of Dawn.

FESTIVALS

Athens Festival

4 Months	Athens Festival Box Office
June–September	4, Stadiou Street
	GR-10564 Athens
Op, Orch, Chor, Cham, Rec,	Tel: 01/323 0049
Org, Th, Dance	Fax: 01/322 4148

The ancient 5000-seat amphitheater at the foot of Athens' Acropolis is the site of this festival, which has drawn artists and audiences from all over the world since 1955. Operas are presented by companies such as the Kirov of Leningrad and the National Opera of Greece, with productions including Tchaikovsky's *Queen of Spades* and Donizetti's *Maria Stuarda*. Orchestral music favors the nineteenth century, while chamber music tends toward the contemporary. An especially rich offering of dance features companies such as the Bolshoi, Hamburg, Paris Opera, and Royal Danish Ballet companies. The concurrent Epidaurus Festival offers classical drama in that city's equally ancient (and much larger) amphitheater. **Recent Performers:** Zubin Mehta conducting the New York Philharmonic Orchestra, the Academy of St. Martin in the Fields, Pierre Boulez conducting the Ensemble Intercontemporaine, Martha Graham Dance Company. **Venues:** Odeon of Herodes Atticus. **Performances:** Nearly 60.

ONGOING EVENTS

National Lyric Opera

Op

National Lyric Opera
59 Academias Street
Athens
Tel: 01/361 2461

The sole opera company in Greece, the National Lyric Opera presents a season of international operas, giving special attention to the works of Greek composers. In addition to its regular season, the company performs during the Athens festival from June to September. **Performances:** Mid-October–April.

PATRAS
120 miles W of Athens

Laid out in an attractive pattern of neoclassical squares and arcades, Patras is Greece's third-largest city and its largest western port. The cathedral contains the silver-mounted skull of St. Andrew, who was crucified on this site. Few ancient monuments are left in Patras, although the Roman Odeion and the city's Archeological museum are both impressive.

FESTIVALS

Patras International Festival

2 Months
Late June–Mid-August

Orch, Chor, Cham, Jazz,
Dance, Th, Film, Ex,
Sem

Patras International Festival
P.O. Box 1184
GR-26110 Patras
Tel: 061/336 390
Fax: 061/332 578

This highly imaginative festival has grown rapidly since its inception in 1985, and is now one of the longest and most diverse in Europe. One central theme—"Freedom and the Arts," "The Myth of Europe" to give two recent examples—is explored through music, theater, dance, film, and the visual arts. Events make use of sites that represent centuries of history, including the ancient amphitheater, medieval castles, a nineteenth-century industrial complex, and a twentieth-century mansion. The music ranges from Dowland to Dvořák to the works of Greece's most gifted young composers, with performers ranging from solo guitarist to symphony orchestra. **Recent Performers:** Warsaw Sinfonia conducted by Yehudi Menuhin, soprano Victoria de los Angeles, trumpeter Wynton Marsalis, singer Joan Baez.   **Venues:** Ancient Amphitheater, Castle of Patras, Castle of Rion, Municipal Gallery, Barry Warehouse, National Stadium, boats (!), and squares.   **Performances:** 30.

IRELAND

Harpist at the Knappogue Castle (courtesy of the Irish Tourist Board).

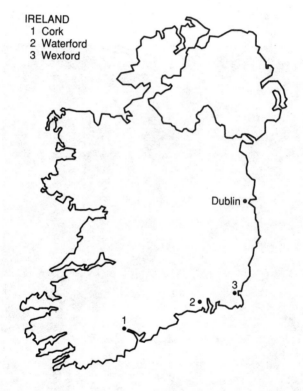

IRELAND
1 Cork
2 Waterford
3 Wexford

Dublin

CALENDAR

APRIL

Cork International Choral Festival, **Cork**

MAY

Cork International Choral Festival, **Cork**

SEPTEMBER

Waterford International Festival of Light Opera, **Waterford**

OCTOBER

Wexford Opera Festival, **Wexford**

NOVEMBER

Wexford Opera Festival, **Wexford**

The international telephone country code for Ireland is (011) 353. City codes have the prefix 0, which is dropped when dialing from abroad.

CORK
130 miles SW of Dublin

Spanning the River Lee in the south of Ireland, Cork is a cultural center with drama, film, and choral festivals on its annual calendar. Pubs, boutiques, and restaurants abound here, and the city is in the vicinity of some of Ireland's most historic sites. The most popular side trip from Cork is to Blarney Castle, where the legendary Blarney Stone is said to bring everlasting eloquence to those who kiss it.

FESTIVALS

Cork International Choral Festival

4 Days	Cork International Choral
Late April–Early May	Festival
	P.O. Box 68
Orch, Chor, Rec, Dance, Ex	Cork, Ireland
	Tel: 021/312296

Since 1954 this festival has championed the very special repertoire of choral music, sponsoring national and international competitions that range from school groups to professional ensembles. A seminar on contemporary choral music encourages the awareness and appreciation of new music, and gala concerts are given both at lunchtime and in the evenings. **Venues:** Cork City Hall, plus other locations throughout the city. **Performances:** 4 main, evening gala concerts, other shorter daytime performances; events daily.

ONGOING EVENTS

Cork Orchestral Society

Orch, Chor, Cham, Rec

Cork Orchestral Society
Pro Musica
Oliver Plunkett Street
Cork

This series of concerts has brought major symphony orchestras and chamber music groups to Cork since the 1950s. Music from the classical era through the present day is programmed, including newly commissioned works. **Recent Performers:** Cork Symphony Orchestra, RTE Symphony Orchestra, RTE Vanbrugh String Quartet, Cork Brass Trio. **Venues:** City Hall, Aula Maxima, University College of Cork, St. Francis' Church, St. Fin Barre's Cathedral. **Performances:** 18; at 8:00 P.M. several matinees.

DUBLIN

In a country that prides itself on friendly small villages and vast sheep-covered meadows, Dublin is an appropriately genial urban capital. Its modern buildings blend nicely with the lovely Georgian houses and squares that are the city's trademark, and the fashionable Grafton Street area features enough boutiques, galleries, and cafes to keep one busy for days. In the center of Dublin is St. Stephen's Green, a 22-acre park complete with swans, weeping willows, and a pond. All of the stories about Dublin's pubs are true—pubs are the center of social activity not only here, but throughout the country, and there is simply no better place to get to know the Irish.

ONGOING EVENTS

Gaiety Theatre

Op, Orch, Rec, Dance, Th

Gaiety Theatre
South King Street
Dublin 2
Tel: 01/77 17 17
Fax: 01/77 19 21

Refurbished in 1984, this grand, Victorian theater presents a wide range of entertainment, from opera and drama productions to business conferences and large-scale fashion shows.

National Symphony Orchestra of Ireland

Orch, Chor

National Symphony Orchestra of Ireland
National Concert Hall
Earlsford Terrace
Dublin 2
Tel: 01/711533

Inaugurated in January 1990, this exciting new orchestra was created to serve audiences throughout Ireland. The ensemble presents a wide range of repertoire, touching upon both the best-loved and the lesser-known compositions of the orchestral literature, and has invited soloists and guest conductors of prominent standing. **Recent Performers:** principal conductor George Hurst, conductors Sir Charles Groves and Simon Rattle, pianist Barry Douglas. **Venues:** National Concert Hall in Dublin, and various venues throughout Ireland and Northern Ireland, including City Hall, Cork Leisureland, Galway, and Ulster Hall, Belfast. **Performances:** 160 concerts; year-round.

WATERFORD
90 miles SW of Dublin

Waterford is a rewarding destination for history buffs with an eye for a bargain. Located on the Suir River, its origins are Viking and go back to the ninth century. A highlight of the city is Reginald's Tower, built by Reginald the Dane in 1003 and now open as a museum. Best known for the crystal which bears its name, Waterford today is a growing port and capital of the South East Region of Ireland.

FESTIVALS

Waterford International Festival of Light Opera

2 Weeks
Late September

Op

Waterford International Festival of Light Opera
60 Morrissons Avenue
Waterford
Tel: 051/75437

Conceived in 1959, the Waterford Festival was designed exclusively for the amateur operatic societies of England, Scotland, Wales, Northern Ireland, the Republic of Ireland, and the United States, and is the only one of its kind. Both the spirit of competition and the love of light opera bring these societies together, and the festival's hospitality has contributed to its fame and success. Capacity crowds are drawn to the intimate Theatre Royal, and patrons may also enjoy the many fringe events which take place throughout Waterford. **Venue:** Theatre Royal Waterford. **Performances:** 16; evenings.

WEXFORD
70 miles S of Dublin

The Vikings gave Wexford its name ("harbor of the mud flats") when they settled the hilly terrain by the Slaney River in 850. A penitent Henry II of England came to Wexford in 1170 following the murder of Thomas à Becket. Now a soaring church spire rises above narrow streets that slope down to the harbor, where brightly colored fishing boats are reflected in the calm waters.

FESTIVALS

Wexford Opera Festival

3 Weeks	Wexford Opera Festival
Late October–Mid-November	Theatre Royal
	High Street
Op, Cham, Rec, Th, Fringe	Wexford
	Tel: 053/22144
	Fax 053/24289

Those who enjoy hearing less familiar repertoire will be drawn to the Wexford Festival, which is famed for its productions of lesser-known works by composers past and present. The three productions mounted each year are as notable for their diversity as for their relative obscurity—a recent season featured Boieldieu's *La Dame Blanche*, Leoncavallo's *Zaza*, and Nicholas Maw's *The Rising of the Moon*, commissioned for the 1970 Glyndebourne Festival. In addition, there are lunchtime concerts, afternoon recitals, late night revues, and opera scenes. A fringe program offers concerts, theater, parades, and fireworks. **Venue:** 550-seat Theatre Royal. **Performances:** 18; evenings.

ITALY

Verona Arena (courtesy of the Italian Government Travel Office).

ITALY

1 Aosta
2 Asolo
3 Bergamo

14 Martina Franca
15 Modena

22 Piacenza
23 Primervo
24 Ravello
25 Ravenna
26 Reggio Emilia
27 Rimini
28 Riva del Garda
29 Salerno
30 Savona
31 Sermonetta
32 Siena
33 Spoleto
34 Stresa
35 Taormina
36 Torre del Lago
   Puccini
37 Trieste
38 Turin

4 Bologna
5 Brescia
6 Cagliari
7 Como
8 Cortina
  d´ Ampezzo
9 Cremona
10 Fermo
11 Fiesole
12 Genoa
13 Latina

16 Montepulciano
17 Naples
18 Orta San Giulio
19 Palermo
20 Parma
21 Pesaro

39 Verona
40 Vicenza

CALENDAR

APRIL

Florence May Music Festival, **Florence** (Tuscany)
International Piano Festival of Brescia and Bergamo, **Bergamo**
(Lombardy)

MAY

Florence May Music Festival, **Florence** (Tuscany)
International Piano Festival of Brescia and Bergamo, **Bergamo**
(Lombardy)
Song of the Stones, **Como** (Lombardy)

JUNE

Cusius Festival of Early Music, **Orta San Giulio** (Piedmont)
Festival of Two Worlds, **Spoleto** (Umbria)
Florence May Music Festival, **Florence** (Tuscany)
International Music Weeks, **Naples** (Campania)
Music in the Courtyards, **Milan** (Lombardy)
Music in the Museums, see **Venice** (Venetia)
Musica in Villa, **Milan** (Lombardy)
Operetta Festival, **Trieste** (Friuli-Venezia Giulia)
Pontino Festival, see **Rome** (Latium)
Salerno Festival, **Salerno** (Campagnia)
Song of the Stones, **Como** (Lombardy)

JULY

Aosta Art and Music, **Aosta** (Valle d'Aosta)
Baths of Caracalla, **Rome** (Latium)
Concerts on the Capitoline Hill, **Rome** (Latium)
Estate Musicale Chigiana, **Siena** (Tuscany)
Fermo Festival, **Fermo** (The Marches)
Festival of Two Worlds, **Spoleto** (Umbria)
Florence May Music Festival, **Florence** (Tuscany)
Music in the Courtyards, **Milan** (Lombardy)
Music in the Museums, see **Venice** (Venetia)
Musica in Villa, **Milan** (Lombardy)
Musica per Velia, **Salerno** (Campagnia)
Musica Riva, **Riva del Garda** (Trentino-Alto Adige)
Operetta Festival, **Trieste** (Friuli-Venezia Giulia)
Pontino Festival, see **Rome** (Latium)
Puccini Festival, **Torre del Lago Puccini** (Tuscany)
Ravello Music Festival, **Ravello** (Campagnia)
Ravenna Festival, **Ravenna** (Emilia-Romagna)
Salerno Festival, **Salerno** (Campagnia)

Summer in Fiesole, see **Florence** (Tuscany)
Taormina Arte, **Taormina** (Sicily)
Valle d'Itria Festival, **Martina Franca** (Apulia)
Verona Arena, **Verona** (Venetia)

AUGUST

Aosta Art and Music, **Aosta** (Valle d'Aosta)
Asolo and Cortina Chamber Music Festival, **Asolo** (Venetia)
Baths of Caracalla, **Rome** (Latium)
Estate Musicale Chigiana, **Siena** (Tuscany)
Fermo Festival, **Fermo** (The Marches)
International Meeting Place for the Arts, see **Siena** (Tuscany)
Malatestiana Music Festival, **Rimini** (Emilia-Romagna)
Musical September, **Turin** (Piedmont)
Operetta Festival, **Trieste** (Friuli-Venezia Guilia)
Puccini Festival, **Torre del Lago Puccini** (Tuscany)
Ravenna Festival, **Ravenna** (Emilia-Romagna)
Rossini Opera Festival, **Pesaro** (The Marches)
Salerno Festival, **Salerno** (Campagnia)
Siena Music Week, **Siena** (Tuscany)
Stresa Music Weeks, **Stresa** (Piedmont)
Summer in Fiesole, see **Florence** (Tuscany)
Taormina Arte, **Taormina** (Sicily)
Valle d'Itria Festival, **Martina Franca** (Apulia)
Verona Arena, **Verona** (Venetia)

SEPTEMBER

Asolo and Cortina Chamber Music Festival, **Asolo** (Venetia)
Autumn Music Festival, **Como** (Lombardy)
Baroque Music Concerts, **Bergamo** (Lombardy)
Cremona Festival, **Cremona** (Lombardy)
Donizetti and His Age, **Bergamo** (Lombardy)
Malatestiana Music Festival, **Rimini** (Emilia-Romagna)
Musical September, **Turin** (Piedmont)
Musical September on San Giulio, **Orta San Giulio**
   (Piedmont)
Song of the Stones, **Como** (Lombardy)
Stresa Music Weeks, **Stresa** (Piedmont)
Taormina Arte, **Taormina** (Sicily)
Verdi Festival, **Parma** (Emilia-Romagna)

OCTOBER

Autumn Music Festival, **Como** (Lombardy)
Baroque Music Concerts, **Bergamo** (Lombardy)

Donizetti and His Age, **Bergamo** (Lombardy)
Rendez-vous with New Music, **Brescia** (Lombardy)
Song of the Stones, **Como** (Lombardy)

The international telephone country code for Italy is
(011) 39. City codes have the prefix 0, which is dropped when
calling from abroad.

AOSTA (Valle d'Aosta)
480 miles NW of Rome

Aosta is the capital of the Valle d'Aosta, a region that rewards
the traveler with breathtaking views of the towering Alpine
peaks, including Mont Blanc and the Matterhorn. The town
was founded by the Romans in 25 B.C. and became a major
trading post on the route between Italy and France. Aosta's
street layout is identical to the original Roman plan, and
centuries of history are reflected in its buildings, including
the Arch of Augustus (constructed in the year of the city's
founding), the Pretorian Gate, an ancient Roman theater of
which sections still remain, and the tenth-century Church of
Sant'Orso. Aosta is considered the gateway to the Gran Paradiso National Park.

FESTIVALS

Art and Music

6 Weeks	Arte e Musica
Mid-July–Late August	Tourist Information Office
	Piazza Chanoux 8
Orch, Cham, Rec, Org,	11100 Aosta
Dance	Tel: 0165/236154
	Fax: 0165/34657

This program brings together quasi-autonomous festivals
of classical music, jazz, and fine arts, as well as an international festival for organ. A multifaceted "happening," this
unique event began as an experiment in the mid-1980s and
has become well established in the 1990s. **Recent Performers:** Leningrad Symphony Orchestra, Vienna String Sextet,
Pro Musica Antiqua, Manhattan Transfer. **Venues:** Arena
Croix Noire di Aosta, Church of Aosta, Teatro Giacosa, Teatro
Romano. **Performances:** 17; 2 weekly.

ONGOING EVENTS

Cultural Season

Orch, Chor, Cham, Rec, Th, Film	Saison Culturelle Assessorato della Pubblica Istruzione Piazza Deffeyes, 1 11100 Aosta Tel: 0165/35655 Fax: 0165/236200

Music, theater, and special artists such as mime Marcel Marceau are all part of the active cultural season in this region of Italy. Both native and visiting musicians perform in concerts ranging from the panpipe to Puccini. **Recent Performers:** Choir and Orchestra of the University of Paris–Sorbonne, Aosta Chamber Orchestra, Crakow Chamber Orchestra, pianist Andrei Gavrilov. **Venues:** Théâtre Giacosa, Eglise Collégiale de Sante-Ours, Auditorium of Pont-Saint-Martin. **Performances:** about 70; October–June.

ASOLO (Venetia)
370 miles N of Rome

A castle presides over this attractive small town where fresco-covered palaces line the streets. The town charmed Robert Browning, who spent time here, and was the birthplace of actress Eleonora Duse.

FESTIVALS

Asolo and Cortina Chamber Music Festival

3 Weeks	Asolo Musica
Mid-August–Early September	«Casa Pase»
	Via Browning 141
Cham	31011 Asolo
	Tel: 0423/950150

The rich musical heritage of Venetia serves as the inspiration for this young festival, which presents concerts in both Asolo and Cortina. From its beginning in 1979, this program has taken very seriously its mission of presenting the very best, and its offerings justify the pride of its organizers. This is an ideal setting in which to hear the masterworks of the chamber repertoire. **Recent Performers:** Salzburger Soloisten, cellist Yo-Yo Ma, I Virtuosi di Roma. **Venue:** Church of San Gottardo in Asolo, Hotel Savoia in Cortina. **Performances:** 9; all at 9 or 9:30 P.M.

BERGAMO (Lombardy)
375 miles NW of Rome

Set in the Alpine foothills of Lombardy, Bergamo is an unusual town divided into two levels, the modern, commercial lower city and the walled, medieval upper city. The narrow streets and gracious piazzas of Old Bergamo are lined with medieval and Renaissance buildings that recall a rich heritage. The lower city draws visitors to the splendid Carrara Academy, one of Italy's finest museums. Bergamo was the birthplace of Gaetano Donizetti, and both he and Bellini conducted their operas in the Teatro Ricordi, now the Teatro Donizetti. Donizetti's home is now open to the public.

FESTIVALS

Baroque Music Concerts

4 Concerts
Late September–Early
  October

Orch, Chor

Concerti di Musica
  Barocca
Azienda Autonoma di
  Turismo
Via Paleocapa, 2
24100 Bergamo
Tel: 035/24 22 26

An unusual outgrowth of the Bergamo International Piano Festival, this series of concerts has presented chamber orchestras in the monumental churches of Bergamo for nearly 20 years, all *sans* piano! Although the title promises "Baroque," these programs include choral and instrumental works of Mozart and Haydn, as well as music of such earlier masters as Vivaldi, Albinoni, and Tartini. Concerts are given in the upper town in the twelfth-century Basilica of Santa Maria Maggiore, where the interior is remarkable for its baroque ornamentation and magnificent Florentine tapestries. **Recent Performers:** I Pomeriggi Musicali di Milano, Chamber Orchestra of Padua and Venice, Chamber Orchestra of the Brescia and Bergamo International Piano Festival. **Venue:** Basilica di S. Maria Maggiore. **Performances:** all at 9 P.M.; free admission.

Donizetti and His Age

4 Weeks	Donizetti e il suo Tempo
Mid-September–Early	Teatro Donizetti
October	Piazza Cavour, 14
	24100 Bergamo
Op, Orch, Chor, Cham, Rec	Tel: 035/249631
	Fax: 035/217560

The birthplace of one of Italy's most prolific and most beloved composers, Bergamo has hosted this annual homage to Donizetti since 1982. The opera production, which is the centerpiece of the festival, also opens the annual opera season in Bergamo. Music for the church, chamber, and theater by Donizetti and his contemporaries can be heard in concerts throughout the festival. Recent productions include *Maria Stuarda* and *Elisabetta al Castello di Kenilworth* in its first modern production in Italy. **Recent Performers:** Myung-Shun Chung conducting the Maggio Musicale Fiorentino, sopranos Renata Scotto and Katia Ricciarelli. **Venues:** Teatro Donizetti, Basilica di S. Maria Maggiore, Sala Piatti, Teatro Sociale. **Performances:** 14.

International Piano Festival of Brescia and Bergamo

6 Weeks	Festival Pianistico Inter-
Mid-April–Late May	nazionale di Brescia e
	Bergamo
Orch, Rec	c/o Teatro Grande
	1-25121 Brescia
	Tel: 030/29 55 66

Both Bergamo and Brescia play host to the recitals and orchestral concerts of this 30-year-old festival. A special theme is often chosen for the festival, and a recent year's programs were devoted to the music of Beethoven. **Recent Performers:** Rafael Frübeck de Burgos conducting the Orchestra Sinfonia Varsovia with pianist Alicia de Larrocha, Aldo Ceccato directing the Bergen Philharmonic Orchestra, pianist Gerhard Oppitz. **Venues:** Teatro Donizetti in Bergamo; Teatro Grande in Brescia. **Performances:** 18 in each city.

ONGOING EVENTS

Teatro Donizetti

Op, Dance	Teatro Donizetti
	Piazza Cavour, 14
	Bergamo
	Tel: 035/249631

This theater, overlooking the grand Piazza Matteotti in the lower town, is the home of Bergamo's opera and ballet season, with productions such as Puccini's *Tosca* and Piccinni's *Cecchina ovvero La Buona Figliola*. **Performances:** 8–10 monthly; season begins in October.

BOLOGNA (Emilia-Romagna)
235 miles NW of Rome

Bologna, home of the oldest European university (founded in 1050), was settled by the Etruscans in the sixth century B.C. and has evolved with each wave of political change that has swept through this country in the course of its turbulent history. It is also the center of epicurean delights, where the original recipes for lasagna and ragu were born and where many excellent restaurants attest to its culinary heritage.

ONGOING EVENTS

Teatro Comunale

Op, Orch, Rec

Teatro Comunale
Largo Respighi 1
40126 Bologna
Tel: 051/529999
(Monday–Friday 3:30–7 P.M.,
Saturday 9:30–12:30; 3:30–7)

Not surprisingly, Verdi, Puccini, and Bellini are at the fore in the Teatro Comunale opera season, joined by Strauss, Wagner, and Vacchai. These productions also travel to other cities throughout the region of Emilia Romagna (Ravenna, Ferrara, Parma, Reggio Emilia, Modena). Orchestral concerts are given by the resident orchestra as well as guest ensembles, and programs feature renowned soloists in a well-rounded repertoire. **Recent Performers:** conductor Jeffrey Tate with the English Chamber Orchestra, Carlo Maria Giulini conducting the La Scala Philharmonic Orchestra, pianist Martha Argerich, soprano Edita Gruberova. **Performances:** 75; October–June.

BRESCIA (Lombardy)
335 miles NW of Rome

This ancient town in the northern lake district is second only to Milan in its economic importance in the province of

Lombardy. Until the eighteenth century Brescia supplied countries throughout Europe with arms and armor, leading to a prosperity that is still visible in a wealth of medieval and renaissance buildings. The Roman Museum here is home to an impressive collection of sculptures, including the revered first-century "Winged Victory." Adjoining the museum are the ancient ruins of the Capitoline Temple built in A.D. 73 by Emperor Vespasian. Brescia's proximity to Lake Garda makes day trips to the waterside a tempting possibility.

FESTIVALS

Rendez-vous with New Music

1 Month	Incontri con la nuova musica
October	Nuovi spazi sonori
	Associazione Italiana per la
Cham, Rec	Musica Contemporanea
	Via Vitt. Emanuele II, 60
	25122 Brescia
	Tel: 030/43237
	Fax: 030/43237

This young festival, founded in 1987, features contemporary music, and intersperses its chamber music concerts with conferences exploring this special genre. Performers include the winners of the Camillo Togni International Competition for Composers.   **Venue:** Pietro da Cammo Concert Hall.   **Performances:** 5–6.

ONGOING EVENTS

Teatro Grande

Op	Teatro Grande
	25122 Brescia
	Tel: 030/42400

Brescia's active opera season takes place in this theater, where the repertoire includes such lesser-known composers as Cimarosa and Facchinetti, as well as Puccini and Verdi. **Performances:** 4–6 monthly; season begins in October.

CAGLIARI (Sardinia)

Cagliari is the capital and largest city of Sardinia, the Mediterranean's second largest island. Its strategic location and its natural harbor have made it an important stop in international sea trade since the days of the Carthaginians. Sun-drenched beaches and intimate coves attract an exotic mix of international sun worshippers, who flock to the many luxurious hotels. Artistic and architectural evidence of many cultures is evident in the Old Town, the Castello, and in the National Archeological Museum.

ONGOING EVENTS

Opera Season

Op

Istituzione P.L. Da Palestrina
Piazza Porrino
Cagliari
Tel: 070/662850

The busy opera season here ranges from *Don Pasquale* and *Suor Angelica* to somewhat unexpected productions of Gluck's *Orfeo ed Euridice* and Strauss's *Salomé*. **Performances:** 8–10 monthly; season begins in November.

COMO (Lombardy)
380 miles NW of Rome

The Lombardy town of Como sits on the southern tip of Lake Como, one of Europe's deepest and most picturesque lakes. An industrial town, Como is filled with buildings attesting to longtime prosperity largely attributable to its centuries-old silk industry. This is the usual starting point for a tour of Lake Como, surrounded by magnificent villas, gardens, and cathedrals dating back to the Middle Ages.

FESTIVALS

Autumn Music Festival

4 Weeks
Early September–Early
   October

Orch, Chor, Cham, Rec, Dance

Autumno Musicale a Como
Villa Olmo Via Cantoni, 1
22100 Como
Tel: 031/571150
Fax: 031/570540

Although festivals planned around one or more chosen themes are common now, when this festival was founded in 1967 its aim for homogeneity made it something of an innovation. The careful planning is still evident today, and the diversity achieved within this context was evident in a recent season, when topics ranged from medieval music drama to Clara

Schumann. While concentrating on music, the programs often include the other performing arts, especially dance, theatre, and marionettes. Performances take advantage of Como's resplendent venues, including the gardens of villas facing the lake. **Recent Performers:** Orchestra Stradivari, Baroque Ensemble of Nice, Ravel Trio, soprano Cecilia Gasdia. **Venues:** Teatro Sociale, Villa Olmo, eleventh-century Basilica of San Carpaforo, churches in Como and surrounding area. **Performances:** 30.

Song of the Stones

8 Weekends
Mid-May–Mid-June
Mid-September–
   Mid-October

Il Canto delle Pietre
Villa Olmo Via Cantoni
22100 Como
Tel: 031/572800
Fax: 031/570540

Chor, Th

The stones in question here are those with which the magnificent holy places throughout Lombardy have been built. These churches, chapels, cathedrals, and crypts have long resounded with the choral and dramatic works associated with Christian liturgy. Reflecting on the importance of sacred structures as gathering places in medieval society, this festival explores the repertoire of the tenth to the fifteenth centuries, focusing as well on the interconnection between music, text, site, iconography, and spirituality. **Recent Performers:** Gothic Voices, Schola Hungarica, Ensemble für Frühe Musik. **Venues:** Churches throughout Lombardy, in the provinces of Bergamo, Brescia, Como, and Cremona. **Performances:** 24; Saturday and Sunday. Free; reservations suggested.

CREMONA (Lombardy)
320 miles NW of Rome

Situated in the fertile Po River plain south of Milan, Cremona has long been known for the incomparable stringed instruments made here. In the seventeenth century, such masters as Amati, Guarneri, and Stradivari crafted hundreds of violins, cellos, and other instruments, many of which are played today by the world's greatest musicians. The legacy lives on in Cremona thanks to the renowned violin-making school, Scuola Internazionale di Liuteria.

FESTIVALS

Cremona Festival

2 Weeks   Cremona Festival
Mid-September   Teatro Comunale "Amilcare
                                     Ponchielli"
Orch, Cham, Rec   C.so Vittorio Emanuele, 52
                                 26100 Cremona
                                 Tel: 0372/407273

Those who associate Cremona with the great instrument makers who flourished here will be gratified by the special attention given to stringed instruments on this festival's programs. Although the repertoire is broad, a current theme, such as a recent focus on Russian music, brings unity to the offerings. **Recent Performers:** Orchestra of St. Cecilia, Orpheus Chamber Orchestra, Takacs Quartet. **Venues:** thirteenth-century Palazzo Cittanova, Teatro Comunale Ponchielli. **Performances:** 11; evenings.

ONGOING EVENTS

Teatro Comunale Ponchielli

Op, Orch, Rec, Dance   Teatro Comunale Ponchielli
                                Piazza del Comune n.8
                                26100 Cremona
                                Tel: 0372/407273
                                (4–7 P.M.)

Painstaking renovation has returned this theater to its eighteenth-century splendor while maintaining its extraordinary acoustics. The house is ideal for the primarily Italian opera repertoire that is offered here (5 productions), as well as orchestra concerts, recitals, dance productions (4) and theater (13 plays). **Recent Performers:** pianist Jörg Demus, mezzo-soprano Brigitte Fassbaender, Martha Graham and Merce Cunningham Dance Companies. **Performances:** 70; October–May.

FERMO (The Marches)
160 miles NE of Rome

The lovely hilltop town of Fermo is graced with a historic medieval district whose jewel is a remarkable thirteenth-century

Duomo. The Plaza in front of the Cathedral affords equally magnificent views of the Adriatic to the east and the Apennine mountains to the west. Fermo is one of the cultural centers of the Marches, a diverse region whose other cities include Pesaro and Ancona.

FESTIVALS

Fermo Festival

6 Weeks	Festival di Fermo
Mid-July–Late August	Commune di Fermo
	Assessorato alla Cultura
Op, Orch, Chor, Cham	63023 Fermo

Premieres and rediscoveries are an important part of this festival, which also presents operatic and orchestral favorites. A European premiere of Varèse's *Etude pour espace*, and revivals of Paisiello's *Le Due Contesse*, Jommelli's *Don Falcone*, and Palma's *I Vampiri* were highlights of a recent season, along with *La Traviata* and major orchestral works. Also heard for the first time in over a century were choral works by Haydn, Rossini, and Cherubini. Many of the opera performances are given in the open-air theater of the Villa Vitali. **Recent Performers:** pianist Vladimir Ashkenazy conducting the Royal Philharmonic Orchestra, Lorin Maazel conducting the Orchestre da Definire. **Venues:** Teatro all'Aperto di Villa Vitali, Tempio di San Francesco, Piazza del Popolo, Palazzo Sassatelli. **Performances:** 25; all at 9:15 P.M.

FLORENCE (Tuscany)
170 miles NW of Rome

The Tuscan sun on the jewel-like walls of the Duomo and the red tile roofs of the surrounding buildings create a magic that even the twentieth-century bustle cannot dispel. Although the Medici made this city powerful, it was the artists that made it immortal. So abundant are the riches of Renaissance art in Florence that the entire city might be deemed one of Europe's most historic treasures. The city that fostered the Renaissance in painting was also the cradle for a new birth in music, for the nobles and gifted amateurs meeting together here at the end of the sixteenth century created a new art form—opera—and with it paved the way for the music we term baroque.

FESTIVALS

Florence May Music Festival

9 Weeks	Maggio Musicale Fiorentino
Late April–Early July	Biglietteria del Teatro
	Comunale
Op, Orch, Rec	Corso Italia 16
	50123 Firenze
	Tel: 055/2779236
	(Tuesday–Saturday,
	9 A.M.–1 P.M.)

Florence reverberates with the music of this renowned festival for more than two months. It would be hard to imagine a more stellar assemblage than that which gathers here to present 5 opera productions augmented by ballet, orchestra concerts, and recitals. The Festival's history goes back to 1933, and it has achieved an almost unrivaled brilliance. **Recent Performers:** tenor Luciano Pavarotti with Zubin Mehta conducting *Il Trovatore*, conductors Seiji Ozawa, Sergiu Celibidache, Carlo Maria Giulini, pianists Maurizio Pollini and Vladimir Ashkenazy. **Venues:** eighteenth-century Teatro della Pergola, Teatro Comunale, Teatro Verdi, Teatro della Compagnia, Piazza SS. Annunziata. **Performances:** 40; evenings.

ONGOING EVENTS

Teatro Comunale

Op, Orch	Teatro Comunale
	Biglietteria
	Via Solferino 15
	50123 Firenze
	Tel: 055/2779236
	(Tuesday–Saturday,
	3:30–6 P.M.)

Zubin Mehta is the principal conductor of the resident orchestra here, which also hosts guest artists of equal stature. The Teatro Comunale, Teatro Verdi, Piccolo Teatro, and Teatro della Campagnia provide varied settings for operas such as *Rigoletto* and Boito's *Mefistofele*, as well as orchestra concerts. **Recent Performers:** conductor Eduardo Mata, choreographer Rudolf Nureyev, soprano Ashley Putnam. **Performances:** more than 20 each month.

Orchestra della Toscana (O.R.T.)

Orch   Orchestra della Toscana
                              Box Office
                              Via della Pergola 10 A/r
                              Florence
                              Tel: 055/24 23 61

Founded in 1980, the O.R.T. has rapidly become a major force in the Italian musical scene. International conductors and soloists join the 45-member ensemble for concerts in the Church of San Stefano at the Ponte Vecchio, and Principal Conductor Donato Renzetti leads the orchestra in concerts throughout Italy. The diverse repertoire includes refreshingly unfamiliar works by composers such as Brahms and Busoni, as well as recent commissions. Special programs include a Sunday morning series during the autumn and a competition for young conductors. **Recent Performers:** oboist Heinz Holliger, hornist Barry Tuckwell, soprano Cecilia Gasdia. **Venue:** Church of San Stefano near the Ponte Vecchio (Florence's oldest bridge). **Performances:** 17; November–July.

Teatro della Pergola

Op, Cham, Rec, Th   Teatro della Pergola
                              Via della Pergola 12
                              50137 Firenze
                              Tel: 055/2476351
                              Fax: 055/610141

This jewel-like theater is one of the oldest in Italy. Built in 1600, the 1000-seat hall has perfect acoustics for chamber opera and chamber music, as well as for recitals and intimate theater productions.

IN THE AREA

Summer in Fiesole

2 Weeks   Estate Fiesolana
Late July–Early August   Ente Teatro Romano
                                 di Fiesole
Orch, Cham, Dance, Th   Villa La Torraccia
                              Via delle Fontanelle, 24
                              S. Dominico de Fiesole
                              50014 Firenze
                              Tel: 055/599983

Chamber music and ballet are the focus at this festival held in the first-century Roman Amphitheater and the Cloister of the Fiesole Abbey. Perched in the hills 5 miles N of Florence, the small town of Fiesole affords a welcome retreat and provides magnificent views over Florence and the Arno Valley. The festival is now in its fifth decade. **Recent Performers:** Orchestra Villa Lobos (12 cellos!), Ysäye Quartet, violinist Enzo Porta. **Venues:** Teatro Romano, Chistro della Badia Fiesolana (a former Benedictine convent rebuilt in the fifteenth century under the patronage of the Medicis). **Performances:** 14; at 9:30 or 9:45 P.M.

GENOA (Liguria)
310 miles NW of Rome

Rising up from the Gulf of Genoa, this city is Italy's largest seaport and reflects a history of maritime prosperity. Art and architectural treasures abound here, mixing nicely with the city's continuous modernization. Genoa's history is easy to trace by simply starting with its lowest point, the large medieval section that lines the harbor, then moving up to the hillsides, which are filled with dozens of Renaissance palaces. Still higher on the hills are the modern sections, lined with grand boulevards affording panoramic views of the city. Genoa is a popular point of departure for trips along the Italian Riviera.

ONGOING EVENTS

Carlo Felice Opera House

Op, Orch

Teatro dell'Opera Carlo Felice
Box Office
Via I. Frugoni 15/6
1612 Genoa
Tel: 010/5381225
Fax: 010/5381233

It is possible to hear not only operas such as *Turandot* and *Adrianna Lecouvreur* in Genoa's opera house, but also orchestral concerts that have included Mahler's Symphony no. 1. The artistic directors of this house demonstrate their interest in special programs by projects such as the 1991-92 "Columbus Season" in celebration of the 500th anniversary

of the discovery of America. **Performances:** Approx. 50;
November–June.

Teatro Comunale

Orch, Chor, Cham, Rec,
   Dance

E. A. Teatro Comunale dell'
   Opera
Ufficio Biglietteria
Via Frugoni, 15/6
16121 Genoa
Tel: 010/53811

Despite its name, this theater is home to concerts and ballet, but not to opera, which takes place in the new Carlo Felice
Opera House. Orchestral concerts offer some refreshing addi-
tions to the standard repertoire, including music by Delius,
Granados, and Ginastera. Chamber music and choral concerts are given in various Genoa churches. **Recent Performers:** conductor Antonio de Almeida, violinist Ruggiero Ricci,
baritone John Shirley-Quirk. **Performances:** 5–6 monthly;
November–June.

IN THE AREA

Teatro Chiabrera (Savona)

Op

Teatro Chiabrera
Piazza Diaz, 2
Savona
Tel: 019/820409

Expect the unexpected in this neoclassical opera house
30 miles W of Genoa, where recent productions have included Rossini's *Torvaldo e Dorliska*, G. Apollini's *L'Ebreo*,
and Luigi and Federico Ricci's *Crispino e la Comare*. **Performances:** 6–8 monthly; season begins in October.

MARTINA FRANCA (Apulia)
325 miles SE of Rome

This Apulian town midway across Italy's boot is set in the
heart of the Trulli region, named for its odd, white houses
capped by conical stone roofs. In Martina Franca itself one
can trace the influences of the Goths, Byzantines, French, and
Spanish, who all contributed to the city's lively cultural mix.
Today the town's architecture is mostly baroque, with fanciful
decorations adorning even the most modest homes.

FESTIVALS

Valle d'Itria Festival

3 Weeks   Festival della Valle d'Itria
Mid-July–Early August   Biglietteria–Palazzo Ducale
                                1-74015 Martina Franca
Op, Orch, Chor   Tel: 080/701030

Imaginative staging of lesser-known operas are the centerpiece of this festival, which mounts at least two such events each year. Recent productions include Donizetti's *La Favorita*, Piccinni's *Cecchina*, and Bizet's *Pearl Fishers*. Orchestral works such as Beethoven symphonies and choral masterpieces such as Bach's B Minor Mass are also featured. The festival dates from 1975. **Recent Performers:** Orchestra Pro Arte, Orchestra Internazionale d'Italia. **Venue:** Palazzo Ducale. **Performances:** 10; all at 9 P.M.

MILAN (Lombardy)
360 miles NW of Rome

Milan is the dynamic economic center of Northern Italy and the country's second largest city. The Duomo, Milan's majestic Gothic cathedral, dominates the city, and the world's first and probably most posh shopping arcade, the "Galleria Vittorio Emanuele," showcases Milan's elegant fashion industry. Most important to music lovers is the jewel of all European opera houses, La Scala, completed in 1778. Here in this acoustically perfect house many of the operas of Rossini, Bellini, Donizetti, Verdi, and Puccini were premiered and hailed as works of genius. Don't miss the Museo della Scala for a look at memorabilia from famous past productions.

FESTIVALS

Music in the Courtyards

6 Weeks   Musica nei Cortili
Late June–Late July   Comune di Milano
                                Settore Cultura e Spettacolo
Op, Orch, Cham   Via T. Marino 7
                                20122 Milan
                                Tel: 02/862418

Courtyards, cloisters, and piazzas resound with varied ensembles as this festival celebrates both musical and architectural treasures. In addition to outstanding Milanese ensembles such as I Pomeriggi Musicali, the series presents a diverse range of international chamber and orchestral musicians playing music from Bach to Shostakovich. The historic sites often provide a setting for music composed when the walls were erected, but just as frequently provide a stimulating contrast for more recent works. **Recent Performers:** Orchestra Stradivari, Camerata Accademica del Mozarteum di Salisburgo. **Venues:** various courtyards, cloisters, and piazzas. **Performances:** 8; all at 9 P.M.

Musica in Villa–Summer Season

2 Months	Musica in Villa
June–July	I Pomeriggi Musicali di Milano
Orch, Dance, Jazz	Via Guicciardini, 5
	20129 Milan
	Tel: 02/76 00 19 00
	Fax: 02/76 00 45 62

This series provides a unique opportunity to visit more than two dozen palatial homes and villas in and around Milan. Programs emphasize jazz and dance as well as traditional orchestral concerts by I Pomeriggi Musicali. **Recent Performers:** I Pomeriggi Musicali, Sicilian Jazz Orchestra of Palermo, Lombardy Ballet. **Performances:** 32; all at 9 P.M.

ONGOING EVENTS

I Pomeriggi Musicali di Milano

Orch, Cham	I Pomeriggi Musicali di Milano
	Via Guicciardini, 5
	20129 Milano
	Tel: 02/76001900

Since 1945 this chamber orchestra has been one of the most potent forces in the musical life of Italy. Concentrating on repertoire from the baroque to the early nineteenth century, the ensemble has been led by conductors of the stature of Riccardo Muti and Riccardo Chailly. In addition to its regular seasons in Como, Brescia, Cremona, and other cities in Lombardy, the orchestra participates in the "Musica in Villa" series, bringing concerts to nearly 30 historic homes and villas throughout this northern province. **Venue:** Milan Conservatory. **Performances:** 15–16; January–May.

Music and Poetry at S. Maurizio

Orch, Chor, Cham, Rec, Org

Musica e Poesia a San
Maurizio
Comune di Milano
Settore Cultura e
Spettacolo
Ufficio Musica
via T. Marino 7
20121 Milano
Tel: 02/862418

Some of Europe's most noted early music ensembles appear in these concerts, which focus on music of the baroque era. Although sacred vocal works such as Bach cantatas, Handel oratorios, and Monteverdi motets predominate, instrumental works by such composers as Biber, Fontana, and Castello can also be heard. **Recent Performers:** Concerto Köln, Hilliard Ensemble, flutist Frans Brüggen. **Venues:** Church of San Maurizio, twelfth-century Basilica of San Sempliciano. **Performances:** approximately 20; two weekly, March–June, September–November.

Teatro alla Scala

Op, Orch, Dance

Ufficio Biglietteria
Via Filodrammatici, 2
20121 Milano
Tel: 02/80 70 41
(Information only)

This world-renowned theater opened in 1778, and its tier upon tier of boxes, glittering chandeliers, and sumptuous appointments have witnessed musical spectacles ever since. It has been the site of many memorable operatic premieres, and is perhaps most closely associated with Verdi, Puccini, and Toscanini. Today its performances feature the world's most famous singers in productions of a wide variety of the operatic repertoire. La Scala presents not only opera, but ballet, orchestra concerts, and chamber music. **Recent Performers:** conductors Riccardo Muti and Lorin Maazel, pianist Maurizio Pollini. **Performances:** 15–20 monthly; December–May. Written ticket requests are limited to one event per request, which may indicate a choice of three dates.

MODENA (Emilia-Romagna)
250 miles NW of Rome

Ferrari cars and Lambrusco wine are the most widely known of this city's exports, but music lovers know it as the home town of Luciano Pavarotti. Like its neighbor and rival, Bologna, Modena is famed for its cuisine (especially cured meats), its medieval university, and for its treasures of art and architecture.

ONGOING EVENTS

Teatro Comunale Modena

Orch, Cham, Rec

Stagione Concertistica
Servizio Attività Teatrali
  e dello Spettacolo
Via Fonteraso, 1
41100 Modena
Tel: 059/225443

The Teatro Comunale offers an outstanding season of classical music with all of its programs given by artists of international renown. The music ranges from Bach to Schönberg, and from piano solo to symphony orchestra. Seven annual productions bring primarily Italian opera to the stage, and the active dance schedule includes both classical ballet and such modern troupes as the Martha Graham and Merce Cunningham Dance Companies. **Recent Performers:** Bamberg Symphony conducted by Georges Prêtre, St. Paul Chamber Orchestra conducted by Christopher Hogwood, violinst Igor Oistrakh, pianists Alicia de Larrocha, soprano Mirella Freni. **Venue:** Teatro Comunale. **Performances:** 23 concerts, September–May; 22 opera and dance, December–May.

NAPLES (Campania)
140 miles SE of Rome

Despite the urban troubles that have beset even the fairest of Italian cities, the heart and soul of Naples still fill this city with a poignant gaiety. The appreciative eye can easily see beyond the poverty and crime to the fascinating reminders of more prosperous days. Naples was one of the most important centers in the early history of opera, and the neoclassical Teatro San Carlo is still among Italy's operatic meccas. Lying in the shadow of the fearsome Mount Vesuvius, whose volcanic wrath claimed Pompeii and Herculaneum in 79 A.D., the city rises in turbulent beauty above the Bay of Naples.

FESTIVALS

International Music Weeks

3 Weeks	Settimane Musicali Inter-
Mid-June	nazionali
	Riviera di Chiaia 200
Op, Orch, Cham, Rec, Dance	Museo Pignatelli
	80121 Napoli
	Tel: 081/761 28 57

The venues for this festival are unparalleled—the famed San Carlo Opera House, the Teatro Mercadante, and the palatial Pignatelli Museum, a neoclassical villa surrounded by public parkland and filled with an impressive collection of decorative arts. Guest ensembles and solo artists of international standing join the resident ensemble, Musica d'Insieme, for 13 concerts ranging from Boccherini to Brahms. A staged production of *Così fan Tutte*, a concert version of Monteverdi's *L'Orfeo*, and Stravinsky's *Pulcinella* were among the highlights of a recent season. **Recent Performers:** Leipzig Gewandhaus Orchestra conducted by Kurt Masur, pianist Alicia de Larrocha, bass Samuel Ramey. **Venues:** Teatro di San Carlo, Teatro Mercadante, Museo Pignatelli. **Performances:** 16; evenings.

ONGOING EVENTS

Teatro delle Palme

Orch, Cham	Teatro delle Palme
	Associazione "Alessandro
	Scarlatti"
	Piazza dei Martiri, 58
	80121 Naples
	Tel: 081/406011

This theater features exceptional chamber music played by exceptional musicians. Works by Mozart, Britten, Stravinsky, Haydn, Handel, Elgar, Brahms, Bartók, and Schubert were heard during a recent season. Concerts present instrumental soloists with piano, string quartets, and chamber orchestras. **Recent Performers:** cellist Heinrich Schiff with the German Chamber Orchestra, Quarneri Quartet, violinist Itzhak Perlman. **Performances:** 18; January–May.

Teatro di San Carlo

Op, Orch, Cham, Rec

Teatro di San Carlo
Via San Carlo
80121 Naples
Tel: 081/797 2111

This important theater has known several reincarnations since it first opened as a baroque treasure in 1737. A devastating fire in the early nineteenth century resulted in the current neoclassical decor, which was restored following heavy damage during World War II. The theater is home to the opera season in Naples, and is also used for concerts and as an important venue for the International Music Weeks held in June. The repertoire favors Italian composers, though operetta and an occasional French or German work is performed. **Performances:** 5 of each of 7 productions; December–June.

ORTA SAN GIULIO (Piedmont)
340 miles NW of Rome

One of the loveliest parts of Northern Italy is its lake region, which extends through the foothills of the Alps. Lake Orta is one of this region's most captivating, with the charming village of Orta San Giulio adorning its edge. The village boasts elegant seventeenth-century chapels and frescoes, splendid baroque buildings, and the timeless serenity of a nearly perfect lake- and hillside location. From Orta San Giulio one can take a boat to the enchanting island of San Giulio.

FESTIVALS

Cusius Festival of Early Music

10 Days
Mid-June

Chor, Cham, Rec

Festival Cusiano di Musica
    Antica
Azienda Promozione Turis-
    tica del Lago d'Orta
Via Olina, 9/11
28016 Orta San Giulio
Tel: 0322/90355
Fax: 0321/26344

"In the ancient silence nothing is lost of the archaic sounds suspended in time." This lofty sentiment from the festival director sets the tone for this event, which presents early music (baroque and before) in incomparable surroundings. Most concerts are given in the ancient buildings of San Giulio Island, a tiny mist-enshrouded isle that rises from Lake Orta close to the lakeside town of Orta San Giulio. The carefully chosen programs often present music not heard in centuries, and the performers are active in rediscovering both repertoire and performance styles. **Recent Performers:** Ars Italica, Il Virtuoso Ritrovo, Vienna Horn Quartet, trumpeter André Bernard. **Venues:** Basilica (rebuilt in the eleventh century, with fifteenth-century frescos), seventeenth-century Concert Hall of Villa Tallone, Church of Santa Maria Assunta. **Performances:** 9; all at 9:15 P.M.

Musical September on San Giulio

10 Concerts
September

Rec

Settembre Musicale di
S. Giulio
Azienda Promozione Turis-
tica del Lago d'Orta
Via Olina 9/11
28016 Orta San Giulio
Tel: 0322/90355

Piano recitals and programs by vocal and instrumental soloists from all over Italy have brought music to the enchanting island of San Giulio for more than 30 years. An ancient basilica dominates this picturesque spot, also known for its splendid views of the mainland. **Venue:** Sala Eleonora Tallone. **Performances:** Saturday at 9 P.M.; Sunday at 4:30; Sunday concerts are free.

PALERMO (Sicily)
550 miles SE of Rome

Though prominently baroque, Palermo has preserved many of the cross-cultural influences bequeathed by the successive rule of Phoenicians, Romans, Byzantines, Saracens, Normans, Spaniards, and Bourbons. Now the largest port of Sicily, Palermo is also its thriving capital. This city of more than half a million people is enhanced by delightful squares and gardens and a seemingly endless array of Byzantine, Gothic, and baroque churches and buildings.

ONGOING EVENTS

Concert Season

Orch, Chor, Cham, Dance   Comune di Palermo
                                 Assessorato alla Cultura
                                 Via Caltanissetta, 2
                                 90100 Palermo
                                 Tel: 091/6205141

String quartets by Mozart and Beethoven, orchestral music by Brahms, cantatas by Bach, and Renaissance choral music are among the year-round offerings in this city, where programs can also include the Universal Ballet of Korea and the latest American jazz. **Recent Performers:** The Hilliard Ensemble, Kronos Quartet, cellist Mstislav Rostropovich. **Performances:** year-round.

Teatro Massimo

Op, Dance   Teatro Massimo
                                 Piazza Verdi
                                 90138 Palermo
                                 Tel: 091/581512

One of Italy's renowned opera houses, this theater first opened in 1897. A recent season here included Puccini's *La Fanciulla del West*, Nicolai's *The Merry Wives of Windsor*, Alfano's *Risurrezione*, Donizetti's *Maria Stuarda*, and Rossini's *La Cenerentola*, as well as Tchaikovsky's ballet "The Golden Cockerel." **Recent Performers:** soprano Katia Ricciarelli. **Performances:** 12; January–June.

PARMA (Emilia-Romagna)
290 miles NW of Rome

This thriving industrial town is both an economic and gastronomic center, and has given us both Parmesan cheese and the array of dishes described as parmigiana. The city's cultural and intellectual life was shaped by its ruling families, the Farnese and the Bourbons, who brought artists, architects, and musicians from all over Europe. The important mannerist painters Correggio and Il Parmigianino hailed from Parma, which was also the birthplace of conductor Arturo Toscanini. Giuseppi Verdi was born in nearby Roncole, grew up in neighboring Busseto, and settled just a few miles away on his estate at Sant'Agata.

FESTIVALS

Verdi Festival

2 Weeks
Late September

Op, Orch, Cham, Rec, Org

Fondazione Verdi Festival
Biglietteria Teatro Regio
Via Garibaldi 19
43100 Parma
Tel: 0521/218678
Fax: 0521/206156

A long-anticipated project came into being in 1990 when this festival was first held. Verdi's work is celebrated here on his native soil—in Roncole Verdi, where he was born in 1813, in Busseto, where he grew up, and in neighboring Parma, Colorno, and Fidenza. International artists collaborate in three Verdi operas and in orchestral concerts and recitals that include the music of Verdi's contemporaries. The festival has been enhanced by unique offerings such as a "Breakfast with the Duchess" featuring "table music" by pianist Jörg Demus, roundtable discussions with experts that have included Verdi scholar Julian Budden, and special walking tours of the sites of interest to Verdi fans. **Recent Performers:** tenor José Carreras with the English Chamber Orchestra conducted by Luciano Berio, Orchestra and Chorus of the Bastille Opera (Paris) conducted by Myung Whun Chung, baritone Leo Nucci. **Venues:** Parma: Teatro Regio, Palazzo Marchi, Teatro Due, Conservatorio; Busseto: Teatro G. Verdi; Roncole Verdi: Church of San Michele; Colorno: Church of San Liborio; Fidenza: Teatro Magnani. **Performances:** 35; evenings and afternoons.

ONGOING EVENTS

Teatro Regio

Op, Rec, Dance

Teatro Regio
Biglietteria
Via Garibaldi 16
43100 Parma
Tel: 0521/218678

Five opera productions, 1 ballet, and 4 important vocal recitals fill the bill at the Teatro Regio, which opened in 1829 with the music of Bellini. The proximity to Verdi's birthplace draws throngs of his fans, who make this the most critical Verdi house in the country. Some singers claim to lose more

sleep over performances in this house than for those anywhere else in the world. Italian opera predominates, though
a recent season included Massenet's *Werther*. **Recent Performers:** sopranos Cecilia Gasdia and Margaret Price, tenor
Neil Rosenshein, bass Samuel Ramey, all in recital. **Performances:** 26; December–May.

PESARO (The Marches)
190 miles NE of Rome

Basking on the Adriatic coast at the mouth of the river Foglia,
Pesaro's old town preserves much of its sixteenth-century heritage. The massive Ducal Palace and two museums offer visitors a glimpse of its rich past. Pesaro was the birthplace of
Gioacchino Rossini, and his home is now open as a museum.
Pesaro is just 20 miles from the unforgettable town of Urbino,
birthplace of Rafael, and one of the most beautiful Renaissance cities in Italy.

FESTIVALS

Rossini Opera Festival

3 Weeks   Rossini Opera Festival
Early–Mid-August   Via Rossini 37
                              61100 Pesaro
Op, Orch, Chor, Cham, Rec   Tel: 0721/33184

Whereas the operas here are exclusively those of Rossini,
the concerts that are also part of the festival rarely include
Rossini's compositions. This gives the visitor a chance to hear
a variety of music, as well as lesser-known works by this
master. Recent productions have included *La Gazza Ladra,
L'Occasione fa il Ladro,* and *Bianca e Falliero.* The three
venues used for performances offer a delightful variety of
locales. The Teatro Comunale G. Rossini is an elaborate,
horseshoe-ringed opera house with tier upon tier of boxes.
The neoclassical simplicity of the smaller Auditorium Pedrotti shows understated elegance, while the clean, modern
lines of the Palafestival provide a more contemporary setting.
Recent Performers: conductor Riccardo Chailly, soprano June
Anderson, pianist Aldo Ciccolini. **Venues:** Teatro Comunale
G. Rossini, Auditorium Pedrotti, Palafestival. **Performances:**
about 20.

PIACENZA (Emilia-Romagna)
320 miles NW of Rome

Established by the Romans along the Po River, Piacenza is now an industrialized town where an impressive and well-preserved medieval section recalls an era of colorful fairs, commerce, and general prosperity. The town's twelfth-century cathedral is a combination of Gothic and baroque architecture, and the town square, Piazza dei Cavalli, is home to a marvelous, turreted Gothic building that once served as the local government headquarters.

ONGOING EVENTS

Teatro Municipale

Op, Orch, Chor, Cham, Rec, Org, Dance, Th

Biglietteria
Via G. Verdi n. 41
29100 Piacenza
Tel: 0523/492251

Built in 1804 by several aristocratic families of the town, this theater is the centerpiece of Piacenza's cultural life, offering an ambitious season of opera, concerts, ballet, and theater. The concert season runs the gamut from lieder recitals to the Tchaikovsky violin concerto, and ballets offer such unusual productions as a *Butterfly* utilizing music of both Giacomo Puccini and Philip Glass. **Recent Performers:** St. Paul Chamber Orchestra conducted by Christopher Hogwood, Salzburg Bach Choir, soprano Elly Ameling with pianist Dalton Baldwin. **Performances:** 55; October–April.

RAVELLO (Campagnia)
170 miles SE of Rome

This small town, one of the many that line the Amalfi Coast, sits just inland and is often overlooked by visitors. Ravello's secret charms lie in its sumptuous gardens. Especially enticing are those at the medieval ruins of Villa Rufolo, which impressed the visiting Richard Wagner, and those at the Villa Combrone estate, which offer magnificent views of the Gulf of Salerno.

FESTIVALS

Ravello Music Festival

1 Week	Festival Musicale Ravello
Early July	Ufficio Informazioni dell
	E.P.T. di Salerno
Orch, Cham, Rec	Via Velia 15
	84100 Salerno
	Tel: 089/231432

When Richard Wagner visited the gardens of the Villa Rufolo in 1880, he exclaimed: "At last I have found Klingsor's garden." The setting that brought *Parsifal* to Wagner's mind was used for a special commemorative concert by the Orchestra of San Carlo in 1933, and since 1953 has been the site of a festival that celebrates not only Wagner, but a host of his nineteenth-century contemporaries. The San Carlo Orchestra has been joined by other famed ensembles, and since 1977 chamber music has been an integral part of the proceedings. **Recent Performers:** Ensemble Wien (composed of soloists from the Vienna Philharmonic), Munich Chamber Ensemble, Orchestra del Teatro di San Carlo. **Venues:** Garden of the Villa Rufolo, Municipal Gardens, Piazzetta S. Giovanni del Tor (concerts in the last two are free!). **Performances:** 9; late morning and early evening.

RAVENNA (Emilia-Romagna)
225 miles N of Rome

Now an inland city, Ravenna once sat proudly on the Adriatic, an important city and capital of the Western Roman Empire during the fifth and sixth centuries. Known as the "Byzantium of the West," Ravenna is filled with magnificent Byzantine treasures testifying to the Eastern influences that so profoundly affected this city. The exquisite mosaics to be found throughout the city are unparalleled in Europe. Dante died here in 1321, an exile from his native Florence.

FESTIVALS

Ravenna Festival

1 Month	Ravenna Festival
Early July–Early August	Biglietteria del Teatro
	Alighieri
Op, Orch, Chor, Cham, Rec,	Via Mariani 2
Org, Jazz, Dance	48100 Ravenna
	Tel: 0544/32577

Two or three major opera productions are the focal point here, surrounded by other events ranging from early music to Beethoven symphonies to jazz. The performers are world class—Lorin Maazel, Zubin Mehta, Pierre Boulez, and Riccardo Muti all conducted in one recent season. A common theme runs through many of these programs, with a recent focus on "Cherubini and the French School." Also part of the program is the annual organ festival that has taken place at the Church of S. Vitale for more than three decades, featuring organists from all over Europe. Ravenna is especially celebrated for its performance venues, which include three sixth-century basilicas containing some of the world's most extensive ancient mosaics. Operas and ballets are produced in the open-air theater of the Rocca Brancaleone, a fifteenth-century fortress, and in the nineteenth-century splendor of the Teatro Alighieri. Recent productions include *Falstaff, La Traviata, Don Carlos,* and *Fidelio.* **Recent Performers:** Carlos Kleiber conducting the La Scala Philharmonic Orchestra, Musica Antica, The King's Consort, bass Simon Estes. **Venues:** Basilicas of S. Apollinare Nuovo, S. Apollinare in Classe, and S. Vitale, Dante's Tomb, Franciscan Cloisters, Teatro Alighieri, Rocca Brancaleone. **Performances:** 25; all at 9:15 P.M.

REGGIO EMILIA (Emilia-Romagna)
275 miles NW of Rome

The tricolored flag of Italy originated in this city, where it was first flown in 1797. This rich commercial center was also the birthplace of the poet Ariosto, whose *Orlando Furioso* is one of the masterpieces of Italian Renaissance literature. Numerous museums and the Romanesque cathedral contain a wealth of frescos and paintings.

ONGOING EVENTS

Teatro Municipale

Op, Orch, Cham, Rec
Teatro Municipale Valli
Piazza Martiri 7 Luglio
42100 Reggio Emilia
Tel: 0522/43 42 44

This nineteenth-century theater hosts both the opera and concert season in Reggio Emilia. The opera season benefits from the recent trend toward shared productions, and the five works mounted here each season are often coproductions. Thus *La Traviata* comes by way of the Ravenna Festival, while

La Fanciulla del West and *I Capuleti e i Montecchi* involves the theaters of Parma, Bologna, and Covent Garden. Recent recitals have featured soprano Renata Scotto and tenor Luciano Pavarotti. The concert season shows careful planning with a balance of old and new, so that Schubert appears with Schönberg, and Luigi Nono with Josquin des Prez. Concerts are presented in the "Cavallerizza," which means "Riding School." It was used as such until the mid-1970s and now, after extensive renovation, acts as both concert hall and drama theater and seats 300. **Recent Performers:** Pittsburgh Symphony with Lorin Maazel, Chamber Orchestra of Riga with pianist Lazar Berman, The Academy of Ancient Music directed by Christopher Hogwood, soprano Katia Ricciarelli, pianist Maurizio Pollini. **Performances:** October–May.

RIMINI (Emilia-Romagna)
140 miles N of Rome

This seaside resort town is one of the liveliest on the Adriatic coast, attracting beachgoers from every country in Europe. While disco music and the mixed aromas of hundreds of restaurants seem to engulf the town with reminders of the present day, the literary-minded visitor may sense the presence of the eternally embracing ghosts of Paolo and Francesca, the ill-fated medieval lovers in Dante's *Inferno,* who lived and died here. The story of this beautiful young wife's illicit love for her tutor is the basis for Zandonai's grand opera, *Francesca da Rimini.*

FESTIVALS

Malatestiana Music Festival

3 Weeks	Sagra Musicale Malatestiana
Late August–Mid-September	Biglietteria ufficiale
	Ufficio Informazioni del
Orch, Chor, Cham	Comune di Rimini
	Piazza Cavour
	Rimini
	Tel: 0541/704114

Now in its fourth decade, this festival takes its name from the site where many of its programs are given–the magnificent Tempio Malatestiano. Begun in the thirteenth century and almost completely rebuilt during the fifteenth century, this church (*tempio* means "temple") is a Renaissance masterpiece and a testament to the wealth and power of the Malatesta family, whose most famous member, the ill-fated Francesca, was immortalized by Dante. In addition to the concerts given here by major orchestras, this festival provides a forum for young musicians. **Recent Performers:** Leningrad Philharmonic Orchestra, Bamberg Symphony conducted by Georges Prêtre, soprano Gundula Janowitz. **Venues:** Tempio Malatestiano, Sala Ressi. **Performances:** 20.

RIVA DEL GARDA (Trentino-Alto Adige)
290 miles NW of Rome

Perched on the northern shore of Lake Garda, this resort town was built on an important trade route between Verona and the Alps. The caravans of former days have been supplanted by vacationers who are drawn to the crystal blue lake and towering mountains that surround it. For those intent on exploration, there is a turreted medieval castle, the Rocca, completely surrounded by water and containing an interesting civic museum.

FESTIVALS

Musica Riva

2 Weeks	Musica Riva
Mid-July	Via Pilati, 5
	38066 Riva del Garde
Op, Orch, Chor, Cham, Rec,	Tel: 0464/554073
Org	0464/516161
	Fax: 0464/505643

The full title of this festival is Musica Riva—International Meeting of Young Musicians, and since 1984 it has provided a forum for gifted conservatory students to study and perform with internationally known artists. Like similar programs in Salzburg and Siena, the concerts, which are an integral part of the learning process, are also richly rewarding for the audience. Performances have included Haydn's *Creation,* Mozart's Requiem, and masterpieces of the orchestral and chamber music repertoire. **Recent Performers:** violinist Ruggiero Ricci, harpist Nancy Allen, String Quartet of Vienna. **Venues:** Inner Courtyard of the twelfth-century Rocca (fortress), Church of S. Maria Assunta, others in and around Riva. **Performances:** nightly, with two performances on Saturday and Sunday.

ROME (Latium)

It is hard to imagine a more complete sensory inundation than that which awaits the visitor to Rome. The constant splashing of fountains, vistas across the Tiber, famed cuisine, and remnants of an empire at every turn are ever-present reminders that Rome is indeed the Eternal City. Succeeding generations have built directly over and around the preceding ones, with the result that traffic now swirls around the Colosseum, and Michelangelo's splendid Campidoglio is all but hidden by the giant memorial to Victor Emmanuel, presiding over the hubbub of the Piazza Venezia. Here as in many European cities, the best source of information on unexpected musical treats is often to be sought on the walls and billboards—posters announce concerts that make delightful use of courtyards and other private spaces that are seldom found in guidebooks.

FESTIVALS

Baths of Caracalla

3 Weeks   Baths of Caracalla
Late July–Early August   Box Office
     Teatro dell'Opera
Op, Dance   Piazza Beniamino Gigli
     00100 Rome
     Tel: 06/461755

A performance of *Aida* at the Baths of Caracalla is one of the quintessential operatic spectacles. The Baths themselves were built by the Emperor Caracalla in the third century, and were unprecedented in splendor—baths, gymnasiums, gardens, and libraries extended over 25 acres and could accommodate over 1500 bathers at one time. Though in ruins today, they provide a suitable backdrop not only for *Aida,* but for productions such as *Cavalleria Rusticana* and *I Pagliacci* and for classical ballet. The Baths are also used for special events, such as the historic 1990 joint concert of tenors Placido Domingo, José Carreras, and Luciano Pavarotti. **Recent Performers:** soprano Aprile Milo as Aida. **Performances:** 8; evenings.

Concerts on the Capitoline Hill

10 Concerts   Concerti al Campidoglio
July   Accademia Nazionale di
         Santa Cecilia
Orch   Via Vittoria, 6
     00187 Roma
     Tel: 06/6780742

The orchestra of the Academy of St. Cecilia and guest ensembles can be heard in these outdoor concerts given on the most famous of Rome's seven hills—Il Campidoglio. Surrounded by Michelangelo's architectural masterpieces, audiences can revel in the sounds of Respighi's Roman "symphonic poems" and popular favorites of Beethoven, Strauss, and Rossini. **Recent Performers:** Lorin Maazel conducting the Orchestra dell'Accademia di Santa Cecilia, Virtuosi of the Berlin Philharmonic, Soviet Radio Orchestra. **Performances:** all at 9:30 P.M.

ONGOING EVENTS

Accademia Nazionale di Santa Cecilia

Orch, Cham, Rec

Accademia Nazionale di
    Santa Cecilia
Via Vittoria, 6
00187 Roma
Tel: 06/6780742

The programs and performers found here are among the finest in the world. The conductors and soloists appearing with the orchestra and the solo and chamber artists who fill the active chamber music schedule include major recording artists. The repertoire is impressively diverse, representing over 60 composers from Bach to Webern and Busoni to Saponaro. **Recent Performers:** conductors Georges Prêtre, James Levine, pianist Cecile Licad, violinist Midori, cellist Mstislav Rostropovich. **Venue:** Auditorio di Via della Conciliazione. **Performances:** 32 orchestral, 32 chamber; October–June.

Auditorio del Foro Italico

Orch, Chor, Cham

Orbis
Piazza dell'Esquilino 37
00184 Roma
Tel: 06/4827403
CC: 06/36865625

Built in the 1930s as a recording and broadcasting hall, this elegant 800-seat theater is a prime example of the Bauhaus style. Each season 26 concerts by the RAI Symphony Orchestra and Chorus are broadcast live from this hall on Saturday evenings, exploring the repertoire from Mozart to Enescu. **Resident Ensembles:** RAI Symphony Orchestra and Chorus, RAI Chamber Chorus. **Recent Performers:** conductor Dennis Russell Davies, violinist Joshua Bell, soprano

Sheila Armstrong. **Performances:** 100; mostly October–May. Dark Monday and August.

Rome Opera

Op, Dance   Teatro dell'Opera
                            Piazza Beniamino Gigli, 1
                            00184 Rome
                            Tel: 06/461755

The seven productions that make up the operatic season in Rome include works by Strauss, Massenet, Lehár, and other foreign composers, as well as Italian favorites Bellini, Puccini, and Verdi. Productions often draw on the resources of La Scala in Milan and the Teatro Comunale in Florence. The season also offers two ballet productions—a recent year included Prokofiev's "Cinderella" and Tchaikovsky's "Swan Lake." **Recent Performers:** conductor Spiros Argiris, tenor Alfredo Kraus, soprano Leona Mitchell, tenor Chris Merritt. **Performances:** approx 50; December–June.

IN THE AREA

Pontino Festival

4 Weeks   Pontino Festival
Late June–Late July   Campus Internazionale di
                              Musica
Orch, Cham, Rec   Via Ecetra, 36
                            04100 Latina
                            Tel: 0773/663266
                            Fax: 0773/663264

This festival takes place in three quite diverse locales SE of Rome. Piano recitals, chamber orchestras, and string quartets are among the offerings at the imposing Castello Caetani in the small medieval town of Sermoneta, while the city of Latina, founded as an administrative center for the region in 1932, hosts one or two programs. The third venue is the town of Priverno. The consistent factor here is the level of artistry and the delightful diversity of the programs (Boccherini, Berio, and Bottesini shared one recent program for cello and contrabass!). Since 1963 this festival has presented over 100 world premieres, including compositions by Elliott Carter, Luigi Nono, and Heinz Holliger. Concerts are not limited to modern repertoire, however, and Couperin, Mozart, or Schubert may be heard as well as Berio, Schönberg, or Ginastera. **Recent Performers:** The Schubert Ensemble of London, Borodin Quartet, pianist Charles Rosen. **Venues:** Sermoneta: Caetani Castle; Priverno: Fossanova Abbey; Latina: Palazzo della Cultura, Villa di Fogliano. **Performances:** Saturday and Sunday evenings.

Chamber Music Concerts in Latina

Orch, Cham, Rec

Campus Internazionale de
Musica
Via Ecetra, 36
04100 Latina
Tel: 0773/663266
Fax: 0773/663264

The list of renowned artists who have performed in this small town SE of Rome is indeed impressive. The concerts have been held since 1972, and present a wide range of chamber music, from Bach to Martinu. **Recent Performers:** European String Trio, violinist Ruggiero Ricci, clarinetist Gervase de Peyer. **Venues:** Piccolo Teatro, Teatro Ridotto. **Performances:** 12 Fridays; October–December.

SALERNO (Campagnia)
160 miles SE of Rome

Once known as "the city of Hippocrates" for its distinguished medieval medical school, Salerno sits to the south of Naples along the Gulf of Salerno and is a beginning point for the spectacular Amalfi Drive. Although much of the waterfront was destroyed during the Allied invasion in World War II, the medieval Old Town still clings to the side of a castle-topped hill. The town's eleventh-century Romanesque cathedral is one of its landmarks, with an intriguing twelfth-century pulpit and Byzantine doors from Constantinople.

FESTIVALS

Musica per Velia

7 Concerts
Mid–Late July

Orch, Chor, Dance

Musica per Velia
Ente Provinciale per
Tourismo
Via Velia n. 15
84100 Salerno
Tel: 089/224 322

These concerts and ballets are notable for their unusual setting—the archeological area near Salerno—as well as for the chance to hear ensembles such as the Orchestra and

Chorus of San Carlo and the Collegium Musicum Harmonia without charge!

Salerno Festival

9 Concerts	Salerno Festival
Late June–Mid-August	Ente Filharmonico per il
	mezzogiorno
Orch, Cham, Rec	Via Picenza n. 76
	84100 Salerno
	Tel: 089/33 54 94
	(Monday–Friday,
	9–10:30 A.M.)

Prestigious ensembles and soloists gather for these concerts, whose programs have featured Vivaldi and Mozart, Beethoven and Wagner, and Varese and Webern. The site of these events is unusual—the atrium of the Duomo, Salerno's ancient Cathedral, where the diverse cultural influences that have contributed to this city and to this splendid edifice are most clearly seen. **Recent Performers:** Zubin Mehta conducting the Orchestra and Chorus of the Maggio Musicale Fiorentino, Pierre Boulez conducting the Orchestre Nationale de France, soprano Jeanine Altmeyer. **Venue:** Atrium of the Duomo. **Performances:** all begin at 9 P.M.

SIENA (Tuscany)
135 miles NW of Rome

Siena is a place that seems to have ignored the passage of time, a walled medieval city preserving the glory of its thirteenth and fourteenth-century prosperity. Narrow streets lined with Gothic buildings radiate in all directions from the famed Piazza del Campo, covering three hills whose red clay has given us the color sienna. This is a city for art lovers, where mysticism and the influence of the Greeks and Byzantines created a tradition quite different from that of neighboring Florence.

FESTIVALS

Estate Musicale Chigiana

2 Months	Accademia Musicale
July–August	Chigiana
	Via di Città, 89
Op, Orch, Cham, Rec	53100 Siena
	Tel: 055/214992

The title here comes from the Institute of Count Guido Chigi Saracini, whose Renaissance Palace is an important venue for these summer (estate) concerts. Except for the week-long Settimana Musicale Senese in August (see the following), chamber music predominates, presented in historic settings throughout Siena. The city is internationally famous for its extensive summer institutes, and recitals by faculty and students are an important part of the musical calendar. **Recent Performances:** pianist Andrea Martin, soprano Penelope Price Jones, clarinettist Giuseppe Garbarino. **Venues:** Palazzo Chigi Saracini, others. **Performances:** 70; usually at 9 P.M.

Siena Music Week

1 Week	Fondazione Accademia
Mid-August	Musicale Chigiana
	Via di Città, 89
Op, Orch, Rec, Conf	53100 Siena
	Tel: 055/214992 or
	0577/46152

The performances given during this week are the centerpiece of the active musical summer in Siena. Operatic rarities such as Mozart's *Thamos, Re d'Egitto* and Salieri's *Axur, Re d'Ormus* (to a libretto by Mozart's famed collaborator, Da Ponte), share the limelight with piano recitals, new music, and seminars. The festival is nearing its 50th anniversary. **Recent Performers:** Gennady Rozhdestvensky conducting the Russian Philharmonic Orchestra, pianist Andrei Gavrilov. **Venues:** Palazzo Chigi Saracini, Teatro dei Rinnovati. **Performances:** 12; evenings.

ONGOING EVENTS

Micat in Vertice

Orch, Cham, Rec,	Micat in Vertice
	Fondazione Accademia
	Musicale Chigiana
	Via di Città, 89
	53100 Siena
	Tel: 055/214992

This rather unusual title applies to the star-studded winter concert season in Siena. The series has a nearly 70-year history, and its offerings, while concentrated on the nineteenth century, include music both ancient and modern.

Recent Performers: Vienna Chamber Orchestra with pianist Philippe Entremont, Tokyo, Juilliard, and Borodin String Quartets, harpsichordist Gustav Leonhardt. **Performances:** 14; November–April.

IN THE AREA

International Meeting Place for the Arts

10 Days	Cantiere Internazionale
Early August	d'Arte
	Via del Teatro 4
Op, Orch, Cham, Child	53045 Montepulciano (SI)
	Tel: 0578/757089

This highly imaginative festival draws some stellar performers to the town of Montepulciano, 30 miles SE of Siena. The two opera productions in a recent year included Hans Werner Henze conducting his "story for singers and instruments," *La Gatta Inglese* (*The English Cat*), and the world premiere of *Gli Spiriti dell'Aria* by Matteo D'Amico, based on the story of Pulcinella. Orchestra concerts offer repertoire from Vivaldi to Odzil, and chamber music recitals present some interesting combinations, such as Berio and Schubert, or Musgrave and Purcell. Other programs include marionettes, clowns, and mimes. **Recent Performers:** Sir Michael Tippett conducting the Parnassus Ensemble of London, pianist Penelope Roskell. **Venues:** Teatro Poliziano (named for the Renaissance poet Politian, who was born here), Auditorium di San Francesco, Piazza Grande, Teatrino de San Biagio. **Performances:** 34; mornings, afternoons, and evenings.

SPOLETO (Umbria)
80 miles N of Rome

Spoleto is a delightfully well-preserved town whose narrow streets and ancient churches exude the atmosphere of medieval Europe. The town is dominated by a fourteenth-century castle (once occupied by Lucrezia Borgia), which protects the Ponte della Torri. This "Bridge of the Towers" spans a gorge of over 260 feet and affords pedestrians a magnificent view. At the center of town is the Cathedral, with a splendid facade and interior frescoes by Filippo and Filippino Lippi.

FESTIVALS

Festival of Two Worlds

2 Weeks
Late June–Mid-July

Op, Orch, Chor, Cham, Rec,
Dance, Th, Film

Associazione Festival dei
    due Mondi
Teatro Nuovo
Biglietteria Festival
06049 Spoleto (pg)
Tel: 0743/44097
Fax: 0743/43284

The two worlds—old and new—meet both in this festival and in its founder, Italian-born composer Gian Carlo Menotti, who has spent most of his creative life in the United States. Founded in 1958, this festival is one of the most popular among American tourists, in part due to the recognition gained through its sister festival, the Spoleto Festival in Charleston, South Carolina. The diverse programs of the Italian festival include operas ranging from *Le Nozze di Figaro* to Philip Glass's *Hydrogen Jukebox*; concerts featuring Berlioz, Strauss, and Verdi; and dance ranging from classical ballet to African folk dance. Menotti presides in a variety of capacities, from conductor to stage director. **Recent Performers:** Orchestra of the Bastille Opera of Paris conducted by Myung-Whun Chung, Spoleto Festival Orchestra conducted by Spiros Argiris, The Westminster Choir. **Venues:** Teatro Nuova, Teatro San Carlo Melisso, Teatro Romano, Cathedral, Churches. **Performances:** 100–150.

STRESA (Piedmont)
340 miles NW of Rome

Stresa is a pleasant village on the shores of the placid Lake Maggiore, the most famous of Italy's northern lakes. It is a highly popular resort and a departure point for boat rides to the remarkable Borromean islands. The largest of the three enchanting isles is Isola Madre, with magnificent botanical gardens occupied by peacocks, pheasants, and parrots. The most famous island is Isola Bella, graced by the elegant seventeenth-century Palazzo Borromeo and its sumptuous gardens.

FESTIVALS

Stresa Music Weeks

4 Weeks
Late August–Mid-September

Orch, Chor, Cham, Rec, Org

Settimane Musicali
Palazzo dei Congressi
Via R. Bonghi 4
1-28049 Stresa
Tel: 0323/31 095
to purchase tickets in U.S.:
Dailey-Thorp, Inc.
315 West 57th Street
New York, NY 10019
Tel: 212/307-1555
Fax: 212/974-1420

World-class performers, young international competition winners, and incomparable settings mark Stresa's annual festival. Stresa's lakeside location makes it possible for concerts to take place on the spectacular Borromean Islands, famed for their baroque gardens. Here one can listen to the Tokyo String Quartet playing Schubert, or Julian Bream playing Bach, amid the splendor of the Tapestry Hall of the Palazzo Borromeo on Isola Bella. Orchestral concerts, chamber music, and recitals are also given in Stresa itself, also featuring virtuoso performers in an exciting range of repertoire. The festival celebrated its 30th year in 1991. **Recent Performers:** violinist Pinchas Zukerman conducting the English Chamber Orchestra, Beaux Arts Trio, sopranos Eva Johansson and Katia Ricciarelli. **Venues:** Teatro del Palazzo dei Congressi di Stresa, St. Ambrose's Church, Isola Bella, Isola Madre. **Performances:** 20; at 9:15 or 9:30 P.M.

TAORMINA (Sicily)
440 miles SE of Rome

Taormina seizes the senses with such beauty and mystique that it is difficult to determine which aspects of this Sicilian town are the most spectacular. Depicted with eloquent zeal by writers such as Goethe and D. H. Lawrence, the town possesses an astounding ancient Greek theater, which dates to the third century B.C., a multitude of fourteenth and fifteenth century palaces, and a breathtaking panorama of the Ionian Sea, nearby mountains, and the towering presence of Mount Etna—Europe's highest and largest active volcano.

Local goods that include black lava pottery and almond wine are offered in the plentiful array of shops and restaurants.

FESTIVALS

Taormina Arte

8 Weeks	Taormina Arte
Mid-July–Early September	Via Pirandello 31
	98039 Taormina (ME)
Op, Orch, Chor, Cham,	Tel: 0942/21142
Rec, Dance, Th, Film	(9:30 A.M.–12:30 P.M.)
	Fax: 0942/23348

An ancient amphitheater with a backdrop of mountains and sea is the dramatic setting for this spectacular arts event. Giuseppe Sinopoli directs the opera festival, which is a recent addition to a program notable for the diversity of its offerings. Theater, dance, and film tend toward the avant-garde, but musical programs are for the most part nineteenth-century. **Recent Performers:** Erich Leinsdorf conducting the Royal Philharmonic Orchestra, Wolfgang Savallisch conducting the Orchestra and Chorus of the Bavarian State Opera, pianist Enrique Arias, Alvin Ailey American Dance Theater. **Venues:** Greco-Roman Amphitheater, public gardens, conference hall. **Performances:** 50 (music, theater, dance), 50 films.

TORRE DEL LAGO PUCCINI (Tuscany)
190 miles NW of Rome

On the shores of the serene Lake Massaciùccoli, near this pleasant small town, is the estate where Puccini wrote *La Bohème, Tosca,* and *Madama Butterfly*. The composer's villa and tomb are open to visitors during the festival season.

FESTIVALS

Puccini Festival

3 Weeks	Festival Pucciniano
Late July–Mid-August	Belvedere Puccini no. 4
	55048 Torre del Lago Puccini
Op, Dance, Cham, Rec	Tel: 0584/359322

Lake Massaciùccoli forms the backdrop of the spectacular open-air "Teatro all'Aperto," where operas of Puccini and his contemporaries are produced with splendor and imagination. While Puccini operas have been the mainstay of this festival for decades, recently one production each year has been devoted to the work of another composer for the lyric stage. A recent festival mounted *Cavalleria Rusticana* in homage to Mascagni, who in 1930 conducted the first performances of Puccini works in Torre del Lago, where the composer lived and is now buried. Performances in the nearby Villa Borbone offer ballet and chamber music and such offerings as Schönberg's *Pierrot Lunaire.* **Recent Performers:** Bruno Moretti conducting *Madama Butterfly,* Orchestra Villa-Lobos, soprano Eva Marton. **Venues:** Grande Teatro all'Aperto, Villa Borbone. **Performances:** 14 opera; 10 others, all at 9:15 P.M.

TRIESTE (Friuli-Venezia Giulia)
415 miles NE of Rome

The largest port on the Adriatic, Trieste sits at the end of a thin sliver of northern Italy that extends along the beautiful Adriatic coast into Yugoslavia. The historic town was prized by the Celts and the Romans, and much later became the chief port and strategic stronghold of the Hapsburg Empire. This long and diverse history is seen in the Hill of St. Justus, where remnants of the ancient city, a Roman basilica, a Renaissance castle, and a modern war memorial all border the medieval cathedral.

FESTIVALS

Operetta Festival

6 Weeks	Festival dell'Operetta
Late June–Early August	Ente Autonomo
	Teatro Comunale Giuseppe
Operetta, Cham, Dance,	Verdi
Cabaret	Riva Tre Novembre 1
	34121 Trieste
	Tel: 040/62931

This delightfully diverse festival reflects Trieste's synthesis of both Eastern and Western European traditions. Operetta is the mainstay, augmented by dance and cabaret performances. A recent season focused on Hungary's "musical landscape," with its colorful gypsy spirit reflected in works by native composers and those whom they influenced in other countries. Recent Productions include Johann Strauss's *Gypsy*

Baron, and Imre Kálmán's *La Contessa Mariza.* **Recent Performers:** Berliner Ensemble, Ballet de Monte Carlo, tenor Nicolai Gedda. **Venues:** Teatro Comunale Giuseppe Verdi, Politeama Rossetti, Teatro Gristallo, parks and piazzas. **Performances:** 25; evenings.

ONGOING EVENTS

Teatro Comunale Giuseppe Verdi

Op, Orch, Dance

> Teatro Comunale Giuseppe Verdi
> Biglietteria del Teatro
> Piazza Verdi, 1
> 34121 Trieste
> Tel: 040/367816
> Fax: 040/366300

Tchaikovsky and Wagner, as well as Puccini, Rossini, and Donizetti, can be found on the operatic slate in this theater, where orchestral concerts also offer primarily nineteenth-century repertoire. The orchestra and chorus of the Teatro Verdi are joined by guest artists from around the world, while the opera showcases Italian singers and conductors. The theater, built in 1801, was known by several different names until the city spontaneously decided to name it in honor of Verdi following his death. **Recent Performers:** conductors Yoel Levi and Spiros Argiris, pianist Bella Davidovich and Jean-Yvres Thibaudet. **Performances:** 10 performances of each of 7 operas, December–May; 45 orchestral concerts, September–July.

TURIN (Piedmont)
400 miles NW of Rome

The capital of Piedmont, Turin is an important trade and industrial center. The house of Savoy reigned here for nearly a millennium, and the city was the center of the nineteenth-century unification movement. Carefully planned boulevards, parks, and squares belie the heavy industry of the region (Fiat is headquartered here). Among the city's treasures is the Shroud of Turin, believed by many to have been the cloth wrapped around Christ when He was taken down from the cross. Turin's impressive Egyptian Museum is said to be second only to Cairo's.

FESTIVALS

Musical September

4 Weeks   Settembre Musica
Late August–Late September   Vetrina per Torino
                                       Assessorato Cultura
Orch, Chor, Cham, Rec, Org   Piazza San Carlo, 161
                                       10123 Torino
                                       Tel: 011/510 450
                                            011/544 691

A star-studded roster of artists fills the churches, courtyards, and concert halls of Turin during this month-long celebration. From early music to the most contemporary, this festival offers an unusually rich and varied schedule of performers and concerts, including special programs focused on such artists as the Italian composer Franco Donsfoni. **Recent Performers:** Moscow Philharmonic Orchestra with conductor Dmitry Kitaenko, English Chamber Orchestra with conductor and violinist Pinchas Zukerman, Royal Philharmonic Orchestra with conductor and pianist Vladimir Ashkenazy. **Venues:** more than a dozen in and around Turin, including churches, theaters, and concert halls. **Performances:** about 50; two daily, at 4 and 9 P.M.

ONGOING EVENTS

Musical Union

Orch, Chor, Cham, Rec   Unione Musicale
                                       Piazza Castello, 29
                                       10124 Torino
                                       Tel: 011/544523

Those who enjoy the masterpieces of the chamber music repertoire will delight in the concerts given here. Schumann's *Dichterliebe,* Berg's *Lyrische* Suite and sixteenth-century Italian madrigals were among the plentiful offerings of one recent season. **Recent Performers:** I Musici, cellist Lynn Harrell, violinist Igor Oistrakh. **Performances:** 30; January–June.

RAI Auditorium

Op, Orch, Chor   Auditorium RAI
                                       Via Verdi, 16
                                       10124 Torino
                                       Tel: 011/88074653

The Italian Radio Television (RAI) Orchestra performs here in a season of Bach, Beethoven, and Brahms, but just as frequently features composers such as Bartók, Sibelius, and Prokofiev. A Russian production of Tchaikovsky's *The Queen of Spades* was a recent highlight.   **Recent Performers:** conductor Aldo Ceccato, pianist Rudolf Buchbinder.   **Performances:** 24; January–March.

Teatro Nuovo

Dance

Teatro Nuovo
Corso M. D'Azeglio, 17
10100 Torino
Tel: 011/655552

A most intriguing dance season is offered here. New music, new choreography, and new companies appear most appropriately at the Teatro Nuovo ("New Theater"), where music by Debussy and De Falla is likely to be the most "classic" on the program.   **Performances:** 12; January–April.

Teatro Regio

Op, Orch, Chor, Cham, Rec,
   Dance

Teatro Regio Torin
Piazza Castello, 215
10124 Torino
Tel: 011/8815 241
Fax: 011/8815 214

The theater is more than an opera house—it was designed to be the cultural and artistic center for the city of Turin. A recent season opened with Verdi's *Don Carlos* and *Don Carlo*—the French and Italian versions presented on alternating evenings. Other productions have included Zandonai's *Francesca da Rimini*, Puccini's *La Fanciulla del West*, and Berg's *Wozzeck*. The current building was built in 1973 to replace the original eighteenth-century structure destroyed by fire in 1936.   **Recent Performers:** Orchestra and Chorus of the Teatro Regio, sopranos Renata Scotto and Jeannine Altmeyer. **Performances:** Approx. 60; September–June.

VENICE (Venetia)
330 miles N of Rome

Venice is a city of magic, where the boundaries between fancy and fact are obscured, and where the ever-changing play of light on water is reflected on the magnificent palazzos that line the Grand Canal. Hordes of visitors throng St.

Mark's Square in summer, but those who wander among the winding passageways and cross the canals by the footbridges will discover her magic even at the height of the tourist season. This is where Vivaldi was born and Wagner died, and where generations of organists, from Willaert to Monteverdi to Gabrieli, filled the glorious domed spaces of St. Mark's Cathedral with music that influenced composers throughout Europe. The world's first public opera house opened here in 1637, and though it hasn't survived, visitors may still enjoy the unparalleled splendor of La Fenice, the magnificent opera house built in 1792.

ONGOING EVENTS

Teatro La Fenice

Op, Orch, Chor, Cham, Dance	Teatro la Fenice Biglietteria Campo S. Fontin, 1965 30124 Venezia

One of Italy's most renowned and most beautiful theaters, La Fenice has a proud history at the center of Italy's musical life. Its name, "The Phoenix," refers to the resiliency with which it has been resurrected after two disastrous fires. An active and varied calendar proves that the tradition of excellence and perseverance continues. In addition to operas ranging from *Fidelio* to *La Bohème* to *Lohengrin,* there are many orchestral and chamber concerts. The carnival season in Venice is legendary, and La Fenice celebrates with a week-long series of noontime chamber music concerts held in the foyer. The theater is also the site of the prestigious Maria Callas Vocal Competition, with semifinals and finals open to the public in January. Although rebuilt after a fire in the mid-nineteenth century, the hall retains the graceful elegance of its eighteenh-century design. **Resident Companies:** Orchestra and Chorus of La Fenice. **Recent Performers:** soprano Barbara Hendricks, tenor Francisco Araiza, pianist Maurizio Pollini. **Performances:** 100; October–June.

IN THE AREA

Music in the Museums

1 Month Late June–Late July	Musica nei Musei Veneto Musica "Casa Pase"
Cham	Via Robert Browning, 141 31011 Asolo

Bringing together diverse but complementary art forms is the goal of this series. Museums and galleries throughout the province of Venetia are host to chamber music that spans the centuries. It is possible to hear contemporary music in Venice's Peggy Guggenheim Collection, vocal music amid Canova's plaster casts in Possagno, or baroque opera in the civic museum of Bassano. **Recent Performers:** Verona Chamber Orchestra, Karlstadt Chamber Ensemble, Da Ponte String Quartet. **Venues:** 10 museums throughout Venetia. **Performances:** 14; almost all at 9 P.M.

VERONA (Venetia)
310 miles NW of Rome

The strife that brought tragedy to Romeo and Juliet characterized this city long before Shakespeare immortalized its most famous residents. The Roman city was the envy of Frankish tribes, and the rivalry of Guelphs and Ghibellines gave way to a struggle between Milan and Venice. Occupied by Austria in 1814, Verona finally became part of the united Italy in 1866. The city's importance to the Romans can be gauged by its magnificent arena, one of the largest ever built. Despite its turbulent history, Verona has long been an important artistic center, rivaled in Venetia only by Venice.

FESTIVALS

Verona Arena

2 Months	Arena di Verona
July–August	Information Office–Ente Arena
Op, Chor, Dance	Piazza Bra, 28
	37121 Verona
	Tel: 045/590109

This is the site of perhaps the most widely known musical event in Italy, and understandably so. The first-century Roman Arena could seat 25,000 spectators, and was among the largest ever built. Today the immense amphitheater lends itself perfectly to the spectacle of opera and dance—*Aida* here is legendary. **Recent Performers:** tenor Luciano Pavarotti, bass Paul Plishka, conductor Lorin Maazel. **Performances:** 40.

VICENZA (Venetia)
325 miles NW of Rome

Vicenza was transformed in the sixteenth century by one man—architect Andrea Palladio. His many building projects are characterized by simplicity and symmetry, and his combination of classical and Renaissance forms resulted in a style mirrored throughout Europe. Palladio's masterpiece is the Vicenza Basilica, which now contains a museum devoted to its designer. Throughout the area villas in the Palladian style give a formal elegance to the region.

ONGOING EVENTS

The Gold of Veneto

Cham, Dance

L'Oro del Veneto
Via Querini, 10
Mestre/Venezia
Tel: 041/974299

A regional project that seeks to promote both musical life and tourism, this series of concerts takes advantage of villas and palazzos throughout the area while offering the majority of its programs in Vicenza. The programs are as various as the locales, and may include opera arias, New Orleans Jazz, and baroque chamber music. **Recent Performers:** Orchestra Vecchia Vienna, Pro Arte Quartet. **Performances:** 25; August–October.

LUXEMBOURG

Echternach (courtesy of the Luxembourg National Tourist Office).

LUXEMBOURG

CALENDAR

MAY

Echternach International Festivals, **Echternach**

JUNE

Echternach International Festivals, **Echternach**

JULY

Wiltz Open Air Theater and Music Festival, **Wiltz**

The international telephone country code for Luxembourg is (011) 352. Although individual cities do not have area codes, it may be necessary to dial a prefix when calling within Luxembourg. Check the local telephone directory for more information.

ECHTERNACH
20 miles NE of Luxembourg City

A small town on the German border, Echternach lies beside the Sauer river near the German-Luxembourgoise Natural Park. While the mountains entice hikers to well-marked trails, the less venturesome are rewarded by the carefully restored buildings of the town. Medieval walls still stand, and the fourteenth-century Town Hall dominates the central square. From the eighth century to the French Revolution, the Benedictine monks cultivated hymn singing, and now every year on Whittuesday a dance procession in honor of St. Willibord, the founder of the Basilica, traverses the city streets.

FESTIVAL

Echternach International Festival

5–6 Weeks	Festival International
Late May–Late June	Echternach
	P.O. Box 30
Orch, Chor, Cham, Rec,	L-6401 Echternach
Org, Ex	Tel: 72 83 47
	Fax: 72 83 48

Decades of hopes and plans were realized in 1975 when this festival was inaugurated. Internationally known musicians such as Yehudi Menuhin and Claudio Arrau as well as promising young artists are featured in programs that span the repertoire from the baroque to the present. Living composers are especially honored here, and almost every year one or more is present as a guest of the festival. **Recent Performers:** Camerata Bern with oboist Heinz Holliger, Melos Quartet, guitarist Julian Bream, pianist Vladimir Ashkenazy. **Venues:** Basilica of St. Willibord (in the Benedictine abbey), Church of St. Peter and St. Paul, Luxembourg Theater and Conservatory. **Performances:** 18 (3–4 Weekly); 8:30 P.M.

LUXEMBOURG CITY

This pulsating capital enjoys a spectacular location above the Alzette River. The Old Town commands the highest ground and is separated from the newer sections below by ravines spanned by nearly 100 bridges. This strategic spot has been fortified since the days of the Romans, and its history, like that of the country as a whole, tells of the struggles for power that at one time or another have brought almost all the armies of Europe to its territory. Today it serves as a more pacific center, and since 1952 has been the home of the European Community.

ONGOING EVENTS

Municipal Theater

Op, Orch, Chor, Cham, Rec, Dance, Lect, Th	Théâtre Municipal Rond-Point Robert Schumann L-Luxembourg City Tel: 47 08 95 (tickets) 47 96 27 10 (info)

A cultural center of many facets, this theater recently celebrated its 25th anniversary. Lectures and exhibitions complement the performing arts, which range from opera and ballet to folk music and cabaret. Recent productions include *Salome*, *My Fair Lady*, and Brahms' *German Requiem*. **Recent Performers:** Tokyo Philharmonic Orchestra, Bolshoi Ballet, pianist Maria Tipo. **Performances:** Approx. 125; September–May.

WILTZ
25 miles NW of Luxembourg City

This city on the banks of the Wiltz river is a favored tourist center, with more than a dozen chalets located in the surrounding forest. The city is crowned by the château of the Counts of Wiltz, located in the picturesque Upper Town. The château gardens and nearby amphitheater are host to the annual festival of theater and music.

FESTIVALS

Wiltz Open-Air Theater and Music Festival

Weekends	Festival Européen de
July	Théâtre en Plein Air
	et de Musique
Orch, Cham, Rec, Dance,	1, rue du Château
Jazz, Th	L-9516 Wiltz
	Tel: 958 145
	Fax: 958 145

Since 1953 the Wiltz festival has presented well-known artists and promoted young talents. From classical guitar to the National Black Touring Circuit's "I have a Dream," from Carl Orff's *Carmina Burana* with the Introdans Ballet to Anouilh's *Antigone*, there are offerings for every taste. **Recent Performers:** soprano Julia Miguenes, pianist Sviatoslav Richter, singer Ella Fitzgerald. **Venues:** churches, open-air theater, château, concert halls. **Performances:** 12–15; 8:45 P.M.

Monaco

Monaco Casino, home of the Opéra de Monte Carlo (courtesy of the Monaco Government Tourist and Convention Bureau).

MONACO

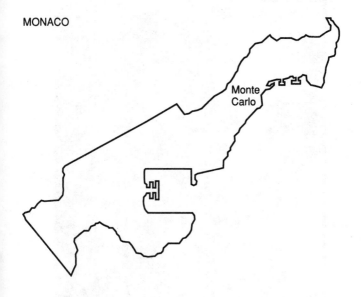

Monte
Carlo

CALENDAR

MARCH

Spring of the Arts, **Monte Carlo**

APRIL

Spring of the Arts, **Monte Carlo**

JULY

Summer Concerts at the Palace, **Monte Carlo**

AUGUST

Summer Concerts at the Palace, **Monte Carlo**

The international telephone country code for Monaco is (011) 33. Monaco shares this code with France.

MONACO

The waters of the Riviera reflect back the glittering splendor of the Principality of Monaco, one of the wealthiest and most glamorous states in Europe. Its less than 500 acres are divided into four areas: Monte Carlo (the New City), where the Casino houses both the Opera House and the famed Gaming Rooms; Monaco (the Old City), site of the crenelated medieval fortress that is the Prince's Palace; La Condamine (the port); and Fontevielle, where a magnificent park and rose garden dedicated to Princess Grace offer respite from the social whirl.

FESTIVALS

Spring of the Arts

1 Month	Direction des Affaires
Late March–Late April	Culturelles
	4, rue des Iris
Op, Orch, Cham, Rec,	ML 98000 Monaco
Dance, Th, Film, Fringe	Tel: 93 30 19 21

This festival is actually a combination of two concurrent events, the Festival of Musical Films and Films of Opera, and the Biennial Sculpture Exhibition. Musical offerings are not limited to movies, however, and live performances have featured famed artists such as Montserrat Caballé as well as the young winners of prestigious international vocal competitions. Recent opera productions have included Gluck's *Alceste* and Handel's *Flavio* on authentic instruments with historically accurate costumes and sets. The orchestral repertoire includes a wide range of music, from Dowland to Dukas and Scriabin to Villa-Lobos. **Recent Performers:** The King's Consort, pianist Claudio Arrau, mezzo-soprano Janet Baker. **Venues:** Princess Grace Theatre, Salle Garnier, Chapel of the Visitation, Center of Congress Auditorium. **Performances:** 23.

Summer Concerts at the Palace

6 Concerts	Palace Concerts
Mid-July–Mid-August	Direction du Tourisme
	2a, Boulevard des Moulins
Orch, Chor	Monte Carlo
	MC 98030 Monaco Cedex
	Tel: 93 30 87 01

The cascading marble staircases and gracefully arched portico of the Palace's Main Quadrangle form the background for the Monte Carlo Philharmonic Orchestra's series of outdoor concerts. Joined by stellar guests, the orchestra performs in what was once the central portion of the thirteenth-century fortress. **Recent Performers:** conductor Rafael Frühbeck de Burgos, pianist Murray Perahia, soprano Katia Ricciarelli. **Venue:** Main Quadrangle of the Palace. **Performances:** 6.

ONGOING EVENTS

Salle Garnier

Op, Orch, Cham, Rec	Atrium du Casino
	Place du Casino
	98007 Monaco Cedex
	Tel: 93 50 69 31
	93 50 76 54

Located in the Monaco Casino, this splendid hall is the home of the Opéra de Monte Carlo. Since its inception in 1879, the Opéra de Monte Carlo has been noted for the artistic integrity of its productions. Directed for many years by Serge de Diaghilev and Raoul Gunsbourg, it has presented premieres by such composers as Berlioz, Massenet, and Puccini, and decors by Rouault, Picasso, and Brayer. Recent productions include *Der Freischütz*, *La Bohème*, *Carmen*, and

La Traviata. Co-productions include those with the Washington Opera, the Teatro la Fenice in Venice, and Barcelona's Gran Teatro del Liceu. **Recent Performers:** sopranos Renata Scotto and Julia Migenes, tenor Luciano Pavarotti, I Solisti Veneti, Juilliard String Quartet. **Venue:** Salle Garnier, a 524-seat theatre designed by the architect of the Paris Opera and considered a jewel of the Belle Epoque for its golden opulence. **Performances:** approx. 12; January–March.

Rainier III Auditorium

Orch, Rec

Rainier III Auditorium
Convention Center
Boulevard Louis II
Monte Carlo
MC 98000 Monaco
Tel: 93 50 93 00

This auditorium is the home of the Monte Carlo Philharmonic Orchestra, which is joined by an impressive roster of guest soloists. Other programs include guest orchestras and recitals by renowned artists. **Recent Performers:** violinist Anne-Sophie Mutter, pianist Martha Argerich, mezzo-soprano Dame Janet Baker. **Performances:** 25; year-round (Philharmonic).

THE NETHERLANDS

The Christian Müller Organ (1738) in St. Bavo's Church, Haarlem (courtesy of E. A. van Voorden).

THE NETHERLANDS
1 Haarlem
2 The Hague
3 Rotterdam
4 Utrecht

Calendar

JUNE

Holland Festival, **Amsterdam**

JULY

Haarlem International Organ Festival, **Haarlem**

AUGUST

Holland Festival—Early Music Utrecht, **Utrecht**

SEPTEMBER

Holland Festival—Early Music Utrecht, **Utrecht**
International Gaudeamus Music Week, **Amsterdam**

The international telephone country code for the Netherlands is (011) 31. City codes have the prefix 0, which is deleted when calling from abroad.

AMSTERDAM

Eccentric yet pragmatic, innovative yet traditional, Amsterdam reflects the spirit of its people in a way rarely matched by other cities. The 164 waterways that weave through the city are lined with gabled mansions built in Amsterdam's golden age, the seventeenth century, evoking images of Venice, the great canal city to the south. But the similarities end there. Progress is to Amsterdam what nostalgia is to Venice—its lifeblood, as is perhaps best illustrated in the resourceful use of many of the city's oldest and most historic buildings as offices and homes, rather than monuments or museums. Not that Amsterdam is in any way lacking in museums! They are in great abundance here, and the Rijkmuseum Vincent van Gogh is highly renowned, featuring the world's largest collection of the Dutch painter's works.

FESTIVALS

The Holland Festival

1 Month	Netherlands Reservation
June	Center
	P.O. Box 404
Op, Orch, Chor, Cham, Rec,	2260 AK Leidschendam
Dance, Film, Th	The Netherlands
	Tel: 070/320 25 00

The Holland Festival, one of the most important events on the Dutch cultural calendar, has presented both standard repertoire and invigorating new works since 1948, showcasing some of the world's most renowned performers. An impressive schedule of opera, concerts, dance, and theater productions is offered in the concert halls and theaters of two of Holland's oldest and most beautiful cities—Amsterdam and the Hague. **Recent Performers:** Royal Concertgebouw Orchestra conducted by Riccardo Chailly, The Netherlands Opera Company, Schönberg Ensemble, soprano Kathleen Battle with pianist Martin Katz. **Venues:** Many sites in Amsterdam and the Hague. **Performances:** Daily.

International Gaudeamus Music Week

1 Week
Early September

Orch, Chor, Cham

International Gaudeamus
Music Week
Swammerdamstr. 38
1091 RV Amsterdam
Tel: 020/94 73 49

Since 1947 the Contemporary Music Center of the Gaudeamus Foundation has used this festival as a showcase for premieres of works by young composers such as Helmut Lachenmann and Joep Straesser. Other events sponsored by the organization include workshops for young composers and musicians, special festivals with concerts, lectures, and panel discussions, Days of Dutch Music in December, and many other activities. **Recent Performers:** Radio Chamber Orchestra, The Hague Percussion Group, Arditti Quartet. **Venues:** Beurs van Berlage, Paradiso, IJsbreker Music Center, Municipal Museum, others. **Performances:** daily.

ONGOING EVENTS

Beurs Van Berlage

Orch, Chor, Cham, Rec

Beurs Van Berlage
Damrak 213
1012 ZH Amsterdam
Tel: 020/6271161
Fax: 020/6270466

This building, formerly the Berlage stock exchange, is now one of the centers of Amsterdam's musical life. Located in the oldest part of central Amsterdam, this historic structure now contains two concert halls, Wang Hall and AGA

Hall, which host the Netherlands Philharmonic Orchestra and the Netherlands Chamber Orchestra under the batons of such conductors as Lukas Foss, Tibor Varga, Frans Brüggen, and Hartmut Haenchen. In addition to the standard orchestral and chamber repertoire, these ensembles participate in the opera productions at the Muziektheater. **Recent Performers:** conductor/cellist Heinrich Schiff, violinist Josef Suk, bass Robert Holl. **Performances:** 120; September–June.

IJsbreker Music Center

Cham

Muziekcentrum De IJsbreker
Weesperzijde 23
1091 EC Amsterdam
Tel: 020/66 81 805
Fax: 020/94 66 07

Since 1980 performances at the IJsbreker have focused solely on modern music, presenting the works of such well-known figures as Carter, Cage, Crumb, Kagel, Ligeti, and Stockhausen, as well as those of many less-famous composers. Events are held in the 150-seat concert hall of this building, designed in 1885 by Van Gendt, the architect of the Concertgebouw. A special treat here is the cafe and terrace overlooking the Amstel river. Bimonthly calendars of the concerts, workshops, master classes, and lectures are available throughout the city. The Center also participates in jointly sponsored events such as a recent opera based on the life of poet William Blake. **Recent Performers:** Schönberg Ensemble, Arditti String Quartet, oboist Heinz Holliger, cellist Heinrich Schiff. **Performances:** approx. 200; September–June.

Netherlands Opera

Op

De Nederlandse Opera
Waterlooplein 22
1011 PG Amsterdam
Tel: 020/5518922
Fax: 020/832350

Founded in 1964, the Netherlands Opera has performed in the newly built Muzeiktheater in the heart of Amsterdam since 1986. The company works principally with the Netherlands Philharmonic Orchestra, but also collaborates with the Rotterdam Philharmonic and Concertgebouw orchestras. Among the company's recent productions are Wagner's

Parsifal, Mozart's *Idomeneo*, and Monteverdi's *Il Ritorno d'Ulisse in Patria*. The Opera shares the 1600-seat Muziektheater with the National Ballet. **Recent Performers:** conductors Nikolaus Harnoncourt, Pierre Boulez, Simon Rattle, Mstislav Rostropovich, director Peter Sellars. **Venue:** Het Muziektheater. **Performances:** 10; September–June.

Royal Concertgebouw

Op, Orch, Chor, Cham, Rec   Royal Concertgebouw
                              Jacob Obrechtstraat 51
                              1071 K J Amsterdam
                              Tel: 020/718 345

The concert hall of this venerable theater is considered by many to have the most perfect acoustics in Europe. Designed in 1888, the building contains both the 2219-seat concert hall and an intimate chamber music hall accommodating just under 500. The name Concertgebouw, however, is synonymous with the resident orchestra, now led by Riccardo Chailly. Ravel, Debussy, Mahler, Richard Strauss, Stravinsky, Schönberg, Hindemith, and Milhaud are among the many composers who have led this renowned orchestra in performances of their own works. In addition to concerts by this ensemble, the Concertgebouw is host to guest orchestras, chamber music programs, recitals, and performances by the National Ballet and Netherlands Ballet Orchestra. **Recent Performers:** Conductors Erich Leinsdorf and Klaus Tennstedt, Tokyo String Quartet, pianist Maurizio Pollini, baritone Dietrich Fischer-Dieskau. **Performances:** approx. 80; August–June.

HAARLEM
15 miles W of Amsterdam

This often overlooked medieval town is one of Holland's most fascinating centers of Dutch history. Standing in Haarlem's main square, the Grote Markt, one is surrounded by such architectural gems as the majestic Renaissance "Meat Market," and an impressive fourteenth-century Town Hall, not to mention dozens of other buildings representing Dutch architecture from the fifteenth through nineteenth centuries. Of particular interest is the fifteenth-century Church of St. Bavo. This imposing church houses one of Europe's most famous organs, an immense instrument played by many a visiting musician, including Handel, Mozart, and Albert Schweitzer. Haarlem's museums are some of Holland's most magnificent, offering hours of exploration.

FESTIVALS

Haarlem International Organ Festival

3 Weeks	Stichting International Orgel
July	Concours
	Postbus 511
Org	2003 PB Haarlem
	Tel: 023/17 12 13

Many music lovers consider the Netherlands an "organ paradise," for no other country harbors such a wealth of historic organs. Of the instruments to be found in every town and village, the organ in St. Bavo's in Haarlem is perhaps the most famous. Designed by Christian Müller and completed in 1738, the fame of this organ soon spread, and both Handel and Mozart were among the musicians who traveled here to play it. The organ and the splendid case by sculptor Jan van Logeren were completely renovated in 1961, restoring the instrument to its original glory. The organ has stimulated a rich musical tradition: the establishment of the centuries-old municipal organ recitals, the International Summer Academy for Organists, and since 1951 the International Organ Improvisation Competition.

Concertgebouw

Orch, Chor, Cham, Rec, Org,	Concertgebouw
Dance, Th	Klokhuisplein 2A
	2011 HK Haarlem
	Tel: 023/320994

The Concertgebouw is the site of many musical activities, and is the home of the North Holland Philharmonic Orchestra. Established as a symphonic orchestra in 1921, the ensemble received its present name in 1953, and has since earned a reputation as one of the best regional orchestras in Holland. There are a number of family concerts with free lemonade and "Promenade Concerts" featuring lighter classical works. **Recent Performers:** Conductor Frans Brüggen, pianist Imogen Cooper, violinist Emmy Verhey. **Venues:** Concertgebouw Haarlem, other sites throughout Holland. **Performances:** Approx. 110; September–June.

THE HAGUE
35 miles SW of Amsterdam

Three majestic royal palaces are evidence that The Hague has been a sophisticated seat of nobility since the thirteenth century. Although it is currently the seat of Holland's government, The Hague is not its capital. Nevertheless, with a fashionable population of half a million, and over 60 embassies, this is one of Holland's most elegant and cosmopolitan cities. Within a short tram ride from town is the highly popular seaside resort of Scheveningen, known for its lively casinos, handsome hotels, and nudist beaches.

ONGOING EVENTS

Dr. Anton Philipszaal

Orch, Chor, Cham, Rec

Dr. Anton Philipszaal
Residentie Orkest
Postbox 11543
2502 AM The Hague
Tel: 070/3609 810

Built in 1987 to house the Residentie Orchestra, this concert hall also hosts outstanding ensembles and soloists from around the world. The Residentie Orchestra itself has a venerable history, and has played under Toscanini, Stokowsky, Stravinsky, and Bernstein. Important premieres are frequent. **Recent Performers:** Riccardo Chailly conducting the Royal Concertgebouw Orchestra, Amsterdam Baroque Orchestra, tenor Peter Schreier. **Performances:** 50; September–June.

ROTTERDAM
35 miles SW of Amsterdam

Although only a short drive from both The Hague and Amsterdam, Rotterdam is vastly different from its neighboring cities. Devastated by a Nazi air raid, this once historic city is now a prime example of postwar and modern architecture. In this sense, Rotterdam proves that Dutch creativity did not begin and end in the seventeenth century. Around town, interesting and unique examples of Cubism blend nicely with an abundance of greenery, evoking the optimistic atmosphere of a city's rebirth.

ONGOING EVENTS

de Doelen Concert Hall

Orch, Chor, Cham, Rec,   Concert en Congresgebouw
    Org, Jazz, Pop   de Doelen
                        Schouwburgplein 50
                        3012 CT Rotterdam
                        Tel: 010/4132490

This spacious theater was built in 1966 to replace the Doelezaal, destroyed during World War II. One of the largest concert halls in the Netherlands, it draws 600,000 audience members a year to stimulating programs that include not only stellar classical performers but more specialized offerings such as youth orchestras, Indian music, and contemporary Dutch composers. Though the regular season runs from September to June, performances are given throughout the summer. **Recent Performers:** Peking Opera, Musica Antiqua Köln, pianist Bella Davidovich. **Performances:** Approx. 130.

Rotterdam Philharmonic Orchestra

Orch   Rotterdam Philharmonic
                        Orchestra de Doelen
                      Kruisstraat 2
                      3012 CT Rotterdam
                      Tel: 010/413 24 90

The international character of Rotterdam is reflected in its celebrated orchestra, where many of the stellar guest artists and more than a third of the orchestral musicians are from abroad. Established in 1918 as "an association of professional musicians for the mutual practice of art," this ensemble began a new era in 1966 with the opening of the de Doelen, one of the finest modern concert halls in the world. **Recent Performers:** Conductor James Conlon, pianist André Watts, soprano Susan Dunn. **Venue:** de Doelen; sites in Amsterdam, The Hague, Utrecht. **Performances:** 70 (in Rotterdam); September–June.

UTRECHT
20 miles S of Amsterdam

Brimming with high-gabled houses and an endless maze of canals, Utrecht (along with Maastricht) is Holland's oldest city. Utrecht's historic treasures almost seem disproportionate to its small size, and an intimate atmosphere prevails. At the forefront of the historic sites is the late-Gothic Domkerk. Built between 1254 and 1517, the cathedral is filled with ancient tombs and brilliant stained glass, but most magnificent is its 365-foot bell tower, Holland's tallest. The city's thirteenth-century wharves and cellars now house delightful boutiques and cafes.

FESTIVALS

Holland Festival—Early Music Utrecht

10 Days	Utrecht Early Music Festival
Late August–Early September	Organisatie Oude Muziek
	Postbus 734
Op, Orch, Chor, Cham, Rec,	3500 As Utrecht
Org, Dance, Fringe	Tel: 030/34 09 21
	030/34 09 81

Since 1982 musicians and music lovers from all over the world have come to this festival, which is at the forefront in the recent revival of interest in early music. In addition to more than 60 principal concerts, over 100 other activities (lectures, workshops, fringe concerts) take place in beautiful, historic venues, including the Vredenburg Concert Hall. **Recent Performers:** Thomas Hengelbrock conducting the Freiburger Barockorchestra, the Hilliard Ensemble, harpsichordist Gustav Leonhardt, sopranos Montserrat Figueras, Emma Kirkby, and Catherine Bott. **Venues:** historic churches throughout Utrecht. **Performances:** 200.

SCANDINAVIA

Olavinlinna Castle (courtesy of the Finnish Tourist Board).

SCANDINAVIA

SWEDEN

FINLAND

•2   5

NORWAY

7

4
6   •3

Oslo

Helsinki

Stockholm

DENMARK

8

1•

•Copenhagen

DENMARK	NORWAY
1 Århus	7 Bergen

FINLAND	SWEDEN
2 Jkväskylä	8 Visby
3 Lahti	
4 Naantali	
5 Savonlinna	
6 Turku	

CALENDAR

APRIL

Tivoli Concerts, **Copenhagen** (Denmark)

MAY

Bergen International Festival, **Bergen** (Norway)
Danish Ballet and Opera Festival, **Copenhagen** (Denmark)
Drottningholm Court Theatre Festival, **Stockholm** (Sweden)
Tivoli Concerts, **Copenhagen** (Denmark)

JUNE

Bergen International Festival, **Bergen** (Norway)
Drottningholm Court Theatre Festival, **Stockholm** (Sweden)
Jyväskylä Arts Festival, **Jyväskylä** (Finland)
Naantali Music Festival, **Naantali** (Finland)
Tivoli Concerts, **Copenhagen** (Denmark)

JULY

Drottningholm Court Theatre Festival, **Stockholm** (Sweden)
Lahti Organ Festival, **Lahti** (Finland)
Savonlinna Opera Festival, **Savonlinna** (Finland)
Tivoli Concerts, **Copenhagen** (Denmark)
Visby Festival, **Visby** (Sweden)

AUGUST

Chamber Music Festival, **Oslo** (Norway)
Drottningholm Court Theatre Festival, **Stockholm** (Sweden)
Helsinki Festival, **Helsinki** (Finland)
Lahti Organ Festival, **Lahti** (Finland)
Savonlinna Opera Festival, **Savonlinna** (Finland)
Tivoli Concerts, **Copenhagen** (Denmark)
Turku Music Festival, **Turku** (Finland)
Visby Festival, **Visby** (Sweden)

SEPTEMBER

Århus Festival, **Århus** (Denmark)
Drottningholm Court Theatre Festival, **Stockholm** (Sweden)
Helsinki Festival, **Helsinki** (Finland)
Tivoli Concerts, **Copenhagen** (Denmark)

OCTOBER

Oslo Contemporary Music Festival, **Oslo** (Norway)

DENMARK

ﾟﾟﾟﾟﾟﾟﾟﾟﾟﾟﾟﾟﾟ

The international telephone country code for Denmark is (011) 45. There is no prefix to the city codes.

ÅRHUS
95 miles NW of Copenhagen

The vivacity of this highly cultural town can be attributed not only to its university, but also to the fact that it is Denmark's second largest city. Particularly appealing are the Old Town, where a reconstructed village presents a glimpse of the sixteenth century, two museums devoted to Scandinavian history, and the magnificent Århus Cathedral, dating from the thirteenth century.

FESTIVALS

Århus Festival

10 Days	Århus Festival
Early September	Musikhuset
	Thomas Jensen Allé
Op, Orch, Chor, Cham, Rec,	DK-8000 Århus C
Dance, Th, Folk, Film,	Tel: 86/12 12 33
Ex, Jazz, Child, Lect,	Fax: 86/19 43 86
Fringe, others	

The Århus Festival, founded in 1965, has blossomed into Scandinavia's largest annual cultural celebration. The festival completely dominates the city throughout its duration, with performances organized by local institutions, societies, and clubs as well as by the festival office itself. Its more than 300 diverse activities run the gamut from the traditional to the futuristic, and are designed to stimulate the intellect as well as to provide entertainment. **Recent Performers:** Royal Concertgebouw Orchestra, Le Mystère des Voix Bulgares, violinist Anne-Sophie Mutter, Chick Corea Acoustic Quartet. **Venues:** concert halls, churches, clubs, theaters, public squares, parks. **Performances:** many daily. Tickets available after 5 August.

COPENHAGEN

Denmark's capital is in many ways an unlikely representative of the rest of the country. In contrast to the relative conservatism of the remote Danish countryside, this port city's famous liberalism makes it comparable in many ways to Amsterdam. Skyscrapers have not been allowed to mar the skyline, and friendly sidewalk cafes and shops on some of Europe's longest arcades are the city's pride. The ever-popular Tivoli Gardens are a pedestrian's paradise of gardens and lakes, perfumed with the scent of over 100,000 flowers.

FESTIVALS

Danish Ballet and Opera Festival

2 Weeks	Danish Ballet and Opera
Late May	Festival
	Det Kongelige Theater Og
Op, Orch, Cham, Dance	Kapel
	Postboks 2185
	DK-1017 Kobenhavn K
	Tel: 33/14 10 02
	Fax: 33/14 46 06

Founded in 1951, the Danish Ballet and Opera Festival features an international roster of ballet companies as well as productions of operas such as *Otello* and *Les Contes d'Hoffman*. Orchestral and chamber music concerts feature music ranging from Couperin to Gershwin. **Recent Performers:** The Cleveland and Hamburg Ballet Companies, dancer Rudolf Nureyev. **Venues:** The Royal Theater, Tivoli Concert Hall. **Performances:** 20.

Tivoli Concerts

5 Months	Tivoli Musikafdelingen
Mid-April–Mid-September	Vesterbrogade 3
	DK-1620 Kobenhavn V
Op, Orch, Dance	Tel: 33/15 10 01
	Fax: 33/15 16 79

Since 1843 Tivoli has been the musical center of Copenhagen throughout the summer. Orchestras, soloists, and opera and ballet companies from all over the world perform in the 2000-seat Concert Hall. **Recent Performers:** Tivoli Symphony Orchestra with conductors Sergiu Commissiona and Aldo Ceccato, Tafelmusik, pianist Andras Schiff, Pilobolus Dance Theater. **Venue:** Concert Hall. **Performances:** nightly.

FINLAND

The international telephone country code for Finland is (011) 358. City codes have the prefix 9, which is deleted when calling from abroad.

HELSINKI

Entertainment can be found on nearly every corner of this vibrant town—from that found in the many pubs, outdoor cafes, and clubs to the concerts offered in the spectacular Finlandia Hall. The very look of the city seems to indicate a dynamic sense of the present and future. Indeed, much of Helsinki's most interesting architecture is not found in the older historic landmarks, but in the lively colors and angles of the newer buildings, whose innovation has brought the Scandinavian style to the forefront of architectural design.

FESTIVALS

Helsinki Festival

3 Weeks	Helsinki Festival
Mid-August–Mid-September	Unioninkatu 28
	SF-00100 Helsinki
Orch, Cham, Rec, Jazz,	Tel: 90/659 688
Dance, Th, Film, Pop, Ex	Fax: 90/656 715

Classical music predominates, but the challenging and innovative offerings of theater, dance, film, and popular music give this festival its highly original character. Contemporary music is represented on almost every concert program, where favorites from Bach to Bartók can also be found. **Recent Performers:** Helsinki Philharmonic Orchestra, Tokyo String Quartet, guitarist Julian Bream. **Venues:** Finlandia Hall, Johannes Church, Espoo Cultural Center, Temppeliaukio Church, Savoy Theater, others. **Performances:** 60 concerts; dozens of other events.

ONGOING EVENTS

Finlandia Hall

Op, Orch, Chor, Cham, Rec, Finlandia Hall
Org, Dance, Th, Film, Ex Lippupalvelu
Bio-Bio's Hall
Mannerheimintie 5
SF-00100 Helsinki
Tel: 90/643043

This sleek, contemporary building designed by Alvar Aalto in 1976 contains a concert hall, chamber music hall, and a recital hall, and is Helsinki's center for both concerts and conferences. The Helsinki Philharmonic Orchestra under the direction of Sergiu Commissiona is in residence here. Music heard in the various halls ranges from Handel to Xenakis. **Recent Performers:** Moscow Chamber Orchestra, soprano Arleen Auger, tenor José Carreras, violinist Joseph Swensen. **Performances:** Approx. 200; September–May.

The Finnish National Opera

Op Finnish National Opera
Bulevardi 23-27
SF-00181 Helsinki
Tel: 90/123401
Fax: 90/1292301

When the New Opera House opened in 1990, Finland for the first time had a theater specially designed for operatic performances. The splendid new buildng combines tradition and modernity in an extensive facility on the shore of the Töölönlahti Bay. The house is the home of the Finnish National Opera, which since 1918 had performed at the Russian Drama Theater. The larger stage and orchestra pit of the New Opera House allows a wider range of repertoire in the 12 annual productions.

JYVÄSKYLÄ
150 miles N of Helsinki

Set in a gorgeous region of lakes, log cabins, and forests, Jyväskylä is one of the picturesque villages highly popular among Finnish vacationers. The town rests on the north shore of Lake Päijänne (Finland's second largest), where an endless stream of pleasure craft arrive and depart on voyages south through the lake's spectacular scenery to the neighboring city of Lahti. Woodworking is an important industry here, directly attributable to the lush surrounding forest, and the town's large university provides a lively cultural community. Not to be overlooked is the unique Alvar Aalto museum, displaying the works of the famous Finnish architect who was born and raised here.

FESTIVALS

Jyväskylä Arts Festival

10 Days	Jyväskylän Arts Festival
Mid-June	Kramsunkatu 1
	SF-40600 Jyväskylä
Orch, Chor, Cham, Rec,	Tel: 941/617 531
Dance, Th, Film, Ex	

This is the oldest continuously occurring arts festival in Finland (founded in 1955). The concerts are stellar, and conferences and symposia on subjects such as "Poetry and Mysticism," "Religious Conversion as an Early Twentieth-Century Literary Phenomenon," and "The Finns—One of Europe's Minorities" are just as important. Ethnic music (Arabic, Estonian, Jewish) as well as more traditional Western repertoire is offered. **Recent Performers:** Kronos Quartet, sitarist Ravi Shankar, fortepianist Malcom Bilson. **Venues:** churches and various concert halls. **Performances:** approx. 60.

LAHTI
60 miles N of Helsinki

Famous for its world-class ski jumps, Lahti is a prominent winter sports town that lies just to the north of Helsinki, on the route to the popular Lake Region. The highest ski jump is of use to more than just brave souls on skis — an observation deck is open to the public during summer months and affords magnificent views of the bordering Lake Region.

FESTIVALS

Lahti Organ Festival

1 Week	Lahti Organ Festival
Late July–Early August	Kirkkokatu 5
	SF-15110 Lahti
Orch, Chor, Cham, Rec,	Tel: 918/23 184
Lec, Master classes	Fax: 918/832 190

Since 1972 the Lahti Organ Festival has been a meeting place for organists as well as fans of organ music. Recent evidence of the commitment to bring new, gifted performers to Lahti was the 1989 organ competition, which drew participants from many countries. The festival often commissions works from young composers. Expect more than just organ music, for programs are well rounded. **Recent Performers:** Estonian State Symphony Orchestra, Tallis Scholars, organist Ton Koopman. **Venues:** The Church of the Cross, Lahti City Theatre, surrounding churches. **Performances:** many daily.

NAANTALI
110 miles W of Helsinki

An idyllic seaside spot easily reached from Helsinki and Stockholm, Naantali offers peace and relaxation enhanced by sun, sea, shady trees, charming old architecture, fine restaurants, and quaint shops specializing in the works of local artisans. The entire old quarter of the city serves as a museum of medieval town planning and Finnish history. There are plenty of places to visit, including the yacht harbor, Copper Mountain, the island of Kilo, and the gardens at the President's summer residence. Throughout the summer a trumpet calls out Vesper hymns from the belfry of the Convent Church at 8 P.M.

FESTIVALS

Naantali Music Festival

2 Weeks	Naantali Music Festival
Mid-June	Puistotie 24, Box 46
	SF-21101 Naantali
Cham, Rec, Org	Tel: 921/75 53 63
	Fax: 921/75 54 25

This chamber music festival, housed in the monumental fifteenth-century Naantali Abbey, has become one of the highlights of the Finnish cultural calendar. First held in 1980, it quickly became an event of international importance under the artistic direction of Professor Arto Noras. The intimate atmosphere that prevails provides the artists and audience with a unique chance to interact. **Recent Performers:** The Academy of Ancient Music, The Academy of St. Martin in the Fields, violinists Isaac Stern and Miriam Fried, cellist Janos Starker. **Venues:** Naantali Abbey, various medieval churches. **Performances:** 25; 2 daily.

SAVONLINNA
190 miles NE of Helsinki

Situated on a group of islands connected by a network of bridges, Savonlinna is a central attraction of the Saimaa Lake District. Its harbor is home for the Saimaa Lake steamers, and the variety of exquisite beaches makes this area a popular vacation resort. Aside from the beauty of the islands, Savonlinna's other marvel is the magnificent medieval castle Olavinlinna, which occupies its own tiny island.

FESTIVALS

Savonlinna Opera Festival

1 Month	Savonlinna Opera Festival
Early July–Early August	Olavinkatu 35
	SF-57130 Savonlinna
Op, Orch, Chor, Cham, Rec,	Tel: 957/514 700
Dance	Fax: 957/21 866

Finland's best-known music festival is truly an international event, with opera companies, ballet troupes, and symphony orchestras from around the globe. Founded in 1912, the festival was given new life in 1967 with a performance of *Fidelio* in the fifteenth-century Olavinlinna Castle. From 1972 to 1980 the event was under the artistic direction of Martti Tavela, and artists of similar renown have continued to build the festival's prestige. A new production is always among the half-dozen operas performed each year by the festival's own company and by visiting companies, which have included the Royal Opera of Stockholm, the National Theater of Prague, and the Central Opera of China. In addition to opera, there are numerous orchestral and chamber music concerts, and recitals by such well-known singers as tenor Nicolai Gedda and soprano Edith Mathis. **Recent Performers:** Czech Philharmonic Orchestra, Bavarian Chamber Opera, soprano Eva Marton, baritone Tom Kraus. **Venues:** Olavinlinna Castle, Music Institute, nearby churches. **Performances:** daily.

TURKU
100 miles W of Helsinki

Situated on the banks of the river Aura, Turku is Finland's oldest city and was once the country's capital. Although a raging fire in 1827 destroyed many of the town's mostly wooden buildings, the structures that remained have been restored. Most notable is the 700-year-old cathedral, which still serves as the seat of Finland's archbishop, and the thirteenth-century castle that was once the seat of government. The Handicrafts museum is a fascinating street of wooden houses spared by the fire that now serve as quarters to potters, weavers, and craftspeople.

FESTIVALS

Turku Music Festival

10 Days	Turku Music Festival
Mid-August	Uudenmaankatu 1
	SF-20500 Turku
Orch, Chor, Cham, Rec, Org, Lec	Tel: 921/511 162

Founded in 1960, the Turku Music Festival is one of Finland's oldest, offering a medley of musical styles and periods from medieval to modern world premieres. A recent season emphasized keyboard instruments, with performers such as harpsichordist Gustav Leonhardt and pianist Murray Perahia. In addition to regular concerts by outstanding artists, the festival often includes a "Night of the Arts" featuring all aspects of the arts in galleries, museums, bookstores, and cafes along the riverside and around the marketplace. **Recent Performers:** London Classical Players conducted by Roger Norrington, the London Philharmonic conducted by Esa-Pekka Salonen, violinist Joshua Bell, soprano Barbara Hendricks. **Venues:** Turku Cathedral and Castle, Concert Hall, Academy Hall, Betel Church, Swedish Theater, Sibelius Museum, Michael's Church. **Performances:** more than 20.

NORWAY

The international telephone country code for Norway is (011) 47. City codes have the prefix 0, which is deleted when calling from abroad.

BERGEN
180 miles NW of Oslo

The native town of Edvard Grieg, Bergen is certainly one of Scandinavia's most picturesque locales. The skyline of magnificent medieval buildings and church steeples is best viewed from atop Mt. Floyen, the steepest and highest of the city's seven surrounding mountains. Among the historic buildings worth coming back down for are the twelveth-century St. Mary's Church, which is Bergen's oldest building, and the remarkably restored thirteenth-century Håkonshallen.

FESTIVALS

Bergen International Festival

2 Weeks	Festspillene i Bergen
Late May–Early June	Box 183
	N-5001 Bergen
Op, Orch, Chor, Cham,	Tel: 05/32 04 00
Dance, Jazz, Folk, Th	

Since 1953, the Bergen Festival has offered extensive and richly varied programs with the motto "Det beste for de fleste," "Quality for the Majority." These diverse activities include the "Music Factory" featuring contemporary music, special events honoring living Norwegian composers, and programs specially designed for young audiences. Music from the baroque to jazz and gospel is performed, as well as works composed by Bergen's native son, Edvard Grieg. **Recent Performers:** Stockholm Philharmonic Orchestra, violinist Isaac Stern, sopranos Elly Ameling and Victoria de los Angeles, the Swingle Singers. **Venues:** Bergen National Theater, Troldhaugen (Edvard and Nina Grieg's home), Lysoen (violinist and composer Ole Bull's summer residence on an island about 24 miles south of Bergen), Håkonshallen (inaugurated by King Håkon Håkonsson in 1261 and now the official reception rooms of the city of Bergen), the Bryggen Museum (featuring medieval Bergen), St. Mary's Church, the Wharf, others. Transportation is available to events outside of the city. **Performances:** as many as 18 daily.

OSLO

Spread out over a vast expanse of fjords, forests, and lakeland, the more than 450 square kilometers that constitute Oslo are a nature-lover's paradise, and congestion is almost an alien concept in this airy and spacious place. The city's central section is a relatively small concentration of diverse architectural styles, dominated by ultra-modern glass and concrete structures. Art can be found everywhere in Oslo, not only in the museums for which the city is most famous, but in countless frescoes that grace the city's walls and captivating sculptures found in the Vigeland Sculpture Park and other parks throughout the city. Sunday afternoon concerts are often given in the chapel of Akershus Palace.

FESTIVALS

Chamber Music Festival

August	Oslo Chamber Music Festival
Cham	P.O. Box 667-Sentrum
	N-0106 Oslo, 1
	Tel: 02/42 28 68

Both Norwegian and foreign musicians participate in Oslo's summer chamber music festival, which takes place in the majestic Akershus Castle and Fortress. Built around 1300 by King Haakon V and rebuilt in the seventeenth century by King Christian IV, this medieval fortress is now used for state and governmental functions.

Oslo Contemporary Music Festival

1 Week	Oslo Contemporary Music Festival
Mid-October	Ny Musikk
	Musikkens Hus
Op, Orch, Cham, Rec	Toftesgt. 69
	N-0552 Oslo, 5
	Tel: 02/37 08 10
	Fax: 02/37 60 27

Thirteen musical institutions collaborate to produce this festival, which includes an international competition for newly composed orchestral works. **Recent Performers:** Oslo Philharmonic Orchestra, the Norwegian Opera.

SWEDEN

The international telephone country code for Sweden is (011) 46. City codes have the prefix 0, which is deleted when calling from abroad.

STOCKHOLM

Seemingly preserved by the sparkling waterways that separate them, the 14 islands that constitute the regal city of Stockholm each represents a somewhat different aspect of the capital's heritage. Even though twentieth-century Stockholm is reflected by the imposing glass edifices of the city's modern financial district (*Norrmalm*), the Old Town (*Gamla Stan*) exists almost as a separate entity, seemingly untouched by the centuries. The Royal Palace dominates this section of town, which contains a multitude of historic buildings. The other islands (all easily accessible by boat or bridge) offer all of the necessary virtues of a well-planned city. One island is covered almost entirely by a beautiful park, while another is devoted entirely to residences and embassies. Magnificent gardens are a feature common to all.

FESTIVALS

Drottningholm Court Theatre Festival

3 Months
Late May--Early September

Op, Orch, Dance, Th

Drottningholms Teatermuseum
"Föreställningar"
Box 27050
S-102 51 Stockholm
Tel: 08/660 8281
08/660 8225

The operas of Mozart and his contemporaries work their magic during this festival, which takes advantage of the exceptionally deep stage and intimate seating area of the eighteenth-century Court Theatre. The theater was the pride and joy of opera-loving Gustaf III, whose murder at the Stockholm opera house in 1792 later became the subject of Verdi's *Un Ballo in Maschera*. The Theatre and its stage machinery have been carefully restored, and the original scenery, now too fragile for use, has been carefully reproduced. Since 1946 the festival has specialized in late eighteenth-century operas and ballets, with an orchestra of authentic instruments. The Royal Stockholm Opera also performs in this memorable setting. **Recent Performers:** conductors Arnold Östman and Thomas Schuback, singers Richard Croft, Anita Soldh, and Aga Winska. **Venue:** Drottningholm Court Theatre. **Performances:** approx 30.

ONGOING EVENTS

The Stockholm Concert Hall

Orch, Chor, Cham, Rec

The Stockholm Concert Hall
Foundation
P.O. Box 7083
S-10387 Stockholm
Tel: 08/102 110
or 244 130

This hall is the home of the Stockholm Philharmonic Orchestra. This venerable ensemble, active since 1914, is celebrated at home and abroad, and it might be termed the Nobel Symphony Orchestra, since it provides music for the famed peace prize ceremonies. A special feature of each season is a festival honoring a contemporary Swedish or foreign composer. Recent honorees include Karl Birger Blomdahl and Soviet composer Alfred Schnittke. **Recent Performers:** conductors Mstislav Rostropovich and Gennady Rozhdestvensky, pianist Maurizio Pollini, violinist Anne-Sophie Mutter. **Performances:** Approx. 80.

Berwald Hall

Orch, Chor, Cham, Rec

Berwald Hall
Swedish National Radio
S-105 10 Stockholm
Tel: 08/784 1800

Berwald Hall is the home of the extensive performing arts programs sponsored by the Swedish National Radio ("Riksradion"). In addition to the 35 annual concerts by the Swedish Radio Symphony Orchestra, there are scores of concerts by guest ensembles and artists and chamber ensembles drawn from the Orchestra and the Stockholm Radio Choir. **Resident Companies:** Swedish Radio Symphony Orchestra and Choir. **Recent Performers:** Danish Radio Symphony Orchestra, Alban Berg Quartet, sopranos Phyllis Bryn-Julson and Margaret Price. **Performances:** 130; August–June.

VISBY
125 miles S of Stockholm

Visby is the capital of one of Sweden's most historic islands, Gotland. Strategically situated on a prominent trade route, the island boasts a prosperous heritage that goes back to the sixth century, when Vikings landed here. The famous medieval wall with its dozens of towers and turrets still surrounds the town's attractive white stone houses. Serving as gateways into the village are lovely thirteenth- and fourteenth-century gates and towers that are original sections of the wall. Today Visby is a thriving year-round cultural center offering much in the way of art, music, cuisine, and nightlife.

FESTIVALS

Visby Festival

5 Weeks	Visby Festival
Mid-July–Mid-August	Tranhusgatan 47
	S-621 55 Visby
Op	Tel: July–August:
	0498/121 44
	September–June:
	0498/110 68

Founded by Friedrich Mehler in 1929, the Visby Festival annually presents the opera *Petrus da Dacia*, especially composed for the open-air stage of the medieval St. Nicholas ruins. Mehler collaborated with writer Josef Lundahl to create a mystic pageant opera about "Sweden's first author," who was the Prior of the Monastery of St. Nicholas during the 1280s and is believed to be buried beneath its choir. A companion exhibit in the city's museum supplies historical background. **Recent Performers:** conductor Peter-Tom Langelaar, singers from the Royal Opera in Stockholm. **Venue:** St. Nicholas ruins. **Performances:** every Monday, Wednesday, and Friday at 9 P.M.

Spain and Portugal

Palau de la Musica Catalana, Barcelona (courtesy of Barceló Fotos).

SPAIN
1 Barcelona
2 Cuenca
3 Figueras
4 Granada
5 Mallorca
6 Montserrat
7 San Sebastián
8 Santander

9 Seville
10 Valencia
11 Zarazoga

PORTUGAL
12 Estoril
13 Sintra

CALENDAR

JANUARY

Canary Islands Music Festival, **Canary Islands**

FEBRUARY

Canary Islands Music Festival, **Canary Islands**
Canary Islands Opera Festival, **Canary Islands**

MARCH

Canary Islands Opera Festival, **Canary Islands**
International Organ Days, **Zaragoza** (Aragon)

APRIL

Canary Islands Opera Festival, **Canary Islands**
Cuenca Week of Religious Music, **Cuenca** (New Castile)
Gulbenkian Encounters with Contemporary Music, **Lisbon**
    (Portugal)

MAY

Gulbenkian Encounters with Contemporary Music, **Lisbon**
    (Portugal)
International Festival of Theater, Music, and Dance, **Zaragoza**
    (Aragon)

JUNE

Castel de Peralada International Music Festival, **Figueras**
    (Cantabrian Coast)
International Festival of Music and Dance, **Granada**
    (Andalusia)
International Festival of Theater, Music, and Dance, **Zaragoza**
    (Aragon)
Musica de l'Emporada International Festival, **Figueras**
    (Cantabrian Coast)
Sintra Festival, **Sintra** (Portugal)

JULY

Castel de Peralada International Music Festival, **Figueras**
    (Cantabrian Coast)
Estoril Festival, **Estoril** (Portugal)
Festivals of Mallorca, **Mallorca** (Balearic Islands)
International Chamber Music Week, **Montserrat** (Catalonia)

International Festival of Music and Dance, **Granada** (Andalusia)
Santander International Festival, **Santander** (Cantabrian Coast)
Sintra Festival, **Sintra** (Portugal)

AUGUST

Estoril Festival, **Estoril** (Portugal)
Festivals of Mallorca, **Mallorca** (Balearic Islands)
International Chamber Music Week, **Montserrat** (Catalonia)
San Sebastian Musical Weeks, **San Sebastian** (Cantabrian Coast)
Santander International Festival, **Santander** (Cantabrian Coast)

SEPTEMBER

Bunyola Music Festival, **Mallorca** (Balearic Islands)
San Sebastian Musical Weeks, **San Sebastian** (Cantabrian Coast)

OCTOBER

Bunyola Music Festival, **Mallorca** (Balearic Islands)
Fiestas del Pilar, **Zaragoza** (Aragon)

NOVEMBER

Bach Festival, **San Sebastian** (Cantabrian Coast)
Bunyola Music Festival, **Mallorca** (Balearic Islands)

SPAIN

The international telephone dialing code for Spain is (011) 34. City codes have the prefix 9, which is deleted when calling from abroad.

BARCELONA (Catalonia)
325 miles NE of Madrid

Wide boulevards crisscross this elegant, international city, Spain's second largest, and one of the Mediterranean's most important seaports. The capital of Catalonia, Barcelona has long been characterized by a mix of languages and cultures and is second only to Madrid as a literary center. The arts are celebrated here with great enthusiasm, and music is as much a part of life as the Catalan language and the famous cuisine.

ONGOING EVENTS

Ibercamera

Orch, Cham

Ibercamera
Gran Via 636, 1r 2a
08007 Barcelona
Tel: 93/301 1104
Fax: 93/301 1104

Ibercamera, a main promoter of classical music in Barcelona, organizes the Temporada Ibercamera, a prestigious season of orchestral and chamber music concerts. Since its inception in 1984, it has attracted outstanding performers from all over the world and has provided a wide range of music from early to contemporary. Concerts are presented in the magnificent Palau de la Música, a building of extraordinary architectural interest built in 1878 by architect Domenech i Montaner in the Modernist style. **Recent Performers:** Philharmonia Orchestra of London with Giuseppe Sinopoli, Israel Philharmonic with Zubin Mehta, Royal Concertgebouw Orchestra with Carlo Maria Giulini, Tokyo String Quartet, violinist Midori, guitarist Julian Bream. **Venues:** Palau de la Música. **Performances:** about 30; October–June.

Gran Teatre del Liceu

Op, Orch, Chor, Rec

Gran Theatre del Liceu
Carrer Sant Pau no. 1
08001 Barcelona
Tel: 93/318 91 22
Fax: 93/302 2979

This is Barcelona's opera house, where the season features not only the resident opera company, but productions from La Scala, Lyric Opera of Chicago, and the Théâtre Royal de la Monnaie of Brussels. The schedule offers a dozen operas from Mozart to Strauss, with star-studded casts and lavish productions. Recitals by such artists as sopranos June Anderson and Aprile Millo and concerts by the resident orchestra and chorus round out the season. Although the theater's name may lead one to expect a large hall, this intimate ninteenth-century opera house accommodates just 500 in gilt and velvet splendor. **Resident Companies:** Opera, Orchestra, and Chorus of the Gran Teatre del Liceu. **Recent Performers:** tenors Placido Domingo and Luciano Pavarotti, sopranos Montserrat Caballé and Mirella Freni. **Performances:** more than 100; September–July.

Palau de la Música Catalana

Op, Orch, Chor, Cham, Rec, Org, Dance, Th, Film

Palau de la Música Catalana
Sant Francesc de Paula, 2
08003 Barcelona
Tel: 93/301 11 04

Orchestra tickets:
Via Laietana 41, pral.
08003 Barcelona
Tel: 93/317 10 96
Fax: 93/317 54 39

In addition to the full season of admirably diverse programs offered by the Orchestra of the City of Barcelona, this magnificent theater is host to many other musical events, including the stellar concerts of the Ibercamera series. Built in 1908 in the Spanish equivalent of Art Nouveau, this colorful and exquisitely designed hall is a luminous, spectacular work of art reflecting the culture of its era and its people. **Resident Performers:** Orchestra of the City of Barcelona, Orfeó Catala, Chamber Orchestra of the Palau de la Música Catalana. **Recent Performers:** Gennady Rohzdestvensky conducting the London Philharmonic Orchestra, guitarist Julian Bream, violinst Pinchas Zukerman, soprano Kiri Te Kanawa. **Performances:** January–December; closed in August.

Temporada Musical Fundacion Caja de Pensiones

Cham, Rec

Temporarda Musical Fundacion Caja de Pensiones
Via Layetana, 56
08003 Barcelona
Tel: 93/258 89 07 or
93/315 17 17
Fax: 93/258 75 82

Since 1980 this organization has sponsored weekly chamber music concerts that focus each year on one chosen instrument. Performances feature established artists and also spotlight young players. Master classes are also part of the Foundation's offerings. **Recent Performers:** Academy of Ancient Music conducted by Christopher Hogwood, Josef Suk Trio, pianist Tatiana Nikolaevna. **Venue:** Concert Hall of the Centro Cultural Fundacion Caja de Pensiones. **Performances:** 30; November–May.

CANARY ISLANDS

Although the name evokes images of an aviary, these islands 65 miles NW of the coast of Africa were named for the wild dogs (*canes*) that greeted a first-century explorer. The dogs seem to have vanished, and this enchantingly beautiful cluster of islands is said to be the remains of the lost continent of Atlantis. The varying topography of the islands ranges from desert-like to the snow-capped top of Spain's highest peak, resembling the diversity in cultures that vary from island to island. But one feature shared by all of the islands is a mild subtropical climate and magnificent beaches that attract visitors from around the world.

FESTIVALS

Canary Island Music Festival

1 Month
Early January–Early February

Orch, Chor, Cham, Rec, Org

Festival de Musica de
   Canarias
SOCAEM
Graciliano Alfonso 13-1
35005 Las Palmas de Gran
   Canaria
Tel: 928/246544 (/5/6)
Fax: 928/246547

This is an ambitious festival, and although chamber music and recitals are very much a part of the whole, the primary emphasis is on major works for large ensembles. This includes choral music, and a recent season offered six works ranging from Haydn's *Missa Caellensis* to Prokofiev's *Alexander Nevsky*. Orchestral programs also tend toward the grand scale, with works by Berlioz, Tchaikovsky, Strauss, and Mahler. **Recent Performers:** Czech Philharmonic Orchestra conducted by Vaclav Neumann, Bach Collegium of Stuttgart conducted by Helmut Rilling, violinist Schlomo Mintz. **Venues:** Teatro Perez Galdos (Las Palmas), Sala Teobaldo Power (Tenerife), churches across the archipelago. **Performances:** 60.

Canary Island Opera Festival

12 Performances
Late February–Mid-April

Op

Amigos Canarios de la Opera
Teatro Perez Galdos
c./Malteses, 22
35005 Las Palmas de Gran
    Canaria
Tel: 928/37 01 25

Two productions by major international companies are the focus of this festival, which mounts works such as *Aida, La Fille du Regiment,* and *Norma.* The Deutsche Oper Berlin offered *Tristan und Isolde* and *Ariadne auf Naxos* in 1990, and an upcoming season promises works of Tchaikovsky and Rimski-Korsakov by the Bolshoi Theater of Moscow. **Recent Performers:** Deutsche Staadsoper Berlin, Orquestra Philarmonica de Gran Canaria, mezzo-soprano Fiorenza Cosotto. **Venue:** Teatro Perez Galdos (Las Palmas). **Performances:** 2 each of 6 productions.

ONGOING EVENTS

Orchestra Sinfonica de Tenerife

Orch, Chor

Orchestra Sinfonica de
    Tenerife
Patronato Insular de Música
Cabildo de Tenerife
Plaza de España
38001 Santa Cruz de Tenerife
Tel: 922/24 20 90 ext. 261
Fax: 922/24 50 02

Under the direction of Victor Pablo, this ensemble presents a varied season, including much of the Spanish repertoire. Major works such as Haydn's *Seasons* and Beethoven's Symphony no. 9 are among the offerings. **Recent Performers:** Chorus of the Czech Philharmonic, violinist Schlomo Mintz, pianist Cecile Ousset. **Performances:** 20; October–May.

CUENCA (New Castile)
75 miles SE of Madrid

Cuenca is a truly enchanting medieval town, perched above the rambling Jucar River on steep hills into which cliffside "Casas Colgadas" (hanging houses) have been built. The town has a magnificent Cathedral containing a mixture of Norman and Gothic architecture, and narrow historic streets lead to the picturesque medieval squares of Descalzos and Merced. The contemporary Museum of Abstract Spanish Art provides a refreshing balance to the abundance of centuries-old art here, its contents providing an interesting contrast to the imposing fifteenth-century building in which they are housed.

FESTIVALS

Cuenca Week of Religious Music

1 Week	Semana de Musica Religiosa
Preceding Holy Week	Cuenca
	Hotel Torremangana
Orch, Chor, Cham, Rec	16002 Cuenca
	Tel: 966/223351
	Fax: 966/229671

Acclaimed ensembles from all over Europe converge on Cuenca in the spring, where for almost 30 years this festival has included familiar favorites, lesser-known Renaissance masterworks, and even a concert version of Wagner's *Tannhäuser*. From Bach cantatas to Brahms' *German Requiem*, these concerts offer a rewardingly broad repertoire. **Recent Performers:** Vienna Academy and Concentus Vocales of Vienna conducted by Martin Haselböck, Tallis Scholars, Vienna Mozart Chamber Orchestra. **Venue:** Ancient Church of San Pablo. **Performances:** daily.

FIGUERAS (Cantabrian Coast)
400 miles NE of Madrid

Renowned surrealist Salvador Dalí lived, died, and is buried in this small town. The Dalí Museum is not only Figueras' main attraction, but is one of Spain's most popular museums, second only to Madrid's Prado. Like the artist it represents, the Dalí Museum is undeniably eccentric, and it is worth a special visit.

FESTIVALS

Castel de Peralada International Music Festival

4 Weeks	Festival Internacional de
Mid-June–Mid-July	Musica de Castell de
	Perelada
Op, Orch, Chor, Cham, Rec,	Peralada (Girona)
Dance	Tel: 972/53 81 25
	Fax: 972/53 80 87

The ancient turreted castle of Peralada and neighboring churches and cloisters form the backdrop for this incomparable festival in the area of Figueras. Cherubini's *Medea* with soprano Montserrat Caballé, song recitals by soprano Victoria de los Angeles and tenor José Carreras, and productions of Handel's *Alceste* and Purcell's *Dido and Aeneas* by the English Bach Festival make this an unforgettable event. **Recent Performers:** Karl Münchinger Chamber Orchestra, European Chamber Orchestra, harpist Nicanor Zabaleta. **Venues:** Churches and the castle. **Performances:** 15; weekends only.

Música de l'Emporadà International Festival

5 Concerts	Festival Internacional de
June	Música de L'Emporadà
	Oficina Municipal d'Infor-
Orch, Chor, Cham, Rec, Ex	mació i Turisme de
	Figueras
	Plaça del Sol
	Figueras
	Tel: 972/50 31 55

Chamber music is the focus here, and the varied ensembles, from winds to brass to chamber orchestra, present a delightful sampling of the repertoire. Music for larger ensembles is also heard, and a recent season included a symphony of Schubert and Mozart's Requiem. **Recent Performers:** New American Chamber Orchestra, English Brass Ensemble, Orquestra Simfònia del Vallès. **Venues:** Municipal Theater. **Performances:** 5; all at 10 P.M.

GRANADA (Andalusia)
250 miles S of Madrid

Perched above the city of Granada is the magical Alhambra Palace complex, one of Europe's most exotic buildings. Completed in the fourteenth century, this sumptuously decorated fortress-palace with its magnificent gardens was once the residence of the Moorish kings. Today Granada is a pleasing city filled with students enrolled in the large university, their youthful exuberance and the colorful presence of gypsies throughout town providing a somewhat Bohemian atmosphere.

FESTIVALS

International Festival of Music and Dance

2 Weeks
Mid-June–Early July

Op, Orch, Chor, Cham, Rec,
Org, Dance

Festival Internacional de
Música y Danza
c/Gracia, 21, 4
18002 Granada
Tel: 958/26 74 42
Fax: 958/26 74 47

For almost 40 years, Granada has hosted this event, bringing together top classical music, ballet, and flamenco performers. Diverse programs juxtapose works such as Monteverdi's *Vespre della Beata Vergine* and Penderecki's Requiem, and orchestral concerts include a surprising number of contemporary works. The venues include one of Spain's finest Renaissance buildings (Palacio de Carlos V) and the fourteenth-century summer home of the Moorish kings (Palacio del Generalife, part of the Alhambra). **Recent Performers:** Philharmonia Orchestra conducted by Luciano Berio, soprano Jessye Norman, Bach Collegium of Stuttgart, Joffrey Ballet, pianist Alfred Brendel. **Venues:** Palacio de Carlos V, Teatro del Generalife, Auditorio Manuel de Falla. **Performances:** 17; daily at 10 or 10:30 P.M.

ONGOING EVENTS

Winter Concerts

Orch, Chor, Cham, Rec

Kiosco Acera del Casino
Centro Cultural Manuel
de Falla
Paseo de los Mártires
Alhambra
18009 Granada
Tel: 958/22 82 89
or 22 21 88

A six-month concert season is offered in the Manuel de Falla Concert Hall, where orchestral and chamber music concerts are given by well-known ensembles. **Recent Performers:** Philharmonic Orchestra of Renanania, Mannheim Chamber Orchestra, Martinú Chamber Orchestra, Colorado String Quartet. **Venue:** Manuel de Falla Concert Hall. **Performances:** 2–4 monthly; October–May.

MADRID (New Castile)

The sunny climate and high altitude of Madrid are just two of the elements that prompt residents to refer to this elegant city as "the gateway to heaven." This city has recently experienced an intense cultural renaissance and it has been proclaimed the Cultural Capital of Europe for the year 1992 by the European Economic Community. The city's Prado Museum is certainly one of Europe's finest, and it is a perfect starting point for exploring the city's vast treasures.

ONGOING EVENTS

Auditorio Nacional de Música

Orch, Chor, Cham, Rec

Auditorio Nacional de Música
Calle Principe de Vergara, 136
Madrid
Tel: 91/337 0100

In addition to its resident ensembles, this concert hall (completed in 1988) hosts an impressive roster of international orchestras and chamber ensembles and an innovative series of contemporary chamber music concerts. Orchestral programs feature the standard repertoire, including many large-scale choral works such as Haydn's *Creation* and Bach's *St. Matthew Passion*. **Resident Ensembles:** Orchestra and Chorus of the Auditorio Nacional de Música. **Recent Performers:** Sergiu Celibidache conducting the Munich Philharmonic Orchestra, James Conlon conducting the Rotterdam Philharmonic Orchestra, Tokyo String Quartet, guitarist Julian Bream. **Performances:** 150; October–May.

Círculo de Bellas Artes

Cham

Círculo de Bellas Artes
Marqués de Casa Riera 2
28004 Madrid
Tel: 91/532 74 27

The Hall of Columns is the site for these chamber music concerts, including many of those sponsored by the "Center for the Diffusion of Contemporary Music." **Recent Performers:** Ópera da Cámara, Trío Monpou.

Teatro Lirico Nacional La Zarzuela

Op, Rec, Dance, Zarzuella   Teatro Lirico Nacional
                                La Zarzuela
                                Jovellanos, 4
                                28014 Madrid
                                Tel: 91/429 82 25

The Teatro Lirico is Madrid's opera house, which presents zarzuellas and ballets in addition to opera. Favorites by Mozart, Verdi, Wagner, and Bellini are complemented by less often heard works by Tchaikovsky, Respighi, and contemporary composers. Eight productions are featured each season, including two mounted in cooperation with other important European theaters. **Recent Performers:** soprano Montserrat Caballé, tenor Placido Domingo, recitals by soprano Renata Scotto, mezzo-soprano Teresa Berganza.

Teatro Monumental

Orch, Chor, Cham, Rec   Teatro Monumental
                            Atocha, 65
                            Madrid
                            Tel: 91/227 12 14

The venturesome programming by the resident ensembles of this hall ensures that a concert by "three Bs" is as likely to include Bartók, Berrea, and Bruck as Bach, Beethoven, and Brahms. International conductors and soloists are featured throughout the season. **Resident Companies:** Symphony Orchestra and Choir of Radio Television de España. **Recent Performers:** conductor Sir Yehudi Menuhin, pianists Katia and Marielle Labeque. **Performances:** 40; October–May, Thursday and Friday at 8 P.M.

MALLORCA (Balearic Islands)

Mallorca is the largest of the Balearic Islands, off the southeast coast of Spain. Visitors come from throughout Europe to the island, drawn by the warm Mediterranean climate and the inviting beaches. The island's capital, Palma, contains the fourteenth-century Castle of Bellver (which housed medieval Mallorcan kings), a remarkable thirteenth-century Gothic cathedral, and the Convent Church of San Francisco with its beautiful cloister.

FESTIVALS

Bunyola Music Festival

2 Months	Festival de Música de
Mid-September–	Bunyola
Mid-November	Oficina d'Informatió
	Turística
Orch, Chor, Ch	Jaime III, 10
	07012 Palma de Mallorca

These weekly concerts present both local and international artists, ranging from soloists to symphony orchestra. **Recent Performers:** Bamberg Symphony, The Consort of Musicke, Symphony Orchestra of the Balearics. **Venue:** Bunyola Church. **Performances:** Saturdays.

Festivals of Mallorca

Concerts a l'Herba
Festival de Pollença
Festival de Música Clássica d'Artà
Festival Internacional de Deià
Festival Internacional de Música al Santuari de Cura
Festival Chopin de Valldemossa
Serenates D'Estiu de Capdepera
Serenates d'Estiu

2 Months	Festivals de Mallorca
July–August	Oficina d'Informació
	Turística
Orch, Cham, Rec	Jaime III, 10
	07012 Palma de Mallorca
	Tel: 971/22 45 37

Mallorca is justly proud of its cultural offerings, and these concurrent festivals provide a summer season of music across the island. Nearing its thirtieth anniversary, the Pollença Festival is the oldest and most extensive, and has given rise in recent years to an abundance of smaller festivals in neighboring towns and villages. Chamber music is most plentiful, especially at the Chopin Festival in Valldemossa, the hillside town where Chopin and George Sand spent the winter of 1838–39. **Recent Performers:** Musica Antiqua Köln, harpist Nicanor Zabaleta, pianist Bella Davidovich, violinist Pinchas Zukerman. **Venues:** Churches, cloisters, and gardens throughout Mallorca. **Performances:** almost daily.

ONGOING EVENTS

Balearic Symphony Orchestra

Orch, Chor

Fundació Pública de la
Balears per a la Música
c/Vicene Joan Rossello
Ribas 22A
07013 Palma
Tel: 971/28 75 65

The varied programs of this ensemble always feature one or more instrumental or vocal soloists. The repertoire includes a surprisingly large proportion of works outside the well-known orchestral literature, though Bach, Beethoven, and Brahms can also be heard. **Venue:** Auditorium de Palma. **Recent Performers:** conductor Luis Remartínez, pianist Walter Hautzig, tenor Nigel Robson. **Performances:** 19; October–June.

MONTSERRAT (Catalonia)
310 miles NE of Madrid

Set at the foot of an astounding wall of rock, the world-renowned monastery of Montserrat ("jagged mountain") has the imposing presence of a truly holy place. Perhaps the awesome appearance of Montserrat is what has lent an air of mystique to the site, giving rise to the legends that associate the Holy Grail with the monastery, which served as the inspiration for Wagner's *Parsifal.* Founded in 880, the monastery has been rebuilt several times in the intervening centuries and now houses several hundred monks. Although the monastery itself is not open to the public, travelers may visit several impressive museums, attend services in the church, and hear the singing of the Escolanía, a boys choir founded in the thirteenth century.

FESTIVALS

International Chamber Music Week

1 Week
Late July–Early August

Cham, Rec

Setmana Internacional de
Música de Camara
Ajuntament de Monserrat
Unión Musical Española
C./Paz 15
València
Tel: 93/332 22 02

Although known to opera lovers as the home of the Knights of the Grail in *Parsifal,* Montserrat hosts music on a much smaller scale than the opera it inspired. There are indeed Teutonic masterpieces to be heard here, but they are the intimate chamber works of Brahms and Beethoven, not the grand music drama of Wagner. **Recent Performers:** Salzburg Chamber Orchestra, Guildhall String Ensemble of London, Valencia Brass Quintet. **Venue:** Plaza de la Iglesia. **Performances:** 10, all at 11 P.M (!).

SAN SEBASTIAN (Cantabrian Coast)
250 miles NE of Madrid

This bayside town captures the truly romantic essence of the Basque country. San Sebastian sits just 12 miles from the French border, tucked between two large mountains that seem to protect it from the rest of the world. Other elements that add to the city's charm are the mild summer climate, exquisitely prepared seafood, and the magnificent beaches, most notably the halfmoon-shaped La Concha, considered by many to be Spain's finest. In addition to its musical offerings, San Sebastian hosts 8 performances of contemporary dance, given each year in May by international dance companies.

FESTIVALS

Bach Festival

5 Days   Bach Festival
Early November   Oficina de Turismo
    c/Miramar 1
Orch, Chor, Cham, Rec   20004 San Sebastian
    Tel: 943/42 62 82

Two Basque cities, San Sabastian and Ordizia, host this tribute to the master of Leipzig, and have done so for more than 20 years. Music by Bach is found on every program, complemented by that of his contemporaries, including Handel, Telemann, Purcell, and others. **Recent Performers:** Orquesta Sinfonica de Euskadi, Coro Donosti de Euskadi, Trio Zarabanda. **Venues:** Salon de Plenos del Ayuntamiento, Parroquia de San Vicente, Basilica de Santa Maria del Coro (all in San Sebastian); Palacio Barrena, Iglesia Parraquial (in Ordizia). **Performances:** 7; evenings.

San Sebastian Musical Weeks

1 Month
Early August–Early
   September

Op, Orch, Cham, Rec, Ballet

Quincenza Musicial de
   San Sebastian
C/República Argentina, s/n
20003 San Sebastian
Tel: 943/48 12 38
Fax: 943/43 07 02

Since 1939 San Sebastian has hosted this important festival, the oldest in Spain. Its two resident orchestras are joined by renowned ensembles from abroad, with conductors such as Riccardo Muti, Sergiu Celibidache, and James Conlon. Opera productions range from *Don Giovanni* to chamber works of Gluck, and recitals feature such artists as soprano Montserrat Caballé. **Recent Performers:** Orquestra Nacional de España conducted by Rafael Frübeck de Burgos, Orfeón Donostiana, pianist Alfred Brendel, soprano Jessye Norman. **Venues:** Teatro Victoria Eugenia de San Sebastian, Museo San Telmo, Baroque Basilica of Santa Maria, Iglesia San Vicente, others. **Performances:** 50; evenings.

SANTANDER (Cantabrian Coast)
215 miles N of Madrid

Destroyed by a tornado and freak fire in 1941, Santander has been rebuilt as a gracious resort town. An extensive harbor gives the city great natural advantages, and the rebuilding has allowed for extensive parks along the waterside. The town's three beaches offer a wide range of vacation activities.

FESTIVALS

Santander International Festival

1 Month
Late July–Late August

Op, Orch, Chor, Cham, Rec,
   Org, Dance, Th, Lect

Festival Internacional
   Santander
Avda Calvo Sotelo, 15-5
39002 Santander
Tel: 942/31 48 19
Fax: 942/314767

One of Spain's oldest and most established festivals, the Santander Festival was begun in 1952 and has grown steadily ever since, involving in one recent season over 1,300 performers and 80,000 audience members. Striving to widen the appeal of all forms of classical music, its programs show a careful balance of standard repertoire and contemporary works, including world premieres and commissions. Venues include a number of unique and unexpected sites. There is a special emphasis on Spanish works and artists. **Recent Performers:** London Symphony Orchestra, Cleveland Quartet, violinist Pinchas Zukerman, tenor José Carrerras. **Venues:** Churches, castles, prehistoric caves (!), and country homes. **Performances:** more than 90.

SEVILLE (Andalusia)
280 miles SW of Madrid

Moorish ramparts and towers, the stunning Alcázar fortress, and an enormous fifteenth-century cathedral help to make Seville a favorite city of travelers to Spain. Only St. Peter's in Rome and the cathedral in Milan are larger than the richly decorated cathedral of Seville, the world's largest Gothic structure. Don Juan is said to have dined near the Alcázar, the great Moorish palace near the cathedral. Set along the rambling Rio Guadalquivir, Seville's charms have inspired such great operas as Bizet's *Carmen* and Rossini's *Barber of Seville.* In August the Plaza de España is the site for open-air opera productions that have included *Carmen,* with Placido Domingo in the cast. Cultural events are listed in the monthly publication *El Giradillo.*

ONGOING EVENTS

Cultural Events

Op, Orch, Cham, Rec, Dance Oficina de Turisme
          Calle Adolfo Rodriquez
          Jurado, 2
          41001 Seville
          Tel: 95/421 1091

Classical music can be found in a variety of locales throughout the city, featuring both Spanish and international performers. Concerts and dance are presented at the Teatro Lope de Vega (Tel: 95/23 21 03). **Recent Performers:** Orquestra Betica Filarmonica, Chorus of the University of Arkansas, Duo Armano (duo pianists). **Venues:** Teatro Lope de Vega, Cathedral, Iglesia del Salvador, Conservatorio, Iglesia de San Alberto, Salón de Actos de El Monte, Parroquia Sagrario.

Teatro de la Maestranza

Op, Zarzuela

Teatro Maestranza
Paseo de Colon, 22-23
41001 Seville
Tel: 95/456 0899

Although the city has been the setting for more than two dozen operas, Seville did not have an opera house until this handsome new structure opened in 1991. Under the direction of Placido Domingo, the opera house began its inaugural season with productions of *Rigoletto, La Bohème, Tosca,* and the Spanish zarzuela *Doña Francisquita.*

VALENCIA (Valencia)
190 miles SE of Madrid

This colorful, lively city on the banks of the River Turia has been prized by the Greeks, Carthaginians, Romans, Visigoths, and Arabs, and an ancient saying described it as "a piece of heaven fallen to earth." The historic beauty of Spain's third largest city is to be found in its old town, where brightly tiled church roofs and the Plaza de la Reina recall the colorful past.

ONGOING EVENTS

Palau de la Música

Orch, Cham, Rec, Org

Palau de la Música
Oficina de Turismo de
    Valencia
Paz, 48
46002 Valencia

This new concert hall is the most important center for the performing arts in Valencia, and its programs showcase not only local ensembles but guest artists from Europe and North America. The resident ensemble is the Orquesta Municipal de Valencia, which presents a season of 10 concerts.

Recent Performers: Christopher Hogwood conducting the St. Paul Chamber Orchestra, Gennady Rozhdestvensky conducting the London Philharmonic, sopranos June Anderson and Lucia Popp. **Performances**: 90; October–March.

ZARAGOZA (Aragon)
170 miles NE of Madrid

Located on the well-traveled route between the Pyrenees and Castile, the industrial city of Zaragoza is the capital of Aragon. Overlooking the river Ebro is the magnificent Basilica of the Virgin of the Pilar, an immense, double-towered baroque edifice that dominates the city's skyline. Francesco de Goya was born in a small village near Zaragoza and left his mark in dozens of glorious frescoes and paintings in churches throughout the city.

FESTIVALS

Fiestas del Pilar

1 Week	Fiestas del Pilar
Early October	Area de Cultura
	Delegacion de Fiestas
Cham, Dance, Folk, Th, Ex	Populares
	Excmo. Auntamiento de
	Zaragoza
	San Jorge, 1-4C
	50001 Zaragoza
	Tel: 976/29 68 38

The feast of St. Pilar is a national holiday in Spain, but it is of special significance here, where St. Pilar is the patron saint. During this week-long outpouring of goodwill, there is entertainment for all in the streets, plazas, parks, and public places. Classical music is but a small part of the proceedings, for this is an event for which "the norms of daily life are set aside—uproar reigns, and clamorous music assumes its assured place." Popular entertainments prevail, from bullfights to folk dance. A special concert entitled "La Muestra Regional de Musica Laudistica" is given during the festivities at the Colegio El Salvador. **Recent Performers:** Rheinland-Pfaltz Philharmonic Orchestra, Stuttgart Philharmonic Orchestra, soprano Terese Berganza. **Venues:** Church of San Carlos (for classical programs), other events take place all over Zaragoza. **Performances:** as many as 40 daily.

International Festival of Theater, Music, and Dance

3 Weeks	International Festival of Theater, Music, and Dance
Late May–Early June	Area de Cultura
Orch, Dance, Th	Delegacion de Fiestas Populares
	Excmo. Auntamiento de Zaragoza
	San Jorge, 1-4C
	50001 Zaragoza
	Tel: 976/29 68 38

Classical music is juxtaposed here with the most contemporary works of theater and dance, all offered by ensembles and composers from Europe and America. Works by Dvořák and Vivaldi can be heard in concert, while those of Bizet, Purcell, and more modern composers are the inspiration for recent choreography. **Recent Performers:** I Musici, Orquesta Filarmonica de Brno (Czechoslovakia), Wim Mertens Ensemble (Belgium). **Venue:** Teatro Principal. **Performances:** 16.

International Organ Days

1 Week	Jornadas Internacionales de Organo
Late March	Area de Cultura
Org, Cham	Delegacion de Fiestas Populares
	Excmo. Auntamiento de Zaragoza
	San Jorge, 1-4C
	50001 Zaragoza
	Tel: 976/29 68 38

This international festival celebrates Zaragoza's rich musical heritage and its longstanding tradition as one of the most important European centers for organists. This reputation dates from the sixteenth century, when a rivalry between the organists of Zargoza's two cathedrals resulted in an era of musical splendor. A recent festival showcased artists from Germany, Spain, Portugal, Italy, England, and Holland. **Venue:** Church of San Gil. **Performances:** daily.

Teatro Principal

Orch, Cham, Rec, Drama, Th	Teatro Principal
	c/o C/Coso. 57, 3
	E-50001 Zaragoza

This theater is at the heart of Zaragoza's lively cultural life, with programs that span classical music, ballet, modern dance, and drama. **Recent Performers:** Iona Brown conducting the Academy of St. Martin in the Fields, soprano Montserrat Caballé, Rudolf Nureyev and the Ballet Theatre Francais de Nancy. **Performances:** September–May.

PORTUGAL

The international telephone country code for Portugal is (011) 351. City codes have the prefix 0, which is deleted when calling from abroad.

ESTORIL
15 miles W of Lisbon

The strip of Portuguese coastline that includes the showy casino towns of Estoril and neighboring Casais has been dubbed the "Portuguese Riviera" for its popularity among wealthy vacationers. The wrath of the Atlantic has made its impact on the steep cliffs of Cabo da Roca and the Boca do Inferno ("Mouth of Hell"), both near Casais. But when the seas are calm, Estoril's gentle beaches are as romantic as they were in the nineteenth century, when exiled kings and queens came here for refuge from political turmoil. A small turreted castle stands on the beach as a reminder of the area's privileged past.

FESTIVALS

Estoril Festival

1 Month Early July–Early August	Festival de Música da Costa do Estoril Casa-Museu Verclades
Orch, Chor, Cham, Rec, Dance	de Faria Av. de Saboia 1146 B Monte Estoril Tel: 01/267 00 76 01/268 56 07

Estoril's renowned festival has offered venturesome programming since 1965, presenting lesser-known works along with the standard repertoire, and it is safe to expect at least one unfamiliar composer on each program. Chamber music is an important part of the offerings. **Recent Performers:** Nova Filarmonia Portuguesa, Festival Strings Lucerne, harpist Zoraida Ávila. **Venues:** Casino, Hotel Palácio, Igreja dos Salesianos (all in Estoril); Teatro Nacional S. Carlos and Aula Magna (in Lisbon); others. **Performances:** 16; all at 8:30 P.M.

LISBON

The wealth of its New World empire poured into Lisbon during the fifteenth and sixteenth centuries, and although this was the time of its greatest prosperity, the city had been an important center even before the Romans arrived in the 2nd century B.C. An earthquake in 1755 all but destroyed Lisbon, so that today the city is a combination of modern, cosmopolitan capital and the classically proportioned Baixa, where the streets and squares rebuilt in the eighteenth century captured the grace and balance of the era.

FESTIVALS

Gulbenkian Encounters with Contemporary Music

2 Weeks	Calouste Gulbenkian
Late April–Early March	Foundation
	Music Department
Orch, Cham, Rec, Dance	Avenida de Berna, 45-A
	1093 Lisbon
	Tel: 01/735 131
	Fax: 01/735 139

Concerts, lectures, seminars, and master classes contribute to this program, which concentrated in a recent year on the music of Karlheinz Stockhausen. Among the special events is "Music in Colorscape," an audiovisual installation in the gardens of the Gulbenkian Foundation. **Recent Performers:** Gulbenkian Orchestra and Choir, Contemporary Music Group of Lisbon, Lisbon String Quartet. **Venue:** Gulbenkian Foundation. **Performances:** 16.

ONGOING EVENTS

Gulbenkian Foundation

Orch, Chor, Cham, Rec,   Calouste Gulbenkian
    Dance, Th, Ex, Child   Foundation
                         Music Department
                         Avenida de Berna, 45-A
                         1093 Lisbon
                         Tel: 01/735 131
                         Fax: 01/735 139

Named for the Armenian-born entrepreneur who bequeathed his fortune for its creation, the Calouste Gulbenkian Foundation sponsors an astonishing array of activities in the fields of health, welfare, education, science, and the arts. The headquarters in Lisbon contains three concert halls, an open-air amphitheater, exhibition galleries, a museum, a library, and a children's pavilion. The Foundation maintains its own orchestra, chorus, and ballet company, and also hosts musicians, dancers, and theater companies from Portugal and abroad. **Performances:** year-round.

Teatro de São Carlos

Op, Orch, Dance   Teatro National de Opera
                         de São Carlos
                         Rua Serpa Pinta, 9
                         Lisbon
                         Tel: 01/327172

This beautiful eighteenth-century theater hosts many of the cultural activities found in Lisbon, including opera, concerts, and ballet. **Performances:** December–May.

SINTRA
15 miles W of Lisbon

Set on the Serra de Sintra's North Slope, Sintra is a place of heights—towering castles and cascading waterfalls make the town a vision of vertical splendor, most eloquently described in Lord Byron's "Childe Harold" as a "glorious eden." And what a lavish garden it is—brimming with thick and colorful plant life that only fresh mountain streams can sustain. Sintra is one of Portugal's oldest and most popular towns, filled with art treasures and architectural delights.

FESTIVALS

Sintra Festival

1 Month	Sintra Festival
Mid-June–Mid-July	R. Alvaro des Reis no. 9-C
	2710 Sintra
Cham, Rec, Dance	Tel: 01/9235401

Romantic chamber music abounds here, where solo piano recitals form the largest portion of the program. Instrumental recitals may feature the violin or clarinet, and concerts occasionally feature orchestral works such as a Schumann symphony or a Beethoven piano concerto. **Recent Performers:** Orquestra Gulbenkian, Wanderer Trio, pianist Catherine Collard. **Venues:** castles, old manor houses, wine cellars (!). **Performances:** 14; evenings.

SWITZERLAND

Richard Wagner's piano in the Wagner Museum at Tribschen (courtesy of the Swiss National Tourist Office).

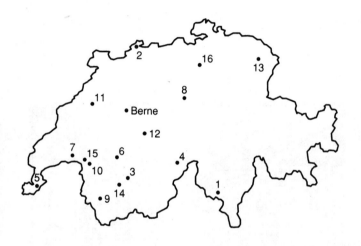

SWITZERLAND

1	Ascona	9	Martigny
2	Basel	10	Montreux
3	Crans-sur-	11	Neuchâtel
	Montana	12	Oberhofen
4	Ernen	13	St. Gallen
5	Geneva	14	Sion
6	Gstaad	15	Vevey
7	Lausanne	16	Zurich
8	Lucerne		

CALENDAR

MARCH

Easter Festival, **Lucerne** (Lucerne)

APRIL

Easter Festival, **Lucerne** (Lucerne)

JUNE

International June Festival, **Zürich** (Zürich)

JULY

Summer Music Festival, **Geneva** (Geneva)
Oberhofen Palace Concerts, see **Berne** (Berne)
Organ Festival, **Sion** (Valais)
Tibor Varga Festival, **Sion** (Valais)

AUGUST

Summer Music Festival, **Geneva** (Geneva)
Festival of the Future, **Ernen** (Valais)
Lucerne International Festival Weeks, **Lucerne** (Lucerne)
Menuhin Festival, **Gstaad** (Berne)
Montreux-Vevey Festival, **Montreux** and Vevey (Vaud)
Musical Weeks, **Ascona** (Ticino)
Organ Festival, **Sion** (Valais)
Tibor Varga Festival, **Sion** (Valais)

SEPTEMBER

Alpengala, **Gstaad** (Berne)
Lucerne International Festival Weeks, **Lucerne** (Lucerne)
Montreux-Vevey Festival, **Montreux** and Vevey (Vaud)
Musical Weeks, **Ascona** (Ticino)
Organ Festival, **Sion** (Valais)
Tibor Varga Festival, **Sion** (Valais)

OCTOBER

Montreux-Vevey Festival, **Montreux** and Vevey (Vaud)
Musical Weeks, **Ascona** (Ticino)

The international telephone country code for Switzerland is (011) 41. City codes have the prefix 0, which is omitted when calling from abroad.

ASCONA (Ticino)
135 Miles SE of Berne

The stretch of Italian-speaking villages and towns that line the northern shores of Lake Maggiore are called the Ticino, and known less formally as the "Swiss Riviera." Renaissance buildings and churches reflect the strong influence of the Italian neighbors on the south shores of the lake and stand out amid postmodern structures built during the recent boom in development. The mild climate and brilliant foliage are reasons why this spot has been a favorite refuge for such illustrious vacationers as Lenin, Jung, and Isadora Duncan.

FESTIVALS

Musical Weeks of Ascona

8 Weeks	Settimane Musicali di
Late August–Late October	Ascona
	Ente Turistico Ascona e
Orch, Chor, Cham, Rec	Losone
	CH-6612 Ascona
	Tel: 093/35 55 44
	Fax: 093/36 10 08

Once a small fishing village, Ascona became a gathering place for artists in the years prior to World War II. This creative energy culminated with the birth of the Music Weeks in 1946. The unique interaction between the performers and the public, coupled with the beautiful scenery, has continued to draw world-class artists throughout the years. The repertoire has included string quartets of Haydn and Schubert, songs by Beethoven and Dvořák, and symphonies by Brahms. **Recent Performers:** Academy of St. Martin in the Fields, Tokyo String Quartet, cellist Yo-Yo Ma. **Venues:** Church of San Francesco in Locarno, Collegio Papio Church in Ascona. **Performances:** 17.

BASEL (Basel)
55 miles N of Berne

With its overwhelming abundance of art treasures, theaters, symphony orchestras, ballet, museums, and the world-renowned Academy of Ancient Music, it's easy to see why Basel is known as the cultural center of Switzerland. The city's Fine Arts Museum is known throughout the world for its collection of early Flemish and German art and for the largest display of Holbein family paintings in existence. Built on the shore of the Rhine River where it first becomes navigable, Basel has been an important port since its founding as a Roman colony. It is close to the borders of France and Germany, and cross-cultural diversity enriches the city. Throughout the nineteenth century Basel was an important stop in the touring schedules of Brahms, Liszt, Mendelssohn, and Robert and Clara Schumann. Today the city is noted for its wealth of both early and contemporary music.

ONGOING EVENTS

Cultural Events

Op, Orch, Chor, Cham, Rec, Org, Dance, Th, Ex, Child	Official Tourist Office Schifflände 5 CH-4001 Basel Tel: 061/261 50 50

From Bach to Britten and Shakespeare to O'Neill, this city boasts an impressive schedule of events throughout the year. Recent offerings included Wagner's *Tristan und Isolde,* Spoerli's ballet *Don Quixote,* and Nielson's Flute Concerto. Monthly schedules are printed by the Tourist Office. **Recent Performers:** Basel Symphony Orchestra, Munich Chamber Orchestra, Beaux Arts Trio. **Venues:** Academy of Music, Casino Concert Hall, Museum of Contemporary Art, various churches and other sites. **Performances:** nearly 50 each month.

Theater Basel

Op, Chor, Dance, Th, Fringe	Theater Basel Billettkasse Postfach CH-4010 Basel Tel: 061/22 11 33 (Mid-August–Mid-June) Fax: 061/22 19 90

This theater is active during the year with many diverse events, from operas of Mozart and Beethoven to theatrical works of Beckett. Within the theater is an "evening café," where musical performances, cabarets, sketches and scenes, and speeches are presented. **Venues:** main stage, small stage, and foyer at Theater Basel; various other locations in the city. **Performances:** 30 productions; September–June.

BERNE (Berne)

Steeped in medieval history, this elegant Swiss capital is so filled with Gothic and baroque architecture that it has been granted world-landmark status by the United Nations. Berne's 4-mile pedestrian arcade is a delightful place to start exploring the city's offerings. The twelfth-century astronomical Clock Tower (which presents a dance of mechanical kings and bears at four minutes before each hour), the Gothic Cathedral of St. Vincent with its tower and flying buttresses, and the Barengraben ("Bear Pit," which houses the animals from which Berne derives its name) are just a few of the appealing features of this lovely city on the Aare River.

ONGOING EVENTS

Berne Symphony Orchestra

Orch, Cham

Berner Symphonieorchester
Konzertkasse Casino
Herrengasse 25
CH-3011 Bern
Tel: 031/22 42 42
        031/22 73 33
Fax: 031/22 62 57

This orchestra presents a full season of concerts, including repertoire from virtually every period. International artists are often featured. The "Casinotte" program serves to showcase rising young talents. **Recent Performers:** conductor Dmitry Kitayenko, oboist Heinz Holliger, violinist Kyung-Wha Chung. **Venues:** Casino Bern, Konservatorium, Restaurant "Zum Aeussern Stand," Empiresaal. **Performances:** 18 symphony concerts, 8 chamber music concerts, 8 "soirées."

Cultural Events

Op, Orch, Chor, Cham, Rec,
    Org, Dance, Th

Tourist Office of Berne
P.O.B.
CH-3001 Bern
Tel: 031/22 76 76
Fax: 031/22 12 12

A wide variety of music is offered in this city, including orchestral works by Mozart, Dvořák, and Bruckner performed by the Berne Symphony Orchestra with conductor Peter Maag. The Tourist Office publishes monthly listings of events. **Venues:** Casino, Cathedral, Municipal Theatre, Rathaus, others. **Performances:** over 70; November–April.

Stadttheater Bern

Op, Orch, Dance, Th

Theaterkasse
Stadttheater Bern
Kornhausplatz 18
CH-3000 Bern 7
Tel: 031/22 07 77

Dating from 1903, this striking 770-seat theater presents theater and opera as well as orchestral concerts. Recent productions have included *Il Trovatore* and *Albert Herring*. **Recent Performers:** Soprano Kathleen Broderick, tenor Lawrence Bakst.

IN THE AREA

Oberhofen Palace Concerts

2 Concerts
Mid-July

Cham

Schlosskonzerte Oberhofen
Verkehrsbüro Oberhofen
STI-Station
Oberhofen
Tel: 003/43 14 19

The rose garden of this castle 15 miles SE of Berne is the visitor's first welcome to an enchanted spot. The path through the garden leads to a chamber overlooking Lake Thun, where intimate concerts feature Swiss artists performing music of Mozart, Bach, and Chopin, among others. First built in the twelfth century and oft-restored in the centuries since, Oberhofen Castle now serves as a historical museum, with rooms decorated in period styles from the Gothic, Renaissance, and baroque to Biedermeier and the Second Empire. **Recent Performers:** pianists Silvia Harnisch, Jan Tomes, violinist Christina Meyer-Bauer. **Venue:** Gartensaal of Oberhofen Castle. **Performances:** 2; at 8:30 P.M.

CRANS-SUR-SIERRE, MONTANA (Valais)
125 miles S of Berne

Set in the heart of the Alps on a vast plateau covered with evergreen forests and lakes are the three neighboring resorts of Crans-sur-Sierre, Montana, and Aminona. Facing the highest mountains in Europe, the Crans-Montana region offers beautiful surroundings and exceptional sports facilities, as well as an exciting social and cultural life.

ONGOING EVENTS

Musical Weeks of Crans-Montana

Orch, Cham, Rec

Semaines Musicales de
Crans-Montana
Case Postale 296
CH-3963 Crans-sur-Sierre
Tel: 027/41 46 40
027/41 27 02

Despite the impression given by its title, this is not a festival, or a weekly series, but a small number of carefully produced concerts featuring outstanding soloists and ensembles. Founded in 1979, the Musical Weeks have offered the Crans-Montana area an impressive roster of musicians performing musical classics from Mozart to Schönberg, Granados to Shostakovich. **Recent Performers:** conductor Daniel Barenboim, mezzo-soprano Teresa Berganza, pianist Alicia de Larrocha. **Venues:** Église Catholique de Montana, Grande Salle du Régent à Crans. **Performances:** 5–6; 3 of which were in February in 1989.

ERNEN (Valais)
75 miles SE of Berne

The meticulous restoration of its ancient buildings has earned Ernen its reputation as the most beautiful and well-kept village of the Valais. Such sites as the Pfarrkirche St. Georg with its famous organ, the Courthouse, and the City Hall are reminders of a richly historic past. This lovely hamlet offers musical activities that attract musicians and music lovers from all over the world.

FESTIVALS

Festival of the Future

10 Days
Mid-August

Festival der Zukunft
Ernen Musikdorf
CH-3995 Ernen

Orch, Cham

Tel: 028/71 15 62

With a name such as this, one might expect a more thoroughly modern musical palette at this festival, founded in 1986. Although music by twentieth-century composers such as Messiaen and Bartók is performed, the spectrum is broad, reaching back in time to include Vivaldi and C. P. E. Bach.

The festival orchestra employs the finest musicians and is led by internationally known conductors. **Venues:** Pfarrkirche St. Georg, Stockalperschloss. **Performances:** 8; 8 P.M.

GENEVA (Geneva)
110 miles SW of Berne

A sense of serenity prevails over the bustling urban landscape of Geneva, encouraging the belief that achieving peace in an often chaotic world is a distinct possibility. Maybe this, more than the allure of Lake Geneva or the stunning surrounding beauty of the Alps, is what has long drawn international peacemakers to this neutral territory for negotiations. But for visitors not sent here to discuss nuclear arms, there is much more to be seen in this cosmopolitan city than round tables. The city's old town has an interesting array of cafes and shops that center around the impressive twelfth-century Cathedral of St. Pierre where John Calvin preached. The philosophically inclined will enjoy the Voltaire and Rousseau Museums.

FESTIVALS

Summer Music Festival

8 Weeks	Summer Music Festival
Early July–Late August	Office du Tourisme de Genève
Orch, Chor	Information Office
	Gare de Cornavin
	CH-1201 Genève
	Tel: 022/45 52 00

Each year Geneva hosts a festival that centers on one specific topic or style of music. A recent season offered Été Italien, presenting a panorama of Italian music, both choral and instrumental, from the Middle Ages to the twentieth century. **Recent Performers:** Orchestre de la Suisse Romande. **Performances:** 8.

ONGOING EVENTS

Cultural Events

Op, Orch, Chor, Cham, Rec, Dance, Th, Film, Ex, Child	Office du Tourisme Case Postale 440 CH-1211 Genève 11 Tel: 022/28 72 33 Fax: 022/21 89 65

Geneva's cultural calendar is filled with a wide variety of the lively arts, from ancient lute to jazz saxophone, and from Monteverdi to musical theater. **Recent Performers:** Orchestre de la Suisse Romande, Emerson String Quartet, guitarist Julian Bream. **Venues:** Victoria Hall, Conservatoire, Cathédrale Saint-Pierre, others. **Performances:** over 50 monthly.

Grand Casino de Genève

Op, Orch, Chor, Rec, Dance Grand Casino de Genève
7, chemin de la Vielle-
   Fontaine
1233 Berne
Genève
Tel: 022/757 31 71
(2–9 P.M.)

Major operatic and dance productions are only a small part of the larger picture here, for the calendar also includes Broadway shows and other performances of special interest. Recent productions include *Nabucco* and *Madama Butterfly*. **Recent Performers:** Ballet and Opera of Kiev, Red Army Chorus, Peking Circus, Mummenschanz. **Performances:** 10 productions; November–April.

Grand Théâtre

Op, Cham, Rec, Dance Grand Théâtre
 Child   Place Neuve
CH-1204 Genève
Tel: 022/21 23 18

While the main thrust here is opera, the season in this late nineteenth-century theater also includes solo and chamber music recitals given by world-famous artists. Among the recent productions were *Elektra, Tales of Hoffman,* and Handel's *Alcina*. **Recent Performers:** Fine Arts Quartet, violinists Pinchas Zuckerman and Schlomo Mintz. **Performances:** 10 productions, 30 concerts; September–June.

Victoria Hall—Sunday Concerts

Orch, Chor   Victoria Hall—Sunday
       Concerts
Rue Général–Dufour 14
CH-Genève

This diverse series of Sunday concerts features European orchestras with guest soloists. The music ranges from

Beethoven to Britten and Bartók. **Recent Performers:** Orchestre de la Suisse Romande, Orchestre Symphonique de Budapest, Orchestre de la Beethovenhalle de Bonn. **Performances:** 9; all at 5 P.M.; October–April.

GSTAAD (Berne)
50 miles SW of Berne

Nestled between four majestic mountains, Gstaad is one of Switzerland's most exclusive resort villages. In winter the surrounding slopes offer world-class skiing, while in summer the narrow streets and Alpine meadows all seem to burst with colorful flowers.

FESTIVALS

Alpengala

2 Weeks	Alpengala
Early September	Office of Tourism
	CH-3780 Gstaad
Op, Orch, Chor, Cham, Rec, Dance	Tel: 030/4 10 55

Nineteenth-century French and Italian symphonic works and operas in concert form are the primary focus of this memorable festival. The programs also include piano and dance recitals and major choral works, all presented in the festival's spectacular concert hall. This modern, tent-like structure is known for its superlative acoustics, and its striking outline provides an arresting contrast to the surrounding scenery. **Recent Performers:** conductors Carlo Maria Giulini and Yehudi Menuhin, soprano Renata Scotto. **Venue:** Festival Tent. **Performances:** 5 evenings.

Menuhin Festival

1 Month	Menuhin Festival
August	Gstaad-Saanen
	Verkehrsbüro
Orch, Chor, Cham, Rec, Org	CH-3780 Gstaad
	Tel: 030/4 10 55

Established in 1956, this festival's early directors were Antal Dorati, Benjamin Britten, and tenor Peter Pears. In more recent years it has been led by violinist Yehudi Menuhin, for whom the festival is now named. New and lesser-known works are often performed by rising young musicians as well as by international stars. Performances are held in the beautiful Church of Saanen, which has a rare fifteenth-century wooden ceiling. Programs range from Bach and Mozart to Gershwin and Ellington. **Recent Performers:** Royal Philharmonic Orchestra, violinist Anne-Sophie Mutter, flutist Eugenia Zuckerman. **Venue:** Church of Saanen. **Performances:** 16; all beginning at 7:30 P.M.

LAUSANNE (Vaud)
65 miles SW of Bernes

This lively, cosmopolitan city overlooking Lake Geneva can trace its history back to the stone age. A more recent view of the city's heritage can be found in its medieval "Cité," with its narrow, winding streets and historic houses. The magnificent thirteenth-century Gothic cathedral here is considered to be Switzerland's finest. At the foot of Lausanne's steep slope is the lakeside town of Ouchy, a delightful village that offers spectacular views and pleasant pubs.

ONGOING EVENTS

Palais de Beaulieu

Op, Orch, Chor, Ballet

Palais de Beaulieu
Case Postale 89
Avenue des Bergières 10
CH-1000 Lausanne 22
Tel: 021/45 11 11
Fax: 021/45 37 11

The impressive schedule at this theater features a vast variety of events and international artists, as well as many Swiss performers. Among the recent presentations were Bach's *Saint Matthew Passion*, and Beethoven's Ninth Symphony. **Recent Performers:** conductors Erich Leinsdorf and James de Priest, Orchestre de la Suisse Romande, pianists Emmanuel Ax and Malcolm Frager. **Performances:** 8–10 monthly.

Théâtre Municipal—Opéra de Lausanne

Op, Chor, Dance

Théâtre Municipal
Case Postale 3972
CH-1002 Lausanne
Tel: 021/32 64 37

The season here includes major operas, choral works, and ballets. Productions have recently included Verdi's *Aida* and Monteverdi's *The Return of Ulysses,* along with performances by the Tokyo Ballet and the Andre Charlet Concert Choral. **Venues:** Théâtre Municipal, Théâtre de Beaulieu, Théâtre du Jorat à Mézières, others. **Performances:** 14 productions; September–June.

LUCERNE (Lucerne)
45 miles E of Berne

Nestled between snow-capped Alpine passes and shimmering Lake Lucerne, this city may be the quintessential Swiss town. A walk down most any of Lucerne's streets reveals flowers cascading from window boxes onto walls graced with swirling frescoes. Lucerne's medieval churches, curiosity shops, cafes, and boutiques are a feast for the senses. Richard Wagner came here in 1866 seeking refuge from his troubles in Munich, and settled on an estate at Tribschen, two miles from town. He stayed for six years, working *on Die Meistersinger, Siegfried,* and *Götterdämmerung.* The villa is now open as a museum, with manuscripts, memorabilia, and musical instruments.

FESTIVALS
Lucerne International Music Festival

3 Weeks
Mid-August–Early September

Orch, Chor, Cham, Rec, Org,
    Dance, Lect, Film, Ex

Luzern Internationale
    Musikfestwochen
Hirschmattstrasse 13
P.O. Box
CH-6002 Luzern
Tel: 041 23 52 72
Fax: 041/23 77 84
To purchase tickets in
    the United States:
Dailey-Thorp Travel Inc.
315 West 57th St.
New York, NY 10019
Tel: 212/307-1555

Considered to have the most spectacular scenery of any music festival in Europe, the Lucerne Festival has also proved to be one of the most highly respected. It began in 1938 as a summer home for the Orchestre de la Suisse Romande, but quickly grew to include many foreign orchestras and solo artists. Conductors Arturo Toscanini and Herbert von Karajan were vital in the shaping of its early years. Various exhibits, lectures, and exhibitions in art museums are also an important part of the festival's appeal. **Recent Performers:** conductor/composer Pierre Boulez, Vienna Philharmonic Orchestras, Tokyo String Quartet, pianist Vladimir Ashkenazy, violinist Isaac Stern. **Venues:** Kunsthaus, Schweizerhof Hotel, Lion Monument, Lucerne Jesuit Church. **Performances:** 40–45; many daily.

Easter Festival

3 Days	Osterfestspiele
March/April	Internationale Musikfestwochen Luzern
Orch, Chor, Cham, Rec, Org, Th	Hirschmattstrasse 13
	Postfach
	CH-6002 Luzern
	Tel: 041/23 52 72
	Fax: 041/23 77 84

Inaugurated in 1988 and an annual event since 1991, this musical celebration of Easter is an outgrowth of the Lucerne International Festival of Music. The festival is planned to complement the religious observances during this holy season, not to compete with them, and two of the musical events are part of liturgical services. Music for the orchestral and choral concerts is chosen with regard to both the contemplative and celebratory nature of this holiday, with composers such as Bruckner, Brahms, and Barber represented by large-scale works. **Recent Performers:** New York Philharmonic Orchestra conducted by Zubin Mehta, organist Marie-Claire Alain, flutist James Galway. **Venues:** Jesuit Church, thirteenth-century Franciscan Church, Hofkirche (a grand building in the Renaissance style, surrounded by Italianate cloisters and containing one of Switzerland's finest organs), Kunsthaus. **Performances:** 7; morning and evening.

ONGOING EVENTS

State Theater (Opera House)

Op, Dance, Th	Stadttheater Luzern
	Theaterstrasse 2
	CH-6002 Luzern
	Tel: 041/23 66 18

Constructed in 1839, this intimate opera house holds an audience of only 564. The resident company performs operas from every period and also premieres new works. Productions have included Mozart's *The Magic Flute*, Poulenc's *Les Dialogues des Carmélites*, and Ingomar Grünauer's *König für einen Tag*. **Performances:** 19 productions, 280–290 performances; August–June.

MARTIGNY (Valais)
75 miles SW of Berne

A well-known alpine crossroad because of its links to Italy by way of the Grand-Saint Bernard mountain pass and to France by the Forclaz mountain pass, the city of Martigny lies between a magnificent forest and vineyard covered hills. Martigny was known to the ancient Romans as an important center of commerce, and many vestiges of the city's history remain, including an ancient amphitheater. Today Martigny prides itself on being the artistic capital of the Valais region.

ONGOING EVENTS

Jeunesses Musicales Martigny

Orch, Chor, Cham, Rec
Jeunesses Musicales
Martigny
Fondation Pierre Gianadda
Rue du Forum
CH-1920 Martigny
Tel: 026/22 39 78

Although the title of this series might lead one to expect artistic newcomers, these concerts actually present some of the world's most renowned and established musicians in a very unique setting. In 1976 Léonard Gianadda discovered the remains of a Gallo-Roman temple, the oldest of its type in Switzerland. When his brother was killed shortly thereafter in a plane crash, Gianadda built a cultural center around the temple to perpetuate his brother's memory. Surrounded by a sculpture park with works of Brancusi, Arp, and Rodin, the temple forms a beautiful natural setting for these concerts. **Recent Performers:** Stockholm Chamber Orchestra, Orpheus Chamber Orchestra of New York, soprano Barbara Hendricks, pianist Alfred Brendel. **Performances:** 9; approximately one a month, October–May.

MONTREUX (Vaud)
50 miles SW of Berne

Montreux's gentle climate has nurtured the wide variety of trees that flourish here in abundance—from cypresses and figs to magnolias and palms. Montreux has been a famed refuge for a number of expatriate authors, Rousseau and Byron among them, and the city's botanical wonders have been more recently documented by novelist Vladimir Nabokov, who spent his last years here. An Edwardian elegance defines much of the city's architecture, while the crooked streets and historic buildings of the old town offer a glimpse of Montreaux's medieval heritage.

FESTIVALS

Montreux-Vevey Music Festival

6 Weeks
Late August–Early October

Orch, Chor, Cham, Rec, Org

Festival de Musique
Rue du Théâtre 5
Case postale 162
CH-1820 Montreux 2
Tel: 021/963 54 50
     021/963 12 12
Fax: 021/963 25 03
To purchase tickets in
    the United States:
Dailey-Thorpe Inc.
315 W. 57th St.
New York, NY 10019
Tel: 212/307-1555

Founded in 1946, this festival has evolved throughout the decades with the support of such artists as Richard Strauss and pianists Robert Casadesus and Clara Haskil. The event began in Montreux and became associated with nearby Vevey in 1954. Both cities boast halls with superb acoustics, and concerts are now also given in other nearby sites, including the Château de Chillon, a moated castle built in the thirteenth century. The festival strives to showcase not only major performers and works, but also young artists and more modern music. As Yves Petit de Voize, a recent director, described it: "the festival, more than an annual social ritual, should be an intelligent celebration where every famous work, every beloved composer should serve as a springboard to a thousand other discoveries." Hence, offerings here span Bach to Berio, Vivaldi to Schönberg and beyond. **Recent Performers:**

Tokyo Philharmonic Orchestra, Orchestre de la Suisse Romande, cellist Yo-Yo Ma, pianist Emmanuel Ax. **Venues:** Montreux, Vevey, Château de Chillon, Martigny, Aigle, St.-Maurice, Corseaux. **Performances:** 30; evenings and afternoons.

IN THE AREA

Arts et Lettres Vevey

Cham, Rec

Arts et Lettres Vevey
Office du Tourisme
Place de la Gare 5
CH-1800 Vevey
Tel: 021/921 48 25
Fax: 021/921 10 65

This series in the town of Vevey features world-famous artists and programs made up of predominantly classical and romantic repertoire. The lovely Italianate Théâtre de Vevey where most concerts take place seats 800. **Recent Performers:** American String Quartet, Trio de Milan, pianist Murray Perahia. **Venue:** Théâtre de Vevey, Casino du Rivage, Salle del Castille. **Performances:** 10; May.

NEUCHÂTEL (Neuchâtel)
25 miles W of Berne

The waters of Lake Neuchâtel lap the quays and waterside parks of this town, nestled among the vineyards that line the lake's shore. Once the domain of the House of Orléans, Neuchâtel retains an inherently French flavor, and the language spoken here is said to be French in its purest form. Neuchâtel's prominent university contributes to the town's vibrant cultural atmosphere, and two impressive museums, the Musée d'Art and the Musée d'Ethnographie, are among the city's most notable attractions.

ONGOING EVENTS

Cultural Events

Op, Orch, Chor, Cham, Rec,
Org, Dance, Th, Lect,
Ex, Child

Office du Tourisme du
Neuchâtel et Environs
Rue de la Place d'armes 7
CH-2001 Neuchâtel
Tel: 038/25 42 42

Some of Switzerland's most splendid castles, churches, and concert halls host a range of concerts that focus on music from the nineteenth century while also including music of earlier and more recent eras. Most performances are given by Swiss artists, and events take place in historic sites throughout the region. **Recent Performers:** Bournemouth Symphony Orchestra, La Camerata Academia du Mozarteum de Salzburg, oboist Heinz Holliger. **Venues:** Théâtre, Temple du Bas, Conservatoire, Musée d'art et de histoire, Château de Neuchâtel, Château du Landeron, Château de Vaumarcus, Château de Valangin, Eglise d'Auvernier, others. **Performances:** 10–20 monthly; September–March.

ST. GALLEN (St. Gallen)
115 miles NE of Berne

This ancient town dates back to the year 720, when the Irish Monk Gallus established a cloister here. The old town is filled with narrow streets, half-timbered houses, and a striking baroque church, considered Switzerland's finest. St. Gallen is known for its needlework and lace and is considered the embroidery capital of Europe.

ONGOING EVENTS

State Theater

Op, Dance, Th, Child

Stadttheater St. Gallen
Billettkasse
CH-9004 St. Gallen
Tel: 071/25 25 11

This theater's exhaustive schedule includes Mozart, Wagner, Prokofiev, and Shakespeare, among others. Swiss performers are featured, and recent productions include *The Magic Flute, Tristan und Isolde, My Fair Lady,* and the ballet "Romeo and Juliet." **Recent Performers:** Städtisches Orchester St. Gallen, Städttheaterchor St. Gallen. **Performances:** 20 productions; year-round.

SION (Valais)
90 miles S of Berne

The historic city of Sion prides itself on being the "Capital of the Violin," in large part due to the contributions of violinist Tibor Varga. Situated in the heart of the Alps, close to world-famous mountain resorts such as Crans-Montana and Zermatt, Sion's natural beauty is enhanced by its excellent wines, savory local cuisine, sunny climate, and its artistic treasures.

FESTIVALS

Tibor Varga Festival

15 Concerts
Early July–Early-Sepember

Orch, Chor, Cham, Rec

Association du Festival
Tibor Varga
Office Tourisme de Sion
Place de la Planta
CH-1950 Sion
Tel: 027/22 85 86
Fax: 027/23 46 62

Named for violinist and conductor Tibor Varga, who performs in several of its programs, this festival has been in existence since 1964, and is associated with Varga's mid-August International Violin Competition. Its well-rounded musical offerings have included works by such diverse composers as Purcell, Prokofiev, Stamitz, and Schönberg. **Recent Performers:** Stockholm Chamber Orchestra, the King's Consort, violinist Joshua Bell. **Venues:** Salle de la Matze, Fondation Pierre Gianadda, Cathédral of Sion, Église des Jésuites Sion, Église du Feydey in Leysin, Grande Salle Aitersheim St. Joseph in La Souste. **Performances:** 17; usually at 8:30 P.M.

International Festival of the Ancient Organ of Valère

3 Months
Early June–Early September

Orch, Chor, Org

Festival International de
L'Orgue Ancien
Case Postale 2088
CH-1950 Sion 2
Tel: 027/22 85 86 or
22 57 67

This festival invites internationally respected performers to explore the repertoire of ancient organ music. Many works by anonymous and lesser-known composers are played, as well as works by masters such as C. P. E. Bach. The Gothic organ that the festival celebrates is the oldest playable organ in the world, dating from the fourteenth century. Restoration of the instrument and its wing doors (painted in 1437 by Peter Maggenberg) was completed in 1968. The Valère cathedral, where the organ is located, is part of the castle of Valeria, whose history can be traced back to the middle of the eleventh century. **Recent Performers:** Lucerne Festival Strings,

Grupo Universitario de Camara-Compostela, organists Kei Koito and André Isoir. **Performances:** Saturdays at 4 P.M.

ZÜRICH (Zürich)
65 miles NE of Berne

Switzerland's largest city, Zürich is best known as a commercial and banking center. Centuries of financial activity have made this Switzerland's richest city, but the second-most desired bars here are made not of gold, but of chocolate, which is produced in great abundance. Despite all of this commerce, Zürich is considered by many to be one of Europe's most elegant cities, with celebrated shopping on the Bahnhofstrasse and magnificent views of Lake Zürich and the Alps.

FESTIVALS

International June Festival Weeks

4 Weeks	International Junifest-
June	wochen
	Tonhalle-Kasse
Op, Orch, Cham, Rec, Org,	Claridenstrasse 7
Dance, Th, Film	Haupteingang T
	CH-0882 Zürich
	Fax: 01/211 39 81

Since 1909, this festival has served to bring all facets of Zürich's cultural life together. A chosen theme unifies the various events and exhibits, such as the recent featuring of Soviet art and culture. Recent musical offerings have included Debussy's *Pelléas et Mélisande,* Mendelssohn's Violin Concerto, and Stravinsky's *Rite of Spring.* **Recent Performers:** Zürich Chamber Orchestra, Leningrad Philharmonic, Bolshoi Ballet, trumpeter Maurice André. **Venues:** Opera House, Tonhalle, Kunsthaus, Stadthaus. **Performances:** 30.

ONGOING EVENTS

Meisterzyklus

Cham, Rec	Meisterzyklus
	Billettzentrale
	Werdmühleplatz
	CH-8001 Zürich
	Tel: 01/221 22 83 or
	251 60 61

Eight concerts make up this impressive series, which focuses chiefly upon classical and romantic repertoire. Programs have recently included such works as Mendelssohn's Octet for Strings and Reinecke's flute sonata "Undine." **Recent Performers:** Beaux Arts Trio, flutist James Galway, violinist Schlomo Mintz. **Venue:** Tonhalle Zürich. **Performances:** 8; October–June.

Tonhalle Zürich

Orch, Chor, Cham, Rec, Org

Tonhalle Box Office
Gotthardstrasse 5
CH-8002 Zürich
Tel: 1/201 15 80
Fax: 1/201 23 64

One of Europe's most spectacular halls, the Tonhalle was designed by Viennese architects Fellner and Hellmer. It was officially opened in 1895 with a concert given by the acclaimed Zürich Tonhalle Orchestra, with guest conductor Johannes Brahms. In addition to concerts by the famed resident orchestra, programs here include those given by guest chamber music performers. The arresting beauty of the hall has provided inspiration to countless world-class performers, and continues to leave its audiences virtually breathless. **Recent Performers:** Orpheus Chamber Orchestra, conductors Neville Mariner and Lorin Maazel, violinist Midori. **Performances:** August–June (closed in July).

Zürich Chamber Orchestra

Orch, Cham

Zürich Chamber Orchestra
Kreuzstrasse 55
CH-8032 Zürich
Tel: 01/252 10 71
Fax: 01/252 10 71

The Zürich Chamber Orchestra is known as one of Europe's finest and most unique musical ensembles. It has established a unity that comes from rehearsing on a daily basis, while still giving ample attention to the artistry of the individual players. Composers recently represented include Bach, Haydn, Beethoven, Prokofiev, and Stravinsky. **Recent Performers:** trumpeter Maurice André, flutist Aurèle Nicolet. **Venues:** Tonhalle, Grosser Saal. **Performances:** 19 concerts; September–June.

Zürich Opera House

Op, Orch, Cham, Ballet,
    Child

Opernhaus Zürich
Falkenstrasse 1
CH-8008 Zürich
Tel: 01/262 09 09
Fax: 01/251 58 96

This opera house, built in 1891 and renovated in 1984, houses a number of innovative companies and programs. Its far-ranging operatic repertoire, usually performed in the original language, includes Berlioz' *Les Troyens,* Tchaikovsky's *Eugene Onegin,* and Johann Strauss's *Der Zigeunerbaron.* Ballet productions include favorites such as *La Sylphide.* The resident orchestra is featured in four concerts, and chamber operas, chamber music, and productions of the famed Zürich International Opera Studio are given throughout the season. **Performances:** 260 performances, 8 productions; September–June.

UNITED KINGDOM

Performance of *Don Giovanni* (courtesy of Pavilion Opera).

ENGLAND
1 Aldeburgh
2 Ambleside
3 Arundel
4 Bath
5 Beverley
6 Bournemouth
7 Brighton
8 Bristol
9 Buxton
10 Cambridge
11 Canterbury
12 Cheltenham
13 Chichester
14 Coventry
15 Cricklade
16 Gloucester
17 Glyndebourne
18 Haslemere
19 Hereford
20 King's Lynn
21 Leeds
22 Lichfield
23 Lincoln
24 Liverpool
25 Ludlow
26 Manchester
27 Newbury
28 Nottingham
29 Oxford
30 Poole
31 St. Albans
32 St. Endellion
33 Salisbury
34 Sevenoaks
35 Southampton
36 Stratford
37 Thaxted
38 Truro
39 Warwick
40 Winchester
41 Windsor
42 Worchester

SCOTLAND
43 Aberdeen
44 Dumfries
45 Dundee
46 Glasgow
47 Perth
48 St. Andrews

WALES
49 Fishguard
50 Gregynog
51 Llangollen
52 Swansea

NORTHERN
IRELAND
Belfast

CALENDAR

FEBRUARY

Gleneagles Weekend with the Scottish Chamber Orchestra, **Perth** (Scotland)
Winter Visitors' Season, **Stratford-upon-Avon** (Warwickshire)

MARCH

Easter at Snape Maltings, **Aldeburgh** (Suffolk)
St. Endellion Easter Festival, **St. Endellion** (Cornwall)
Winter Visitors' Season, **Stratford-upon-Avon** (Warwickshire)

APRIL

Easter at Snape Maltings, **Aldeburgh** (Suffolk)
London Handel Festival, **London**
Mayfield Festival, see **Brighton** (East Sussex)
St. Endellion Easter Festival, **St. Endellion** (Cornwall)

MAY

Back to Beethoven Festival, **Sheffield** (South Yorkshire)
Bath International Festival of Music and the Arts, **Bath** (Avon)
Beverley Early Music Festival, **Beverley** (Humberside)
Brighton International Festival, **Brighton** (East Sussex)
Bristol Proms Festival, **Bristol** (Avon)
Chelmsford Cathedral Festival, see **London**
Dumfries and Galloway Arts Festival, **Dumfries** (Scotland)
Glyndebourne Festival, **Glyndebourne** (East Sussex)
London Festival Orchestra's Cathedral Classics, see
London
Mayfield Festival, see **Brighton** (East Sussex)
Newbury Spring Festival, **Newbury** (Berkshire)
Nottingham Festival, **Nottingham** (Nottinghamshire)
Perth Festival of the Arts, **Perth** (Scotland)
Stately Homes Music Festival, **St. Albans** (Hertfordshire)
Tilford Bach Festival, **Tilford** (Surrey)

JUNE

Aldeburgh Festival of Music and the Arts, **Aldeburgh**
(Suffolk)
Bath International Festival of Music and the Arts, **Bath** (Avon)
Bournemouth Music Festival, **Bournemouth** (Dorset)
Dolmetsch Festival in Haslemere, **Haslemere** (Surrey)
Dumfries and Galloway Arts Festival, **Dumfries** (Scotland)

Glyndebourne Festival, **Glyndebourne** (East Sussex)
Greenwich Festival, **London**
Gregynog Festival, **Gregynog** (Wales)
London Festival Orchestra's Cathedral Classics, see
    London
Ludlow Festival, **Ludlow** (Shropshire)
Lufthansa Festival of Baroque Music, **London**
Nottingham Festival, **Nottingham** (Nottinghamshire)
St. Magnus Festival, **Orkney Islands** (Scotland)
Stately Homes Music Festival, **St. Albans** (Hertfordshire)
Stour Music, **Canterbury** (Kent)
Sevenoaks Summer Festival, **Sevenoaks** (Kent)
Thaxted Festival, **Thaxted** (Essex)
Three Spires Festival, **Truro** (Cornwall)

JULY

BBC Henry Wood Promenade Concerts, **London**
Bournemouth Music Festival, **Bournemouth** (Dorset)
Buxton Festival, **Buxton** (Derbyshire)
Cambridge Festival, **Cambridge** (Cambridgeshire)
Cheltenham International Festival of Music, **Cheltenham**
    (Gloucestershire)
Chichester Festivities, **Chichester** (West Sussex)
Fishguard Music Festival, **Fishguard** (Wales)
Glyndebourne Festival, **Glyndebourne** (East Sussex)
Gower Festival, **Swansea** (Wales)
Handel in Oxford Festival, **Oxford** (Oxfordshire)
The King's Lynn Festival of Music and the Arts, **King's Lynn**
    (Norfolk)
Lichfield Festival, **Lichfield** (Staffordshire)
Llangollen International Musical Eisteddfod, **Llangollen**
    (Wales)
London Festival Orchestra's Cathedral Classics, see
    London
Ludlow Festival, **Ludlow** (Shropshire)
St. Albans International Organ Festival, **St. Albans**
    (Hertfordshire)
Southern Cathedrals Festival, see **Salisbury** (Wiltshire)
Stately Homes Music Festival, **St. Albans** (Hertfordshire)
Thaxted Festival, **Thaxted** (Essex)
Three Spires Festival, **Truro** (Cornwall)
Warwick Arts Festival, **Warwick** (Warwickshire)
Welsh Proms, **Cardiff** (Wales)
York Early Music Festival, **York** (North Yorkshire)

AUGUST

Aberdeen International Festival of Youth, **Aberdeen**
    (Scotland)
Arundel Festival, **Arundel** (West Sussex)
BBC Henry Wood Promenade Concerts, **London**
Buxton Festival, **Buxton** (Derbyshire)
Edinburgh International Festival, **Edinburgh** (Scotland)
Glyndebourne Festival, **Glyndebourne** (East Sussex)
Lake District Summer Music International Summer
    School and Festival, **Ambleside** (Cumberland)
Malting Proms, Aldeburgh (Suffolk), see **Swansea** (Wales)
Royal National Eisteddfod of Wales, see **Swansea** (Wales)
St. Endellion Summer Festival, **St. Endellion** (Cornwall)
Stately Homes Music Festival, **St. Albans** (Hertfordshire)
Summer in the City, **London**
Three Choirs Festival, **Hereford,** Gloucester,
    Worcester (Herefordshire)
Vale of Glamorgan Festival, see **Swansea** (Wales)

SEPTEMBER

Arundel Festival, **Arundel** (West Sussex)
BBC Henry Wood Promenade Concerts, **London**
Cardiff Festival of Music, **Cardiff** (Wales)
Cricklade Music Festival, **Cricklade** (Wiltshire)
Edinburgh International Festival, **Edinburgh** (Scotland)
Salisbury Festival, **Salisbury** (Wiltshire)
Stately Homes Music Festival, **St. Albans** (Hertfordshire)
Windsor Festival, **Windsor** (Berkshire)

OCTOBER

Cardiff Festival of Music, **Cardiff** (Wales)
Canterbury Festival, **Canterbury** (Kent)
Cricklade Music Festival, **Cricklade** (Wiltshire)
Early Music Center Festival, **London**
Stately Homes Music Festival, **St. Albans** (Hertfordshire)
Swansea Festival of Music and the Arts, **Swansea**
    (Wales)
Windsor Festival, **Windsor** (Berkshire)

NOVEMBER

Belfast Festival at Queens, **Belfast** (Northern Ireland)
Huddersfield Contemporary Music Festival, see **Leeds**
    (West Yorkshire)

DECEMBER

Huddersfield Contemporary Music Festival, see **Leeds** (West Yorkshire)

The international telephone country code for Great Britain is (011) **44**. City codes have the prefix 0, which is deleted when calling from abroad.

ENGLAND

꒰ᴥ꒱

ALDEBURGH (Suffolk)
100 miles NE of London

Benjamin Britten set his great opera *Peter Grimes* in this small fishing village, which is even today recognizable as the quiet, simple place it was several centuries ago. The town bustles with activity during the festival, and then returns to its largely unchanged village pace.

FESTIVALS

Aldeburgh Festival of Music and the Arts

2 Weeks	Box Office
Mid-June	Aldeburgh Foundation
	High Street
Op, Orch, Chor, Cham, Rec,	Aldeburgh, Suffolk
Film, Lect, Ex	IP15 5AX
	Tel: 0728/453543

One of the most important European festivals, Aldeburgh has long sought to introduce younger artists along with internationally known performers. The festival was founded in 1948 by Benjamin Britten, Peter Pears, and Eric Crozier to showcase the music of British artists. Even though 8 of Britten's own operas received their premieres here, the Festival honors the spirit of this composer more in the richness of its diversity than in a concentration of his music, though Britten is well represented each year. **Recent Performers:** English Concert, Tokyo String Quartet, soprano

Jessye Norman. **Venues:** Jubilee Concert Hall, Snape Maltings, churches, country homes. The concert hall complex known as Snape Maltings was converted to its present use in 1967 from an old malt brewery barn, and completely rebuilt following fire in 1969. In its new incarnation, it has been called the finest concert hall in Europe. Transportation is available to all events located outside of Aldeburgh. **Performances:** several daily.

Maltings Proms

1 Month	Box Office
August	Aldeburgh Foundation
	High Street
Orch, Cham, Rec, Org, Child	Aldeburgh
	Suffolk IP15 5AX
	Tel: 0728/453543
	Fax: 0728/452715

This newly established concert series brings a great variety of music to the festive atmosphere of Snape Maltings. From medieval music to Caribbean steel drum bands, versatility is the key. **Recent Performers:** BBC Scottish Symphony Orchestra, BBC Big Band, violinist Nigel Kennedy, Britten-Pears Ensemble. **Venues:** Snape Maltings Concert Hall, Framlingham Church. **Performances:** 30 consecutive evening concerts; 7:30 P.M.

Easter at Snape Maltings

5 Days	Box Office
Easter Weekend	Aldeburgh Foundation
	High Street
Orch, Chor, Cham, Rec	Aldeburgh
	Suffolk IP15 5AX
	Tel: 0728/453543
	Fax: 0728/452715

Both sacred and secular works are offered during this festival, which strives to appeal to a broad audience by bringing these two aspects of music together. Performances have included Mozart's Symphony No. 36 (*Linz*), Bach's "Komm, Jesu, Komm!", and chamber music by Brahms. **Recent Performers:** St. James's Baroque Players, Borodin String Quartet, Britten-Pears Orchestra. **Venues:** Snape Maltings, Orford Church. **Performances:** 7; Maundy Thursday to Easter Monday.

ONGOING EVENTS

Snape Maltings Concert Hall

Orch, Chor, Cham, Rec,
Child

Box Office
Aldeburgh Foundation
High Street
Aldeburgh
Suffolk IP15 5AX
Tel: 0728/453543

This world-famous concert hall houses the Aldeburgh Festival of Music and the Arts in June, as well as many other events throughout the year. Warm and intimate, its superlative acoustics have made it a favorite gathering place for musicians and audiences alike. **Performances:** year-round.

AMBLESIDE (Cumberland)
235 miles NW of London

Ambleside is one of the lake district's most enchanting villages. Perched at the northern, quieter end of Lake Windermere (the area's largest lake), the town is a storybook vision of stone buildings, cozy Victorian inns, and charming pubs nestled between towering emerald mountains and the sparkling lake. For centuries, this has been one of England's most popular vacation regions, immortalized by such poets as Wordsworth, Coleridge, De Quincey, and Shelley, who all lived in the area. The Wordsworth house, known as Dove Cottage, is a mecca for scholars of romantic poetry, who gather here throughout the year for seminars and symposiums.

FESTIVALS

Lake District Summer Music—International
Summer School and Festival

2 Weeks
Mid-August

Orch, Chor, Cham, Rec

Lake District Summer Music
Museum Building
97 Grosvenor Street
Manchester MI 7HF
Tel: 061/274 4149
      0629/823733

Ambleside provides the resplendent setting for this festival. It takes place as part of the summer school, where young artists gather to study chamber music and solo repertoire, both vocal and instrumental. Nightly concerts are presented by faculty members and visiting artists as well as by students. Music lovers are invited to enroll as observers of classes and coaching sessions. **Recent Performers:** Manchester Camerata, Franz Schubert String Quartet of Vienna. **Venue:** Charlotte Mason College. **Performances:** nightly.

ARUNDEL (West Sussex)
60 miles S of London

The majestic turrets that tower above this quiet village belong to Arundel Castle, seat of the Dukes of Norfolk, and the medieval town seems to exist as the Castle's tiny kingdom. The present Duke is a very active president of the Arundel Festival Society, and was the driving force behind the first Shakespeare production in 1977. Walks along the River Arun and the lovely Swanbourne Lake offer a peaceful perspective of the town from its central Great Park.

FESTIVALS

Arundel Festival

10 Days Late August–Early September	Arundel Festival Society Festival Box Office The Mary Gate
Orch, Chor, Cham, Rec, Org, Dance, Th, Lect, Film	Arundel Sussex BN18 9AT Tel: 0903/8836901 Fax: 0903/884276

Concerts are a single but significant ingredient in the bountiful feast of activities and events found at this festival, one of the most innovative and exciting in southern England. The open-air theater, built in the shadow of the battlements of Arundel Castle, is the spectacular setting for an annual Shakespeare production as well as jazz and dance performances. Concerts by world-famous artists are given in the Castle's magnificent Baron's Hall, the private Chapel of the Dukes of Norfolk, and in the fourteenth-century parish church of St. Nicholas. The Gothic splendor of the Cathedral houses large-scale orchestral and choral works and a series of celebrity organ recitals. A unique collection of permanent and temporary galleries is set up all over the town to form the Art Gallery Trail, and fireworks, films, and varied fringe activities add to the town's festival atmosphere. For many festival events, food and/or drink are included with admission tickets. **Recent Performers:** London Mozart Players, City of London Sinfonia, Alberni String Quartet. **Venues:** Arundel Cathedral, Parish Church, The American Ground Open Air Theater (Shakespeare and Jazz performances), Priory Playhouse, Buller's Tea Terrace.**Performances:** many daily.

BATH (Avon)
100 miles W of London

This elegant Georgian city is one of England's most beautiful, owing to careful attention on the part of the eighteenth-century architects who laid out its graceful squares and crescent streets. The city's first planners, however, were the Romans, who created an admirable system of baths in the first century A.D., portions of which are still visible. The tradition of chamber music in the Pump Room and Assembly Rooms dates back to the early eighteenth century, when the town first became fashionable.

FESTIVALS

Bath International Festival of Music and the Arts

2 Weeks	Bath Festival Box Office
Late May—Early June	Century House
	4 Pierrepont Street
Op, Orch, Chor, Cham, Rec,	Bath BA1 1LE
Jazz, Lect, Ex	Tel: 0225/463362 or
	466411

The many events of this festival offer world-renowned performers in every conceivable medium, from symphony to sitar, as well as varied fringe events. Programs range from Monteverdi (and before!) to recently commissioned works. The scope of this festival makes it one of the most diversified of the major festivals. **Recent Performers:** English Baroque Soloists, Kent Opera, Tallis Scholars, Beaux Arts Trio. **Venues:** Assembly Rooms, Pump Room, Guildhall, Theatre Royal, Bath Abbey, Wells Cathedral, Christ Church. **Performances:** an average of five each day.

BEVERLEY (Humberside)
170 miles N of London

This small village was once considered the capital of East Riding, and is known locally for its racing events. The spires of its two notable churches—the Minster, a grand Gothic structure, and the Church of St. Mary—rise above the level pasture that surrounds the town.

FESTIVALS

Beverley Early Music Festival

4 Days	Beverley Early Music
Mid-May	Festival
	Box Office
Orch, Cham, Rec, Org, Lect	The Guildhall
	Register Square
	Beverley, HU17 9AU
	Tel: 0482/867430

This very young festival (founded in 1988) brings together some of the country's most respected early music ensembles and includes them in a varied program that ranges from concerts in the splendid Beverley Minster to programs in the local elementary schools. The schedule of concerts is augmented by informal lectures given by specialists in the field of early music. **Recent Performers:** Hanover Band, New London Consort, St. James Baroque Players. **Venues:** Beverley Minster, St. Mary's Church, Art gallery, Guildhall. **Performances:** daily; afternoon and evening.

BIRMINGHAM (West Midlands)
110 miles NW of London

The industrial city of Birmingham, second largest in England, is now a composite reflection of the twentieth century as a result of redevelopment undertaken since World War II, when many of its buildings were destroyed. Although less than picturesque, there is much to do in this bustling city, which has an excellent City Art Gallery, several museums, and a number of beautiful parks, including the 80-acre Cannon Hill Park. Birmingham was the site of an important music festival held between 1768 and 1912, and the list of works premiered here includes Mendelssohn's *Elijah*.

ONGOING EVENTS

City of Birmingham Symphony Orchestra

Orch   City of Birmingham Sym-
                        phony Orchestra
                        Box Office
                        Birmingham Town Hall
                        Birmingham B3 3DQ
                        Tel: 021/236 3889

This orchestra, one of Britain's finest, gives weekly subscription concerts in its home city and manages an active
touring schedule as well. The orchestra also performs at Bed-
worth (4 concerts), Cheltenham (10 concerts), London (Barbican Centre, 3 concerts), and at festivals throughout the
world. **Recent Performers:** conductor Simon Rattle, tenor
Luciano Pavarotti, pianist Emanuel Ax, violinist Gidon Kremer. **Venue:** Birmingham Town Hall. **Performances:** 50;
September–May.

The Creative Facility Series

Orch, Cham   CBSO Society Ltd.
                         Paradise Hall
                         Birmingham B3 3RP
                         Tel: 021/643 2514

This innovative series presents contemporary music—
from the most recent works of Steve Reich to Stravinsky to
Big Band to Afro-Cuban Jazz. Other composers represented
include Varèse, Xenakis, Stockhausen, and Peter Maxwell
Davies. **Recent Performers:** conductors Simon Rattle and
Oliver Knussen, Birmingham Contemporary Music Group,
soprano Linda Hirst. **Venue:** Adrian Boult Hall. **Performances:** 10; October–April.

Music at the University of Birmingham

Orch, Chor, Cham, Rec   Department of Music
                         University of Birmingham
                         P.O. Box 363
                         Birmingham, B15 2TT
                         Tel: 021/414 5782
                             or 472 0622

This active program features many of Britain's finest artists, as well as members of the university community. Programs range from Handel trio sonatas to choral Evensong liturgies to the Verdi Requiem. **Recent Performers:** The Academy of Ancient Music, Fine Arts Brass Ensemble, Sorrell String Quartet. **Venue:** Concert Hall of the Barber Institute of Fine Arts, Great Hall, St. Alban's Church. **Performances:** several weekly throughout the academic year.

Welsh National Opera

Op

Box Office
Birmingham Hippodrome
Hurst St.
Birmingham B5 4TB

This celebrated company provides a brief season of opera in Birmingham with productions of such favorites as *Lucia di Lammermoor*, *The Bartered Bride*, and *Der Freischütz*. **Venue:** Birmingham Hippodrome. **Performances:** 15; 5 each in November, April, June.

BOURNEMOUTH (Dorset)
100 miles SW of London

This seaside resort attracts vacationers year-round to enjoy its agreeable climate, 7 miles of sandy beaches, and diverse entertainment. A relatively new city, Bournemouth was founded in the early nineteenth century and rapidly became a favorite gathering place for wealthy Victorians. The town is now shedding its somewhat staid image, and casinos prosper along with Victorian shops and promenades. The city's gardens are magnificent, covering thousands of acres and providing a delightful invitation to stroll among rhododendrons and azaleas.

FESTIVALS

Bournemouth Music Festival

2 Weeks
Late June–Early July

Orch, Chor, Band

Music Festival Office
Department of Tourism
Westover Road
Bournemouth, BH1 2BU
Tel: 0202/291718

This festival draws over 3000 members of youth and adult bands, choirs, and orchestras from England and abroad to take part in its 300 competition classes. The first week includes the competitions as well as public concerts and recreational events. A national event since 1926, the Festival has been international in scope since 1986. The professional content of the festival continues to expand. **Venues:** Winter Gardens, an 1800-seat concert hall that is the home of the Bournemouth Symphony. **Performances:** many daily.

ONGOING EVENTS

Bournemouth Sinfonietta *see Poole
Bournemouth Symphony Orchestra *see Poole

BRIGHTON (East Sussex)
50 miles S of London

Brighton was once renowned as an extravagant seaside pleasure spot, a reputation attributable to the lavish social whirl that encircled the Prince Regent (later George IV). The magnificent Royal Pavilion, built in 1787 for Prince George and later used as a summer residence by Queen Victoria, is particularly arresting at night. The beautifully appointed interior contains a valuable art collection from the Regency period. Today Brighton is a family resort, with activities for all ages.

FESTIVALS

Brighton International Festival

3 Weeks	Festival Office
Early–Mid-May	Marlborough Hall
	54 Old Steine
Op, Orch, Chor, Cham, Org,	Brighton, East Sussex
Dance, Th, Film, Rec,	BN1 1EQ
	Tel: 0273/28488
	(Theatre Royal)
	0273/674357
	(Dome/Festival)

In a city known for its ability to cater to every taste, it is not surprising that this festival includes virtually every field of the arts. While nineteenth-century repertoire predominates, there is a frequent emphasis on contemporary and avant-garde music, and a few excursions into the past. Myriad dance, theatre, and literary events provide eclectic offerings from around the world. The festival, founded in 1967, offers especially varied fringe events, including programs for children. **Performers:** London Symphony Orchestra conducted by Michael Tilson Thomas, Takacs Quartet, pianist Alfred Brendel. **Venues:** Royal Pavilion, Theatre Royal, churches, dozens more. **Performances:** many daily (over 400 events).

ONGOING EVENTS

Brighton and Hove Philharmonic Society

Orch, Chor, Cham

The Dome Box Office
29 New Road
Brighton BN1 1UG
Tel: 0273/674357
Fax 0273/602292

The Society sponsors a variety of concerts throughout the season, with the Brighton Philharmonic Orchestra featured throughout. Conducted by Barry Wordsworth, this fully professional ensemble boasts a wide repertoire, including works by Tchaikovsky and Elgar. **Recent Performers:** violinist Nigel Kennedy, cellist Julian Lloyd Webber. **Venue:** Dome Concert Hall. **Performances:** 10; September–March.

IN THE AREA

Mayfield Festival

3 Weeks
Late April–Mid-May

Orch, Chor, Cham, Rec, Org
Lect, Ex, Th, Child

Mayfield Festival
Libra Bookshop
West Street
Mayfield
East Sussex TN20 6EB
Tel: 0435/873382

One of the most important cultural events in southeast England, this festival is mounted biennially (even-numbered years) in the small town of Mayfield, 20 miles NE of Brighton. It covers Renaissance through contemporary styles, as well as lighter entertainment. Nonmusical aspects of the festival include children's drama, puppet shows, photography, and painting and sculpture exhibits. The festival aims to bring world-class international artists and varied repertoire to one of the most beautiful old villages in Sussex and, by doing so, has instituted a unique atmosphere of culture, charm, and conviviality. Recent performances have included Bach's B Minor Mass, songs by Dowland, piano music of Chopin, and Stravinsky's *Dumbarton Oaks*, arranged for two guitars. **Recent Performers:** Dowland Consort, bass John Milne, pianist Cecille Ousset. **Venues:** Mayfield Parish Church, thirteenth-century Mayfield Convent Chapel, Concert Hall. **Performances:** 15–20; evenings, some afternoons.

BRISTOL (Avon)
125 miles W of London

Since the eleventh century, Bristol's location at the confluence of the Avon and Frome rivers has made it an important center of trade and commerce. Its location as an inland port made it a haven safe from pirates and contributed much to the city's prosperity. The town reached its zenith in the eighteenth century, when its importance as a seaport was second only to London. The location was also the cause of the port's decline in the nineteenth century, when seagoing vessels proved too large to navigate the Avon. In recent decades Bristol has made a comeback and today is a thriving commercial city with a skyline that combines modern skyscrapers with medieval church spires.

FESTIVALS

Bristol Proms Festival

2 Weeks	Bristol Proms Festival
Mid-May	Box Office
	Colston Hall
Orch, Chor, Cham, Rec	Colston Street
	Bristol BS1 5AR
	Tel: 0272/223686
	Fax: 0272/223681

Variety distinguishes this festival, where Bach, Barber, Basie, and the Beatles can be heard on consecutive evenings. Each concert is devoted to a particular theme, customarily a nationality or a musical style, and the famous "Last Night at the Proms" brings it all to an exciting close. Among the recently performed works are Tchaikovsky's *Romeo and*

Juliet, Dvořák's *New World Symphony*, Gershwin's *Rhapsody in Blue*, and the music of Duke Ellington. **Recent Performers:** Royal Philharmonic Orchestra, BBC Welsh Symphony Orchestra, Stan Tracey Big Band. **Venues:** Colston Hall, St. George's Church, Brandon Hill. **Performances:** 12; evenings.

BUXTON (Derbyshire)
150 miles NW of London

The elegant spa town of Buxton enjoys one of the highest altitudes in England as well as waters famed for their medicinal qualities. Located in the heart of the scenic Peak District National Park, Buxton is just a few miles from Chatsworth, one of England's great historic homes.

FESTIVALS

Buxton Festival

3 Weeks
Late July–Early August

Op, Cham, Rec, Jazz, Th,
    Lect, Film

Buxton Festival Office
Opera House
Buxton, Derbyshire
SK17 6XN
Tel: 0298/78939

This unique festival centers its activities each year around the influence that a creative artist has had on the works of his or her contemporaries and successors. Past festivals have focused on artists as diverse as Shakespeare and Domenico Cimarosa. The festival also boasts its own highly regarded opera company and is noted for its spirited revivals of operatic masterpieces outside the standard repertoire. Productions are given in the city's elegant opera house, which provided the impetus to create the festival after its renovation in 1979. Varied offerings include a busy fringe schedule and events for children. **Recent Performers:** soprano Margaret Price, baritone Thomas Allen, rising young artists. **Venues:** Opera House, Octagon Hall, Pavilion Gardens, other locales. **Performances:** Many daily.

CAMBRIDGE (Cambridgeshire)
60 miles N of London

The Gothic spires of this extraordinary city soar over the bustle of scholars and students as they have for centuries. The beauty of this vibrant town lies in the more than 30 individual colleges that make up the great university, each embodying in its mullioned windows and carefully tended lawns the care and commitment of generations. The Cam River flows languidly through the city, and hosts a seemingly continuous regatta of punts—long open boats that are propelled beneath the overhanging willows by students and tourists alike. The Chapel of King's College is unforgettable, especially when visited during one of the services or concerts given by its superb choir of men and boys.

FESTIVALS

Cambridge Festival

2 Weeks
Mid to Late July

Op, Orch, Chor, Cham, Rec,
    Org, Dance, Th, Ex,
    Film, Child, Fringe

Festival Office
Mandela House
4 Regent Street
Cambridge CB2 1BY
Tel: 0223/357851

One of England's most beautiful university cities quickens its pace during this festival, to which it has played host since 1962. A special theme is chosen each year, such as the recent spotlight on Italian music. From Bach to jazz, and from chapel choir concerts to cabarets and fireworks, the variety of offerings here is considerable. **Recent Performers:** BBC Symphony Orchestra, King's College Choir, Cambridge Opera, Balletto di Toscana. **Venues:** Cambridge Corn Exchange, King's College Chapel, University Music School, Ely Cathedral.

CANTERBURY (Kent)
60 miles SE of London

The center of this ancient town looks much the same as it has for centuries, with half-timbered houses and tiny shops and pubs of the old town surrounding the cathedral in a maze of narrow streets. But it is the great cathedral itself that is the focal point. Archbishop Thomas à Beckett was murdered here in 1170, and soon after travelers such as those immortalized in Chaucer's *Canterbury Tales* made the site of his martyrdom a place of pilgrimage. Canterbury has been a cathedral city since St. Augustine was sent here in the late sixth century, and its earlier importance as a Roman stronghold is evident in remains throughout the city.

FESTIVALS

Canterbury Festival

2 Weeks
Mid-October

Op, Orch, Chor, Cham, Rec,
    Org, Dance, Th, Film,
    Ex, Fringe

Canterbury Festival Box
    Office
59 Ivy Lane
Canterbury
Kent CT1 1TU
Tel: 0227/455600

Canterbury is sometimes referred to as a "Festival City," and these two words truly become synonymous during the weeks of this event. Fireworks and street entertainment mark its opening, and throughout its duration Canterbury is bustling with concerts, plays, master classes, literary events, and exhibitions. From baroque to jazz and Shakespeare to extemporary dance, the opportunities for enjoyment are boundless. Recent offerings have included Mozart's *Magic Flute*, Shakespeare's *Macbeth*, Rachmaninoff's Preludes for Piano, and Britten's String Quartet no. 3. **Recent Performers:** Kent Opera, BBC Symphony Orchestra, London Mozart Players, Tony Coe Jazz Quartet. **Venues:** Marlowe Theatre, Gulbenkian Theatre, Canterbury Cathedral, Shirley Hall. **Performances:** nearly 160.

Stour Music

2 Weekends
Mid-June

Op, Chor, Cham, Rec

Stour Music
Forwood Bookings
37 Palace Street
Canterbury CT1 2DZ
Tel: 0227/455600

Bach to Britten is the range of this festival, which encourages its audiences to stay for dinner at the Festival Marquee and to attend the short "late night" offerings that begin at 10 P.M. The festival was founded in 1963 by countertenor Alfred Deller, and continues to place its greatest emphasis on early music. **Recent Performers:** Kent Opera in a production of Britten's *The Burning Fiery Furnace*, Trevor Pinnock conducting the English Consort, Mark Deller conducting the Canterbury Cantata Choir. **Venue:** Boughton Aluph Church. **Performances:** Friday and Saturday evenings, Sunday afternoons.

CHELTENHAM (Gloucestershire)
100 miles NW of London

A Regency spa town of gracious elegance, Cheltenham is famous for its chestnut-lined boulevards, gardens, and the curative powers of its waters. Gustav Holst was born in this Cotswolds town in 1874, and his music is well represented in the festival programs.

FESTIVALS

Cheltenham International Festival of Music

2 Weeks	Cheltenham International
Early July	Festival of Music
	Box Office
Op, Orch, Cham, Rec, Jazz,	Town Hall
Dance, Lect, Fringe	Imperial Square
	Cheltenham, Glos.
	GL50 1QA
	Tel: 0242/523690

British contemporary music forms the nucleus of this festival's wide-ranging programming, which since 1980 has also included baroque, classical, and romantic music. This was the first of the postwar festivals, opening in 1945 with music composed and conducted by Benjamin Britten, William Walton, and Arthur Bliss. The festival prides itself on premieres and commissions, and has established a Composer-in-Residence program. **Performers:** City of Birmingham Symphony Orchestra, Opera North, mezzo-soprano Dame Janet Baker. **Venues:** Pittville Pump Room, Everyman Theatre, Town Hall, others. **Performances:** many daily.

CHICHESTER (West Sussex)
60 miles SW of London

Although mainly Georgian in character today, Chichester contains the remnants of a 2000-year history. Its Roman origins are apparent in the crossing of its two main streets and in the extensive palace ruins located just west of the city. The splendid medieval cathedral serves as the town's focus, and its striking Victorian spire can be seen for miles. In addition to the music festival, the city is also host to an internationally famed theater festival, which runs from May to September.

FESTIVALS

Chichester Festivities

2 Weeks	Chichester Festivities
Early July	Box Office
	Hammick's Bookshop
Op, Orch, Chor, Cham Rec,	65 East Street
Jazz, Lect, Film	Chichester, West Sussex
	PO19 1HL
	Tel: 0243/780 192

This eclectic festival fills its calendar with both classical and popular music. Each year a theme is chosen, such as the recent motif of "A Touch of Romance." Young artists are featured, joined by world-class performers. A typical evening might offer a choice of Verdi's *Falstaff,* a harpsichord recital, or choral music by Gounod. British artists are featured, with a special spotlight on highly gifted young performers. Established in the 1970s, this is a young and innovative festival. It precedes the Southern Cathedrals Festival, which is held in Chichester every third year (Salisbury and Winchester are the other locations). **Recent Performers:** The Royal Philharmonic Orchestra, The Dolmetsch Ensemble, soprano Arlene Auger. **Venues:** Chichester Cathedral, many other locales. **Performances:** Many daily.

COVENTRY (Warwickshire)
100 miles NW of London

Nearly all of Coventry was leveled during World War II, including the magnificent fourteenth-century cathedral. As a striking memorial to the dead, the shell of the ancient church has been left standing, and a stunning modern cathedral built adjacent to the ruins. The awesome new cathedral provides a spiritual center for this now highly industrialized city.

ONGOING EVENTS

International Celebrity Concert Series

Orch	International Celebrity
	Concert Series
	Box Office/Arts Centre
	University of Warwick
	Coventry CV4 7AL
	Tel: 0203/417417

This series brings 10 major orchestras to Coventry for one of the most outstanding orchestral series in all of Great Britain. The four major London ensembles (London Philharmonic, Royal Philharmonic, BBC Symphony, and English Chamber Orchestra) are joined by orchestras and soloists from around the world. **Recent Performers:** orchestras of Moscow, Budapest, and Cracow, soprano Maria Ewing, cellist Paul Tortelier. **Venue:** The Arts Centre, 3 miles from Coventry. **Performances:** 13; October–May.

CRICKLADE (Wiltshire)
80 miles W of London

Found in an area quintessentially English, Cricklade lies near the headwaters of the Thames. The area offers interesting walks in the renowned gardens at Hidcote and Kiftsgate, or in the arboretum and bird sanctuary at Westonbirty and Slimbridge. If a bit more hustle and bustle is the goal, a brief car ride leads to the cities of Bath, Bristol, Oxford, or Stratford.

FESTIVALS

Cricklade Music Festival

9 Days
Late September–Early
    October

Op, Orch, Chor, Cham, Rec,
    Org, Dance, Child

Cricklade Music Festival
The Coach House
Latton
Swindon SN6 6DP
Tel: 0793/750338

This very versatile event focuses upon a particular theme, usually the music of a given culture, with recent festivals devoted to Spanish, Slavic, and nineteenth-century Russian music. The offerings are further unified by a special emphasis on a given instrument, such as the guitar. Since its beginning in 1975, the Cricklade Festival has offered world-class performers and the finest music at modest prices. Among its varied programs have been quartets by Beethoven and Messiaen, songs by Schumann and Ravel, and guitar music of Handel and Prokofiev. **Recent Performers:** Orion String Quartet, soprano Lucy Shelton, pianist Andras Schiff. **Venue:** St. Sampson's Church. **Performances:** 14; evenings and weekend afternoons.

GLYNDEBOURNE (East Sussex)
50 miles SE of London

Near the East Sussex town of Lewis is the estate on which John Christie and his wife, a singer, founded one of the world's great opera festivals in 1934. The intimate opera house is surrounded by magnificent gardens, and rolling pastureland reaches toward the nearby Downs. A special train from London's Victoria Station arrives in time for tea.

FESTIVALS

Glyndebourne Festival

3 Months
Late May–Late August

Op

Glyndebourne Festival
Lewes
East Sussex BN8 5UU
Tel: 0273/541111

Arguably the most prestigious opera festival in the world, Glyndebourne is equally renowned for the artistic excellence of its productions and the civilized splendor in which they are given. When this festival was created in 1934 by John Christie and his wife on their country estate, the productions under the baton of Fritz Busch were limited to Mozart. The 6 annual productions now encompass both early baroque and contemporary works, all given with the attention to detail and careful rehearsal for which Glyndebourne is famed. The artistic credo of Glyndebourne is summed up in the words of its founder: "Not the best we can do, but the best that can be done anywhere." **Performers:** Although the list of past participants reads like a roster of the world's greatest singers, star billing is an alien concept, and the creation of an ensemble is the first consideration. Young artists join established singers and are encouraged in an atmosphere of artistic collaboration. **Venue:** The 830-seat theatre on the Christie estate. **Performances:** Performances generally begin early to allow for dinner during the long interval. Three fine restaurants are open to patrons, and the picnics amid the gardens are legendary. Evening dress is customary. **Note:** Productions are generally sold-out long in advance through subscriptions and a ballot allocation during the general booking period. Often the best chance of obtaining tickets is to call the Box Office at short notice during the festival in the hope of ticket returns.

HASLEMERE (Surrey)
50 miles SW of London

The town of Haslemere, albeit small, gives an immediate sense of sophistication and propriety. Places of interest in the surrounding areas include the tiny home of George Eliot in Shottermill Common, and, to the north, a center of medieval glass manufacturing in Chiddingford, where many of Westminister Abbey's stained-glass windows were crafted.

FESTIVALS

Dolmetsch Festival in Haslemere

1 Week	Festival Secretary
Mid-June	Dolmetsch Foundation
	Jesses, Grayswood Rd.
Orch, Cham	Haslemere, Surrey GU27 2AS
	Tel: 0428/2161
	(Monday–Saturday: 9 A.M.–
	12:30 P.M.)

Drawing on the resources of the renowned Dolmetsch Library in Haslemere, the festival features music of the sixteenth to eighteenth centuries, often presenting works not heard since their original performances. Innovative programs also include such favorites as Mozart and Scarlatti, and may feature an era ("le Grand Siècle"), an artistic figure (Shakespeare), or a theme ("In Imitation of Birds"). Eminent musicologist Arnold Dolmetsch founded the event in 1925, which makes this one of Britain's oldest festivals. It has been directed for nearly half a century by Carl Dolmetsch, C. B. E. **Venues:** Haslemere Hall and parish churches. **Performances:** daily at 7:30 P.M., Saturday matinee.

HEREFORD (Herefordshire)
125 miles W of London

Although Hereford is a relatively modern town, a number of gracious older buildings and houses have been preserved, and the town still carries on its tradition of serving as a prominent marketplace for the area's main industry—cattle. The central attraction of Hereford is certainly its medieval cathedral, which houses the fascinating *Mappa Mundi*, one of the world's oldest maps.

FESTIVALS

Three Choirs Festival

1 Week
Mid-August
Gloucester: 1992, 1995, ect.
Worcester: 1993, 1996, etc.
Hereford: 1994, 1997, etc.

Orch, Chor, Cham, Rec,
    Org, Fringe

Three Choirs Festival
Festival Ticket Office
Music School
Hereford Cathedral School
13 Castle Street
Hereford HR1 2NN
(after mid-July)
Tel: 0432/263101

Three Choirs Festival
Festival Office
33 Bridge Street
Hereford HR4 9DQ
(before mid-July)

Three Choirs Festival
Festival Office
Community House
College Green
Gloucester, GL1 2LX

Three Choirs Festival
Festival Office
103a High Street
Worcester WR1 2LH

The cathedral cities of Gloucester, Hereford, and Worcester provide the "Three Choirs" referred to here, and the festival rotates annually among them. The first "Music Meeting" of these cities took place in 1712, making this Europe's oldest music festival. Professional ensembles and soloists now join the 300-voice massed choir to present a broad range of repertoire. The focus remains largely upon English music, although other nations are amply represented. Featured works have included Britten's *War Requiem*, Elgar's *Falstaff*, Vaughan William's *Dona nobis pacem*, and Mahler's Eighth Symphony. **Recent Performers:** Royal Philharmonic Orchestra, Royal Liverpool Philharmonic Orchestra, City of Birmingham Symphony Orchestra, English String Orchestra, Hanover Band conducted by Roy Goodman. **Venues:** Cathedral and other sites in host city. **Performances:** Many daily.

KING'S LYNN (Norfolk)
90 miles N of London

This ancient market town sits on a river bank near the Wash, that arm of the North Sea that extends down into East Anglia. In addition to the charms of this historic town, the nearby Norfolk Lavender farm provides a diverting side-trip.

FESTIVALS

The King's Lynn Festival of Music and the Arts

1 Week	The King's Lynn Festival
Late July	Box Office
	King Street
Orch, Chor, Cham, Rec,	King's Lynn Norfolk
Child	PE30 1HA
	Tel: 0553/773578
	(after mid-June)

King's Lynn aims to provide audience and artists alike with the chance to "cross over" from classical to jazz, from performer to audience—to see and hear the traditional in an innovative way. The music ranges from late Beethoven quartets to choral music of Elgar, while maintaining a focus on the work of young composers. **Recent Performers:** Sir Michael Tippett and Andrew Lloyd Webber conducting their own work, the Scottish Chamber Orchestra, the Endellian Quartet. **Venues:** St. Nicholas Chapel, Town Hall, Guildhall of St. George, Corn Exchange, others. **Performances:** about 10 a day.

LEEDS (West Yorkshire)
180 miles N of London

As one of Yorkshire's largest industrial towns, Leeds is like Birmingham in that its architecture leans more toward postwar, twentieth-century design than that of a bygone era. It is Britain's fourth largest city and offers parks, museums, and comfortable accommodations. Possibly its greatest attribute, however, is its proximity to the famed Brontë landscapes of West Yorkshire, where enthusiasts can explore the lush countryside immortalized in the sisters' novels and visit the Brontë museum in neighboring Haworth. The Leeds Piano Competition is the most prestigious in Britain.

ONGOING EVENTS

Opera North

Op

Opera North
Grand Theatre
46 New Briggate
Leeds LS1 6NU
Tel: 0532/459351 or
444971
Fax: 0532/440418

Formed in 1978, Opera North gives approximately half of its performances in Leeds and the other half in the northern cities of Manchester, Hull, York, and Nottingham. The company, which also tours extensively throughout Europe, is committed to the expansion of the boundaries of opera, and presents innovative productions as well as traditional ones. Recent productions have included Gluck's *Orpheus and Eurydice*, Puccini's *Gianni Schicchi*, Paul Dukas's only opera, *Ariane and Bluebeard*, and the British premiere of Verdi's *Jerusalem*. **Venues:** Grand Theatre in Leeds; Palace Theatre in Manchester; Theatre Royal in Nottingham, New Theatre in Hull; Theatre Royal in York. **Performances:** 16 productions annually.

IN THE AREA

Huddersfield Contemporary Music Festival

10 Days
Late November-Early
December

Op, Orch, Chor, Cham,
Rec, Org, Lect,
Film, Ex, Fringe

Huddersfield Contemporary
Music Festival
Box Office
Tourist Information Centre
Albion Street
Huddersfield
West Yorkshire HD1 2NW
Tel: 0484/422288
ext: 2026/7
(after 5:15 P.M. and Saturday:
0484/423877)
Fax: 0484/516151

Inaugurated in 1978, this program has become one of the world's leading festivals of new music. Huddersfield itself, located 15 miles SW of Leeds, has emerged as a cultural center, and each November it bursts with activity, hosting concerts, exhibitions, workshops, visits by distinguished composers and performers, and music lovers from around the world. While new music is certainly featured, theater, visual arts, jazz, ethnic music, and a fringe festival broaden the appeal immensely. **Recent Performers:** BBC Symphony Orchestra, composers Karlheinz Stockhausen, Pierre Boulez, John Cage, Oliver Messiaen. **Venues:** St. Paul's Hall, Huddersfield Town Hall, Art Gallery, others. **Performances:** 50–60.

LICHFIELD (Staffordshire)
100 miles NW of London

"The most sober, decent people in England" live in the town of Lichfield, according to Dr. Samuel Johnson, the writer and social critic born here in 1709. His birthplace on Breadmarket Street, in the cobbled Market Square, is now a Johnsonian Museum. Dominating the landscape is the Cathedral in the heart of old Lichfield, surrounded by elegant homes and gardens. Built during the thirteenth and fourteenth centuries and dedicated to St. Mary and St. Chad, this red sandstone structure is unique for its three spires, collectively known as the "Ladies of the Vale."

FESTIVALS

Lichfield Festival

10 Days	Lichfield Festival
Early July	Festival Office
	7 The Close
Orch, Chor, Cham, Rec, Org,	Lichfield
Th, Film, Ex	Staffordshire WS13 7LD
	Tel: 0543/257557
	Fax: 0543/415137

This extensive program features a broad spectrum of repertoire presented by world-class performers. Many concerts are presented in the spectacular Lichfield Cathedral, which has undergone three centuries of careful restoration. Programs have included music of Bach, Franck, and Ellington, as well as a discussion session with the festival's composer-in-residence, films, show jumping, and fireworks. **Recent Performers:** BBC Philharmonic Orchestra, pianist Alfred Brendel, guitarist John Williams, Jaguar Cars Band. **Venues:** Lichfield Cathedral, Civic Hall, Guild Hall, Beacon Park. **Performances:** 40.

LINCOLN (Lincolnshire)
130 miles N of London

Britons, Romans, Danes, and Normans all fought for control of Lincoln, referred to by William the Conqueror as the fourth most important city in Britain. The old city's rich history is evident at every turn, but perhaps nowhere quite so overwhelmingly as at the city's Cathedral. Constructed as a Norman church in 1185 and rebuilt after an earthquake and fire during the thirteenth and fourteenth centuries, its tower contains a 5-ton bell, "Great Tom of Lincoln," which still rings on the hour. Adorned with splendid statuary and stained glass, the cathedral is one of England's largest and most spectacular. Lincoln Castle, with its thirteenth-century execution tower and prison chapel (where prisoners could see the pulpit but not each other) is of equal historical and cultural significance.

ONGOING EVENTS

Opera 80

Op

Opera 80
Theater Royal Lincoln
Clasketgate
Lincoln LN2 1JJ
Tel: 0522/25555 or
/34570
Fax: 0522/545867

Instituted in 1980, Opera 80 is regarded as one of Britain's leading touring opera companies, showcasing young and talented artists from across the country. Two new fully staged productions are mounted each year, and 16 singers and 25 orchestral players are brought to areas in Britain where professional operas would not normally be heard. All performances are sung in English. Opera 80 also sponsors a thriving educational program designed to introduce children to opera. Productions have included *The Marriage of Figaro* and *Eugene Onegin*. **Venues:** Theater Royal in Lincoln; over 20 venues throughout Britain. **Performances:** 20; February–May.

Pavilion Opera

Op

Pavilion Opera
Thorpe Tilney Hall
Lincoln LN4 3SL
Tel: 05267/231
Fax: 05267/315

Information on performances in the United States:

Mrs. Lucy Tittmann
102 Estabrook Rd.
Concord, MA 01742
Tel: 508/369-1152
Fax: 508/369-7919

One of the most innovative opera companies to be found, Pavilion Opera was born when its founder, Freddie Stockdale, staged a performance of *Così fan tutte* in the garden pavilion of his Lincolnshire home. He wanted the quality of the singing and the emotions of the characters to be compelling to an audience seated only a few feet from the singers. Accompanied by a piano, the company of young singers presents operas suited to ballrooms, galleries, and drawing rooms large enough for 150 people, though they have performed for as few as a dozen guests. Productions range from Mozart's *Don Giovanni* and *The Marriage of Figaro* to Offenbach's *Tales of Hoffman* and Rossini's *The Barber of Seville*, all sung in the original languages. **Venues:** Private houses, stately homes throughout the countryside, London, the continent, the United States, Australia, and the Far East. **Performances:** 120, April–December.

LIVERPOOL (Lancaster)
180 miles NW of London

To most people, the name Liverpool conjures up one of two images—the Beatles or heavy industrialization. Yet Liverpool is one of Britain's most important trans-Atlantic ports and sustains an active cultural community. The city is home to two twentieth-century cathedrals—the neo-Gothic Anglican Cathedral, which is the largest church in Britain, and the contemporary Roman Catholic Cathedral of Christ the King, which seems to reach upward to its crown of brilliant stained glass.

ONGOING EVENTS

Liverpool Empire Theatre

Op, Th

The Box Office
The Empire Theatre
Lime Street
Liverpool L1 1JE
Tel: 051/709 1555 or
051/709 8070

Although musical theater and popular music are most often featured here, one can also enjoy classic theater and opera. Recent programs included Shakespeare's *A Midsummer Night's Dream*, Weber's *Der Freischütz*, and Smetana's *The Bartered Bride*. **Recent Performers:** Welsh National Opera, Royal Shakespeare Company. **Performances:** each show has a different run, usually approximately one week; year-round.

Philharmonic Chamber Concerts

Cham, Rec

Philharmonic Hall
Hope Street
Liverpool L1 9BP
Tel: 051/709 3789

This series offers international artists and ensembles in the impressive setting of Philharmonic Hall. A wide spectrum of repertoire is represented, from Haydn to Webern. Recent concerts have featured string quartets of Mozart, Beethoven, and Bartók, and piano music by Schubert and Scriabin. **Recent Performers:** Trio Ravel, Smetana Quartet, pianist Melvyn Tan. **Venue:** Philharmonic Hall. **Performances:** 8 Tuesday; October–April.

Royal Liverpool Philharmonic Orchestra

Orch, Chor

Philharmonic Hall
Box Office
Hope Street
Liverpool L1 9BP
Tel: 057/709 3789
Fax: 051/709 0918

This, one of Britain's finest orchestras, has a reputation for its bold and innovative programming, as well as for its exceptional interpretation of the standard literature. It is the world's fifth oldest concert-giving organization, dating back to 1840, when the Liverpool Philharmonic Society was created. From Beethoven to Schnittke, the orchestra and its music director Libor Pešek span the repertoire and offer concerts with world-famous soloists. **Recent Performers:** pianist/conductor Vladimir Askhenazy, violinist Young Uck Kim, pianist Alfred Brendel. **Venue:** Philharmonic Hall. **Performances:** 50, both in Liverpool and on tour; September–May.

LONDON

London is a city of such vast diversity that one could easily visit dozens of times and leave with an entirely different impression on each occasion. A visit to the maddening thrill of Picadilly Circus and the Theater District can leave one's senses somewhat shaken, while literally days could be spent strolling through the elegant tranquility of Mayfair, Belgravia, or Knightsbridge. London has long been a magnet for musicians, especially German-speaking ones. Handel spent most of his life here, and Mozart came as a child and was greatly influenced by another expatriate, Johann Christian Bach (Johann Sebastian's youngest son). Haydn wrote 12 of his most glorious symphonies in commemoration of his visits to this city, which has been the home at one time or another to a host of composers, native and foreign.

FESTIVALS

BBC Henry Wood Promenade Concerts

2 Months
Mid-July–Mid-September

Orch, Chor, Cham, Org

BBC Henry Wood Promenade Concerts
Royal Albert Hall
Kensington Gore
London SW 7
Tel: 071/589 8212

Founded by Sir Henry Wood in 1895, these concerts first took place at the old Queen's Hall and were designed to allow students and others who could not afford costly opera and concert tickets to be a part of London's musical life. In 1942, the series was moved to Royal Albert Hall, where it is still presented today. World-class performers are featured, and repertoire ranges from the sixteenth century to world premieres, from sacred music to jazz. **Recent Performers:** conductor Sir Georg Solti, cellist Paul Tortelier, baritone Dietrich Fischer-Dieskau. **Venue:** Royal Albert Hall. **Performances:** 1, sometimes 2 daily, nearly 70 in all.

Early Music Centre Festival

10 Days
Early October

Op, Orch, Cham, Rec

The Early Music Centre
Charles Clore House
17 Russell Square
London, WC1B 5DR
Tel: 071/580 8401
Fax: 071/323 2133

An exceptional feature of this festival is the fact that its concerts are presented in venues that provide an appropriate historical setting for the program being offered. Both large- and small-scale productions can be heard, and the festival devotes itself to a different aspect of the repertoire each year, focusing on such topics as the English choral tradition in medieval and Renaissance music. Preconcert talks given by established scholars serve to illuminate the historical contexts of the music. Programs include Scarlatti sonatas for harpsichord, songs by Dowland, and Purcell's opera *Dido and Aeneas*.   **Recent Performers:** Westminster Abbey Choir, Gabrieli Consort and Players, the Hilliard Ensemble.   **Venues:** St. John's Church, Smith Square; St. James's Church, Piccadilly; St. George's Church, Hanover; Wigmore Hall.   **Performances:** 10; afternoons and evenings.

English Bach Festival

Variable	English Bach Festival
	15 South Eaton Place
Op	London, SW1 9ER
	Tel: 071/730 5925
	Fax: 071/730 1456

Although the early festivals, under the leadership of Albert Schweitzer and Igor Stravinsky, included very new music (Xenakis, Messiaen, Ligeti) as well as that of Bach and his contemporaries, the focus is now on the production of baroque opera. Not a festival in the traditional sense, the English Bach Festival has no permanent home or set schedule, but takes its productions to events and venues throughout Europe. Harpsichordist Lina Lalandi established the present festival in 1962 and remains as its director.   **Recent Productions:** operas by Gluck, Rameau, Handel.   **Venues:** Royal Opera House, Covent Garden, Versailles, international music festivals including Monte Carlo, Athens, and Granada.   **Performances:** at least one production annually.

Greenwich Festival

2 Weeks	Greenwich Festival
Early June	151 Powis Rd.
	London, SE18 6JL
Orch, Chor, Cham, Rec, Jazz,	Tel: 081/317 8687 or
Th, Film, Ex	081/855 5900

Classical music is but a portion of this wide-ranging festival of the arts, which focuses each year on a special theme—Spain, or the 200th anniversary of the French Revolution, to name but two. The offerings range from the *St. Matthew Passion* to gamelan concerts to the cuisine of Dutch Indonesia. **Recent Performers:** Chandos Baroque Players, the Tallis Scholars, duo-pianists Katia and Marielle Labeque. **Venues:** Greenwich Borough Hall, Royal Naval College Chapel, St. Alfege Church, West Greenwich House, others. **Performances:** almost daily; usually at 7:30, but with some afternoon programs.

London Festival Orchestra's Cathedral Classics, A Summer Festival of Music in Cathedrals

5 Weeks
Late May–Early July

Orch, Chor, Org

Festival Box Office
P.O. Box 1234
London SW2 2TG
Tel: 081/671 7100
Fax: 081/671 3988

This "roving" festival, conceived by London Festival Orchestra director Ross Pople in 1985, takes place in the glorious cathedrals to be found throughout England. The celebration brings the Orchestra and international soloists to large audiences, while involving the choirs and choirmasters of the host cathedrals. Sponsored by British Gas, the festival now reaches literally millions of music lovers, both through the more than 20 venues in which performances are given and also through BBC broadcasts. The wide span of repertoire includes music of Bach, Haydn, Dvořák, Milhaud, and Bernstein. **Recent Performers:** mezzo soprano Elizabeth McCormack, percussionist Evelyn Glennie. **Venues:** Cathedrals in Winchester, Glasgow, Durham, Nottingham, Canterbury, Chichester, Bradford, St. Albans, Windsor, and many others. **Performances:** 25.

London Handel Festival

1 Week
Spring (variable)

Orch, Chor, Cham

London Handel Festival
31 Davies Street
London W1Y 1EN
Tel: 071/629 3391

Instituted in 1978 by Denys Darlow, this festival featuring the London Handel Orchestra strives to present both the famous and the still neglected works of Handel. An annual theme is chosen, usually a particular year in the life and creative output of this master composer. Concerts are presented in the intimate St. George's Church of Hanover Square, Handel's own parish church. Works performed at recent festivals include *Saul*, excerpts from *Dardanus*, *Israel in Egypt*, and many chamber works. **Recent Performers:** London Handel Choir and Orchestra with conductor Roy Goodman, harpsichordist Maggie Cole. **Venue:** St. George's Church, Hanover Square. **Performances:** 4 evening performances.

Lufthansa Festival of Baroque Music

1 Month	Festival Office
June	St. James's Church
	197 Piccadilly
Orch, Chor, Cham	London WIV 9FL
	Tel: 071/434 4003

Conceived in 1985, this festival is primarily a celebration of the seventeenth and eighteenth centuries, with performers playing period instruments. Concerts are presented in the heart of Piccadilly, at Christopher Wren's glorious Church of St. James. The festival is entirely funded by Lufthansa German Airlines. Recent programs have included Bach cantatas, trio sonatas of Telemann and Buxtehude, and Handel's *Alexander's Feast*. **Recent Performers:** The English Concert with Trevor Pinnock, Musica Antiqua Köln, St. James's Baroque Players. **Venue:** Church of St. James. **Performances:** 10; all at 7:30 P.M.

Summer in the City

1 Week	Summer in the City
Mid-August	Barbican Center for Arts and Conferences
Orch, Chor, Child	Silk Street
	London EC2Y 8DS
	Tel: 071/638 8891
	Fax: 071/920 9648

This lively celebration, in existence since 1984, includes many family events and free activities. Music stays mainly within the realms of popular and classical favorites, and concerts and entertainment continue throughout the daytime and evening. Events take place in the Barbican Hall, the Terrace Foyer, and Cinema 1, all within the Barbican Center for Arts and Conferences. **Recent Performers:** King's Singers. **Venue:** Barbican Center. **Performances:** one concert and many other events each day.

ONGOING EVENTS

BBC Symphony Orchestra

Orch

BBC Symphony Orchestra
Room 426
16 Langham St.
London W1A 1AA
Tel: 071/927 4296

The BBC Symphony Orchestra is one of Europe's most prominent ensembles, and is the United Kingdom's leading orchestra in the field of contemporary music, with a strong commitment to the commissioning of new works. Recent programs have included Berio's *Passaggio* and Szymanowski's *King Roger*, as well as standard repertoire pieces. The orchestra is in great demand by music festivals throughout the British Isles and can be heard in many locations during the summer months. **Recent Performers:** conductor Andrew Davis, composer Luciano Berio. **Venue:** Royal Festival Hall. **Performances:** 16; October–May.

Barbican Centre for Arts and Conferences

Orch, Cham, Rec, Ex,

Barbican Centre for Arts and
    Conferences
Silk Street
Barbican
London EC2Y 8DS
Tel: 071/628 8795
Fax: 071/920 9648

Termed "The City's Gift to the Nation" by the Lord Mayor of London, Sir Christopher Leaver, upon its opening in 1982, the Barbican Centre is the largest complex of its kind in Western Europe. It contains the famed Barbican Hall, 2 smaller theaters, and numerous other facilities. The home of the London Symphony Orchestra and the London base for the Royal Shakespeare Company, the Centre also has a close connection with the Guildhall School of Music and Drama. The Theater hosts a great many visiting artists, both from Britain and from abroad. Many small festivals, featuring individual artists, nationalities, or styles of music, are held throughout the year. **Recent Performers:** BBC Symphony Orchestra, Leipzig Gewandhaus Orchestra, Orchestre de Paris, pianist Daniel Barenboim, violinist Anne-Sophie Mutter. **Performances:** many concerts and events daily; year-round.

London Coliseum

Op, Dance

London Coliseum
St. Martin's Lane
London, WC 2
Tel: 071/836 3161

Since 1968 the London Coliseum has been the home of the English National Opera, famed for its innovative, English-language productions of an exceedingly wide repertoire. Built in 1904, this lavish hall is the largest theater in London, and it hosted Diaghilev's Ballet Russe, actress Sarah Bernhardt, and American musicals before it became the London base of the ENO. The company presents about 20 productions each season, and recent repertoire has included *Pelléas and Mélisande*, *Così fan tutte*, *Love for Three Oranges*, and *Madame Butterfly*. **Performances:** almost daily; August–June (ENO); other events April–May.

The London Philharmonic

Orch, Chor

The London Philharmonic
35 Doughty Street
London WC1N 2AA
Tel: 071/833 2744
Fax: 071/837 1224

One of Britain's foremost orchestras, the London Philharmonic performs a full season of varied repertoire with international soloists. Concerts take place in the Royal Festival Hall, and performances have recently included Mahler's Ninth Symphony, Ravel's *La Valse*, and Tippett's Concerto for Double String Orchestra. **Recent Performers:** violinist Itzhak Perlman, violinist Kyung Wha Chung, pianist Dmitri Alexeev. **Venue:** Royal Festival Hall. **Performances:** nearly 60; September–May.

The London Symphony Orchestra

Orch, Chor, Rec

London Symphony Orchestra
Barbican Centre
Silk Street
London EC2Y 8DS
Tel: 071/638 8891
Fax: 071/374 0127

This world-renowned orchestra presents a full range of orchestral literature and employs first-class soloists throughout its extensive season. Critically acclaimed festivals celebrating particular composers and their works are presented, such as "Shostakovich: Music from the Flames," and "The Flight of the Firebird: Rimsky-Korsakov and St. Petersburg." **Recent Performers:** conductors Michael Tilson Thomas and Seiji Ozawa, conductor/cellist Mstislav Rostropovich, violinist Cho-Liang Lin. **Venue:** Barbican Hall, Barbican Center. **Performances:** 80 concerts, September–June (regular concerts) and August (summer pops concerts).

Mobil Concert Season

Orch, Chor, Cham

Greenwich Entertainment
Service
151 Powis Street
London SE18 6JL
Tel: 081/317 8687

Under the sponsorship of Mobil, these concerts offer chamber music of the highest caliber in the neoclassical chapel of the Royal Naval College. **Recent Performers:** guitarist John Williams with the Bournemouth Sinfonietta, Roger Norrington conducting the London Classical Players, Choir of King's College, Cambridge. **Venue:** Chapel of the Royal Naval College. **Performances:** 6; October–April.

Monteverdi Choir and English Baroque Soloists

Op, Orch, Chor

Monteverdi Choir and
Orchestra Ltd.
Bowring Building
P.O. Box 165
Tower Place
London EC3P 3BE
Tel: 071/480 5183
Fax: 071/480 5185

One of Europe's leading chamber choirs and period-instrument orchestras, this ensemble, conducted by John Eliot Gardiner, tours extensively throughout the world. Repertoire is not limited to early music, as the name may suggest—many classical and early romantic composers are programmed, and the season includes a Mozart Opera Festival. Recent works include Bach's Mass in B Minor, Mozart's *Idomeneo* and *La Clemenza di Tito*, and Beethoven's *Missa Solemnis*. **Venues:** Royal Festival Hall, Queen Elizabeth

Hall, Barbican Center in London; many other locations.   **Performances:** many year-round, including about 6 in London.

Royal Albert Hall

Orch, Chor, Dance

Royal Albert Hall
Kensington Gore
London SW 7
Tel: 071/589-8212

This huge Victorian hall seating 8000 people opened in 1871 with a concert conducted by Gounod. Since 1945 the Hall has been the site of the Henry Wood Promenade Concerts, so popular that tickets for the "Last Night at the Proms" have to be allotted by ballot. The Hall is also used for jazz and pop concerts, sporting events, religious rallies, and political meetings. The notoriously bad acoustics have been improved by the installation of sound baffles.   **Recent Performers:** conductor Sir David Willcocks, English National Opera Chorus, Orchestra, and Soloists, Ukrainian Dance Group. **Performances:** almost daily; year-round.

Royal Choral Society

Orch, Chor, Org

Royal Choral Society
Ticket Secretary
69 Lanchester Road
Highgate N6 45X
Tel: 081/365 2209
(24 hours)
Fax: 081/749 6342

Under the musical direction of Laszlo Heltay, the Royal Choral Society presents major choral works with international soloists and orchestras. The choir was formed in 1871 under the title of Royal Albert Hall Choral Society, but at the request of Queen Victoria changed its name to the Royal Choral Society. Its membership includes 230 singers, although the touring ensemble involves a smaller group of 150–180. Recent programs have included Beethoven's *Missa Solemnis*, Verdi's Requiem, Walton's *Belshazzar's Feast*, and performances by the Fanfare Trumpeters of Her Majesty's Royal Marines Commander-in-Chief Fleet.   **Recent Performers:** London Philharmonic, Philharmonia Orchestra, organist John Birch (Royal Choral Society choir organist), soprano Margaret Price. **Venues:** Royal Albert Hall, Royal Festival Hall. **Performances:** 7; November–June.

The Royal Opera

Op, Rec, Dance

The Royal Opera
Box Office
48 Floral Street
London WC2
Tel: 071/240 1066
    071/240 1911
Fax: 071/836 1762

One of the world's truly stunning opera houses, the Royal Opera House at Covent Garden houses the Royal Opera and the Royal Ballet. The very finest singers and conductors appear here, and the operatic literature is thoroughly explored, from Mozart through the nineteenth century to contemporary works. The company strives to present lesser-known works, many of which have never been heard in London, as well as the best-loved operas in both new productions and in revivals. For all foreign-language operas, English surtitles are projected over the stage. Recent productions include Wagner's *Der Ring des Nibelungen*, Beethoven's *Fidelio*, Bizet's *Carmen*, Saint-Saëns' *Samson et Dalila*, and Mussorgsky's *Boris Godunov*. **Recent Performers:** soprano Dame Joan Sutherland, tenor Placido Domingo, soprano Dame Kiri te Kanawa, conductors Zubin Mehta, Colin Davis, and Christof von Dohnányi. **Performances:** over 300 performances of 20 productions; September–July.

Sadler's Wells Theatre

Op, Dance, Th, Child

Sadler's Wells Theatre
Rosebery Avenue
London EC1R 4TN
Tel: 071/278 8916
    071/278 5450
(recorded information)
Fax: 071/837 0965

This theater has a rich history that dates back to the late seventeenth century, when a builder named Richard Sadler discovered ancient medicinal wells in the area. Lillian Baylis gave the theatre new life when she took over the management, and the current building was constructed in the early 1930s as a counterpart to the Old Vic. A second theater, named in her honor, was opened in 1988. All varieties of lyric theater are performed, including opera, operetta, ballet, international theater, and musical theater. The New Sadler's

Wells Opera Company and the Sadler's Wells Theater Company are in residence here, and others, such as the Sadler's Wells Royal Ballet and the English Shakespeare Company, utilize the theater as their administrative base. Recent productions have included Donizetti's *Lucia di Lammermoor* and Lehár's *The Merry Widow*. **Performances:** season varies; no performances on Sunday, Monday irregular.

St. John's Smith Square

Op, Orch, Chor, Cham, Rec, Org

St. John's Smith Square
Box Office
London SW1P 3HA
Tel: 071/222 1061
Fax: 071/233 1618

This baroque church, built in 1728, was partially destroyed during World War II and was rebuilt as a concert hall, following the original design, between 1965 and 1969. With a total of 780 seats on the ground floor and in the gallery, this magnificent hall boasts excellent acoustics and a fine restaurant in the crypt. Concerts involve international artists and repertoire from all periods, including music of Bach, Mozart, Verdi, Brahms, and Bartók. **Recent Performers:** The English Concert, harpsichordist Trevor Pinnock, Israel Piano Trio. **Performances:** concerts nightly except August.

St. Martin in the Fields

Orch, Chor, Cham, Rec, Org

St. Martin in the Fields
Music Office
Trafalgar Square
London WC2N 4JJ
Tel: 071/839 1930

This series of concerts takes place at the Church of St. Martin in the Fields, and is quite independent from the Academy of St. Martin in the Fields. Lunchtime concerts are presented Mondays, Tuesdays, and Fridays at 1:05 P.M., and there is a full program of evening concerts each month. Young performers embarking on careers as soloists are showcased. In existence since the 1950s, this prestigious series attracts large and enthusiastic audiences. Additional pleasures include a superb cafe in the crypt, a book/gift shop, brass-rubbing center, courtyard market, and art gallery. **Recent Performers:** London Soloists Chamber Orchestra, London Musici, Vivaldi Concertante. **Performances:** year-round.

South Bank Centre: Royal Festival Hall
Queen Elizabeth Hall
Purcell Room

Orch, Chor, Cham, Rec, Jazz,   South Bank Centre
   Th, Film, Ex   Box Office
                                 Royal Festival Hall
                                 London SE 1 8XX
                                 Tel: 071/928-8800

Spread out along the Thames at the foot of the Waterloo Bridge, the South Bank Centre houses three of London's most important concert venues, as well as the Royal National Theatre, The National Film Theater, exhibition galleries, craft shops, record and book shops, and restaurants. The Royal Festival Hall (seating 3400) hosts recitals by international artists in addition to concerts by the London Philharmonic, Royal Philharmonic, Philharmonia, and BBC Symphony Orchestras, as well as other large-scale instrumental and choral programs. Queen Elizabeth Hall (seating 1100) houses a similar range of events. The Purcell Room is a recital hall with 370 seats that is also used for lectures and films. Special events include festivals marking composers' birthdays, lunchtime recitals, and daily "Foyer Events"—free programs that feature classical music and jazz, given at 12:30 in the Festival Hall. In one recent month alone, the special festivals included "Brave New Worlds: The Rebellious Generation, 1945–1968," "Tippett/Beethoven," "Robert and Clara," and an International Piano Series. **Recent Performers:** Vienna Philharmonic conducted by Riccardo Muti, Orchestra of the Age of Enlightenment conducted by Frans Brüggen, pianists Alfred Brendel and Peter Serkin, violinist Nigel Kennedy. **Performances:** several daily; year-round.

Wigmore Hall

Cham, Rec   Wigmore Hall
                                 36 Wigmore Street
                                 London W 1
                                 Tel: 071/935 2141

When this 600-seat theater opened in 1901, it was the home of the Bechstein instrument makers. It has since become one of London's premier chamber music venues, and it is often used by young artists making their London debuts. **Recent Performers:** Academy of Ancient Music conducted by Christopher Hogwood, Nash Ensemble, soprano Arleen Auger. **Performances:** September–July.

IN THE AREA

Chelmsford Cathedral Festival

1 Week	Chelmsford Cathedral
Mid-May	Festival
	Box Office
Orch, Chor, Cham, Rec, Film,	Chancellor Hall
Ex, Fringe, Child	Market Road
	Chelmsford CM1 1XA
	Tel: 0245/265848

Since 1984 this festival, held 35 miles NE of London, has flourished as a melange of concerts, poetry, films, exhibitions, wine tasting, and much more, all presented in intriguing venues. Music ranges from pre-baroque to Britten, and programs have included such works as Handel's *Trumpet* Suite, choral music of Byrd and Holst, and chamber works of Schumann, Poulenc, and Brahms. **Recent Performers:** Gabrieli Consort, Guildhall Orchestra, Westminster Cathedral Choir. **Venues:** Chelmsford Cathedral, The Maltings, Centre Square, County Hall Atrium, Chelmsford Railway Station, Cathedral Chapter House. **Performances:** 12–14; afternoons and evenings.

LUDLOW (Shropshire)
110 miles NW of London

Set amid the hills and dales of the Shropshire countryside, Ludlow preserves a timeless tranquility on the banks of the Corve and Teme rivers. Although the town's black and white half-timbered buildings are exceptionally well preserved, the most spectacular site is the eleventh-century Ludlow castle. The town grew up around the castle, where Milton's *Comus* was first performed in 1634. The ashes of poet A. E. Housman are kept in the fifteenth-century parish church.

FESTIVALS

Ludlow Festival

2 Weeks	Box Office
Late June–Early July	Ludlow Festival
	Castle Square
Op, Orch, Cham, Rec, Film,	Ludlow Shropshire SY8 1AY
Th	Tel: 0584/2150

The events of this festival revolve around the annual open-air production of a Shakespearean play, which is presented nightly in the town's medieval castle, where Edward V spent his childhood. Musical events might range from the Verdi Requiem to *Madama Butterfly* to Schubert trios in nearby country houses. The festival was established in 1960. **Recent Performers:** London Opera Players, London Mozart Players, Schubert Ensemble. **Venues:** Ludlow Castle, Parish Church (one of the largest in the country, and old enough to be rebuilt in the fifteenth century), country houses. **Performances:** several daily.

NEWBURY (Berkshire)
60 miles W of London

Centrally located between London, Bath, Winchester, and Oxford, Newbury is on the natural crossroads linking these cities and has long been an important coach stop. Once a center of Britain's textile industry, it is now a bustling market town that retains much of its historic charm. The fourteenth-century Donnington Castle, site of a Civil War battle in 1644, the sixteenth-century Church of St. Nicholas, and the attractive and well-known racecourse provide ample grist for the tourist mill.

FESTIVALS

Newbury Spring Festival

10 Days	Newbury Spring Festival
Mid-May	Suite 3, Town Hall
	Newbury, Berkshire
Op, Orch, Chor, Cham, Rec,	RG14 5AA
Org, Dance	Tel: 0635/49919
	Fax: 0635/528690

Featuring renowned performers from Britain and abroad, this festival offers a wide range of music, from Bach suites to Debussy songs to jazz. There is a special emphasis on chamber music and recitals, but orchestral concerts and opera are also offered. The festival was founded in 1978. **Recent Performers:** Academy of St. Martin in the Fields, Philharmonia Orchestra, English Chamber Orchestra, cellist Ofra Harnoy, guitarist John Williams. **Venues:** several country homes, village halls, and historic churches, including St. Nicolas Church. **Times:** In addition to evening performances, of which there are several each day, a series of lunchtime recitals is given at 1 P.M. at the Newbury Methodist Church.

NOTTINGHAM (Nottinghamshire)
120 miles NW of London

Although steeped in the legend of Robin Hood, Nottingham is rich in history of a more verifiable nature, as displayed in the city's enchanting castle, which sits in the center of town. Various art galleries and half-timbered houses make Nottingham a pleasant place, well worth exploration. Just outside of town is the former home of Lord Byron, Newstead Abbey. The home and its lavish gardens are now open to the public.

FESTIVALS

Nottingham Festival

2 Weeks	Nottingham Festival
Late May–Early June	Arts Department
	51 Castle Gate
Op, Orch, Cham, Rec, Jazz,	Nottingham NG1 6AF
Th, Film	Tel: 0602/483504

This diverse festival offers classical, folk, and ethnic music ranging from Debussy and Delius to the music of India, Africa, and Asia. **Recent Performers:** Opera North with productions of *Boris Godunov* and *The Pearl Fishers*, English Baroque Soloists conducted by John Eliot Gardiner, cellist Julian Lloyd Webber. **Venues:** Nottingham Castle, Royal Concert Hall, Theatre Royal, others. **Performances:** many daily.

OXFORD (Oxfordshire)
60 miles W of London

Whether watching crew races on the Thames, examining the magnificent architecture, or reveling in the academic atmosphere of past and present, the visitor is captivated by the magic of this city. Although Oxford has experienced much growth from the manufacture of cars and steel, it is the University that has made Oxford famous. First founded in the twelfth century, the University is comprised of 35 colleges, each with its own buildings and grounds.

FESTIVALS

Handel in Oxford Festival

10 days	Music at Oxford
Early July	Cumnor Hill
	Oxford OX2 9HA
Orch, Chor, Rec, Org	Tel: 0865/864056
	(24 hours)

This festival celebrates Handel's performance at the Sheldonian Theatre in 1733. From *Messiah* and the *Water Music* to concerti for organ and oboe, Handel's music is well represented, and these performances on authentic instruments also include works by other baroque composers. Fireworks concerts featuring the Handel Festival Orchestra are given in the lovely lakeside setting at Radley College, and conclude, of course, with the *Music for the Royal Fireworks*. **Recent Performers:** The Hanover Band, soprano Arlene Auger, harpsichordist Trevor Pinnock. **Venue:** The Sheldonian Theatre. **Performances:** 20.

ONGOING EVENTS

Music at Oxford

Orch, Chor, Cham, Rec, Org, Child	Music at Oxford
	Cumnor Hill
	Oxford OX2 9HA
	Tel: 0865/864056
	(24 hours)
	Fax: 0865/863088

Bach, Mozart, Ravel, and Cage are but a few of the composers represented on this very extensive schedule. Both local and international artists are featured, and repertoire tends toward the traditional while still incorporating a few surprises. Recent performances have featured Bach's *Easter Oratorio,* Mozart symphonies, Schoenberg's *Pierrot Lunaire*, and piano music of Schubert and Liszt. **Recent Performers:** Bournemouth Symphony Orchestra, the King's Singers, Gabrieli Consort and Players. **Venues:** Sheldonian Theatre (designed by Christopher Wren), Holywell Music Rooms, Christ Church Cathedral. **Performances:** 120; year-round.

IN THE AREA

The Stables

Cham, Rec, Child

The Stables
Wavendon
Milton Keynes MK17 8LT
Tel: 0908/583928
Fax: 0908/281024

The music series at "The Stables," once part of William Butterfield's Old Rectory at Wavendon (35 miles NE of Oxford), has flourished since its institution in 1969. The basic premise here is to break down the barriers between the various styles of music; hence the inclusion of jazz, flamenco, and big band concerts along with the string quartets of Beethoven and Bartók, guitar music of Haydn, and Brahms' violin sonatas. The Stables itself has been expanded over the years to accommodate an audience of 300 and now includes advanced stage facilities. The atmosphere, however, is still intimate. **Recent Performers:** St. James Baroque Players, flutist James Galway, vocalist Cleo Laine. **Venue:** The Stables Concert Hall. **Performances:** nearly 150; year-round (except August).

POOLE (Dorsetshire)
100 miles SW of London

As one of the busiest ports on Poole Harbor, this town has witnessed centuries of seafaring vessels arriving and departing from its docks. The historic old cove section of Poole is dotted with lovely eighteenth-century houses, and the town's waterfront location makes it a popular vacation resort.

ONGOING EVENTS

Bournemouth Sinfonietta

Orch

Bournemouth Sinfonietta
Box Office
Poole Arts Center
Kingland Road
Poole BH15 1UG
Tel: 0202/685222
Fax: 0202/687235

Since its founding in 1968, this chamber orchestra has been recognized as one of the United Kingdom's finest. The orchestra travels extensively throughout the South and West of England and appears regularly in London and at many British festivals, although the main concert season is presented at its base in Poole. **Recent Performers:** conductor Roger Norrington, pianist Andras Schiff. **Venues:** Wessex Hall in Poole; summer concerts throughout the South and West. **Performances:** 20 evenings; October–May. (Details of summer concert series and European tours from the Orchestra's Concerts Information Hotline: 0202/685064).

Bournemouth Symphony Orchestra— Winter Concert Season

Orch, Chor

> Bournemouth Symphony Orchestra
> Poole Arts Centre Box Office
> Kingland Road
> Poole BH15 1 UG
> Tel: 0202/685222

Formed in 1893 in Bournemouth, the orchestra today enjoys an international reputation with its principal conductor, Andrew Litton. Subscription series are presented in 9 major cities throughout the South and West of Britain, including Bristol, Portsmouth, Plymouth, and Southampton. The orchestra is based in Poole, where it presents its most extended season. Repertoire ranges from the classical to the contemporary. **Recent Performers:** conductor Roger Norrington, cellist Lynn Harrell, pianist Murray Perahia. **Venue:** Wessex Hall in Poole; summer concerts in Bournemouth. **Performances:** 20 evenings; October–May. (Details for summer concert series and European tours are available from the Orchestra's Concerts Information Hotline: 0202/685064.)

ST. ALBANS (Hertfordshire)
20 miles N of London

Considered the "jewel of Hertfordshire," St. Albans sits by the banks of the River Ver. The town's heritage goes back even further than its imposing eleventh-century cathedral, for the city boasts a vast collection of Roman relics discovered in the course of continuing archeological digs. Scholars have unearthed such stunning finds as a Roman theater and an intricate heating system.

FESTIVALS

St. Albans International Organ Festival

1 Week	International Organ Festival
Mid-July (Biennial: odd years)	Box Office
	P.O. Box 8O
Orch, Chor, Cham, Rec, Lect,	St. Albans AL3 4HR
Ex	Tel: 0727/65133

Since its founding in 1963, this festival has demonstrated the versatility of the organ as a solo instrument, and has sought to dispel its "stuffy" image. The music presented is not limited to traditional repertoire and is augmented by guest artists and innovative dramatic and visual programs. At the heart of the festival are the prestigious competitions for which it is famous. **Recent Performers:** organist Peter Hurford, Musica Antiqua Köln, London Brass. **Venues:** Cathedral, churches, St. Albans School. **Performances:** many daily.

Stately Homes Music Festival

6 Months	Stately Homes Music Festival
May–October	P.O. Box No. 1
	St. Albans
Op, Orch, Cham, Rec, Dance	Hertfordshire AL1 4ED
	Tel: 0727/37799 or
	66533
	Fax: 0727/51676

This "traveling" festival presents concerts in various stately homes throughout the United Kingdom, offering programs that are appropriate to the period of the particular venue. Since 1980, over 75 homes have provided the historical setting for music from the Renaissance, baroque, classical, and early romantic eras. **Recent Performers:** English Concert, Academy of St. Martin in the Fields, Brandis Quartet, Consort of Music. **Performances:** approximately 1 per week.

ST. ENDELLION (Cornwall)
200 miles SW of London

This tiny Cornish hilltop town has few inhabitants, but draws many visitors from vast distances, who come to the Shrine of

St. Endelienta. Sculpted in the blue-black slate called Cataclewse, it is a source of mystery and inspiration to many. The surrounding area of Cornwall offers spectacular scenery ranging from beach resorts to cliffs and moorland and has provided asylum for many artists throughout history.

FESTIVALS

St. Endellion Easter and Summer Festivals

1 Week at Easter	St. Endellion Festivals
2 Weeks in Early August	Rock House
	Delabole
Orch, Chor, Cham, Th	Cornwall
	Tel: 0840/213242

St. Endellion has welcomed the many modern pilgrims in its village church, which is said to "give the impression that it goes on praying day and night whether there are people in it or not." In 1959, such a pilgrim named Roger Gaunt was rehabilitating the rectory for use by various university groups and clergy when he and his companions were heard singing madrigals and motets in the gardens. He was asked to hold a festival at the church the following year, and so began the St. Endellion festivals. Programs offer a wide variety of music, from Bach to Bernstein and beyond. Liturgical music also plays a part, as do poetry readings. **Recent Performers:** Richard Hickox, director; cellist Alexander Baillie; soprano Catherine Pierard. **Venue:** St. Endellion Church. **Performances:** 6 during Easter Week, 9 in summer.

SALISBURY (Wiltshire)
75 miles SW of London

Although this county town is clearly dominated by the glorious cathedral that bears its name, Salisbury rewards the wanderer with glimpses of its 700-year history. Surrounding lawns give a sense of space and lightness to the thirteenth-century Cathedral, whose 404-foot spire is the tallest in all of England. Salisbury is a favored center from which to visit Stonehenge, Thomas Hardy country, the Dorset coast, Winchester, and many stately homes.

FESTIVALS

Salisbury Festival

Two Weeks	Salisbury Festival
Early September	Box Office
	Salisbury Playhouse
Orch, Chor, Cham, Rec, Film,	Maltose Lane
Lect	Salisbury, SP2 7RA
	Tel: 0722/25173

Truly an interdisciplinary affair, Salisbury organizes its many events around a central theme (a recent four-year series focused annually on one of the four elements—earth, air, fire, and water). The far-reaching program includes both performing and visual arts, with an active artists-in-residence program and a special focus on young talent. The program for young people is extensive and varied. Performances can range from Bach's B Minor Mass to Britten's *Noye's Fludde*. **Recent Performers:** conductor John Eliot Gardiner with the Monteverdi Choir and the English Baroque Soloists, English Guitar Quartet, organist Thomas Trotter.   **Venues:** Cathedral, St. Thomas Hall, Medieval Hall, Youth Hostel, others.

SEVENOAKS (Kent)
25 miles S of London

Beautifully situated in the Greensand Hills, Sevenoaks is a small village with great appeal. Here one finds England's largest house, Knole, built by the Archbishop of Canterbury in 1456 and later enlarged by Thomas Sackville in 1603. Some portions of the home, which has 365 rooms, 52 staircases, and 7 courtyards, as well as a glorious 1000-acre park, are open to the public. The village's treasures also include a thirteenth-century church, a fifteenth-century school, and the Vyne Wicket, England's oldest cricket field.

FESTIVALS

Sevenoaks Summer Festival

10 Days	Sevenoaks Summer Festival
Mid–Late June	Sevenoaks School
	Sevenoaks
Op, Orch, Chor, Cham, Rec,	Kent TN13 1HU
Org, Dance, Th, Film,	Tel: 0732/455133
Ex, Child	Fax: 0732/456143

This festival was created with the intent of bringing world-renowned performers to the community of Sevenoaks, particularly to the young. Pupils from the Sevenoaks School are featured along with both international artists and young professionals. Patrons are encouraged to broaden their artistic palates, whether it be within the realm of music or in drama, dance, or other special events. Music includes works by Bach, Schubert, Respighi, and Cole Porter. **Recent Performers:** pianist Vladimir Ashkenazy, Borodin String Quartet, cellist Julian Lloyd Webber. **Venues:** Aisher Hall and Sackville Theater, Sevenoaks School; Stag Theater; St. Nicholas Church; Knole. **Performances:** several daily.

STRATFORD-UPON-AVON (Warwickshire)
95 miles NW of London

Shakespeare's hometown is a tidy (if somewhat touristy) Tudor village, where even modern hotel rooms are dedicated to the Bard. As its name suggests, Stratford is, in fact, upon the Avon River, which meanders through town amid tourbuses and theaters like the playwright's verse, constantly flowing and unaffected by time. William Shakespeare was born, raised, lived, and died here, where the humble, half-timbered homes of his mother, Mary Arden, his wife, Anne Hathaway, and his daughter, Susanna, can still be found. The houses are all museums open to the public. A production by the world-renowned Royal Shakespeare Company at the Royal Shakespeare Theatre on the Avon River should not be missed.

FESTIVALS

Winter Visitors' Season

6 Weeks	Winter Visitors' Season
Early February–Mid-March	Royal Shakespeare Theatre
	Box Office
Op, Orch, Cham, Rec, Jazz,	Stratford-upon-Avon
Th, Child	CV37 6BB
	Tel: 0789/295623

Touring companies specializing in music, drama, and comedy provide the basis for this short season, which has something for all ages and all interests. **Recent Performers:** Royal Philharmonic Orchestra, Glenn Miller Orchestra, Travelling Opera (*La Bohème*, *Don Pasquale*), Lindsay String

Quartet.   **Venues:** Royal Shakespeare Theatre, Swan Theatre.
Performances: nightly except Mondays; some evening performances.

THAXTED (Essex)
40 miles NE of London

An example of the splendor that once filled Thaxted is displayed in the intricate carvings that may be seen on the exterior of the town's church. These riches were accrued as a
result of the importance this town held in the trade of cutlery
and lumber. Traveling the short distance east of Thaxted to
Finchingfield provides an opportunity to view "field" villages
typical of Essex.

FESTIVALS

Thaxted Festival

3 Weeks   Thaxted Festival
Late June–Mid July   Ticket Office
                                 Thaxted Galleries
Op, Orch, Chor, Cham, Rec,   1, Newbiggen Street
    Ex   Thaxted
                                 Essex CM6 2QS
                                 Tel: 0371/830350

This collection of concerts features a diverse repertoire
performed by international artists. Most performances take
place in the Thaxted Church, which has been actively hosting concerts since the mid-1950s. Programs have included
orchestral music by Mozart and Elgar, vocal music of Purcell and Vaughan Williams, and chamber music of Beethoven
and Walton.   **Recent Performers:** Academy of St. Martin
in the Fields, St. James's Baroque Players, Prometheus Ensemble, Ionian Singers.   **Venues:** Thaxted Church, Bolford
Hall, Barn Theatre, Little Easton.   **Performances:** 3–4 concerts each weekend.

TILFORD (Surrey)
30 miles SW of London

The tranquility that pervades this lovely small village is best
represented by the venerable King John's Oak Tree, said to be

several centuries old. Of historic interest are the two medieval bridges that span the River Wey. In the neighboring town of Farnham, a Norman castle was the residence of the Bishops of Winchester for 800 years, from the twelfth century until 1927.

FESTIVALS

Tilford Bach Festival

3 Concerts
Mid-May

Op, Orch, Chor, Cham

Tilford Bach Festival
Old Quarry House
Seale Lane
Farnham, Surrey
GU10 1LD
Tel: 02518/2167

Located three miles from the old town of Farnham, Tilford provides an idyllic village setting for this festival of baroque music. The London Handel Orchestra, using authentic orchestration and instruments, forms the nucleus of the festival, and concerts are given in Tilford's acoustically superb Victorian church. **Recent Performers:** London Handel Orchestra. **Venue:** Tilford Church. **Performances:** evenings.

ONGOING EVENTS

Tilford Bach Society

Orch, Chor, Cham, Rec

Old Quarry House
Seale Lane
Farnham, Surrey
GU10 1LD
Tel: 02518/2167

The Tilford Bach Society was founded in 1953 to promote "the music of Bach, his predecessors, contemporaries, and successors, in a manner consistent with the style and demands of the period." Performances maintain a high professional standard within an intimate and informal setting, featuring both young and well-established artists. **Recent Performers:** London Handel Orchestra and Choir. **Venues:** The Great Hall, Farnham Castle, Tilford Church, Hunters Music Room, Frensham. **Performances:** monthly; Saturday evenings.

TRURO (Cornwall)
250 miles SW of London

Situated beside the River Truro, this town rivaled Bath during its eighteenth-century heyday, catering to high society in its elegant Georgian Assembly Rooms. Today this part of Cornwall is thronged with artist colonies, gardens, and historical monuments. A cathedral city, Truro is still unofficially considered the county seat of Cornwall.

FESTIVALS

Three Spires Festival

2 Weeks
Late June–Early July

Orch, Cham, Rec, Org,
    Dance, Th, Film, Ex

Festival Office
Three Spires Trust, Ltd.
Bryher, Norway Lane
Perranarworthal
Truro
Cornwall TR3 7NU
Tel: 0872/863346

Founded in 1980, this international festival features a wealth of fine music combined with new and exciting ventures into the allied arts. The site for most events is Truro Cathedral, a resplendent Victorian Gothic structure seating 1200. Music ranges from Bach, Mozart, and Berlioz to Barber, Gershwin, and Ives. **Recent Performers:** Bournemouth Symphony Orchestra, City of London Sinfonia, pianists John Lill and Fouts'ong. **Venues:** Truro Cathedral, Alverton Manor Hotel, Royal Institute of Cornwall, Princess Pavilion, Falmouth City Hall. **Performances:** 18 events.

WARWICK (Warwickshire)
85 miles NW of London

Just down the River Avon from Stratford sits the equally historic, if less-heralded village of Warwick. Dominated by its fourteenth-century castle, where towers, turrets, and a torture chamber are among the intriguing features, the town itself is equally noteworthy for its unspoiled charm. St. Mary's Church, rebuilt during the seventeenth and eighteenth centuries, is considered to represent some of the finest work of that period. Also worth exploring is the Lord Leycester Hospital. Built during the early fifteenth century and designated in 1571 as a home for old soldiers, it still houses ex-servicemen today.

FESTIVALS

Warwick Arts Festival

10 Days	Warwick Arts Festival
Early–Mid-July	Advance Booking Office
	Northgate
Orch, Chor, Cham, Rec, Org,	Warwick CV34 Y51
Th, Ex, Child	Tel: 0926/410747
	Fax: 0926/492468

This festival features chamber music, and offers it almost continuously. Although each year two or more general themes are chosen, for example, the Italian baroque and nineteenth-century Czech nationalism, the programming is general enough to include other periods as well. Since its founding in 1980, the Warwick Festival has showcased young artists at the threshold of major careers as well as established artists. **Recent Performers:** soprano Emma Kirkby, Endymion Ensemble, Locke Consort, pianist Jean Bernard Pommier. **Venues:** Warwick Castle, country houses, St. Mary's Church, Unitarian Chapel, Shire Hall, Kenilworth Castle (open-air). **Performances:** 30–40 events, including evening, lunchtime, and coffee concerts.

WINCHESTER (Hampshire)
60 miles SW of London

The venerable Winchester Cathedral dominates this Wessex town, whose rich and well-preserved history is displayed throughout its narrow streets. The Cathedral, built by Norman invaders, is merely the crown jewel in a town resplendent with historic gems. These include a sixteenth-century prison and the ruins of the medieval Great Hall—a Norman Castle which, according to Henry VIII, contains King Arthur's Round Table.

FESTIVALS

Southern Cathedrals Festival

5 Days	Box Office
Mid-July	Southern Cathedrals Festival
	10d The Close
Orch, Chor, Cham, Rec,	Winchester
Fringe	Hampshire SO23 9LS
	Tel: 0962/53224

This festival, which rotates every three years among Winchester, Salisbury, and Chichester, presents a wide variety of church music, both ancient and newly commissioned. Concerts are presented in the cathedrals of Winchester, Salisbury, and Chichester, all stunning examples of English Gothic architecture. Programs feature the choirs of the three cathedrals and have included choral works of Byrd, Bruckner, Vaughan Williams, and Ian Shaw, as well as organ works by Bach, Franck, and Messiaen. **Recent Performers:** Bournemouth Symphony Orchestra, Bremen Collegium Musicum, organist Martin Neary. **Venues:** Cathedrals of Winchester, Salisbury, and Chichester. **Performances:** several daily. Wine, tea, and buffets are frequently served between concerts.

WINDSOR (Berkshire)
25 miles W of London

The town of Windsor lies on the south bank of the Thames, less than an hour from London. Begun by William the Conqueror in 1070, Windsor Castle is the largest inhabited castle in the world and is today used as an official residence of the Royal Family. When unoccupied, the royal Apartments are available for public inspection, as are the many priceless works of art that adorn the castle walls. Other sites of interest within the castle include St. George's Chapel, beneath which several English monarchs were laid to rest, and the Queen's dolls' house, a gift to Queen Mary in 1924. In the nearby small town of Eton is Eton College, England's most famous public school. Founded by Henry VI in 1440, its remarkable chapel contains fifteenth-century wall paintings and old brasses.

FESTIVALS

Windsor Festival

2 Weeks
Late September–Early
  October

Orch, Chor, Cham, Rec, Org,
  Dance

Windsor Festival Box Office
Theater Royal
Windsor SL4 1PS
Tel: 0753/851696

Since 1969, this festival has offered eclectic programs featuring international performers. Dance programs, classical music, lectures, and exhibitions are part of the offerings each fall. Musical works performed recently include Handel's *Messiah*, Haydn's *Creation*, songs of Schubert and Puccini, and chamber music of Mozart and Dvořák. **Recent Performers:** Orchestra of the Royal Opera House, London Mozart Players, Bach Choir. **Venues:** Waterloo Chamber, Windsor Castle; St. George's Hall and Chapel; Eton College Chapel; Eton School Hall. **Performances:** approximately 20.

YORK (North Yorkshire)
200 miles N of London

England's "second city" until 1800, York is indisputably one of Great Britain's most historic cities. Thriving first as Emperor Hadrian's Roman city, York came into its own during the Middle Ages, when York Minster, northern Europe's largest medieval cathedral, was built. Standing majestically in the center of York's well-preserved medieval section, it is surrounded by half-timbered buildings and cobblestone alleyways. York offers a variety of museums that include the Jorvik Viking Centre, an underground Viking city found by archaeologists.

FESTIVALS

York Early Music Festival

10 Days	York Early Music Festival
Mid-July	De Grey House
	Exhibition Square
Chor, Cham, Rec, Lect	York, Y01 2EW
	Tel: 0904/658338

Early music is broadly defined in this case, and may include Mozart, Beethoven, and Schubert. Each year a special theme is chosen, such as "Vienna: Six Centuries of Imperial Music," with programs ranging from candlelit quartet concerts to oratorio performances in splendid medieval halls. **Recent Performers:** Musica Antiqua Köln, soprano Emma Kirkby, harpsichordist Malcolm Proud. **Venues:** Medieval churches, Guildhall, Betty's Tea Rooms, others. **Performances:** several daily.

NORTHERN IRELAND

❧

BELFAST

Nicknamed the "Athens of the North" for its cultural flow-
ering in the late eighteenth century, Belfast nonetheless remained a small town until the late nineteenth century, when
linen and shipbuilding contributed to a sevenfold increase in
its population. The city enjoys a spectacular location on the
River Lagan where it flows into the sea, and extensive quays
still bustle with activity. The Grand Opera House, St. Anne's
Cathedral, Queen's University, and the Ulster Museum and
Art Gallery are among the landmark buildings.

FESTIVALS

Belfast Festival at Queens

3 Weeks	Belfast Festival at Queens
Early November	Festival Booking Office
	25 College Gardens
Op, Orch, Cham, Rec,	Belfast, BT9 6BS
Dance, Th, Film	Tel: 0232/66 55 77

Diverse and international are but two ways to describe
this far-ranging festival, which owes its name to the University that houses it. Major classical artists share the program
with such popular favorites as La Gran Scena Opera Company di New York (an all-male ensemble that spoofs operatic favorites). **Recent Performers:** Budapest Symphony Orchestra, the Endellion String Quartet, organist Simon Preston.
Venues: Grand Opera House, Ulster Hall, Harp Folk Club, others. **Performances:** many daily.

ONGOING EVENTS

Grand Opera House

Op	Booking Office
	Grand Opera House
	Great Victoria Street
	Belfast BT2 7HR
	Tel: 0232/241919

Copious gilding, ornate cornices, and a painted ceiling make this extravagant Victorian theater one of the most beautiful in Great Britain. It is the home of Opera Northern Ireland, which relies on regional artists for its productions of operas from the standard repertoire as well as for gala concerts comprised of operatic excerpts. Pre-performance talks are sometimes given, and productions have included Mozart's *Don Giovanni* and Johann Strauss's *Die Fledermaus*. **Venue:** Grand Opera House.   **Performances:** 12; March and September.

Ulster Hall

Orch, Chor, Rec, Org

Ulster Hall
Bedford Street
Belfast BT2 7FF
Tel: 0232/323900
Fax: 0232/247199

Ulster Orchestra Ticket
    Office
BBC Shop
21A Arthur Street
Belfast BT1 4GA
Tel: 0232/233240

Built in 1862 by architect W. J. Barre, the Hall is in a Victorian shoe-box style with a wrap-around balcony and superlative acoustics. The main hall, home of the Ulster Orchestra, houses a Mulholland grand organ built by William Hill. There is also a group theater, used primarily by amateur drama companies. The Ulster Orchestra focuses on a different nationality or style of music each year, and gives 30 concerts in Belfast in addition to 20 during its touring season. **Recent Performers:** Belfast Philharmonic Society, conductor Sir Charles Groves, pianist Christina Oritz. **Performances:** 50; year-round except July (Ulster Orchestra, October–May).

SCOTLAND

❦

ABERDEEN (Aberdeen)
100 miles N of Edinburgh

Austere granite buildings constructed of rock from nearby quarries are the trademark of Scotland's third-largest city, Aberdeen. Set in the upper northeast corner of the country, Aberdeen has been a thriving seaport for centuries and in more recent years has become an important base for North Sea oil drilling. Also known for its magnificent parks and gardens, Aberdeen is proximate to the Highlands, with some of Scotland's most breathtaking countryside. Forty enchanting castles can be explored in the nearby area, appropriately known as "castle country." Aberdeen was the birthplace of soprano Mary Garden, who created Debussy's Mélisande and gave the American premiere of Massanet's *Thaïs*.

FESTIVALS

Aberdeen International Festival of Youth

10 Days	Aberdeen International
Mid-August	Youth Festival
	Town House
Op, Orch, Chor, Cham,	Aberdeen AB9 1AQ
Dance, Th, Ex, Fringe	Tel: 0224/642121

This unique festival features amateur groups made up of artists and performers under the age of 23 from all parts of the world. Although they are young, these ensembles are of the highest caliber and come to the Festival to perform as well as to meet and to learn from their international peers. A wide repertoire is covered, and the visual arts are a significant element of this event. **Recent Performers:** University of Texas Jazz Orchestra and Dance Repertory Theater, University of the Phillipines Concert Chorus, Little Flowers of Taiwan, Tel-Aviv Music Academy Chamber Orchestra. **Venues:** His Majesty's Theater, Aberdeen Arts Center, Music Hall, Mitchell Hall, Beach Ballroom. **Performances:** 2–3 events daily.

ONGOING EVENTS

Music Hall Aberdeen

Orch, Chor

Aberdeen Box Office
Union Street
Aberdeen AB1 1QS
Tel: 224/641122

Since its complete renovation in 1986, the Music Hall Aberdeen has won the favor of performers and audiences alike. Orchestral concerts are heard regularly, and many popular groups appear here as well. The main hall has a capacity of 2500, and there are also three main conference rooms, a "square room," a "round room," and extensive bar and catering facilities. **Recent Performers:** Scottish National Orchestra, Scottish Chamber Orchestra.

DUMFRIES (Dumfries)
80 miles S of Edinburgh

Dumfries is a small Scottish village probably best known as the resting place of the country's national poet, mentor, and hero—the beloved Robert ("Rabbie") Burns. This is the last stop of the Burns heritage trail, which follows the writer's path through the bogs and villages of Scotland. Burn's House, where the poet died in 1796, is open to the public, and his tomb can be found in St. Michael's Churchyard. The town's Nith river is spanned by a thirteenth-century, six-arched bridge, which was a gift from the founder of Balliol College at Oxford, Devorguilla Balliol.

FESTIVALS

Dumfries and Galloway Arts Festival

10 Days
Late-May–Early June

Op, Orch, Cham, Jazz, Folk,
    Dance, Th, Ex

Dumfries and Galloway
    Arts Festival
Festival Office
Gracefield Arts Centre
28 Edinburgh Rd.
Dumfries DG1 1JQ
Tel: 0387/56479
(After May 2)

In the years since its founding in 1980, the aims of the Festival have remained the same: "to bring the best in the arts to the southwest of Scotland." The festival has grown dramatically and now includes a fringe program. The very diverse offerings include operatic scenes and arias, early music, and the classics. **Recent Performances:** BBC Scottish Symphony Orchestra, Antwerp Chamber Orchestra, pianist Barry Douglas. **Venues:** many locales in and around Dumfies, including the sixteenth-century Bonshaw Tower. **Performances:** Classical music accounts for approximately one quarter of the more than 50 programs.

EDINBURGH

This "Festival City," the fairest city in Europe according to some, it is actually two cities in one—the Old Town, primarily medieval—and the New Town, chiefly Georgian. Presiding over both is Edinburgh Castle, perched high upon a craggy rock, as spectacular a view as it is a viewing point. From the Castle one may follow the Royal Mile, the Old Town's row of streets lined with historical buildings, down the ridge to the Palace of Holyroodhouse. Originally an abbey, it is now still the official royal residence in Scotland.

FESTIVALS

Edinburgh International Festival

3 Weeks	Edinburgh International
Mid-August–Early September	Festival
	21 Market Street
Op, Orch, Chor, Cham, Rec,	Edinburgh EH1 1BW
Dance, Th, Ex, Film,	Tel: 031/226 4001 or
Fringe	031/225 5756

Founded immediately following World War II and considered by many to be the most comprehensive festival of the arts in Europe, the Edinburgh Festival involves the entire city in a celebration that encompasses music, dance, visual arts, and theater, as well as exhibitions, conferences, and master classes of every kind. Artists and performers are of the highest caliber, and programs offered are as diverse as the international audiences that they entice. The Festival Fringe is virtually equal in scope to the main program itself, and provides a special focus upon innovative theater and comedy. Additional appeal is provided by a spectacle of military bands and exhibitions known as "the Tattoo," festivals of film, books, jazz, and television that run concurrently with the main festival, and other events. **Recent Performers:** Bolshoi Opera of Moscow, Prague Symphony Orchestra, San Francisco Symphony, cellist Yo-Yo Ma, soprano Arleen Auger, dancer Rudolf Nureyev. **Venues:** Usher Hall, Queen's Hall, King's Theater, Playhouse Theater, Royal Museum of Scotland, St. Cecilia's Hall (a restored eighteenth-century concert hall containing an impressive collection of historic harpsichords and clavichords), many others. **Performances:** many daily.

ONGOING EVENTS

The Georgian Concert Society

Cham, Rec

The Georgian Concert
Society
Queen's Hall Box Office
Clerk Street
Edinburgh EH8 9JG
Tel: 031/668 2019 or
The Georgian Concert
Society
3 East Castle Road
Edinburgh EH10 5AP
Tel: 031/229 8018

This organization presents a series of concerts performed on period instruments (or, as they profess, on "good copies" or working reproductions). International artists perform both well known and obscure works in authentic performance style. Many concerts are presented in the Greyfriars Church where the National Covenant was signed in 1638. Recent performances included works by Couperin, Rameau, Purcell, and Carissimi. **Recent Performers:** Gabrieli Consort, Purcell Quartet, oboist Paul Goodwin. **Venues:** St. Cecilia's Hall, Greyfriars Church (where the Presbyterian Church was declared independent from the Scottish government in 1638). **Performances:** 6; October–April.

The Queen's Hall

Orch, Chor, Cham, Rec,
    Child

Box Office
The Queen's Hall
Clerk Street
Edinburgh EH8 9JG
Tel: 031/668 2019

A highly diverse and active schedule is featured in this intimate hall, which was once a church. It is here that Scotland's finest soloists and ensembles, as well as international artists, can be heard. From baroque to jazz, programs at Queen's Hall cater to every musical taste. Special attractions include afternoon tea concerts and folk dances and children's programs. **Recent Performers:** Scottish Chamber Orchestra, London Festival Orchestra, Scottish Early Music Consort, Allegri String Quartet. **Performances:** nearly 25 concerts monthly.

Scottish Chamber Orchestra

Orch, Chor, Cham, Child

Scottish Chamber Orchestra
Queen's Hall Box Office
Clerk Street
Edinburgh EH8 9JG
Tel: 031/668 2019
Fax: 031/557 6933

One of the world's most celebrated young orchestras, the Scottish Chamber Orchestra has attained a reputation of musical excellence. It prides itself on innovative programming and extensive community outreach, offering special concerts for remote communities, the handicapped, and children. Since its inception in 1974, the orchestra has toured considerably and holds regular seasons in Edinburgh, Glasgow, St. Andrews, and Aberdeen. **Recent Performers:** conductor/composer Sir Peter Maxwell Davies, violinist Nigel Kennedy, pianist Barry Douglas. **Venues:** Queen's Hall and Usher Hall, Edinburgh; City Hall, Glasgow; Music Hall, Aberdeen; several others. **Performances:** 20 concerts in Edinburgh, 20 in Glasgow, 8–10 in Aberdeen during main season (October–May), plus summer tours.

Scottish Early Music Consort

Cham, Rec

Scottish Early Music
    Consort
Freepost
Edinburgh EH8 OLW

or Queen's Hall Box Office
Clerk Street
Edinburgh EH8 9JG
Tel: 031/668 2019

This versatile ensemble performs repertoire from the thirteenth century through the present, and has traveled extensively throughout the world. With seasons in both Glasgow and Edinburgh, this active group is a vital element in Scotland's musical life. Concerts often revolve around a particular theme, such as "The Virtuoso Cello" and "The Songbook of Louis de France." **Recent Performers:** cellist Anner Bylsma, lutenist Martin Eastwell. **Venue:** Queen's Hall. **Performances:** 4; evenings, October–March.

Scottish Ensemble

Orch, Cham, Rec

Scottish Ensemble
Queen's Hall Box Office
Clerk Street
Edinburgh EH8 9JG
Tel: 031/668 2019

The Scottish Ensemble consists of eleven string players who perform without a conductor. The group is often augmented by wind players and by distinguished visiting soloists. The Ensemble has performed extensively throughout Scotland, giving concerts in major concert halls as well as in historic venues. From Vivaldi to world-premier works by contemporary composers, all periods are represented. **Recent Performers:** cellist Paul Tortelier, saxophonist Tommy Smith. **Venues:** Queen's Hall, Hopetoun House, Drumlanrig Castle, National Gallery of Scotland, Edinburgh Castle. **Performances:** 8 Sundays at 2:00 P.M. (Lunch is served at 1:00 P.M.); October–May.

GLASGOW (Lanark)
45 miles W of Edinburgh

Scotland's largest city, and the third largest in all of Great Britain, Glasgow is home to nearly half of Scotland's population. An industrial center that once contained infamous slums, Glasgow has worked hard to change its image. The city was designated the Cultural Capital of Europe for 1990, and it drew 4 million visitors to its year-long celebration. The worldwide attention gained during that event-filled year (4000 programs!) has made Glasgow an attractive destination for arts-loving travelers. The Burrell Collection, one of Europe's most outstanding private art collections, is open to the public year-round. The city's cathedral, built in 1136, is said to be Scotland's finest Gothic building, and it was the only Scottish mainland church to escape pillaging during the religious struggles of the sixteenth century.

ONGOING EVENTS

King's Theatre

Op, Orch, Dance, Th

King's Theatre
Bath Street
Glasgow G2 4JN
Tel: 041/248 5332
Fax: 041/221 2642

tickets:
Ticket Center
City Hall
Candleriggs
Glasgow
Tel: 041/227 5511
Fax: 041/552 1605

A prime example of Edwardian architecture, this magnificent three-tiered theater has been beautifully preserved. A great variety of programs is presented, from classical music to pantomime.

Scottish National Orchestra

Orch, Chor

Scottish National
  Orchestra
Freepost
Ticket Center
Glasgow G1 1BR
Tel: 041/429 0022
Fax: 041/331 2703

This highly acclaimed orchestra presents full seasons in Glasgow, Edinburgh, Dundee, and Aberdeen. A wide range of orchestral literature is presented, and preconcert talks are offered at many concerts. Recently programmed were works of Mozart, Elgar, Ravel, and Schoenberg. **Recent Performers:** violinists Cho-Liang Lin and Midori, conductor Yuri Temirkanov. **Venues:** City Hall, Glasgow; Usher Hall, Edinburgh; Music Hall, Aberdeen; Caird Hall, Dundee. **Performances:** 26 concerts in each series.

Scottish Opera

Op

Scottish Opera
Box Office
Theatre Royal
Glasgow
Tel: 041/331 1234
Fax: 041/332 3965

The Scottish Opera presents an extensive season of varied operatic literature. Young talent is encouraged, and operas are performed in their original language. Productions have included Mozart's *The Marriage of Figaro*, Verdi's *La Forza del Destino*, Janáček's *Jenufa*, and Bartók's *Bluebeard's Castle*. **Venues:** Theater Royal, Glasgow; performances in Edinburgh, Newcastle, and Aberdeen. **Performances:** 9 productions, 50 performances in Glasgow, typically 6 performances at each tour venue, October–June (broken into three smaller seasons: October–December, January–March, and April–June).

ORKNEY ISLANDS
200 miles N of Edinburgh

This cluster of 67 islands sits several miles from Scotland's northern coast, separated from it by the Pentland Firth. On the 29 inhabited islands are the archeological and architectural remains of centuries. Stone-age ruins, including a mystical Stonehenge-like circle, are found throughout the lush countryside, and the heritage of the ancient Norse kingdom is kept alive through festivals and tradition. The sandy coves and spectacular pink sandstone cliffs that line the North Sea are frequently drenched in generous amounts (by British standards) of sun, yet are subject to sporadic sea squalls. The islands' center of civilization is Mainland, where the two prominent villages of Kirkwall (the capital) and Stromness have retained much of their medieval character.

FESTIVALS

St. Magnus Festival

1 Week
Late June

Op, Orch, Chor, Cham, Rec,
  Org, Dance, Th, Ex,
  Lect, Child

St. Magnus Festival
Strandal
Nicolson Street
Kirkwall
Orkney KW15 1BD
Tel: 0856/2669

This varied festival, initiated in 1977, features both international and local artists performing a wide span of repertoire, including newly commissioned works. Programs have included Mozart's Requiem, Philip Glass's opera *The Fall of the House of Usher*, piano music of Beethoven, Liszt, and Berg, a lecture by Sir Peter Maxwell Davies, and jazz concerts. **Recent Performers:** Scottish Chamber Orchestra, Music Theater Wales, pianist Peter Donohue. **Venues:** St. Magnus Cathedral, Hoy Kirk, Phoenix Cinema, Stromness, Pier Arts Center. **Performances:** approximately 20 events, lunchtime and evenings.

PERTH (Perth)
40 miles N of Edinburgh

Referred to as the "Heart of Scotland" and "The Fair City," this former capital city is rich in history and intrigue. Sir Walter Scott found inspiration here for *The Fair Maid of Perth*, and Scottish kings from Kenneth II to James VI were crowned at Scone Palace, 2 miles to the north. The famed coronation stone, the Stone of Destiny, now rests in Westminster Abbey. Nearby are Huntingtower Castle, formerly Ruthven Castle, and Kinnoull Hill, which affords spectacular views and a pleasant nature walk.

FESTIVALS

Perth Festival of the Arts

2 Weeks	Perth Festival Box Office
Late May	Perth Theater
	185 High Street
Op, Orch, Chor, Cham, Rec,	Perth PH1 5UW
Dance, Ex	Tel: 0738/21031

This distinctive program features a wide variety of concerts, art exhibits, lectures, and special attractions. World-class performers can be heard in evening performances, and young talent is featured in mid-day recitals. From Mozart's *Don Giovanni* to Porter's "Begin the Beguine," every musical whim is satisfied. **Recent Performers:** Scottish National Orchestra, Moscow Radio Orchestra, Alberni String Quartet. **Venues:** Perth Theater, Perth City Hall, St. John's Kirk, Station Hotel, Scone Palace. **Performances:** 30 concerts and events.

WALES

❦

CARDIFF

The capital city of Cardiff is a bustling commercial center with plentiful cultural and arts-related offerings. These include the Welsh Folk Museum, the National Museum of Wales, a variety of impressive theaters, and the Welsh National Opera Company's lavish New Theater. A visit to the Cardiff castle, a composite of Roman, Norman, and Victorian architecture, should not be missed, if only for the sheer, gluttonous delight of taking in one of the famous "medieval" banquets held there daily except Sunday. Cardiff had a choir school as far back as the ninth century; the present one dates from 1880.

FESTIVALS

Cardiff Festival of Music

2 Weeks	Cardiff Festival
Mid-September–Early October	Box Office, St. David's Hall
	The Hayes
Op, Orch, Chor, Cham, Rec,	Cardiff, CF1 2SH
Film	Tel: 0222/23 59 00
	(Monday–Saturday, 10 A.M.
	to 8 P.M.)

When the Festival was begun in 1967 its title was "The Cardiff Festival of Twentieth-Century Music," but since 1979 the name and the programming have reflected a broader range of music. While maintaining its original aim to spotlight the vitality of Welsh musical life, the Festival is now a forum where new music is juxtaposed with works of composers such as Haydn, Brahms, and Poulenc. Three major productions by the Welsh National Opera Company are offered along with major symphonic concerts. **Recent Performers:** Welsh National Opera, BBC Welsh Symphony Orchestra, London Symphony Orchestra, Cardiff Philharmonic Orchestra, flutist James Galway. **Venues:** St. David's Hall, University Concert Hall, Welsh Folk Museum, Llandaff Cathedral, others. **Performances:** 16; afternoons and evenings, but not daily.

Welsh Proms

1 Week	Welsh Proms
Mid-July	Box Office
	St. David's Hall
Orch, Chor	The Hayes
	Cardiff CF1 2SH
	Tel: 0222/371236

Major orchestral works are featured in these concerts, which are augmented by "Foyer Music"—clowns, mimes, and puppeteers who add to the festive atmosphere. **Recent Performers:** BBC Welsh Symphony Orchestra, Halle Orchestra, London Philharmonic. **Venue:** St. David's Hall. **Performances:** 6; evenings.

ONGOING EVENTS

St. David's Hall

Orch, Cham, Rec	St. David's Hall
	The Hayes
	Cardiff CF1 2SH
	Tel: 0222/37 12 36

This splendid new facility hosts an active concert season featuring famed orchestras from around the world with internationally known soloists. **Recent Performers:** Tokyo Philharmonic Orchestra, Royal Philharmonic Orchestra conducted by Sir Yehudi Menuhin, pianist Alfred Brendel, flutist James Galway. **Performances:** 50; September–May.

Welsh National Opera

Op	Welsh National Opera
	John Street
	Cardiff
	CF1 4SP
	Tel: 0222/464666

This highly esteemed company was founded in 1946 and tours extensively throughout Britain, with performances in Cardiff, Birmingham, Oxford, Southampton, Liverpool, Bristol, Swansea and occasional seasons in London. Casts include young stars from Britain and the United States, and the company has recently been invited to perform in Japan. Six productions are offered each year, and repertoire has included *Rigoletto*, *Carmen*, and *La Fanciulla del West*. **Venues:** New Theater in Cardiff. **Performances:** approx. 25; September–

October, February–March, May–June in Cardiff; 125 in other cities.

FISHGUARD (Pembrokeshire)
90 miles NW of Cardiff

Merely a short trip from Ireland, Fishguard rests along the coastal path surrounding the Pembrokeshire National Park. The old town itself, called Lower Fishguard, is nestled around an attractive fishing harbor, while the newer section sits atop a steep hill that affords panoramic vistas. Slightly north and west, on the Pen Caer peninsula, one finds Iron Age forts and prehistoric remains that hint at the scope of the area's ancient history. Within the nearby Pembrokeshire National Park, breathtaking cliffs, profuse wildflowers, and abundant rare birds are a naturalist's delight.

FESTIVALS

Fishguard Music Festival

1 Week	Festival Office
Late July	Fishguard
	Pembrokeshire
Orch, Chor, Cham, Rec, Org,	SA65 9BJ
Film, Ex, Child	Tel: 0348/873612
	(24 hours)

Since 1970 the dramatic Welsh coastline has provided the backdrop for an exciting program of concerts and recitals as well as exhibits featuring local artisans. The music includes standard repertoire interspersed with contemporary works, and young performers are often featured with major artists. Recent highlights include Bach's Mass in B Minor, Beethoven's *Emperor* Concerto, and symphonies by Mozart and Panufnik. **Recent Performers:** BBC Welsh Symphony Orchestra with conductor Tadaaki Otaka, London Mozart Players, violinist Dmitri Sitkovetsky. **Venues:** twelfth-century St. David's Cathedral, School Concert Hall, local churches. **Performances:** 12; morning and evening.

GREGYNOG
75 miles N of Cardiff

Built in the nineteenth century in the style of the grand Tutor manor houses, Gregynog is now a residential educational center of the University of Wales. Its tradition of artistic activity was begun by its former owners, and is continued with both public and private support. The mansion is set on 750 acres of lawns, wooded parkland, and farmland.

FESTIVALS

Gregynog Festival

1 Week	Gregynog Festival
Late June	Newtown
	Montgomeryshire
Orch, Chor, Cham, Rec, Org	Powys SY16 3PW
	Mid Wales
	Tel: 0686 87/224

Under the directorship of tenor Anthony Rolfe Johnson, this festival brings outstanding artists to this spectacular setting in Mid-Wales. Music from Handel to Mahler to Walton is heard in the splendid music room of this stately home. **Recent Performers:** Orchestra of the Golden Age, Northern Chamber Orchestra, organist John Birch. **Performances:** nightly except Monday.

LLANGOLLEN (Denbighshire)
100 miles N of Cardiff

Llangollen lies beside the Dee River in the beautiful Dee Valley. One may enter the town via one of the "Seven Wonders of Wales," a medieval bridge over the river, and a ride down the Llangollen canal offers vistas of the local hills and vales. Plass Newydd, a home once owned by Eleanor Butler and Sarah Ponsby, the "Ladies of Llangollen," is a most unique attraction. During the late eighteenth and early nineteenth centuries, these two ladies, along with their maid "Molly the Basher," were hostesses to guests that included Wordsworth and Sir Walter Scott.

FESTIVALS

Llangollen International
Musical Eisteddfod

1 Week	Llangollen International
Early July	Music Eisteddfod
	Eisteddfod Office
Chor, Dance, Child	Llangollen
	Clwyd
	North Wales LL20 8NG
	Tel: 0978/860236

Every July since 1947 the small town of Llangollen has come to life with thousands of folk singers and dancers, as well as choral competitions characterized by very high standards and friendly rivalry. Nearly 30 countries are represented, the majority appearing in national costume, and the 8000 competitors from the United Kingdom and abroad perform for audiences of approximately 120,000. Events take place in a giant marquee-pavilion. **Recent Performers:** Wayne State University Men's Glee Club; Chernobrivets Folk Song and Dance Group, Ukraine; Rodina Choir, Bulgaria. **Venue:** Eisteddfod Ground. **Performances:** several daily.

SWANSEA (Glamorganshire)
40 miles W of Cardiff

On the southeast entrance to the Gower Peninsula, along the Tawe River, stands Swansea, Wales' second largest city. A port city famous for its industry, Swansea sustained heavy damage during World War II. When it was rebuilt, great pains were taken to limit the advances of industrialization and to preserve the natural heritage of breathtaking cliffs and unspoiled beaches. These scenic treasures helped earn Swansea its designation as Great Britain's first "Area of Outstanding Natural Beauty." The city now has 48 parks. Poet Dylan Thomas was from this area.

FESTIVALS

Gower Festival

2 Weeks	Gower Festival
Late July	Civic Information Office
Chor, Cham, Rec	Singleton Street
	Swansea SA1 3QG
	Tel: 0792/47 00 02

Begun in 1976, this festival presents music in intimate settings throughout the Gower Peninsula. The programming is primarily baroque and classical, though more contemporary works are also included. **Recent Performers:** Deller Consort, Swansea Bach Choir, New Chamber Ensemble of Wales. **Venues:** Parish churches. **Performances:** Nightly at 8 P.M.

Swansea Festival of Music and the Arts

1 Month	Swansea Festival
October	City Centre Booking Office
	Singleton Street
Op, Orch, Chor, Cham, Rec	Swansea SA1 3QG
	Tel: 0792/47 00 02

An important festival with a special emphasis on orchestral music, the Swansea Festival began in 1948 with Sir Adrian Boult conducting the London Philharmonic. The primary focus is on standard repertoire, with major orchestras playing Beethoven, Brahms, and Tchaikovsky, and the Welsh National Opera offering such favorites as *Lucia di Lammermoor,* and *Der Freischütz.* **Recent Performances:** London Philharmonic conducted by Klaus Tennstedt, Tokyo Philharmonic, Hanover Band. **Venues:** Brangwyn Hall, St Mary's Church. **Performances:** evening; almost daily.

Royal National Eisteddfod of Wales

1 Week	Royal National Eisteddfod
Early August	Eisteddfod Ticket Office
	41, Hanbury Road
Orch, Chor, Th, Ex, Child	Bargoed
	Mid-Glamorgan CF8 8SQ
	Tel: 0443/821677

An "eisteddfod," in its modern translation, refers to a public gathering for the purpose of competition in the fields of music and the arts, with great emphasis placed on the honor of winning and not the prize itself. The spirit and pagentry of the Royal National Eisteddfod in Mid-Glamorgan, 30 miles E of Swansea, has made it a mainstay in the cultural life of Wales, and the event has become a magnet for artists, performers, and artisans of all disciplines. Many family-oriented events are held on the 18-acre site where the Eisteddfod takes place. Conducted entirely in Welsh, the proceedings are simultaneously translated for the enjoyment of local patrons and visitors alike. The festival culminates in the magnificent Crowning and Chairing of the Bard ceremonies. **Recent Performers:** BBC Welsh Symphony Orchestra, National Youth Orchestra of Wales, Cwm Rhtymni Massed Male Voice Choirs. **Venues:** The main festival site includes a theater, literature and craft pavilions, and smaller marquees and pavilions. Local chapels, halls, and schools are also used. **Performances:** events daily.

Vale of Glamorgan Festival

3 Weeks	Vale of Glamorgan Festival
Mid–Late August	St. Donats Arts Centre
	St. Donats Castle
Op, Orch, Chor, Cham, Rec	Llantwit Major
	South Glamorgan CF6 9WF
	Tel: 0446/794848
	(24 hours)
	Fax: 0446/79416883

Instituted in 1968, the Vale of Glamorgan Festival fills the castles and country homes of this quiet area 30 miles SE of Swansea with some of the world's finest music and musicians. Music from twelfth-century choral pieces to newly commissioned works and modern jazz are performed by international and local artists. Concerts are presented in scenic and historic sites throughout the Vale of Glamorgan, and the festival has been celebrated for its "instinctive gift for matching music and environment." In addition to St. Donats Castle, former home of American millionaire William Randolph Hearst, concerts are presented in the glorious Bradenstoke Hall as well as the Tythe Barn, a fourteenth-century structure that has been converted into a center of performances and exhibitions with bar and restaurant facilities. Works performed have included *The Fall of the House of Usher* (a chamber opera by Philip Glass), songs by Schubert and Liszt, and chamber works of Mozart and Metcalf. **Recent Performers:** Amsterdam Bach Soloists, cellist Paul Tortelier, Moscow Virtuosi, Allegri String Quartet. **Venues:** St. Donats Castle, Tythe Barn, churches, cliff-top castles, and historic country houses. **Performances:** 12–14.

EASTERN EUROPE

Smetana Theatre, Prague (courtesy of Cedok, Czechoslovak Travel Bureau, Inc.).

EASTERN EUROPE

CALENDAR

MARCH

Budapest Spring Festival, **Budapest** (Hungary)

MAY

Prague Spring International Music Festival, **Prague**
    (Czechoslovakia)

JUNE

Prague Spring International Music Festival, **Prague**
    (Czechoslovakia)

JULY

Budapest Summer Festival, **Budapest** (Hungary)
Dubrovnik Festival, **Dubrovnik** (Yugoslavia)

AUGUST

Budapest Summer Festival, **Budapest** (Hungary)
Dubrovnik Festival, **Dubrovnik** (Yugoslavia)

SEPTEMBER

Bratislava Music Festival, **Bratislava** (Czechoslovakia)
Budapest Arts Weeks, **Budapest** (Hungary)
Budapest Music Weeks, **Budapest** (Hungary)
Warsaw Autumn International Festival of Contemporary
    Music, **Warsaw** (Poland)

OCTOBER

Bratislava Music Festival, **Bratislava** (Czechoslovakia)
Budapest Arts Weeks, **Budapest** (Hungary)
Budapest Music Weeks, **Budapest** (Hungary)
Music of Our Age, **Budapest** (Hungary)

The following festivals are all members of the European
Association of Music Festivals. While it is difficult to predict
the future of the many arts events in this part of Europe, the
festivals discussed below are all well established, and are
likely to continue.

The telephone numbers for these festivals are given as
they should be dialed from the United States. When calling
from other countries or from another part of the country in
question, check with the local operator before dialing.

CZECHOSLOVAKIA

ᏅᏃᎷᎥᏃᎯ

BRATISLAVA

Bratislava Music Festival

2 Weeks
Late September–Mid-October

Op, Orch, Chor, Cham, Rec,
   Folk, Dance, Film, Child

Musikfestspiele Bratislava
Michalská 10
CS-81536 Bratislava
Tel: (011) 42 7/334528 or
   (011) 42 7/334559
Fax: (011) 42 7/332652

Approaching its 4th decade, this festival offers one of the most extensive rosters of international artists of any festival in Europe. More than 6 symphony orchestras, 25 conductors and artistic directors, 40 ensembles and vocal soloists, and numerous chamber ensembles participate. **Recent Performers:** London Philharmonic, Hungarian National Philharmonic Orchestra, conductors Rafael Frühbeck de Burgos and Pinchas Zukerman, Opera and Ballet of the Slovakian National Theater, Consortium Musicum Wien, Mozarteum Orchestra of Salzburg, guitarist Julian Bream.

PRAGUE

Prague Spring International Music Festival

3 Weeks
Mid-May–Early June

Op, Orch, Chor, Cham, Rec,
   Org, Dance

International Music Festival
"Prague Spring"
Bohemia Tickets Inter-
   national
P.O.B. 534
Prague 1-11121
Tel: (011) 42 2/26 37 47
Fax: (011) 42 2/73 46 32

Five opera productions and eight guest orchestras help make this one of Europe's most ambitious festivals. Operas by Donizetti, Tchaikovsky, Mozart, Verdi, Martinu, Mussorgsky, and Penderecki include both repertoire favorites and lesser-known works, and orchestral concerts offer a similar range of musical fare. **Venues:** concert halls, St. Vitus Cathedral, St. James's Church. **Recent Performers:** Sergiu Celibidache conducting the Munich Philharmonic, Czech Philharmonic Orchestra, Moscow Philharmonic, Cleveland Quartet, tenor Peter Schreier. **Performances:** 60.   Tickets must be ordered in December and January.

HUNGARY

BUDAPEST

Interart Festival Center

Orch, Chor, Cham, Rec

Interart Festival Center
P.O. Box 80
H-1366 Budapest
Tel: (011) 36 1/1179910
Fax: (011) 36 1/1179910

This central office can provide information on the many festivals held annually in Budapest. These include the **Budapest Spring Festival** (10 days, mid–late March), **Budapest Summer Festival** (2 months, July–August), **Budapest Arts Weeks** (2 months, September–October), **Music of Our Age** (10 days, early October), and **Music Weeks** (1 month, late September–late October). International performers appear in historic venues throughout Budapest and the surrounding area.

POLAND

WARSAW

Warsaw Autumn International
Festival of Contemporary Music

10 Days
Mid-September

Orch, Cham, Rec

International Festival of
    Contemporary Music
Warsaw Autumn
Rynek Starego Miasta 27
PL-00272 Warszawa
Tel: (011) 48 22/310607

Five or more symphony orchestras participate in this celebration of twentieth-century music, joined by chamber musicians and recitalists from Eastern and Western Europe and the United States. **Recent Performers:** National Philharmonic Orchestra of Warsaw, Moscow Philharmonic, Cracow Philharmonic Orchestra, Kronos Quartet, Steve Reich and Musicians.

YUGOSLAVIA

DUBROVNIK

Dubrovnik Festival

6 Weeks
Mid-July–Late August

Op, Orch, Cham, Rec, Th,
   Folk

Dubrovnik Festival
Od Sigurate 1
YU-5000 Dubrovnik
Tel: (011) 38 50/27995
Fax: (011) 38 50/27944

Theater is as important as music at this festival, and productions often include Shakespeare and Euripides as well as contemporary works. Recent operatic productions have included Mozart's *Bastien und Bastienne* and *Der Schauspieldirektor* and Verdi's *Attila*. The festival is in its fifth decade. **Recent Performers:** Dresden Baroque Soloists, Cleveland and Cincinnati Choruses, Moscow State Symphony, soprano Montserrat Caballé.

EUROPEAN GOVERNMENT
TOURIST BOARDS—NEW YORK OFFICES

The Tonhalle in Zurich (courtesy of the Swiss National Tourist Office).

Austria
Austrian National Tourist
    Office
500 Fifth Avenue
New York, NY 10110

Tel: 212/944-6880

Belgium
Belgian Tourist Office
745 Fifth Avenue
New York, NY 10151

Tel: 212/758-8130

France
French Government Tourist
    Office
610 Fifth Avenue
New York, NY 10020

Tel: 900/990-0040

Germany
German National Tourist
    Office
747 Third Avenue
New York, NY 10017

Tel: 212/308-3300

Greece
Greek National Tourist
    Organization
645 Fifth Avenue
Fifth Floor
New York, NY 10022

Tel: 212/421-5777

Ireland
Irish Tourist Board
757 Third Avenue
New York, NY 10017

Tel: 212/418-0800

Italy
Italian Tourist Office
630 Fifth Avenue
New York, NY 10111

Tel: 212/245-4822

Luxembourg
Luxembourg National
    Tourist Office
801 Second Avenue
New York, NY 10017

Tel: 212/370-9850

Monaco
Monaco Government Tourist
    and Convention Bureau
845 Third Avenue
New York, NY 10022

Tel: 212/759-5227

The Netherlands
Netherlands Board of Tourism
355 Lexington Avenue
21st Floor
New York, NY 10017

Tel: 212/370-7367

Northern Ireland
Northern Ireland Tourist
    Board
276 Fifth Avenue
Suite 500
New York, NY 10001

Tel: 212/686-6250

Portugal
Portuguese National Tourist
    Office
590 Fifth Avenue
New York, NY 10036-4704

Tel: 212/354-4403

Scandinavia
Scandinavian Tourist Board
655 Third Avenue
New York, NY 10017

Tel: 212/949-2333

Spain
Tourist Office of Spain
655 Fifth Avenue
New York, NY 10022

Tel: 212/759-8822

Switzerland
Swiss National Tourist
    Office
608 Fifth Avenue
New York, NY 10020

Tel: 212/757-5944

United Kingdom
British Tourist Authority
Suite 320
40 West 57th Street
New York, NY 10019

Tel: 212/581-4700

EASTERN EUROPE

Czechoslovakia
Cedok Travel Bureau*   Tel: 212/689-9720
10 E 40th Street
Suite 1902
New York, NY 10016

Hungary
Ibusz Hungarian Travel Co.*   Tel: 201/592-8585
1 Parker Plaza
Suite 1104
Fort Lee, NJ 07024

Poland
Orbis Polish Travel Bureau   Tel: 212/867-5011
342 Madison Avenue
Suite 1512
New York, NY 10173

Yugoslavia
Yugoslav National Tourist   Tel: 212/757-2801
    Office
630 Fifth Avenue
New York, NY 10111-0021

* Indicates private organizations.

OPERA IN EUROPE

Opéra Comique, Paris (copyright Agnes Bonnot/Agence Vu Paris Opéra Comique 02/90).

Festivals appear in italics; opera houses and opera companies are in regular type.

Austria

Bad Hall—*Operetta Festival* (see Linz)
Bad Ischl—*Operetta Weeks*
Baden—*Operetta Summer*
Bregenz—*Bregenz Festival*
Graz—*Styriarte Graz*
  Graz Opera
Innsbruck—*Festival of Early Music*
Linz—*International Bruckner Festival*
  Brucknerhaus
Mörbisch—*Operetta Festival*
Ossiach—*Carinthian Summer Festival*
Salzburg—*Easter Festival*
    Hellbrunn Festival
    Mozart Week
    Salzburg Culture Days
    Salzburg Festival
    Festival Theaters
Vienna—*Spectaculum*
   Vienna Festival
   Vienna's Musical Summer
   Wien modern
   Jugendstil Theater
   State Opera
   Theater an der Wien
   Volksoper

Belgium

Antwerp—*Flanders Festival*
   De Vlaamse Opera
Bruges—Municipal Theater
Brussels—*Europalia*
   Flanders Festival
   Balconop
   Théâtre Royal de la Monnaie
Ghent—De Vlaamse Opera
Liège—Opéra Royal de Wallonie

France

Aix-en-Provence—*Aix-en-Provence Festival*

Albi—*Albi Festival of Music*

Avignon—*Avignon Festival*
    Opéra d'Avignon et des Pays de Vaucluse

Beaune—*Beaune International Meeting of Baroque and Classical Music*

Bordeaux—Grand-Théâtre de Bordeaux

Dijon—Grand Théâtre de Dijon

Evian-les-Bains—*Musical Encounters*

Fontevraud l'Abbaye—Cultural Center for Western France

Lille—*Lille Festival*

Lyon—*Berlioz Festival*
    L'Auditorium Maurice Ravel
    L'Opéra de Lyon

Marseille—Opéra de Marseille

Menton—*Menton Festival of Music*

Metz—*International Meeting of Contemporary Music*
    Théâtre Municipal de Metz

Montpellier—*Festival of Radio France and Montpellier*
    Montpellier Opera

Mulhouse—*Mulhouse Bach Festival*

Nancy—Opéra de Nancy et de Lorraine

Nantes—*Festival Atlantique*

Nice—Théâtre de l'Opéra de Nice

Orange—*Chorégies d'Orange*

Paris—*Paris Autumn Festival*
    Musique in Sorbonne
    Opéra Comique
    Paris Opera—Bastille

St.-Céré—*St.-Céré Festival*

Strasbourg—*Strasbourg Music Festival*
    Théâtre Municipal

Sully-sur-Loire—*Sully International Music Festival*

Toulon—Toulon Opéra

Vaison-la-Romaine—*Vaison-la-Romaine Festival*
    (see Orange)

Germany

Amerang—*Amerang Castle Concerts* (see Munich)
Augsburg—*Open-Air Stage at the Red Gate*
   Stadttheater
Bad Hersfeld—*Opera in the Abbey Ruins*
Bayreuth—*Richard Wagner Festival (Bayreuth Festival)*
   Stadthalle
Berlin—*Berlin Festival Weeks*
   Berlin Comic Opera
   German Opera of Berlin
   German State Opera
   Theater des Westens
Bonn—Bonn Opera
Cologne—Cologne Opera
Darmstadt—State Theater
Dresden—*Dresden Festival*
   Semper Opera House
Düsseldorf—German Opera on the Rhine
Duisburg—German Opera on the Rhine (see Düsseldorf)
Essen—Aalto Theater
Frankfurt—Municipal Stages
Freiburg—Freiburg Theater
Hamburg—Hamburg State Opera
Hannover—*Music and Theater in Herrenhausen*
   Lower Saxon State Theater
Heidelberg—*Heidelberg Castle Festival*
Karlsruhe—*Handel Festival*
   Baden State Theater
Leipzig—Leipzig Opera
Ludwigsburg—*Ludwigsburg Castle Festival*
Mainz—State Theater
Mannheim—National Theater
Munich—*Munich Opera Festival*
   National Theater
   State Theater
Nuremberg—Municipal Theaters
Regensburg—City Theater
Schwetzingen—*Schwetzingen Festival* (see Heidelberg)
Sindelfingen—City Hall (see Stuttgart)
Stuttgart—State Theater
Ulm—Ulm Theater

Weissenburg—*Weissenburg Summer Festival*
   (see Nuremberg)
Wiesbaden—*International May Festival*
   Bach Weeks
   Hesse State Theater
Würzburg—*Würzburg Mozart Festival*
   Würzburg City Theater
Xanten—*Summer Festival in the Archeological Park*

Greece

Athens—*Athens Festival*
   National Lyric Opera

Ireland

Dublin—Gaiety Theatre
Waterford—*Waterford International Festival of Light Opera*
Wexford—*Wexford Opera Festival*

Italy

Bergamo—*Donizetti and His Age*
   Teatro Donizetti
Bologna—Teatro Comunale
Brescia—Teatro Grande
Cagliari—Istituzione P. L. Da Palestrina
Cremona—Teatro Comunale Ponchielli
Fermo—*Fermo Festival*
Florence—*May Music Festival*
   Teatro Comunale
   Teatro della Pergola
Genoa—Carlo Felice Opera House
Martina Franca—*Valle d'Itria Festival*
Milan—*Music in the Courtyards*
   Teatro alla Scalla
Montepulciano—*International Meeting Place for the Arts*
   (see Siena)
Naples—*International Music Weeks*
   Teatro di San Carlo
Palermo—Teatro Massimo
Parma—*Verdi Festival*
   Teatro Regio

Pesaro—*Rossini Opera Festival*
Piacenza—Teatro Municipale
Ravenna—*Ravenna Festival*
Reggio Emilia—Teatro Municipale
Riva del Garda—*Musica Riva*
Rome—*Baths of Caracalla*
       Rome Opera
Siena—*Estate Musicale Chigiana*
       Siena Music Week
Savona—Teatro Chiabrera (see Genoa)
Spoleto—*Festival of Two Worlds*
Taormina—*Taormina Arte*
Torre del Lago Puccini—*Puccini Festival*
Trieste—*Operetta Festival*
       Teatro Comunale Giuseppe Verdi
Turin—RAI Auditorium
       Teatro Regio
Venice—Teatro la Fenice
Verona—Verona Arena

Luxembourg

Luxembourg City—Municipal Theater

Monaco

Monte Carlo—*Spring of the Arts*
       Salle Garnier

Netherlands

Amsterdam—*Holland Festival*
       Netherlands Opera
       Royal Concertgebouw
Utrecht—*Holland Festival*

SCANDINAVIA

Denmark

Århus—*Århus Festival*
Copenhagen—*Danish Ballet and Opera Festival*
       Tivoli Concerts

Finland

Helsinki—Finlandia Hall
Savonlinna—*Savonlinna Opera Festival*

Norway

Bergen—*Bergen International Festival*
Oslo—*Oslo Contemporary Music Festival*

Sweden

Stockholm—*Drottningholm Court Theater Festival*
Visby—*Visby Festival*

SPAIN AND PORTUGAL

Spain

Barcelona—Gran Teatro del Liceu
　　　　　Palau de la Música Catalana
Canary Islands—*Canary Island Opera Festival*
Figueras—*Castel de Peralada International Music Festival*
Granada—*International Festival of Music and Dance*
Madrid—Teatro Lirico Nacional La Zarzuela
San Sebastian—*San Sebastian Musical Weeks*
Santander—*Santander International Festival*
Seville—Teatro de la Maestranza

Portugal

Lisbon—Teatro de Sao Carlos

Switzerland

Basel—Theater Basel
Berne—Stadttheater Bern
Geneva—Grand Casino de Genève
　　　　Grand Théâtre
Gstaad—*Alpengala*
Lausaane—Palais de Beaulieu
　　　　　Théâtre Municipal
Lucerne—State Theater

Neuchâtel—see Cultural Events
St. Gallen—State Theater
Zürich—*International June Festival Weeks*
        Zürich Opera House

UNITED KINGDOM

England

Aldeburgh—*Aldeburgh Festival*
Bath—*Bath International Festival*
Birmingham—Welsh National Opera
Brighton—*Brighton International Festival*
Bristol—Welsh National Opera (see Cardiff)
Buxton—*Buxton Festival*
Cambridge—*Cambridge Festival*
Canterbury—*Canterbury Festival*
        Stour Music
Cheltenham—*Cheltenham International Festival*
Chichester—*Chichester Festivities*
Cricklade—*Cricklade Music Festival*
Glyndebourne—*Glyndebourne Festival*
Huddersfield—*Huddersfield Contemporary Music Festival*
        (see Leeds)
Leeds—Opera North
Lincoln—Opera 80
        Pavilion Opera
Liverpool—Empire Theatre
London—*Early Music Centre Festival*
        English Bach Festival
        London Coliseum
        Monteverdi Choir and English Baroque Soloists
        Royal Opera
        Sadler's Wells Theatre
        St. John's Smith Square
Ludlow—*Ludlow Festival*
Manchester—Opera North (see Leeds)
        Welsh National Opera (see Cardiff)
Newbury—*Newbury Spring Festival*
Nottingham—*Nottingham Festival*
        Opera North (see Leeds)

Oxford—Welsh National Opera (see Cardiff)
St. Albans—*Stately Homes Festival*
Sevenoaks—*Sevenoaks Summer Festivals*
Southampton—Welsh National Opera (see Cardiff)
Stratford-upon-Avon—*Winter Visitors' Season*
Thaxted—*Thaxted Festival*
Tilford—*Tilford Bach Festival*
York—Opera North (see Leeds)

Northern Ireland

Belfast—*Belfast Festival at Queens*
   Grand Opera House

Scotland

Aberdeen—*Aberdeen International Festival of Youth*
   Scottish Opera (see Glasgow)
Dumfries—*Dumfries and Galloway Arts Festival*
Edinburgh—*Edinburgh International Festival*
   Scottish Opera (see Glasgow)
Glasgow—King's Theatre
   Scottish Opera
Orkney Islands—*St. Magnus Festival*
Perth—*Perth Festival of the Arts*

Wales

Cardiff—*Cardiff Festival*
   Welsh National Opera
South Glamorgan—*Vale of Glamorgan Festival*
   (see Swansea)
Swansea—*Swansea Festival of Music and the Arts*
   Welsh National Opera (see Cardiff)

EASTERN EUROPE

Czechoslovakia

Bratislava—*Bratislava Music Festival*
Prague—*Prague Spring International Music Festival*

Hungary

Budapest—*Budapest Summer Festival*

Yugoslavia

Dubrovnik—*Dubrovnik Festival*
Ljubljana—*Ljubljana International Summer Festival*

INDEX

❦

Aachen, Germany, 139
Aberdeen, Scotland, 329–393, 398
Aix-en-Provence, France, 68–70
Albi, France, 70–71
Aldeburgh, England, 337–339
Alpirsbach, Germany, 145
Altenberg Abbey (Austria), 21
Altotting, Germany, 164
Ambleshire, England, 339–340
Ambras Castle (Austria), 18
Ambronay Abbey (France), 87–88
Amerang, Germany, 162–163
Aminona, Switzerland, 315
Amsterdam, Netherlands, 259–262, 265
Antwerp, Belgium, 47–48, 56, 57
Aosta, Italy, 199–200
Århus, Denmark, 270
Arundel, England, 340–341
Ascona, Switzerland, 312
Asolo, Italy, 200–201
Athens, Greece, 186–187
Attergau, Austria, 34
Augsburg, Germany, 121–122
Aulne, Belgium, 55–56
Austria, 5–42, 416, 420
Avignon, France, 71–73

Baden, Austria, 10–11
Baden-Baden, Germany, 124
Bad Hall, Austria, 19–20
Bad Hersfeld, Germany, 122–123
Bad Ischl, Austria, 9–10
Bad Kissingen, Germany, 123–124
Bad Reichenhall, Germany, 164
Bad Teinach, Germany, 157
Bamberg, Germany, 125–126
Barcelona, Spain, 286–289
Basel, Switzerland, 312–313
Bath, England, 341
Bayreuth, Germany, 126–128

Beaune, France, 73–74
Belfast, Northern Ireland, 390–391
Belgium, 43–62, 416, 420
Benediktbeuer Cloister (Germany), 163
Berchesgaden, Germany, 164
Bergamo, Italy, 201–203
Bergen, Norway, 278
Berlin, Germany, 129–133
Berne, Switzerland, 314–315
Beverley, England, 342
Birmingham, England, 342–344, 402
Bologna, Italy, 203
Bonn, Germany, 133–134
Bordeaux, France, 74–75
Bournemouth, England, 344–345
Brabant, Belgium, 62
Bratislava, Czechoslovakia, 412
Bregenz, Austria, 11–12
Breiteneich Castle (Austria), 11
Brescia, Italy, 203–204, 214
Brighton, England, 345–347
Bristol, England, 347–348, 379, 402
Brittany, France, 75
Bruges, Belgium, 48–50, 56, 57
Brühl Palace (Germany), 135–136
Brussels, Belgium, 50–55, 57, 62
Budapest, Hungary, 413
Busseto, Italy, 221
Buxton, England, 348

Caen, France, 75–77
Cagliari, Italy, 204–205
Cambridge, England, 348–349
Canary Islands, Spain, 289–290
Cannes, France, 77–78
Canterbury, England, 349–350, 365
Cardiff, Wales, 401–403
Chamonix, France, 78–79

Chartres, France, 79
Chelmsford, England, 374
Cheltenham, England, 351
Chichester, England, 351–352,
    365, 388
Chimay, Belgium, 62
Coburg, Germany, 126
Colmar, France, 110
Cologne, Germany, 134–136,
    139
Colorno, Italy, 221
Como, Italy, 205–206, 214
Copenhagen, Denmark, 271–272
Cordes-sur-Ciel, France, 80
Cork, Ireland, 191–192
Coventry, England, 352–353
Crans-sur-Sierre, Montana,
    Switzerland, 315–316, 327
Cremona, Italy, 206–207, 214
Cricklade, England, 353
Cuenca, Spain, 290–291
Czechoslovakia, 412–413, 418,
    427

Darmstadt, Germany, 136–137
Denmark, 270–272, 424
Dijon, France, 80–81
Dillengen, Germany, 170
Dinant, Belgium, 55–56, 61
Divonne-les-Bains, France, 81
Dresden, Germany, 137–139
Dublin, Ireland, 192–193
Dubrovnik, Yugoslavia, 414
Duisburg, Germany, 140
Dumfries, Scotland, 393–394
Dundee, Scotland, 398
Düsseldorf, Germany, 139–140

Eastern Europe, 409–414, 418,
    427–428
Echternach, Luxembourg,
    247–248
Edinburgh, Scotland, 394–397,
    398
Eggenburg, Austria, 11
Eisenstadt, Austria, 12–15
England, 337–389, 426–427
Epidaurus, Greece, 186
Ernen, Switzerland, 316–317

Essen, Germany, 140–141
Estoril, Portugal, 304–305
Ettal Abbey (Germany), 146
Eutin, Germany, 172
Evian-les-Bains, France, 82

Fayence, France, 78
Feldkirch, Austria, 12
Fermo, Italy, 207–208
Fidenza, Italy, 221
Fiesole, Italy, 210–211
Figueras, Spain, 291–292
Finland, 272–277, 425
Fishguard, Wales, 403
Flanders, Belgium, 56–57
Flensburg, Germany, 171, 172
Florence, Italy, 208–211
Föhr, Germany, 172
Fontaine de Vaucluse, France,
    73
Fontevraud l'Abbaye, France,
    82–83
Forchheim, Germany, 126
France, 63–113, 416, 421
Frankfurt, Germany, 142–143
Freiburg, Germany, 144–145
Fréjus, France, 83

Garmisch-Partenkirchen,
    Germany, 145–146
Geneva, Switzerland, 317–319
Genoa, Italy, 211–212
Georgsmarienhütte, Germany,
    166
Germany, 115–182, 416,
    422–423
Ghent, Belgium, 48, 56, 57–58
Glasgow, Scotland, 365,
    397–399
Gloucester, England, 356
Glücksburg, Germany, 172
Glyndebourne, England, 354
Gmünd, Austria, 11
Göttingen Germany, 146–147,
    155
Grafenegg Castle (Austria), 22
Granada, Spain, 292–293
Graz, Austria, 15–17
Greece, 183–188, 416, 423

Gregynog, Wales, 403–404
Gstaad, Switzerland, 319–320

Haarlem, Netherlands, 262–264
The Hague, Netherlands, 260,
    264, 265
Hainut, Belgium, 62
Halbturn Palace (Austria),
    14–15
Hamburg, Germany, 147–148,
    171, 172
Hannover, Germany, 148–149,
    155
Haslemere, England, 355
Hasselt, Belgium, 57
Heidelberg, Germany, 150–151
Heilbronn, Germany, 151–152
Hellbrun Palace (Austria), 28
Helsinki, Finland, 272–273
Hereford, England, 355–356
Herne, Germany, 141
Herzogenburg, Austria, 23
Hohenems, Austria, 12
Hohenlohe, Germany, 152–153
Horn, Austria, 11
Huddersfield, England, 358
Hungary, 413, 418, 428
Husum, Germany, 172
Huy-Durbury, Belgium, 62

Innsbruck, Austria, 17–18
Inzell, Germany, 164
Ireland, 189–194, 416, 423
Italy, 195–244, 416, 423–424

Jyväskylä, Finland, 273–274

Karlsruhe, Germany, 153–154
Kartause Gaming, Austria, 21
Kiel, Germany, 171, 172
King's Lynn, England, 357
Kortrijk, Belgium, 56, 57,
    58–59
Kraainem, Belgium, 57
Kronach, Germany, 126

Lackenhoff, Austria, 21
Lahti, Finland, 274–275
La Hulpe, Belgium, 57

Las Palmas, Canary Islands,
    Spain, 290
Latina, Italy, 230
Lausanne, Switzerland,
    320–321
Laxenburg Castle (Austria), 42
Leeds, England, 357–359
Leipzig, Germany, 154–155
Leuven, Belgium, 57
Lichfield, England, 359
Lichtenfels, Germany, 125–126
Liège, Belgium, 52, 59–60,
    61, 62
Lier, Belgium, 57, 60
Lilienfeld, Austria, 23
Lille, France, 84
Limburg, Belgium, 57
Lincoln, England, 360–361
Linz, Austria, 18–20
Lisbon, Portugal, 305–306
Liverpool, England, 361–362,
    402
Llangollen, Wales, 404–405
Locarno, Switzerland, 312
Lockenhaus, Austria, 15
London, England, 363–374, 402
Lorient, France, 110
Lourmarin, France, 70
Lower Saxony, Germany,
    155–156
Lübeck, Germany, 171, 172
Lübeck-Travemünde, Germany,
    171
Lucerne, Switzerland, 321–323
Ludlow, England, 374–375
Ludwigsburg, Germany,
    156–157
Luneburg, Germany, 172
Luxembourg, 245–249, 417, 424
Luxembourg City, Luxembourg,
    248
Lyon, France, 84–88

Madrid, Spain, 294–295
Maeght Foundation (France),
    106–107
Mainz, Germany, 157
Mallorca, Spain, 295–297
Manchester, England, 358

Mannheim, Germany, 158
Marseille, France, 88
Martigny, Switzerland, 323
Martina Franca, Italy, 212–213
Mayfield, England, 346–347
Mazauges, France, 69
Mechelen, Belgium, 56, 57,
    60–61
Melk, Austria, 23–24
Menton, France, 88–89
Mettlach, Germany, 170
Metz, France, 89–90
Milan, Italy, 213–215
Millstatt, Austria, 24–25
Modare, Belgium, 62
Modena, Italy, 216
Monaco, 251–255, 417, 424
Mondsee, Austria, 25
Mons, Belgium, 62
Montauroux, France, 78
Monte Carlo, 253
Montepulciano, Italy, 234
Montpellier, France, 91–93
Montreux, Switzerland,
    324–325
Mont Saint Michel, 90–91
Montserrat, Spain, 297–298
Mörbisch, Austria, 25–26
Mulhouse, France, 93–94, 110
Munich, Germany, 158–164

Naantali, Finland, 275
Namur, Belgium, 55, 62
Nancy, France, 94
Nantes, France, 95
Naples, Italy, 216–218
Netherlands, 257–266, 417,
    424
Neuchâtel, Switzerland,
    325–326
Neuenkirchen, Germany, 170,
    171
Neumünster, Germany, 172
Neustadt-Pelzerhaken,
    Germany, 171
Newbury, England, 375–376
Nice, France, 95–97
Northern Ireland, 390–391,
    417, 427

Norway, 277–279, 425
Nottingham, England, 358, 365,
    376
Nuremberg, Germany, 164–166

Oberhofen, Switzerland, 315
Oostende, Belgium, 57, 60
Orange, France, 97–98
Orkney Islands, Scotland,
    399–400
Orleans, France, 110
Orta San Giulio, Italy, 218–219
Oslo, Norway, 278–279
Osnabrück, Germany, 155,
    166–167
Ossiach, Austria, 26–27
Ottenstein Castle (Austria), 11
Oxford, England, 376–378, 402

Palermo, Italy, 219–220
Paris, France, 98–104
Parma, Italy, 220–222
Patras, Greece, 187–188
Perth, Scotland, 400
Pesaro, Italy, 222
Piacenza, Italy, 223
Plon, Germany, 171
Plymouth, England, 379
Poland, 413–414, 418
Poole, England, 378–379
Portsmouth, England, 379
Portugal, 283–286, 304–307,
    417, 425
Prague, Czechoslovakia, 412–413
Priverno, Italy, 230

Raabs, Austria, 22
Ravello, Italy, 223–224
Ravenna, Italy, 224–225
Regensburg, Germany, 167–169
Reggio Emilia, Italy, 225–226
Rendsburg, Germany, 171, 172
Rimini, Italy, 226–227
Riva del Garda, Italy, 227
Rome, Italy, 228–231
Roncole, Italy, 221
Rotterdam, Netherlands,
    264–265
Roussillon, France, 73